THE VICTORIAN WORLD PICTURE

David Newsome is renowned as a social and ecclesiastical historian of the Victorian period, as well as a biographer *sans pareil*. He retired from the Mastership of Wellington College in 1989. Until 1979 he was headmaster of Christ's Hospital and prior to that a Fellow of Emmanuel College, Cambridge, and University Lecturer in Ecclesiastical History. His previous books include *Godliness and Good Learning* ('Social history at its richest and most rewarding', *TLS*), *On the Edge of Paradise*, which won the Whitbread Prize for biography ('A critical tour de force . . . biography at its best', *The Times*), *The Parting of Friends* ('A narrative masterpiece', Lord Runcie) and *The Convert Cardinals* ('A brilliant piece of reconstruction and a fascinating read', *Sunday Telegraph*).

Further praise for *The Victorian World Picture*:

'A splendid read, a tour de force.'

JOHN WALSH

'In *The Victorian World Picture*, David Newsome examines the new sense of life in the context of broad cultural change; the Victorians believed that they were part of an age of transformation; and he depicts the intense self-consciousness of the individual as part of the self-consciousness of the period itself. It was a time of "excessive acceleration" in every conceivable direction with the most salient characteristic, according to one contemporary, of "SPEED". It is an insight which Newsome himself takes forward in his disquisition on class relations as well as transport, on religion as well as political economy . . . Newsome takes a broad view and his narrative is necessarily circumspect on the tender issues of sensibility and conduct; but his transitions are very delicate and graceful. It provid............................ an interesting "diorama" . . . [a.................................... self manifold and contradictor............................... multitude of conflicting impu...................................rocess of life itself.'

YD, *The Times*

'Newsome draws on an amazingly wide stock of references and incidents to flesh out his history, and makes good use of novels to illustrate points ... [He] has succeeded in painting his Victorian world picture in its many vibrant colours.' *Economist*

'[An] admirable survey of the perceptions of the great and the good of the nineteenth century.'

THOMAS PAKENHAM, *Sunday Times*

'An exceptionally sympathetic and moving evocation of a period which many people in the late 20th century find hard to understand or like ... Thank goodness for a historian who can be diverted from the great figures of the age by the image of Darwin's tiny daughter Annie pirouetting round her father on their daily walk together.' MICHAEL HALL, *Country Life*

'It is the familiarity and the remoteness – the two together – that make David Newsome's *The Victorian World Picture* so relevant to our time and so vivid as history ... This is a book full of insights, fascinating to the general reader. David Newsome is a splendid writer, both stylish and good company; immensely readable, at once both brisk and discursive.' ISABEL QUIGLY, *The Tablet*

'A wonderful evocation of the Victorian mind ... Graceful and learned.' *The Good Book Guide*

'Newsome's book captures the complicated times perfectly ... He engages with his subject broadly and his readers ingeniously.'

CRAIG MORRISON, *Birmingham Post*

'Deserves the closest attention ... an important contribution to cultural history.' MICHAEL WHEELER, *Church Times*

DAVID NEWSOME

The Victorian World Picture

Perceptions and Introspections
in an Age of Change

FontanaPress
An Imprint of HarperCollins*Publishers*

Fontana Press
An imprint of HarperCollins*Publishers*
77–85 Fulham Palace Road
Hammersmith, London w6 8jb

This paperback edition, 1998
1 3 5 7 9 8 6 4 2

First published in Great Britain by
John Murray (Publishers) Ltd, 1997

Copyright © David Newsome 1997

David Newsome has asserted the moral right to
be identified as the author of this work

isbn 0 00 686360 4

Set in 11/13 Monotype Baskerville by Servis Filmsetting Ltd

Printed and bound in Great Britain by
Caledonian International Book Manufacturing Ltd, Glasgow

A catalogue entry for this book is available in the British Library

Contents

Illustrations

The author and publisher wish to acknowledge the following for permission to reproduce illustrations: Plate 1, Illustrated London News Picture Library; 3 and 13, Tate Gallery; 4, Royal Archive © Her Majesty the Queen; 5, Manchester City Art Gallery; 9, Royal Academy of Arts; 11 and 14, Royal Photographic Society Picture Library; 12, Royal Collection © Her Majesty the Queen; 15, Girton College Archive.

Preface

THE ORIGIN of this book goes back thirty years, when I was invited to Toronto to address the newly-founded Victorian Society of Canada, choosing as my subject 'The Early Victorian World Picture'. This was a first attempt to gain an understanding of some of the anxieties, hopes and expectations of the first generation of Victorians by viewing the problems that confronted them as far as possible through their own eyes. To develop such a theme, however, and to try to exhibit the extent to which the culture, literature and thought of those times were conditioned by the observations of contemporaries of what was happening in the world around them, clearly required a much fuller treatment than could be offered in the compass of a single lecture. This, then, is my excuse for undertaking that more detailed study now, while at the same time extending the boundaries of the exercise to cover the almost constantly changing scene of the whole of the Victorian period.

The extent of the coverage must also be my excuse for the restriction of my researches to printed sources; and – within that abundantly rich treasure-house – for a selection which some may feel is somewhat arbitrary and subjective. Nevertheless every contemporary observation constitutes evidence; and no apology can be needed for the extent to which I have drawn from the letters, diary extracts and reminiscences that are supplied in such profusion within the multi-volume 'Lives' and 'Letters' of Victorian worthies, compiled so often within months of the death of the subject in question as an act of filial obligation, and therefore all the more revealing because of the minimal attention paid to judicious selection, editing and pruning. The writings of the acknowledged sages are, of course, of primary importance, as is the formidable range of contemporary literature, compelling the historian to pick and choose as may appear to suit his purpose.

In the course of my attempts to synthesize what does not easily admit of synthesis I have had to recognize certain almost unavoidable limitations in my coverage. For instance, although the difference of attitude between the north and south of England cannot simply be ignored, the focus of this study is very plainly Anglo-centric, with scant regard to the different vantage points of those who lived in Wales and Scotland. Similarly, since the central theme of this book is concerned with the observations of contemporaries, such historical background as I supply has had to be pruned and condensed, so that it may seem at times over-simplified and therefore deficient in its recognition of the volume of specialist revisionist studies offered in recent years.

It will be very clear, from the pages that follow, that whatever originality in approach this study may presume to claim, an enormous debt must be acknowledged to certain distinguished scholars, on both sides of the Atlantic, who have done so much to illuminate our understanding of the culture and civilization of the Victorian period. For me personally, a first reading of G.M. Young's *Victorian England: Portrait of an Age* was the moment of conversion from medieval studies to the field of nineteenth-century England; and I doubt whether I could have considered embarking upon this present theme without the help gained from the writings of W.L. Burn, George Kitson Clark and Asa Briggs; or from the equally stimulating American contribution to the study of Victorian culture in the various scholarly offerings of Gertrude Himmelfarb, Walter Houghton and Jerome Buckley.

In addition to the formal acknowledgements listed elsewhere, I should like especially to thank Dr John Walsh of Jesus College, Oxford, for his kindness in reading through my completed typescript and making several helpful suggestions; Dr Peter Nockles of the John Rylands University Library of Manchester, for allowing me to use its magnificent facilities and for searching out various obscure titles at my request; and the patient and genial staff of Keswick Library for procuring books for me through the British Library service. Finally I owe a special debt of thanks to Grant McIntyre (of John Murray) and Stuart Proffitt (of HarperCollins) for the pressure they put upon me to write this book. Roger Hudson, in particular, deserves acknowledgement for his assistance over the selection of illustrations, and for drawing my attention to certain extracts from his own Folio Society publication, *The Jubilee Years*, which provided me with some invaluable material for the coverage of the closing decades of the century.

Thornthwaite, Cumbria   David Newsome

INTRODUCTION

Observation of One's Times

'The world is a looking-glass, and gives back to every man the reflection of his own face.'

W.M. Thackeray, *Vanity Fair*

WHEN DID the Victorians come to regard themselves as 'Victorians' and to use the word as an adjective descriptive of the period in which they were living? The answer appears to be sometime in 1851, the year of the Great Exhibition, fourteen years after the accession of the Queen.[1] Several decades earlier, however, the notion was becoming widely accepted that some momentous events and upheavals at the end of the eighteenth century – and the French Revolution of 1789 was the most momentous of all – constituted a watershed in the history of modern times. The world was never to be quite the same again. Therefore the years that followed heralded a period of unique significance which had a distinctive identity and character all its own. Whether one regarded this changing world with hope and exhilaration, or with mounting apprehension, there was general acknowledgement among contemporary thinkers and commentators that they were destined to live in uncommonly stirring times. 'We have been living ... the life of three hundred years in thirty,' Thomas Arnold, Headmaster of Rugby, observed in 1832.[2] A year later, Edward Bulwer [Lytton] commented that 'Every age may be called an age of transition – the passing-on, as it were, from one state to another never ceases; but in our age the transition is *visible*.'[3] There was never a moment during Victoria's reign that observers thought otherwise. The key-word seems to have been 'transitional'.[4]

As late as 1885, T.H.S. Escott, editor of *The Fortnightly Review*, in a somewhat ponderous work of social analysis, *England: Its People, Polity, and Pursuits,* fastened on precisely that word to describe the character of late Victorianism;[5] and the Preface to *Lux Mundi,* the symposium volume of Anglican theological writings on the doctrine of the Incarnation, published four years later, contains the following reflection:

> We have written with the conviction that the epoch in which we live is one of profound transformation, intellectual and social, abounding in new needs, new points of view, new questions.[6]

This consciousness of dynamism and of living in a distinctive period of history gave rise to the popularization of a relatively new abstraction: the concept of the 'spirit of an age'. An early example is found in Shelley, when he salutes the 'comprehensive and all-penetrating spirit' of the poets of his own times, such ability to 'sound the depths of human nature' being 'less their spirit than the spirit of the age.'[7] The phrase appears again as the title of a book of contemporary character sketches by William Hazlitt in 1825; and in 1831 John Stuart Mill, in the first of five articles for *The Examiner* under the same title, reflected as follows:

> The 'Spirit of the Age' is in some measure a novel expression. I do not believe that it is to be met with in any work exceeding fifty years in antiquity. The idea of comparing one's own age with former ages, or with our notion of those which are yet to come, had occurred to philosophers; but it never before was itself the dominant idea of any age.

Why? he asked; because 'it is an idea essentially belonging to an age of change.'[8]

In the same decade, the young Thomas Babington Macaulay, in his earliest historical essays written for *The Edinburgh Review,* had come to realize that the understanding of the spirit of any particular age, and of how that spirit changed from one epoch to another, was one of the first requirements of an historian. Once grasped, this concept dominated Macaulay's 'approach to both history and the contemporary scene', John Clive has written, 'since it was closely tied in his mind to a general schema of the growth of civilization'.[9] In Disraeli's *Coningsby* (1844), 'the spirit of the age' had become sufficiently established as a facile slogan for it to be caricatured in a dialogue on the nature of character between Coningsby and 'the stranger' at the Forest Inn.[10]

Some thirty years later Matthew Arnold, with his love of Germanisms, substituted the word *Zeitgeist* for the same concept, carrying the meaning of some controlling force which determined the culture of a particular age. That shrewd critic of so many of the writers of the time, R.H. Hutton, was not impressed, however, by invocations of such abstractions:

> To my mind [he wrote], the *Zeitgeist* is a will-o-the-wisp, who misleads us as much as he enlightens ... It breathes on us, and we can no longer see a truth which was clear yesterday. It breathes again, and like invisible ink held to the fire, the truth comes out again in all its brightness.[11]

Nevertheless, if it was the firm conviction of the wiser minds of the nineteenth century that their age was somehow different in character from anything that had preceded it, different too in the way that it reacted and responded to the specific challenges of the times, then this posed a series of questions which could hardly be ignored. How had this come about, and when? More pertinent still, what would be the end thereof? One hardly needed to be a sage or an historian to supply the more obvious answers to the first question. The final defeat of Napoleon in 1815 and the restoration of the Bourbon monarchy, albeit for only fifteen uneasy years, might have suggested a return to the old political *status quo*, but what had happened in France, and the fear of what might at any time occur again, left a legacy of profound unease and of both social and political tension lasting well into Victoria's reign. No section of society was untouched by the vast increase in population (it practically doubled between 1801 and 1851), a fact which meant – as Dr Kitson Clark observed – that 'if nothing else had happened in the first half of the nineteenth century, this alone would have secured that Victorian England was decisively different in a hundred and one ways from the Georgian England of 1800.'[12]

The most powerful impact of all, however, was the massive advance of technology and industrialization which was visibly reshaping both the landscape and the social structure of the whole country. Fully to understand what was happening, and to be able to offer reasonably informed speculation as to the answer to the second question – 'where are we going?' – demanded a deeper appreciation of the whole historical context within which this transformation had been taking place. It required an exercise of sober reflection through observation: 'look here, upon this picture, and on this'.

And well might people marvel, when they put the two pictures side by side; such was Prince Albert's message on the eve of the Great Exhibition. In a speech at the Mansion House before a great assemblage of ambassadors and civic officers, called together to launch this enterprise in 1850, he had this to say:

> Gentlemen – I conceive it to be the duty of every educated person closely to watch and study the time in which he lives, and, as far as in him lies, to add his humble mite of individual exertion to further the accomplishment of what he believes providence to have ordained. Nobody, however, who has paid any attention to the peculiar features of our present era, will doubt for a moment that we are living at a period of most wonderful transition, which tends rapidly to accomplish that great end, to which, indeed, all history points – the realization of the unity of mankind.[13]

'Watch and study' – pay attention to 'peculiar features' – discover, through observation, the lessons that history appears to be teaching: these injunctions, delivered in a spirit of sublime optimism, were the means by which Prince Albert thought the fullest opportunities could be gained from what seemed to be the blessings of Providence. It is interesting, and in itself indicative of one of the main differences between the Victorian age and earlier times, that Walter Bagehot, writing three years later, in an essay on Bishop Butler, observed that this was precisely what the eighteenth century failed to do. This was a generation that was altogether too 'comfortable'. 'The stir and conflict in which we live had barely commenced ... They did not "look before and after", nor "pine for what was not".'[14]

Failure 'to look before and after' denoted a lack of a sense of history in that one could neither explain how a situation had arisen nor guide one's generation in the journeys that lay ahead. It was exactly this perception of the duty of the historian that prompted A.P. Stanley, in his biography of his former headmaster and lifelong hero, to salute Thomas Arnold's contribution to the study of history and his inspirational teaching:

> Striving to fulfil in his measure the definition of man, in which he took especial pleasure, 'a being of large discourse, looking before and after', he learned more and more, whilst never losing his hold on the present, to live also habitually in the past and for the future.[15]

The Victorian age was certainly not deficient in men of 'large discourse'; and just because they were living in a visibly changing world, probably most people at some stage in their lives, according to their individual circumstances and within the compass of their faculties, paused to ask themselves the question 'what does all this mean to me?' The answer given might be as negative, but none the less genuine, as the conclusion of Stephen Blackpool in Dickens' *Hard Times*: "'tis a muddle, a' a muddle!'[16] Nevertheless he was giving expression to his own world picture. To that extent, every generation may be said to have a world picture, and perhaps there are as many world pictures as there are people who seek a meaning in the events around them. The answers, whether supplied by the fictional Stephen Blackpool, or Prince Albert at the Mansion House, or Thomas Arnold, will tend to have at least one thing in common: an inescapable subjectivity. As Thackeray shrewdly observed: 'The world is a looking-glass, and gives back to every man the reflection of his own face.'[17]

Any attempt to define the 'Victorian World Picture', then, has to be undertaken in full awareness of various qualifications which should be registered at the outset. In the first place, the phrase itself may be open to question. When Professor E.M.W. Tillyard published his celebrated little book on *The Elizabethan World Picture* in 1943, a work of seminal significance for the study of sixteenth- and early seventeenth-century England, his use of the phrase 'world picture' was meticulously exact. He was concerned with demonstrating the extent to which medieval geocentric cosmology, with its conviction of a hierarchy of creation and a divine Chain of Being, survived unchallenged into the age of Milton. This present study, although it cannot avoid some consideration of the Darwinian and post-Darwinian concept of the universe, is not really concerned with cosmology at all. 'World Picture' is the best that the English language can offer for what the Germans would render as *Zeitanschauungen*, literally 'observations of one's times'.

How did the Victorians observe their own times? What troubled or excited them, as they looked at their internal problems and crises? How did they see themselves and their country in relation to what was happening in Europe and elsewhere? What did history tell them as a guide to the future (when they 'looked before and after', in fact)? Furthermore, since the Victorian age was unquestionably religious in terms of its prevailing spirit and the extent to which religious issues influenced public affairs, the process of looking into the future inevitably involved a looking into the 'beyond' and therefore highly-fraught controversies over the nature of life hereafter. As the century drew to its close, the world picture began to take on a conspicuously un-Victorian aspect, so that the period of the *fin de siècle* saw the focus of people's attentions turning to the question of what lay ahead.

Watersheds in history are rarely, if ever, determined by the fortuitous dates of the beginning and end of a particular reign, and therefore the label 'Victorian' can only really be justified if one recognizes that the longest reign in British history actually encompassed two-thirds of the nineteenth century, and also that the Victorians themselves came to develop such a keen sense of their own identity. Attitudes and modes of thinking, which have come to be regarded as quintessentially Victorian, in many instances antedated the accession of the Queen. Thomas Arnold was imbuing his pupils with the virtues of earnestness and the obligations of the work ethic from the moment that he became Headmaster of Rugby in 1828; and if his name has gone down to posterity, largely through Lytton Strachey's influence, as an 'Eminent Victorian', it should be remembered that barely five years of his life – he died, aged only 47, in 1842 – coincided with Victoria's reign. As A.O.J. Cockshutt has observed: 'He was not a Victorian, but he trained Victorians ... In an odd way he seems more typical of the decades that followed his death than of any period in his own lifetime.'[18]

If one considers who were the truly formative writers and thinkers who shaped the minds and inspired the actions of the early and mid-Victorian generations, few were still living in 1837. Five of the founding fathers of the Victorian age died in the early 1830s: in 1832, Walter Scott and Jeremy Bentham, the pioneer of Utilitarianism; in 1833, William Wilberforce, the Emancipator; in 1834, Coleridge, the Sage of Highgate; and in 1835, the radical polemicist William Cobbett. Bentham and Coleridge had been – as John Stuart Mill appraised them – creative geniuses who represented the 'two opposite poles of one great force of progression'.[19] Something of the vitality of early nineteenth-century Evangelicalism died with the Emancipator. 'No more Clapham Sect nowadays', James Stephen lamented ruefully in 1845.[20] No more Waverley novels, either, with the death of Scott, arguably the early Victorians' favourite author. With the death of Cobbett, the voice of the boldest champion of popular Radicalism was silenced. A recital of these names goes far to substantiate the claim of Professor J.E. Baker that 'almost everything that grew to maturity' in mid-Victorian times had 'its roots in the first quarter of the century'.[21]

The Romantic Movement, however, had not died by 1837. Indeed, it is questionable whether the nineteenth century ever witnessed its complete demise. But the great age of Romanticism in England, commonly confined to the years 1780 to 1830, had left only two survivors – at least among the poets – into Victoria's reign: Robert Southey and William Wordsworth. Wordsworth's fame was still at its height, but neither man had anything further of significance to offer, honoured though they both were by the Queen with successive laureateships; desiccation of their poetic inspiration seemed to coincide with the reposeful respectability consequent upon the receipt of public pensions. Southey died in 1843 and Wordsworth in 1850.

Hence the impression of many contemporaries that the country was undergoing the unfamiliar experience of a temporary intellectual hiatus. Connop Thirlwall, later Bishop of St David's, expressed this view as early as the 1820s:

> The want of a right direction of intellectual energies is perhaps the greatest [defect] that England now suffers [he wrote to Baron Bunsen in Germany]. For the age appears to me to be scarcely less fruitful of men of extraordinary power than any in our history.[22]

Similar views were expressed in the 1830s,[23] though not shared by Carlyle, Macaulay, Mill or Dickens, none of whom could be said to have been an excessively modest man; and all of whom had published works of some substance by 1837. But when great names leave the stage, their devotees are apt not to notice those waiting in the wings. In 1880 Leslie Stephen, creator of the *Dictionary of National Biography* and father of Virginia Woolf, reflected sadly that 'certainly there is no one now who is to the rising generation what Mill and Carlyle were to us; nor have we a really good novelist or any poet of high rank to replace the old idols.'[24] George Eliot died in 1880, and she had no successor; but Stephen's view would not have been echoed by admirers of Browning, Swinburne, or Meredith, and the names of Stevenson, Hardy, Henry James and Conrad would soon be on many people's lips.

This excursion into the 1880s leads naturally to a necessary qualification about the title of this study: is it possible to make generalizations about the Victorian period as a whole? It is generally accepted by historians that this reign of over sixty years, at a time when society, religious beliefs, and dominant ideas were in a constant state of flux, cannot effectively be assessed without appreciating that it actually divides into three reasonably distinct periods. The first, marked by acute political and social unrest, is deemed to end sometime between 1848 (the last ineffective gasp of the Chartist movement) and 1851 (the year of the Great Exhibition). On the limits of the prosperous and relatively stable mid-Victorian period – the so-called 'Age of Equipoise' – historians differ, some placing the beginning of the late-Victorian age in 1867 (the Second Reform Bill), others choosing the early 1870s, with the onset of the 'Great Depression'. Certainly by 1880 there were sufficient indications that the Victorian age was moving into its 'flash Edwardian epilogue'.[25]

At that stage one is looking at a very different world. E.E. Kellett, whose memories went back to the last decades of the century, wrote:

> I have seen no such rapid or complete change as that which took place in the eighties and nineties. It is like one of those catastrophes which the geologist used to postulate in order to explain the alterations in the earth: sudden, immense, and, I think, irrevocable ... There is far more difference between the mind of 1900 and that of 1800 than between 1880 and 1640.[26]

It is clear from the context that Kellett was recalling the intellectual transformation that had taken place during the aftermath of the Darwinian revolution in the 1860s. But retrospective contemplations of technological and social transformations sound the same note. As early as 1860 Thackeray, looking back to his youth in the 1820s, wrote:

> It was only yesterday, but what a gulf between now and then. *Then* was the old world. Stage-coaches, more or less swift riding-horses, pack-horses, highwaymen, Druids, Ancient Britons ... all these belong to the old period. I will concede a halt in the midst of it and allow that gunpowder and printing tended to modernize the world. But your railroad starts a new era ... We who lived before railways and survive out of the ancient world, are like Father Noah and his family out of the Ark.[27]

Thackeray died only three years after writing this passage, in 1863. But what of the memories of someone who lived through the entire period, whose boyhood antedated Queen Victoria, and who survived into the twentieth century? Goldwin Smith was one such, born in 1823 and surviving until 1910. He was Regius Professor of History at Oxford in the early 1860s until he accepted a professorial post at Cornell University, and then spent the rest of his life in Canada. He recalled the old cheese fairs in the Forbury in Reading, the watchman calling the hour of the night, his bedroom fire lit with a tinder-box, the sight of a man sitting in the stocks at Caversham. 'From this state of things', he wrote, 'I have lived into an age of express-trains, ocean greyhounds, electricity, bicycles, globe-trotting, Evolution, the Higher Criticism, and general excitement and restlessness.'[28] He would have seen, although curiously never mentions it, the revolution wrought by the internal combustion engine: at one end of his life, the stage-coach; at the other, the motor-car. Looking back to his boyhood in Reading, he observed: 'Between that state of things and the present there is only a single lifetime; yet I feel as if I were writing of antiquity.'[29]

Any attempt to recreate the Victorian world picture requires the awareness of pitfalls easy enough to identify, but not so easy to avoid. The first is the need to distinguish between attitudes that were changing, and the particular themes which recur practically throughout the century irrespective of the three time-honoured divisions into periods. It has also to be borne in mind that the observations of contemporaries are only opinions, and may not always be accurate representations of the facts. It is true that the most penetrating observers are also likely to be the most articulate and tend to be, explicitly or implicitly, critics of what they observe and therefore didactic in tone (none more so than Thomas Carlyle, Matthew Arnold and John Ruskin). Didacticism, indeed, was the norm. Trollope, for instance, in his *Autobiography*, was quite clear on the duty of the novelist. 'The writer of stories must please, or he will be nothing', he wrote. 'And he must teach whether he wish to teach or no.'[30]

Now if one is relying upon the writings of critics and moralists in order to gain an accurate picture of the mores and values of a society, it is important to recognize the distinction between the attitudes or actions criticized and the positive substance of the critic's homiletic. This may seem too obvious to be even worth mentioning. It is sometimes forgotten, however. In his celebrated study *Religion and the Rise of Capitalism*, R.H. Tawney pointed the lesson in his analysis of the economic values of the Middle Ages. To those living in the present-day capitalistic economy, there might seem to be something worthy of respect, even a slightly grudging admiration, for the way in which medieval writers and preachers inveighed against covetousness, profit-seeking and usurious rates of interest, holding up ideals of charity, fair dealing and the Just Price. They were prepared to call a spade a spade. 'Men called these vices by their right names, and had not learned to persuade themselves that greed was enterprise and avarice economy.'[31] What this actually reveals, however, is that usury was the medieval besetting sin.

Moving into the mid-Victorian period, we may also regard the abundance of exhortations, either spoken or written, on the virtues of honesty, industry, chastity, temperance and thrift with a feeling of slight guilt at our own half-heartedness, even diffidence, over proclaiming such values today. We have to remember, however, as W.L. Burn has pointed out, that the insistence on these virtues 'was dictated by the threats of dishonesty, sensuality, drunkenness and improvidence; the virtues were flags to which men rallied in battle, not decorations for ceremonial parades'.[32]

It is an argument that can work both ways. An interesting example of its inversion has been given recently by Michael Mason in his study on *The Making of Victorian Sexual Attitudes*, writing of Victorian sentimentality. *The Saturday Review*, according to its historian, launched an attack in the 1860s on the sentimentality of the age, expressing the conviction that 'it may reasonably be doubted whether there has ever been a more thoroughly sentimental time than the present.'

> Our first reaction is to agree [Michael Mason writes]. Our second reaction should be to wonder if Victorian England really can have been as 'thoroughly sentimental' as we suppose, if the tendency was consistently deplored at the time by so powerful an organ of opinion.[33]

A further problematical area is encountered when one begins to move down the scale from the most articulate to the least; from Carlyle, for instance, to the lesser Carlyles, who may in fact have been more representative of the thoughts and aspirations of their times than the acknowledged sages. There are two separate considerations to be borne in mind here. The first is the simple problem of regional variation. England, throughout the nineteenth century, was still very much 'two nations', and not only in the sense that Disraeli used the term to signify the division between the rich and the poor. Those living north of the Trent had a self-conscious identity of their own. Just as a Scotsman or a Welshman understandably resented the way in which the designation 'Britain' was too often employed as interchangeable with 'England', so a northerner rejected the notion that England was, in essence, London and the south. They saw things differently in the north. Keith Robbins has called to mind the observation of John Thornton in Elizabeth Gaskell's *North and South,* that

> Unlike the men of Oxford, who reverenced the past, the men of the North could be defined as those who wanted 'something which can apply to the present more directly.' His 'Milton' might be situated in deepest 'Darkshire', but he was confident that it pointed the way to the England of the future. The men of his county hated to have their laws made at a distance, that is to say in the South.[34]

The second consideration is the difficulty of ascertaining the actual thoughts and feelings of those at the bottom of the scale – John Bright's 'submerged sixth'. They were not, of course, without their spokesmen. But even here one must tread warily. Sometimes we find the echo of an authentic voice in witness supplied to a Royal Commission. Sometimes a fictitious character, such as Jo, the crossing-sweeper in *Bleak House,* can be identified as the actual fourteen-year-old George Ruby who was examined at the Guildhall on 8 January 1850.[35] Although Dickens took acceptable liberties in the development of his character and the unhappy situations in which he found himself, at least something of the real predicament of the juvenile crossing-sweeper, as well as his actual speech, can be recovered. On the other hand, both the second-hand reports of reformers and the liberties of dramatization taken by novelists have a propagandist purpose.[36] 'Reformers must prove their point; novelists must interest their public.'[37]

Working-class literacy was increasing throughout the century, and the press was not slow to exploit the ever-widening market, as will be seen later. Every section of the community came to be fed with material deemed to be appropriate to its needs, or to gratify its wants, by some organ of the press. All governments were sensitive to that indefinable abstraction 'public opinion' – indefinable because, as Mark Pattison, Rector of Lincoln College, Oxford and a notoriously mordant critic of his times, once observed in a sermon on 30 April 1865, it is in fact 'the opinion of no one in particular; it is each appealing to every one else. Men lean against each other and the whole community stands upright, though no separate member of it is in equilibrium.'[38] But however difficult it may be to trace public opinion to its source, or to gauge how truly representative it may be of either individual or group convictions, it is none the less a force to be reckoned with in any assessment of the world picture current at any particular time.

One conclusion, therefore, is inescapable. The world picture of the Victorians, compounded of so many reflections from so many different vantage points, must inevitably turn out to be a collage rather than an ordered composition. Furthermore, granted the dynamism of the age and the extent to which the one constant factor was its changing face, the collage must also be a moving picture. Something of significance can surely be discerned; it is what one fails to see, through the unavoidable process of generalization, that can cause distortion. An uncomfortable parallel suggests itself. In 1897, E.F. Benson witnessed one of the last great feats of nineteenth-century invention: the cinematograph. The Diamond Jubilee procession was captured on film – moving pictures, too, displaying faint adumbrations of the west front of St Paul's Cathedral. It was a wonder. The Queen could be identified and the Princess of Wales, slightly obscured by their parasols. But he had to admit there were imperfections. A significant moment of history had been memorialized and rendered visible, but 'through a blizzard of flashes and winks and large black dots ... all very trying for the eyes'.[39]

CHAPTER 1

Looking Inwards

I

'It has all been so sudden.'

W. Cooke Taylor in 1842

'For sure, th'world is in a confusion that passes me or any other man to understand.'

Nicholas Higgins in E. Gaskell, *North and South*

IT WAS once thought that the visitation of a comet was a presage of the death of kings. A survey of the events immediately leading up to the death of William IV on 20 June 1837 and the accession to the throne of the eighteen-year-old Princess Victoria, however, would suggest that this change of monarch was the culmination of a series of disasters. It all began with a violent snowstorm on the evening of Christmas Day, 1836 – the heaviest fall of snow in living memory. There were drifts of up to fifty feet in depth, it was said. The bitter wintry conditions prevailed into the new year, the inauspicious start of which was compounded by the onset of a virulent epidemic of influenza. At least one man of rising eminence was laid low by it – John Henry Newman, in Oxford, on 9 January, and in view of the large number of fatalities that it claimed, he was lucky to survive after an incapacitation of one week.[1] London was the worst hit. The deaths there were so many, according to one official account, that 'there was scarcely an undertaker not employed, and many unable to accomplish their orders.'[2]

London was again the scene of a shocking episode in May, the *Annual*

Register recorded. This was the execution outside Newgate Prison of James Greenacre, for the wilful murder of Hannah Brown, whose mutilated body had been discovered in the Edgware Road. Even by the standards of an age accustomed to public blood-lettings and visible horrors, the behaviour of the onlookers appalled those endeavouring to maintain order and decorum. A crowd of more than two thousand had waited through the night to view the spectacle, some clinging to lamp-posts. When the deed was over,

> the crowd seemed as if they never could satisfy themselves with gazing on the hanging murderer. The women were, if possible, more ruthless than the men. As the period for taking down the body approached, a fierce conflict ensued between two crowds, one leaving the place of execution, and the other rushing towards it. The pressure became so great in the narrow passages, that several fell in a state of exhaustion, and some narrowly escaped being trampled to death.[3]

The month of June, as the King lay dying, seemed to go from bad to worse. The boiler of a steam-vessel at Hull burst, and nineteen people were killed in the explosion. This was followed by the official report on the nation's 'State of Trade', and a gloomier picture could hardly be imagined. *The Morning Chronicle* published its findings:

> At Manchester it is stated there are 50,000 hands out of employ, and most of the large establishments are working only half time. At Wigan, which is not a large place, there are 4000 weavers totally unable to get work. Unless a stimulus is shortly given to commerce, persons who have the means of forming the most correct opinions say, that half a million of hands, at least, will be idle in the manufacturing districts in the very worst time of the year.

In the same month a public meeting was held in Birmingham to consider possible measures 'to relieve the present appalling state of commercial distress'.[4]

Was there anything uplifting to record in this doleful year? There were certain literary landmarks. Thomas Carlyle had started to give public lectures in London, and published his monumental *History of the French Revolution.* Charles Dickens brought out *Pickwick Papers* in book form, and *Oliver Twist* began to appear in monthly instalments towards the end of the year. A definite change for the better in the character and tone of the Court, which had not been exactly an inspiring source of moral example for several decades, soon began to make its effect. One keen observer of his times, however, expressed a reservation. Thomas Arnold reflected to Julius Hare on the role of a woman as Head of the English Church, doubting that such a circumstance would help to cure its current divisions, torn asunder as it seemed to him by the essentially sectarian stance of Newman and his disciples at Oxford. 'A female reign', he said, 'is an unfavourable time ... for pressing strongly the doctrine of the Crown's Supremacy.'[5]

One doubts whether Queen Victoria, at any stage of her reign, would have appreciated the force of this. As to the more immediate problems that confronted the Queen, and the country at large, Arnold's observations were extremely pertinent. There was nothing of the Tory in Arnold; not a great deal of the Whig, either. He strenuously sought to distance himself from all parties, believing the Whigs to be over-influenced by the Utilitarian doctrines of Jeremy Bentham, and the Tories to be so resistant to reform that they threatened to destroy the very institutions they strove to uphold.[6]

But he was deeply concerned, as he looked about him, that a process of change was taking place in almost every aspect of life, and that the pace of the changes tended to be faster than society could assimilate. Everything seemed to be on the move: population growth, industrialization, the clamour of the Radicals to attain universal suffrage and to push forward to the realization of democracy. In such a state of excessive acceleration, society could easily go off the rails (to which it had recently taken). Civilization would become 'overheated'.[7] This was where the historian's ability to 'look before and after' should be invoked for the guidance of his contemporaries. 'Our future course', Arnold stated in one of his lectures as Regius Professor of History at Oxford, 'must be hesitating or mistaken, if we do not know what course has brought us to the point where we are at present.'[8]

No one could quarrel with that. But what answer could the early Victorians give to the most perplexing question of all? They knew that the population had increased and was continuing to increase; but they did not know why. Indeed, although historians, economists and demographers have been analysing the available statistics from Victorian times to the present day, no incontrovertible conclusion has been reached. It is clear that the increase began in the middle years of the eighteenth century, accelerated from about 1770, and moved into top gear between 1801 and 1851, when the population of England and

Wales rose from nearly 9 million to about 18 million. It continued to rise thereafter, but at a slightly slower rate, reaching 23 million in 1871, after which date both birth and death rates began to fall. The possible explanations can only be a declining death-rate or a rising birth-rate, or the impact of immigration, or – as is most likely – a combination of all three circumstances. Research has suggested that immigration and emigration figures tended to cancel each other out. The vast majority of immigrants were Irish, especially during the 1840s, when it was calculated that 400,000 Irish men and women fled from the starving conditions of their homeland in the hope of finding work and sustenance in expanding industrial cities such as Manchester, Glasgow and Liverpool, or by enrolling as navvies wherever railway construction was under way. Some exchanged a position of hopelessness at home for a plight no less hopeless in the rookeries of London. Many stayed, but some moved on; and doubtless a fair number of Irish are included in the large emigration figures (averaging 198,000 a year between 1852 and 1867), some assisted by the Colonial Land and Emigration Commissioners (from 1847 onwards), and the bulk of them making for Australasia.[9]

The main issue of the debate centres on the validity of the contention made by G.T. Griffith in 1926, and confirmed with reservations by T.H. Marshall, that the major cause of the population growth was the decline in the death-rate, arising from the advance of medical science, perhaps the most significant contribution being the discovery by Jenner of vaccination as a precaution against the notorious killer, smallpox. The effect of this, however, would have made little impact until the early years of the nineteenth century. In recent years emphasis has tended to switch to the rising of the birth-rate, partly as a result of women marrying younger (according to analysis in 1981 by E.A. Wrigley and R.S. Scholfield into what economists describe as 'nuptuality' statistics).[10]

An increasing demand for labour at a time when industry was expanding might also have encouraged larger families. But the rapidity with which booms were followed by slumps during the nineteenth century presents such a picture of fluctuating fortunes that this last argument seems difficult to sustain. Furthermore, different environments created different situations. This has been borne out by recent research into the lowering of the age at which women married. Just a single instance will suffice, for the year 1861. In Sheffield – the centre of the steel and cutlery industry – 85 per cent of the female population were married by the age of 30; whereas in Keighley, a wool textile town, the percentage was only 69. It is a reasonable deduction that women living in centres of heavy industry, where there was little opportunity for employment, would marry at an earlier age than their counterparts in textile towns where they could more easily obtain paid work.[11]

As far as contemporaries were concerned, the population problem aroused intense emotions primarily because a notorious diagnosis of the problem had been provided by Thomas Malthus in 1798 in his *Essay on the Principle of Population*, reproduced in several revised editions until 1817. Malthus was an Anglican clergyman, with a great distaste for the Utopian humanitarianism of such thinkers as Condorcet in France and William Godwin, an avowed atheist. He therefore set out to shatter the notion that nature was essentially benevolent and that civilization could look forward to the realization of some heavenly city on earth. The truth was quite the opposite; and he attempted to prove this with an irritating mathematical exactness. His underlying premiss was that 'population has a constant tendency to increase beyond the means of subsistence';[12] and since it increases in a demonstrable geometrical ratio, there was no hope that subsistence could ever catch up with the inexorable multiplication of the number of mouths to be fed. The only remedies, if such they could be called, were the cataclysmic interventions of plague or famine, and decimation of populations by war. Apart from these, the mandatory response of civilization under threat was some self-imposed restriction on the birth-rate. There were certain things that a government might do, and the first essential was to desist from Poor Relief, because the protection of the pauper or the out-of-work labourer by assisting him from the Poor Rates was a positive encouragement to him to remain economically unproductive, and certainly no deterrent to his reproducing.

These gloomy prognostications were, on the whole, well received by other political economists, especially David Ricardo, and by most Utilitarians. Stranger bedfellows, perhaps, were Unitarians like the sanitary reformer Thomas Southwood Smith and Harriet Martineau (who launched an angry attack on Charles Dickens for presuming to lampoon Malthus), and several prominent Evangelicals, the most articulate of whom was the Scottish divine and eminent preacher, Thomas Chalmers.

What appealed to Chalmers, and to many other Evangelicals, was the corollary that could be drawn from Malthus' mathematical calculations – that one sure, and saintly, way to achieve fewer births was by sexual restraint. He therefore became one of Malthus' leading missionaries, perceiving – in Boyd Hilton's words – that:

> Faced with the immediate threat of wars, famine and pestilence, men were being *forced* 'to elevate their minds above their passionate flesh', and such self-denial put them in a proper mental condition for the receipt of divine grace.[13]

This was a sad trial indeed for the poorer sections of society, who had few enough pleasures as it was. They were now being told to refrain from sexual activity even in the conjugal bed, for fear of bringing children into the world.

Francis Place, no lover of Malthus, countered by issuing handbills advocating the vaginal sponge as an effective contraceptive. Richard Carlile tirelessly continued the same crusade in a work entitled *Every Woman's Book*, and by lecturing up and down the land. It does not appear that they had much success. Perhaps ignorant working people were suspicious of the application of unnatural artificial devices. Even in the later decades of the century, when proselytizing of birth-control became more open, there was a general apprehension in left-wing circles that, in some subtle way, the upper and middle classes were trying to force birth-control on their inferiors in order to maintain 'an inegalitarian *status quo*'.[14]

The symbol of everything hateful about Malthusianism was – to the section of the population most affected by it – the Poor Law Amendment Act of 1834. There was to be no more relief for paupers, that is to say, the so-called 'idle poor'; at a time of 'over-population' (the Malthusian term for unemployment), no help to those unable to obtain work. What they were offered instead was the seemingly heartless 'Workhouse Test', based on the principle of 'Less Eligibility', which – in language that the poor could understand – meant simply this: 'Take it or leave it. If you won't work, or if you can't work, or if you choose to be a pauper (which is not the same thing as being poor), you can come inside the workhouse, and we shall do our best to make your life that much less congenial than anything you can find for yourself outside. We won't have people coming here to shirk work.' Little fear of that. Although the application of the new Poor Law was never so universally rigorous as it threatened to be and Poor Relief still continued in many places,[15] this did not mean that it was hated any the less; and what was most resented was the intention that lay behind it.

The anti-Malthusians were not without their spokesmen. Coleridge was one of the first to speak out. In the *Table-Talk*, he summarized the Malthusian attitude as the equivalent of saying to a man: 'You have no claim upon me: you have your allotted part to perform in the world, so have I . . . I cannot afford you relief: *you must starve.*' What would be the man's answer?

> You disclaim all connection with me: I have no claims upon you? *I can then have no duties towards you*, and the pistol shall put me in possession of your wealth. You may leave a law behind you which shall hang me, but what man who saw assured starvation before him, ever feared hanging?[16]

Carlyle thundered against Malthus in *Sartor Resartus*, inventing a disciple called Hofrath Heuschrecke who set up an Institute for the Repression of Population.

> Enough for us to understand that Heuschrecke is a disciple of Malthus; and so zealous for the doctrine, that his zeal almost literally eats him up. A deadly fear of Population possesses the Hofrath; something like a fixed-idea; undoubtedly akin to the more diluted forms of Madness.[17]

William Cobbett was even more forthright. In an open letter to Malthus, he addressed him as follows: 'Parson, I have, during my life, detested many men; but never any one so much as you.'[18]

All these diatribes were actually written before Victoria came to the throne. They form part, however, of the Victorians' inheritance. As Humphrey House observed, in analysing the strain of pessimism in the world picture of these times, Malthus' theory 'overshadowed and darkened all English life for seventy years'.[19]

It is reasonable to suppose that because the growth of population and the Industrial Revolution proceeded, as it were, in tandem, there must have been some causal connection between them. This is not necessarily so. Population growth was a European phenomenon, but only France experienced anything remotely approaching what happened in Britain in terms of technological advance and industrial and commercial expansion in the century between 1750 and 1850. The two movements appear to have occurred simultaneously. What lay behind Britain's unique situation was a whole complex of favourable circumstances. Of primary significance, of course, was a series of technological 'break-throughs', especially in the field of metallurgy, and in inspired experiments in the use of steam-power resulting in the invention of machinery which revolutionized the various processes in the manufacture of textiles. To be able to obtain maximum advantage of these inventions, however, there were other pre-requisites, all – as it happened – properties with which, during these years, Britain was abundantly blessed: ample natural resources, especially coal and iron-ore, and easy proximity to water; surplus capital wealth and the willingness of investors to make this available; vastly improving communications within the country, and also beyond it, in the supply of shipping to serve international markets; and – more important still – a certain market both at home and abroad for the consumption of mass-produced goods.

A growing population would undoubtedly be a contributory advantage. The introduction of machinery for factory production still required a large labour force, if – for many – labour of a very different kind. This hit hard upon the skilled workers in the textile trade, especially the handloom weavers, whose services became increasingly redundant. On the other hand, an expanding economy, with particular demands for increased labour in railway-construction, the mines and all sections of the building industry, could only profit from population growth. Furthermore, the larger the population, the wider the home market: more mouths to feed, more houses to keep warm, more people to clothe.

Nature does nothing by a jump, it is said. But to the British people living at the time, it seemed as if the world they knew had vanished almost overnight. Quite apart from the awesome revolution in transport and communications – a separate issue to be considered later – it was the suddenness of the changes that was the dominant note in the writings and reflections of contemporaries. Even the word 'industry', in the sense understood today, was a novelty. Adam Smith, towards the end of the eighteenth century, seems to have been the first to endow it with a capital letter and an institutional meaning, embracing the combination of manufacture and productivity.[20] In Carlyle's *Sartor Resartus* (1835), the word 'industrialism' appears for the first time. Five years later, in *Chartism*, the concomitant social problems of the industrial age are by Carlyle given a label, soon to become almost a catch-phrase – 'the Condition of England Question'.[21] 'It has all been so sudden' is the theme of W .Cooke Taylor in his *Notes of a Tour in the Manufacturing Districts of Lancashire* in 1842:

> The steam-engine had no precedent, the spinning-jenny is without ancestry, the mule and the power-loom entered on no prepared heritage: they sprang into sudden existence like Minerva from the brain of Jupiter.[22]

If the coming of the railways served to foster almost a new time-dimension, the whole process of life being speeded up beyond men's imaginations, then the Industrial Revolution was fast creating new perspectives of size. Everything seemed to be getting bigger. Here, however, the reactions of contemporary observers have to be treated with caution. The new factories and cotton mills sprouted into life alongside the domestic workshops, putting only a few in a limited number of trades out of business. The craft-structure of work actually steadily expanded throughout the century, in step with industrialization.[23] But the gaze of contemporaries, quite understandably, fastened upon the new features that were disfiguring the urban landscape, and upon the consequent transformation in the scale and nature of their work force. 'Operatives' worked in factories – a word denoting such depersonalization that it made Coleridge's hackles rise. 'Mark this word,' he said, 'for words *in this sense* are things.'[24] Furthermore, the edifices required to house these operatives were awe-inspiringly massive and testified to the inescapable fact that the industrial towns were expanding at an alarming rate.

No city could rival the size of London; no city in the whole of the world. By the end of the seventeenth century it had become the largest city in Europe. During the eighteenth century the population of Greater London increased by 222 per cent overall.[25] Dickens had to rely on his imagination when he described Gabriel Varden's approach to the city at night in *Barnaby Rudge*, the year in question being 1775.

> The great city lay outstretched before him like a dark shadow on the ground, reddening the sluggish air with a deep dull light, that told of labyrinths of public ways and shops, and swarms of busy people ... tall steeples looming in the air, and piles of unequal roofs oppressed by chimneys.[26]

London never ceased to fascinate Dickens, especially its magnetic pull upon migrants from all quarters of the British Isles, drawn there by the often forlorn hope of finding work. The statistics confirmed his observations: it was calculated, in the 1850s, that 40 per cent of all Londoners had been born elsewhere.[27] In *Dombey and Son,* written in 1848, Dickens cast Harriet Carker as his witness, contemplating the steady stream of travellers approaching the city, 'gazing fearfully at the huge town before them.'

> Day after day, such travellers crept past, but always, as she thought, in one direction – always towards the town. Swallowed up in one phase or other of its immensity, towards which they seemed impelled by a desperate fascination, they never returned. Food for the hospitals, the churchyards, the prisons, the river, fever, madness, vice, and death – they passed on to the monster, roaring in the distance, and were lost.[28]

Hippolyte Taine viewed the monster with wonder mingled with awe in 1862: 'Three million five hundred thousand inhabitants: it adds up to twelve cities the size of Marseilles, ten as big as Lyons, two the size of Paris, in a single mass ... Enormous, enormous – that is the word which recurs all the time.'[29]

But London, even as it swelled ever bigger, was not the creation of the Industrial Revolution. It was not strictly speaking an industrial city at all, even though large industrial concerns could be found within it. It was a huge mart, with vast shipyards and docks that could cope with 2,000 vessels at a time; gasworks, specialized engineering workshops, breweries, builders' yards, shops and traders of every description, and also the financial centre of the Western world. For the towns converted into cities by the Industrial Revolution, one had to travel north; for the supreme example – to Manchester.

In 1745 Manchester was a small town of 17,000 inhabitants. By 1801 it had grown to 70,000. Fifty years later, its population had risen to 303,000. 'All roads led to Manchester', Asa Briggs has written. It was the 'shock city of the age'.[30] Cotton had made it so, and the early Victorian phase of the Industrial Revolution was dominated by that single commodity, both in manufacturing and in commerce. Manchester was 'Cottonopolis'. Both Alexis de Tocqueville and Hippolyte Taine, those keen observers of all things English, made their way to Manchester. De Tocqueville, in 1835, was appalled by what he saw.

> A sort of black smoke covers the city. The sun seen through it is a disc without rays ... A thousand noises disturb this damp, dark labyrinth ... From this foul drain the greatest stream of human industry flows out to fertilize the whole world. From this filthy sewer pure gold flows. Here human-

ity attains its most complete development and its most brutish; here civilization works its miracle, and civilized man is turned back into a savage.[31]

In 1861, Taine described the city as a 'Babel built of brick':

> The factories extend their flanks of fouled brick one after another, bare, with
> shutterless windows, like economical and colossal prisons. The place is a
> great jerry-built barracks, a 'work-house' for four hundred thousand people,
> a hard-labour penal establishment; such are the ideas it suggests to the mind.
> One of the factory blocks is a rectangle six storeys high, each storey having
> forty windows: and inside, lit by gas jets, and deafened by the uproar of their
> own labour, toil thousands of workmen, penned in, regimented, hands
> active, feet motionless, all day and every day, mechanically serving their
> machines. Could there be any kind of life more outraged, more opposed to
> man's natural instincts?[32]

Manchester was not alone in its aspect of industrial squalor. Birmingham, because of its much greater diversity of occupation, with
many more small workshops than factories, might seem to offer to its
work force a blissful existence compared with the lot of a Mancunian.
But Birmingham 'was the hub of the small metal trades of the west
Midlands',[33] and products such as small arms, screws, nails, even
buttons, require forges and furnaces. Both de Tocquville and Dickens
were nauseated by the belching fumes and the incessant 'sound of
hammers' and of 'the whistle of steam escaping from boilers', the
lasting impression that Birmingham made upon their minds.[34] When
Dickens came to write *Hard Times*, depicting a fictional Gehenna called
'Coketown', it would appear that he put together two recollections of
the contemporary industrial scene. One was of the weavers' strike in
Preston, 'a nasty place', which he had recently visited.[35] The other was
his memory of a visit to Birmingham, which supplied the image of
tongues of flame leaping up from great furnaces and the 'smoke', which
Josiah Bounderby so proudly exhibited to James Harthouse as our 'meat
and drink'.[36]

Then there were the lesser Manchesters, mostly north of the Trent,
which were scarcely less squalid and all experiencing a staggering rapidity of growth. East of the Pennines, in the centre of the woollen and
worsted industries, Bradford had grown in thirty years from 29,000
inhabitants to 77,000; Halifax from 63,000 to 110,000; Huddersfield
from 15,000 to 34,000; Leeds from 53,000 to 123,000.[37]

What this tells us is that population was not only growing, it was also on the move. Much of this movement was migration from rural communities into the towns. The extent, however, is difficult to assess. On the one hand, the population growth obviously affected all sections and areas of the community, and the Census figures for 1851 revealed that the number of persons working in agriculture had reached what later proved to be the maximum for the whole century – 2.1 million. In 1801, it had been reckoned at 1.7 million. On the other hand, the proportion of the total work force represented by those employed on the land had fallen from 35.9 to 21.7 per cent.[38] This can be expressed in another way. In 1865, it was calculated that the urban population in England was nearly 50 per cent greater than the rural, 'and [that] more than one person out of every four ... lived and worked in a city of 100,000 inhabitants upwards'.[39]

The chief reason for this relative depopulation appears to have been a lowering of the standard of living of the agricultural labourer, compounded by the cumulative effect of literally thousands of private Enclosure Acts undertaken by landlords in order to bring uncultivated land into use, or to turn common land and former open fields into private land-units, all of which served to increase both the size of their farms and the profits from cultivation. This is yet another example of the smaller giving way to the larger, and also of increasing depersonalization. The days when a group of farm-workers would all eat together round the kitchen table in the farmhouse were fast disappearing. The injurious effect of the Enclosure Acts – the accusation, for instance, that peasants were thereby thrown out of their holdings *en masse* and that many then found themselves unemployed or forced into wage labour – has been challenged in recent years.[40] The most that one can safely say is that, during a period of economic transformation, the hardest hit were likely to be those least capable of bearing the changes.

The observations of two contemporaries are of interest here. In 1862, Taine came to the conclusion from his various enquiries that 'there can be no doubt the class of agricultural labourers is ... the most wretched and the most backward of all.'[41] Edward Bulwer, thirty years earlier, had said much the same, but his sympathies were for those who, in migrating, were making such a poor exchange of one misery for another. 'The physical condition of the Working Classes in Manufacturing Towns', he wrote, 'is more wretched than we can bear to consider.' In comparison with the worker on the land, 'it is not that he *dies sooner* than the labourer; he lives *more painfully*.'[42]

There was one other aspect of population on the move that exacerbated urban grievances and intensified the element of depersonalization. This was the inexorable exodus of the employer, for entirely understandable reasons, from accommodation in close proximity to his mill or factory (and therefore also his work force) to a grander house and less impure air in the suburbs. This is what bothered Mary Barton's father, John, in Elizabeth Gaskell's novel.

> At all times [he grieved] it is a bewildering thing to the poor weaver to see his employer removing from house to house, each one grander than the last, till he ends in building one more magnificent than all, or withdraws his money from the concern, or sells his mill to buy an estate in the country.[43]

By 1861 the distribution of the adult work force in England and Wales looked something like this: workers on the land (farms, forestry and fisheries were traditionally lumped together) still comprised the largest total of any single group, but their percentage of the whole had dropped to 14.6, compared to 34.1 in industry. The largest single groups within industry were the textile workers (1.7 million), metal workers, engineers and shipbuilders (700,000), workers in the building industry (600,000), those engaged in tailoring and boot-and-shoe making (516,000) and miners and quarry-workers (just under half a million).[44] Ranking very high in the list of employments were domestic servants – nearly a million resident female servants of all ages, and another 214,000 washerwomen and charwomen. Male servants, including private coachmen, numbered 95,000.[45] The number in domestic service continued to rise steadily thereafter. In 1881 it was reckoned that over two million were in resident domestic service (12 per cent of the total female population). This certainly suggests that the gap between the rich and the poor was ever-widening.[46]

What these figures do not reveal, however, is the volatile nature of the economy. There were boom years and corresponding slumps. The nine years from 1848 to 1857, for instance, marked a period of almost unprecedented prosperity following the collapse of the Chartist Movement, the discoveries of Californian and Australian gold, and years of extraordinary buoyancy in domestic investment and overseas trade.

The extent to which a rising standard of living was enjoyed by all classes of society has been the subject of much debate among social and economic historians. On the whole recent research, especially that based on analyses of consumption expenditure within the working classes,[47] has established that living standards were rising gradually from the middle years of the century, and that 'lower-income segments shared in economic growth'. Furthermore, 'real income per head for a population which itself more than trebled is estimated to have quadrupled.'[48] On the other hand, as Professor Martin Daunton has pointed out:

> It is impossible to know how much weight contemporaries themselves placed upon money income in comparison with a broader definition of the quality of life. How did they judge the change from rural domestic work to waged factory work and urban residence? ... What is certain is that urban residents who were breathing polluted air and drinking contaminated water were more likely to die at a younger age than their rural counterparts ... It is possible that workers experienced a psychological decline even if economic welfare improved.[49]

Clearly, however, both the level of wages and standards of living varied according to the type of employment and the locality of the workers. In her novel *North and South*, Elizabeth Gaskell drew a significant contrast between the predicament of workers in the industrial north and those elsewhere. During a boom the textile workers enjoyed a temporary place in the sun; not, alas, for long. This is how her character Nicholas Higgins put it, looking first at the southerners:

> If work's sure and steady theer, labour's paid at starvation prices, while here we've rucks of money coming in in one quarter, and ne'er a farthing the next. For sure, th'world is in a confusion that passes me or any other man to understand.[50]

Bad times could be very bad indeed. In the early and middle periods of Victoria's reign, the years *not* to have lived in were 1837–42, 1847–8, 1857 and 1866. The worst slump of all coincided with the first five years of the Queen's reign, a premonition of which had been the report on the 'State of Trade', quoted earlier. Among other distresses, it was a period of bad harvests, and the only people who could find it in them to smile were the farmers protected by the Corn Laws while everybody else sank deeper and deeper into depression.[51]

It was in the aftermath of these grim years that the 'Condition of England Question' provoked a whole spate of so-called 'Social Novels'. Disraeli's *Sybil* was the first in 1845, followed by Elizabeth Gaskell's *Mary Barton* and Charles Kingsley's *Yeast* in 1848. Kingsley repeated the dose in 1850 with *Alton Locke*. Then came Dickens' *Hard Times* in 1854 and Mrs Gaskell's *North and South* in 1855. The most faithful picture of the industrial problems of the north, however, came from the pen of Elizabeth Gaskell. Although born and bred in Knutsford (the setting of *Cranford*), she married the Manchester-based Unitarian minister, William Gaskell, in 1832. Thereafter Manchester was her home, and she knew it as intimately as Dickens knew London. When she wrote in *Mary Barton* of Manchester's terrible years from 1839 to 1842, she was describing what she had personally witnessed.

> Whole families went through a gradual starvation. They only wanted a Dante to record their sufferings. And yet even his words would fall short of the awful truth; they could only present an outline of the tremendous facts of the destitution that surrounded thousands upon thousands.

What would it all lead to? The most ominous consequence was a growing 'feeling of alienation between the different classes of society'.[52]

In the 1850s, it has been said, the 'Condition of England Question' gradually ceased to be the great social issue.[53] This may be so; but there remained many questions that society would be required to answer. One thing is certain, however. In the world picture of the Victorians formed from looking inwards at the problems of their own country, somewhere – either in the forefront or in the background, according to their different circumstances and different points of view – there would be found a representation of the ugliest feature of industrialization: the dark Satanic mills.

II

> 'You see, Tom, ... the world goes on at a smarter pace now than it did when I was a young fellow ... It's this steam, you see.'
> Mr Deane to Tom Tulliver in George Eliot, *The Mill on the Floss*

Also within that picture there would surely have been a train. Cotton may have been the symbol of the Industrial Revolution as the product which determined the prosperity or otherwise of British manufacture; but to the minds of the Victorians the momentum of industrialization, the force which actually revolutionized industry itself, was steam power. Again it was in the north of England, but this time east of the Pennines, in the coal-mining area of Northumberland and Durham, that – from small beginnings – the miracle was wrought.

Primitive so-called 'atmospheric engines' had been used at the mines since about 1770. By 1790 James Watt had pioneered a more efficient steam engine for pumping and winding work at the pithead. Then George Stephenson, the son of a colliery fireman in Northumberland, acquired from his experience working as a boy with Watt's invention sufficient knowledge to see its potentiality as a traction locomotive. By the time he moved to Killingworth mines, north of Newcastle, in 1804, the first experiments had begun. In 1812 he became engine-wright to the colliery, and two years later he had produced a locomotive to carry coals along six miles of rails to the river Tyne. It was observed by one John Rennie as it made its sluggish progress at seven miles an hour, carrying a burden of twenty tons, and he made a prophetic remark: 'Something more will come out of this hereafter.'[1]

A lot more was to come, but at first extreme scepticism was expressed at the possibility that passengers might be conveyed by an iron horse. The Stockton–Darlington Railway, engineered by Stephenson, was opened in 1825, and an experimental passenger-coach trundled along it pulled by horses – otherwise, people said, how could you get it to stop, and what would happen going downhill without a drag? This was not quite such a foolish question as it might seem. When Stephenson won a prize for his high-speed 'Rocket' (it could travel at 28 miles per hour) and the Manchester-Liverpool line was opened for passenger use in 1830 by an extremely sceptical Duke of Wellington, tragedy occurred. As the Rocket stopped to take on water at Parkside, William Huskisson, MP for Liverpool, rashly disembarked, and panicked when he saw that the engine was still moving. He ran on to the line and was crushed to death.

This was an inauspicious start, but the railways had come to stay, and to expand at a fantastic rate, though the early arrangements for passenger conveyance were somewhat makeshift and even grotesque. Guards had to be posted on the outside of carriages to make sure that couplings did not disengage; sometimes they would lock the carriage doors in order to discourage the over-curious or those who might in panic try to alight when the train was in motion. Gentry were allowed to remain in their own private coaches, hoisted and fastened on to a flat truck. The journey itself could prove extremely uncomfortable. Richard Monckton Milnes took his first trip by train in the summer of 1831, and described the experience to his mother:

> We went quick enough (36 miles in an hour and twenty minutes), but it made you so giddy to look on the ground, and the dust flew so disagreeably in your eyes, that unless one slept all the way, a long steam journey would be anything but pleasant ... I cannot conceive a possible accident if you only sit still; for if the boiler was to burst, it could not hurt those in the inside of the carriages. I believe a good many engineers are killed.[2]

How could the stage-coach compare with this, notwithstanding the substantial improvement in the surfacing of major routes by Telford and Macadam? The fastest run was from London to Manchester on 'Peveril of the Peak'. Richard Cobden timed his journey in 1828 at 20 hours;[3] John Bright, on the return route in 1832, took two hours longer.[4] Ten miles an hour was considered par for the course on good roads, but with stoppages for meals this would reduce to nine – the timing by Thomas Sopwith on the Newcastle to London run in 1837.[5] Terrain and weather would, of course, make a difference. On a visit to James Spedding at Mire House in Cumberland in 1835, Tennyson went with his host by coach from Keswick to Kendal. This was a journey of five hours to cover about forty miles – beautifully scenic, but also circuitous, and requiring several stops to apply the drag.[6]

The trains did not kill the stage-coach until well into the mid-Victorian period. Charles Kingsley travelled from Hungerford to Devizes by coach as late as April 1857, although he admitted beforehand that the experience of 'three hours in a real coach will be a second childhood in these roaring and rattling railroad days.'[7] Not surprisingly, the unequal competition was intensely resented by the thousands employed in the whole network of trades involved in what was inevitably a dying concern. Dickens put in the mouth of Mr Weller senior, in *Master Humphrey's Clock*, a stream of vituperative invective against 'the nasty, wheezin', creakin', gaspin', puffin', bustin' monster' that was taking away his livelihood. What made matters worse, his only experience of travelling by rail had been 'locked up in a close carriage with a living widder',[8] a very dangerous and disagreeable breed of womanhood, as he once advised his son, Sam.[9]

> 'I consider', said Mr Weller, 'that the rail is unconstitootional and an inwasion o' priwileges ... As to the pace, wot sort o' pace do you think I, Tony Veller, could have kept a coach goin' at, for five hundred thousand pound a mile, paid in adwance afore the coach was on the road?'[10]

Mr Weller rather exaggerated the cost of railway track per mile, although it was still exceptionally high – about £4,000 per mile in addition to what might have to be paid for land purchase, which could be exorbitant. The owners of land crossed by the line from London to Birmingham, for instance, were enriched by £750,000.[11] The rapidity of the construction of the railway network was staggering. Between December 1844 and January 1849 – the years of the railway boom – track mileage increased from 2,240 to 5,447.[12] During the next forty years the system extended to 13,000 miles.[13]

The passenger statistics are even more revealing. In 1845, 33,391,253 journeys were taken by train; in 1849 this had nearly doubled, to 60 million. In 1880 the grand total had risen to 587,230,641.[14] During the 1840s most of the great railway companies came into being. In 1839 Bradshaw first published his timetable, which immediately caused problems over the continuance of 'local time', still jealously maintained in many parts of the country. Not until the late 1840s did the railway companies succeed in enforcing Greenwich Standard Time for the network; and local time was not officially abolished nationwide until 1880.[15]

For the speculator, the railway boom of the 1840s seemed to offer unimaginable riches almost overnight. The passion to get rich quick gripped the nation. George Hudson was the most unscrupulous in his exploitation of investment fever, and he hoodwinked thousands, including eventually himself, into frenzied speculation almost unparalleled in its euphoric expectations. When the bubble burst, in the years 1847–9, it was calculated that the loss to the investors was of the order of £800,000,000.[16]

The public had also become almost besotted with the sensation of speed. Between 1839 and 1880 the average speed of express trains advanced from thirty-six to forty-eight miles per hour. The record in 1880 was the London to Swindon run by the 'Flying Dutchman', averaging 53.25 m.p.h.[17] 'The world is getting faster and faster', lamented

James Anthony Froude in 1864[18] – a fact that bothered many of his contemporaries. Matthew Arnold in *The Scholar-Gypsy* looked back wistfully to a time

> ... when wits were fresh and clear,
> And life ran gaily as the sparkling Thames:
> Before this strange disease of modern life,
> With its sick hurry, its divided aims.

'A fool always wants to shorten space and time', Ruskin complained: 'a wise man wants to lengthen both.'[19] Then again: 'It does ... a man, if he be truly a man, no harm to go slow: for his glory is not at all in going, but in being.'[20] His generation paid little heed. In 1875, W.R. Greg contributed his analysis of the temper of his age in an article entitled 'Life at High Pressure'. The conclusion he came to was this: 'the most salient characteristic of life in this latter portion of the 19th century is its SPEED.'[21]

'Not quite so fast next time, Mr Conductor, if you please,' said Prince Albert, as he alighted from his coach on his first journey by train.[22] This was not bad advice, in view of the alarming number of accidents reported year after year. *The Household Narrative*, which appeared monthly as a supplement to Dickens' *Household Words* between 1852 and 1855, contained a special section on 'Accidents and Disasters', and grisly reading these entries make. During a period of six months in 1852, 113 persons were killed on the railways and 264 injured, some through misconduct or trespass, some for 'causes beyond their control'; the majority, however, were servants of companies or contractors. In 1853, in the first half-year, 148 had been killed and 191 injured.[23] Some of the worst accidents were caused by collapsing tunnels or embankments. Eight people were killed in the Sonning Hill cutting near Reading in December 1841 ('awful and tremendous, as all railway mishaps are', Lord Melbourne reported to the Queen).[24]

This new cause of death provided a handy way for novelists to dispose of their characters. So, in Elizabeth Gaskell's *Cranford*, 'Captain Brown' is reported to have been killed 'by them nasty cruel railroads!' (he was reading the latest number of *Pickwick Papers* at the time – a nice touch).[25] Dickens himself experienced an appalling accident in 1865, travelling from Folkestone to London, when approaching the viaduct at Staplehurst at a speed of fifty miles an hour on a downward gradient. The train jumped the rails because two had been temporarily removed by workers on the line, the foreman having consulted the wrong timetable. All the first class carriages except one plunged down into the river-bed below. The one that was spared, hanging perilously over the bridge, happened to be the one occupied by Dickens. He was not likely to forget the horror of that moment. 'I never thought I should be here again', he said when he returned to his home in Gad's Hill Place.[26] Seventeen years earlier he had disposed of one of his own villains – Mr Carker in *Dombey and Son* – by having him run down by a train.[27]

Dickens had no love for railways, but they fascinated him. He pictured them thrusting their way into the heart of London, flinging down anything that blocked their path, slicing through Camden Town, even bisecting the building that had once been his school, and always with 'a rattle and a glare', their fearful cacophony a mixture of 'a hiss, a crash, a bell, and a shriek'.[28] That awful engine whistle: it was like the 'scream that they say Catharine of Russia gave on her deathbed'.[29]

The Victorians were compulsive observers of their times. One such was William Johnston, a barrister, who produced a two-volume survey in 1851 entitled *England As It Is*. 'The most important event of the last quarter of a century in English history', he wrote, 'is the establishment of Railroads.' He continued:

> The stupendous magnitude of the capital they have absorbed – the changes they have produced in the habit of society – the new aspect they have given, in some respects, to the affairs of government – the new feeling of power they have engendered – the triumphs and disappointments of which they have been the cause – above all, the new and excessive activities to which they have given rise – must lead all who reflect upon the subject to admit that the importance of the general result of these great undertakings can scarcely be exaggerated.[30]

In terms of the economy, the balance sheet showed an overwhelming surplus on the credit side. A vast new field of employment was opened up, ranging from engineers and transport workers to the huge force of navvies required for the heavy manual construction work. All the heavy industries prospered. The output of British iron, for instance, doubled between 1835 and 1845, and the number of men employed in mining, metallurgy, machine and vehicle building rose by nearly forty per cent between 1841 and 1851.[31] Whole new towns were created: Middlesbrough by the iron industry; Swindon, Crewe and Barrow-in-Furness by railway companies. It was not until the middle years of the 1850s, following the invention of the Bessemer convertor, that the steel industry rose into prominence with a new capacity for mass-production; and again it was the railways that stimulated the demand for a metal of tougher durability than iron.

The coal industry expanded rapidly. The domestic consumption was already vastly increasing as a result of the rise in population. Some conception of the huge demand for the major source of household fuel can be gained from the fact that the coal consumption of a large Victorian mansion (of about thirty bedrooms) was over a ton a day.[32] The railways fed on coal too, and their appetite was insatiable. Furthermore, the transformation in the ease and speed of communications led to a reduction in transport costs. The benefits extended far beyond the coal industry, however. The creation of a railway network, rendering speedier delivery of a wide range of commodities, and especially foodstuffs, proved advantageous to all sections of the community. The cost of consumer goods was reduced, and the quality of meat, milk and vegetables delivered, by being so much fresher, was immeasurably improved.

All this made for buoyant home markets. But great profits were being made overseas by British railway engineers, technologists and the heavy industry companies. It was not textiles alone that Britain sold abroad. Legislation during the eighteenth century had prohibited the export of machinery for the sound reason that this could be giving away industrial secrets to foreign competitors. It was a difficult set of laws to enforce, and during the 1820s and 1830s the export of machine tools became so obviously profitable that the inhibitions were gradually removed; and finally so in 1843. Marine engines were the first to cross the Channel, but locomotives soon followed, to be laid on British-made rails. In 1841 Thomas Brassey took a small army of navvies with him to embark upon the construction of the French railway system. During the next twenty years he was building railways in Belgium, Italy, Austria, Denmark and Canada. In the 1860s, 100,000 tons of British rolling stock and ironwork were exported to India to begin the construction of the Delhi Railway.[33] The profits were high and fortunes were made. In time, however, the question had to be asked whether the British economy had really served itself well by providing to potential competitors the wherewithal to challenge the country's commercial and industrial supremacy.

One other technological development occurred, coincidentally with the creation of the internal railway network, which was to lead in time to consequences of as dramatic significance as the invention of steam traction. This was the first practical application of electricity, in the invention of the electric telegraph. It came about by the mutual acknowledgement of the railway companies and the pioneers of the device known as the 'galvanometer' that each could profit – but for different reasons – by co-operating in experiments in electro-magnetism. In June 1837 W.F. Cooke and Charles Wheatstone, who had worked independently on devices to transmit messages by passing an electric current through a wire, came together and obtained a patent for their 'electric telegraph'. What they needed, however, was the means by which they could instal mileages of wire without having to pay a huge sum to take the wire across private property. The railway companies, however, having met that cost for their own purposes, possessed the ideal medium for running lengths of wire, if need be, across the length and breadth of the whole country. And these companies had an interest of their own: the installation of a more efficient and cost-effective means of operating a safe signalling system. It was the GWR of I.K. Brunel that took the first plunge in 1838, concluding an agreement with Cooke and Wheatstone whereby they were empowered to run their telegraph over railway property at a peppercorn rent, with the railway company having the right to transmit messages free of charge, and reciprocating by allowing the wires to be used for public messages. The first lengths were laid between Paddington and West Drayton; if successful they were to be extended to Maidenhead:[34] tentative beginnings of what was to prove a revolution in communications.

Rowland Hill, a postal expert and a director of a railway company, was the first to perceive the momentous potential of this innovation for the conduct of general business. In 1851 a cable was laid linking Dover and Calais, and the Stock Exchanges of London and Paris were soon in telegraphic contact.[35] Internal security was transformed, too. No more primitive signalling of war's alarms through linked semaphores, visible only in daylight and clear weather; and if there were signs of possible armed insurrection in Manchester, London could be alerted on the instant and troops despatched by train. Further dramatic developments were to follow. With the completion of the Atlantic cable in 1865 and – four years later – the opening of a cable-link with India, the whole process of communication of news from abroad was transformed. 'News could now come in a matter of minutes rather than weeks', Lucy Brown has written: 'the greater the distance the more dramatic the saving. By 1870 the basic technical conditions which underlie modern newspaper production had come into existence.'[36]

In other respects, and for society in general, the railways brought an escape from enforced parochialism. Even at Arnold's Rugby, in the early 1830s, there were boys in the school who had never seen the sea.[37] In 1841, however, a Baptist missionary by the name of Thomas Cook conceived the notion of organizing excursions at a cheap rate for the less affluent, and entered into negotiations with the Midland Railway Company to lay on special trains for private outings for temperance clubs (Cook himself was an ardent temperance crusader) and for Sunday schools. Such arrangements having been successfully concluded, the obvious profits that could accrue both to tour operators and to railway companies rapidly led to undreamt-of recreational opportunities for the working classes. Thousands were taken by train to the Crystal Palace in 1851; and once Saturday half-holidays had become the normal practice in the 1860s, trips were organized to places like Scarborough, Whitby, Blackpool and Southport. The unbelievable luxury, for the lowest-paid, of family holidays away from home had now become a possibility.

Within cities and towns, municipal transport took a long time to become established. London had its cabs, of course: in 1837, some 1200 'hooded gigs', which gave way to the hansom cab in the 1850s. These, however, were only for the well-to-do. Londoners, both employers and employees, walked to work. It was estimated in 1837 that 90,000 people crossed London Bridge, walking in either direction, on a single day.[38] An enterprising French company introduced a reasonably cheap horse-drawn bus service within the City in 1855, although so crowded were the streets that it was often maintained that it was quicker to walk. The electric tram, running on rails, was pioneered in the provinces, Birkenhead leading the way in 1860; again this was the inspiration of a foreign engineer, an American with the felicitous name of George Train.[39] By this time work had begun in London on the Metropolitan Railway, opened in 1863. By 1884 the Inner Circle Line had been completed. The construction of London's 'underground' proved another propitious field for investors, although there were some burnt fingers. Gladstone, so notoriously niggardly and cautious in matters of public finance, was sometimes less prudent in his private dealings. In 1884 he lost £25,000 through an 'excessive holding of Metropolitan District Railway stock'. He had bought his shares, as he ruefully admitted, 'before it was in a paying condition'.[40]

In the whole vast enterprise of expanding communications there were, perhaps inevitably, both winners and losers. The village remote from a railway station felt more isolated than before: no regular calls from the likes of Mr Weller senior to pass on the gossip and scandals of the day. Some east-coast ports declined with the diminution of coal-bearing sea traffic, but a new and ultimately highly prosperous source of trade was opened up by the emergence of popular seaside resorts. The winners greatly outnumbered the losers. The benefits extended across the whole social range, from the landowner who made a lucrative sale of land to the company traversing his property with the permanent way, to the Manchester mill-worker who could now enjoy an outing to Blackpool.

So why the jeremiads? Why despair? R.S. Surtees, in his novel *Mr Facey Romford's Hounds* (1864), saw every reason for rejoicing.

> Among other great advantages afforded by railways has been that of opening out the great matrimonial market, whereby people can pick and choose wives all the world over, instead of having to pursue the old Pelion on Ossa or Pig upon Bacon system of always marrying a neighbour's child. So we now have an amalgamation of countries and counties, and a consequent improvement in society – improvement in wit, improvement in wine, improvement in 'wittles', improvement in everything.[41]

Macaulay had used rather grander language:

> Every improvement of the means of locomotion benefits mankind morally as well as materially . . . [It] not only facilitates the interchange of the various productions, of nature and art, but tends to remove national and provincial antipathies, and to bind together all the branches of the great human family.[42]

Fine words, carrying no conviction to those who refused to be convinced. In ascending order of disquiet, the apprehensions may be summarized as threefold. The first has been encountered earlier – the potentially calamitous effect of ever-increasing speed. Even as late as 1869, Trollope was sending up warning flares. The analogy in *Phineas Finn*, although taken from the past, clearly has the present in mind:

> Unless the coach goes on running, no journey will be made. But let us have the drag on both wheels. And we must remember that coaches running downhill without drags are apt to come to serious misfortune.[43]

The second apprehension was more an outright condemnation. Society's whole scale of values was being inverted by the contemporary mania for railways and industrialization, with the result that materialism was blighting true culture. Its two leading spokesmen were Matthew Arnold and John Ruskin. In *Culture and Anarchy*, Arnold deplored the false Gods of his time – 'railroads and coal'.[44] Ruskin, in *The Crown of Wild Olive*, fastened on 'coal' as the symbol of materialism. 'Civilisation is the economy of power, and English power is coal. If it be so then "ashes to ashes" be our epitaph! and the sooner the better.'[45]

The third rejection was the anguished cry of the cataclysmic school – anguished because they thought they discerned in the whole complex of disintegrating forces within society the imprint of the Devil. It is no coincidence that the third decade of the nineteenth century witnessed a strong revival of Millennialism, especially in what is known as its 'pre-millennial' form, of which the most strident advocate was Edward Irving. The message of the pre-millennials has been described by Sheridan Gilley as 'catastrophic and pessimistic, seeing both the world and the churches as so lost that only Christ's Second Coming could redeem them ... This wicked world would be rendered Christian not by Christians but by Christ, in his Second Coming to an unconverted world.'[46]

If this has more than a touch of the lunatic fringe, it should be recognized that it was not inconsiderable in strength; and the sense of an approaching Armageddon was not confined to the millennialists. Samuel Wilberforce, later to become Bishop of Oxford, could certainly not be so described. In 1837, however, he wrote to his friend Charles Anderson to express his abhorrence of the alliance between Utilitarians and Liberals, blaming them for almost all the infamies of the day. Modern Liberalism, he wrote, 'is the Devil's creed: a heartless steam-engine'. Its highest aims appeared to be 'to multiply such miserable comforts as going very fast through the air on a railroad'. Its advocates would 'worship the very Devil if his horns were of gold and his tail were a steam-engine'.[47]

Two of the most famous hymns of the late 1820s and early 1830s echo this note of impending doom, while appealing to God to guide the faithful through terrible times ahead. 'Lead kindly light', wrote Newman in 1833, 'amid the encircling gloom'. In the second verse of the Evangelical H.F. Lyte's 'Abide with me' occur two lines which, since they were written, have been sung by millions, unaware of the actual context of the sombre words:

> Change and decay in all around I see,
> O Thou who changest not, abide with me.

Common to all these expressions of deep unease is the yearning for stability, some safe and sure anchorage within a frighteningly fast-changing world. Margaret Hale, the heroine of Elizabeth Gaskell's *North and South*, expresses the sentiment perfectly:

> I begin to understand now what heaven must be – and, oh! the grandeur and repose of the words – 'The same yesterday, to-day, and for ever'. Everlasting! 'From everlasting to everlasting, Thou art God.' That sky above me looks as though it could not change and yet it will.[48]

If there was a single image that symbolized to the Victorians the divide between the old world and the new, it was the train. This was progress to some; to others, it was decay. In the Tate Gallery may be seen a huge panoramic picture painted by John Martin in 1853, the subject 'The Last Judgement'. It depicts two sets of people divided by a great gulf, and on the horizon, bathed in celestial light, there is an angelic host. Those on the left of the picture, attired in sober Protestant garb, have an air of smugness about them, as they look to the light in joyous expectation. Those on the right, however, are scrabbling desperately on a cliff face to prevent themselves from slithering into the fiery pit below. An avenging angel hovers above them to remind them that their frantic efforts are in vain. These are the reprobates, some in gorgeous raiment, and one looking more uncomfortable and more affronted than the others, with the papal tiara on his head. The picture repays careful study. Sure enough, a train is there. It is just about to plunge headlong into the abyss from which there can be no return.

III

'The poor in a loomp is bad.'
> Tennyson, 'Northern Farmer, New Style'

A farm house, not far distant from Manchester, forms part of the back-cloth of the opening scene of Elizabeth Gaskell's *Mary Barton*. It has a little garden attached to it, 'crowded with a medley of old-fashioned herbs and flowers, planted long ago ... and allowed to grow ... in most republican and indiscriminate order.'[1] The use of the adjective 'republican' dates the setting. The garden is a disorderly one, and to an early Victorian 'disorder' was equated with civil disturbance; and civil disturbance evoked memories of those who had rejoiced to see the French Revolution – men like William Godwin and Thomas Paine, fomenters of violent upheavals threatening the monarchy, the Church and the established order.

Riots and sporadic insurrectionary risings seem to have been endemic during the Napoleonic wars and for several decades thereafter. Indeed, they had been frequent occurrences during the eighteenth century, whether anticipations of Luddism or demonstrations in support of John Wilkes and Liberty. But the French Revolution, and especially the events of 1789 in Paris, marked a turning-point in the attitude of governments towards them, and in the amount of apprehension they excited in the country at large. In the early nineteenth century the sources of unrest and the violence to which they gave rise differed both in character and in the degree of menace that they represented. When Tennyson put into the mouth of his 'Northern Farmer, New Style' the warning 'Taake my word for it, Sammy, the poor in a loomp is bad', he was expressing his fears of 'Captain Swing' and the angry, desperate rick-burnings by gangs of the agricultural poor. The Luddite machine-smashing, in the closing years of the Napoleonic wars, was not the work of the poor in a lump. Luddism was the outraged response of skilled workers, deprived of their livelihood and therefore their status – men such as the Nottinghamshire framework-knitters – accustomed to working in small workshops, and to whom the machine-operating factories were the cause of their miseries.

These were not 'mobs' in the sense that G. Rudé, in his analysis of *The Crowd in the French Revolution*, used the term. The poor might riot over the high price of bread, and frequently did until the Repeal of the Corn Laws, and this could lead to something very like mob violence. But a mob-rising, such as happened in the anti-Catholic Gordon Riots in London in 1780, was an orchestrated insurrection, behind which lay manipulating influences – political or sectarian – exploiting the mob in order to attain some particular end.[2]

A mob, in this sense, is an urban phenomenon; and what made the mob violence of the early nineteenth century potentially explosive, and perhaps ultimately uncontainable, were three developments arising from the changing social, economic and political conditions of the time. In the first place, the poor were being more and more concentrated in an urban rather than a rural lump. Secondly, the industrial revolution had brought about new grievances and sufferings on an unprecedented scale; and thirdly, these social and economic forces were tending by a process of coalescence to move towards an agitation with definite political aims. Furthermore, the reactionary legislation associated with the upholders of 'old corruption' – especially the repressive Tory administration of Lord Liverpool – served in the long run to create precisely the situation that it was intended to avert: a growing sense of solidarity among the underprivileged, and therefore ominous signs of an approaching class war.

This is why an event which took place on 16 August 1819 in St Peter's Field, Manchester was so significant both at the time and for many years to come. Opinions may differ as to the accuracy of the term 'the Peterloo massacre'. Eleven were killed or died from injuries inflicted by the armed forces of law and order, despatched to disperse a crowd of 60,000 who had assembled to hear the words of Orator Hunt and other Radical spokesmen, determined to whip up indignation against the deprivation of fundamental political rights. It was hardly a revolution; but some of the Manchester Yeomanry – local manufacturers and merchants on horseback, armed with cutlasses – behaved as if it were. They enjoyed the opportunity of slashing at recalcitrant and defenceless employees with impunity, thereby teaching trouble-makers a salutary lesson. Doubtless the tales of the horrors grew in the telling; and memories died hard. As Magdalen Goffin has written: 'What is thought to have happened is in its way as important for history as what actually happened. The propaganda value of Peterloo was incalculable.'[3]

Thereafter the anxieties over the enormous resources of the disaffected that could be marshalled within the growing towns and cities ascended into genuine fears. In the year of Peterloo, Lord Liverpool had said: 'What can be stable with these enormous towns? One serious insurrection in London and all is lost.'[4] The poor in a lump acquired the emotive term 'the masses'. Dire warnings came from the pens of leading writers – Southey, Macaulay and Carlyle. In his *Chartism*, it has been said, Carlyle showed himself 'not only an angry but a frightened man'.[5] In *Barnaby Rudge*, Dickens had chosen the Gordon Riots as the perfect setting for illustrating the psychology of the crowd, hot tempers turning into a madness of wilful destruction through the sheer pressure of numbers; and in *The Old Curiosity Shop*, the Dickensian rhetoric of horrified fascination was given full vent in his description of the menacing group of unemployed labourers in the heart of the industrial Midlands: 'maddened men, armed with sword and firebrand, spurning the tears and prayers of women who would restrain them, rushed forth on errands of terror and destruction.'[6] Birmingham was a centre for the manufacture of small arms, and this fact deeply troubled a lawyer of that city with whom de Tocqueville had converse. 'The press of 150,000 work people crowded together so near the capital', he said, 'and with an immense store of arms is a very serious matter.'[7]

There were specific times of acute danger, when – for instance – economic crisis coincided with political agitation: 1830 was just such a year. Industry was suffering from one of its severest slumps. It was reported that thousands of workers in the Huddersfield area were having to exist on twopence-halfpenny a day.[8] Across the Channel, the barricades went up again in the Paris streets, and the Bourbon monarchy was ousted to make way for the accession of the 'Citizen King'. In June that year George IV died, making a general election inevitable. Agitation was mounting throughout the country on the issue of electoral reform and the extension of the franchise, the Radicals determined to use all their power of intimidation to prevent the return of the Tories under the Duke of Wellington. As early as 1827, in *The Edinburgh Review*, Macaulay – although no Radical – had warned his fellow-countrymen of the consequences of a perpetuation of extreme Toryism: 'A revolution, a bloody and unsparing revolution – a revolution which will make the ears of those who hear of it tingle in the remotest countries, and in the remotest time.'[9]

The election of a Whig administation under Lord Grey did not result, however, in any easing of the tension. No mercy was shown to the rioters. Between November 1830 and March 1831, 1,400 rioters were brought before the courts, and 9 were sentenced to be hanged, 657 imprisoned and 464 transported.[10] And when the House of Lords rejected the Reform Bill, and William IV was initially reluctant to force their hand by creating extra peers, it looked as if Macaulay's prophecy was about to be fulfilled. There was rioting in Cambridge, and the élite club of 'The Apostles', with Tennyson one of their number, armed themselves with staves to help restore order.[11] Nottingham and Derby erupted. But the worst scenes of all occurred in the autumn of 1831 in Bristol, where the Bishop's Palace and the Mansion House were burned down, houses and shops looted and the prisoners set free from the gaol. Charles Kingsley was at school in Clifton at the time and he never forgot the sight of the burning city below. Years later he described the scene to one of his former private pupils at Eversley. Kingsley was only 13 at the time, but he could not resist running down from Clifton to get a closer view of the mayhem. It was the stuff of nightmare:

> The brave, patient soldiers sitting ... motionless on their horses, the blood streaming from wounds on their heads and faces, waiting for the order which the miserable, terrified Mayor had not courage to give: the savage, brutal, hideous mob of inhuman wretches plundering, destroying, burning; casks of spirit broken open and set flaming in the streets, the wretched creatures drinking it on their knees from the gutter, till the flame from a burning house caught the stream, ran down it with a horrible rushing sound, and, in one dreadful moment, the prostrate drunkards had become a row of blackened corpses.

The sight of the 'shamelessness and the impunity of the guilty' and 'the persecution and the suicide of the innocent' – Kingsley told his friend – 'made me a Radical.' When asked by his friend, 'Whose fault is it, that such things can be?', Kingsley replied: 'Mine ... and yours.'[12]

Research by D.J. Rowe into the papers of the Radical reformer Francis Place definitely supports the view that some of the disturbances between 1830 and 1832 were orchestrated. Government was to be presented with a single choice: 'the [Reform] bill or a revolution'. When the Bill had been passed, Place wrote, 'We were within a moment of general rebellion and had it been possible for the Duke of Wellington to have formed an administration, the King and the people would have been at issue.'[13] J.A. Roebuck later recalled a speech by Place, prior to a deputation to Lord Grey. He had used these words: '*We must frighten them* ... No reality we can create will be sufficient for our purposes. We must work on Lord Grey's imagination. We must pretend to be frightened ourselves.'[14] This may have been bluff, of course. The truth will never be known. One result, however, of the Reform Bill riots is incontestable. Although nothing quite so appalling as the Bristol riot of 1831 occurred during Victoria's reign, those who – like Kingsley – had witnessed the scenes at an impressionable age, and who grew to maturity in Victorian times, could never rid their minds of the possibility of something similar or even worse happening again.

Such thoughts were dismissed by the coolly sceptical Lady Charlemont in 1835. She told de Tocqueville that

> One should not judge our situation by the fears that are expressed; since I have been in the world, I have heard it said each year that we are going to have a revolution, and at the end of the year we always find ourselves in the same place.

De Tocqueville was not entirely convinced. Might one not reply 'We have heard it said all our lives that we must die, and we do not die. Does this mean that we are immortal?'[15]

Most of the owners of grand houses in cities, however, took precautions, and continued to do so throughout the century. A hooded chair was placed by the main entrance to protect the footman-porter from the draught as he kept watch through the night; and he was usually armed.[16] Kingsley's household at Eversley did not run to a night-porter, but he kept pistols and blunderbusses handy, which he had to use on one occasion when F.D. Maurice, the Broad Church theologian and Christian Socialist, was staying with him and thieves attempted to break down the back door.[17] During the original troubles of 1830, the Duke of Buckingham had a cannon removed from his yacht and set it up in readiness should there be an assault upon his property.[18] In 1851, William Johnston still believed that a day of reckoning lay in store for the well-to-do. 'God's justice is requiting, and will yet further requite, those who have blown up this country into a state of unsubstantial opulence at the expense of the health and morals of the lower classes.'[19]

Between 1837 and 1842 there could have been an explosion at any time. The combination of events that had made the years 1830–2 so precarious recurred in almost every particular. In the years preceding the

Queen's accession, Chartism had been born, expressive of the realization by the unfranchised that their lot was not one whit better than it
had been before. Indeed, to many it seemed that it was far worse, since
one of the first legislative measures of the reformed Parliament was the
1834 Poor Law Amendment Act, interpreted by the underprivileged as
a fresh declaration of class war. The People's Charter, with its Six Points
aimed at securing universal suffrage and adequate measures to ensure
the freedom to vote without intimidation, was drawn up in 1836, following the formation of the London Working Men's Association. Its co-
founders, William Lovett, James Watson and John Cleave, had
revolutionary aims, but they conscientiously eschewed violence as a
means of attaining them. By 1838, however, the leadership had effectively changed hands; and, even more ominously, the centre of activities
had moved to the northern industrial areas. To the Chartists' self-
appointed spokesman, the Irish demagogue Fergus O'Connor, the attitude of the Londoners seemed altogether too tepid. With O'Connor,
and his own newspaper the *Northern Star*, 'physical force' Chartism came
into being, under its sinister slogan: 'Peacefully if we may, forcibly if we
must.'[20]

A political objective had therefore been identified, coinciding – as it
happened – with the worst industrial depression of the century: a
succession of bad harvests, with wheat prices rising by a third; bank failures; and the closure of several cotton mills. The number of unemployed rose to a new height, as did the amount of Poor Relief (from £4
million in 1836 to £5.2 million in 1842). In some areas the situation
became so desperate that people were forced to eat boiled nettles. It was
reported that in one village the inhabitants dug up the putrid carcase of
a cow.[21] Lord Melbourne sent a grim report to the Queen on 17 August
1842:

> Lord Melbourne hopes [he wrote] that these tumults in the manufacturing
> districts are subsiding, but he cannot conceal from Your Majesty that he
> views them with great alarm – much greater than he generally thinks it
> prudent to express.[22]

The crisis passed. The cool head of Sir Charles Napier, sent to
command the northern division of the army, augmented by contingents
from Ireland, helped. The armed strikers in Lancashire were very much
aware of his presence and the forces he commanded. They were also

aware that he was reluctant to unleash the military unless obliged to. There were a lot of hot words uttered, and threats of strikes on a major scale when the Chartist Petition of 1839 was politely ignored. But apart from the imprisonment of some 400 Chartists, no more decisive action was taken on either side, despite an ugly rising in Newport in South Wales in November of that year and several outbreaks of rural violence and vandalism – the so-called 'Rebecca riots' – which persisted into the middle years of the 1840s.

But then followed 1848 – 'that awful year', as F.D. Maurice described it, looking back.[23] 'God help us!' Absolom Watkin wrote in his diary as news came of the fresh *coup d'état* in France, followed by risings, revolutions, loss of thrones and the flight of eminent statesmen into exile, all over Europe.[24] It was just the stimulus that the Chartists wanted, and Fergus O'Connor, now a Member of Parliament (elected for Nottingham in 1847), summoned his supporters – as he himself put it – to their 'tents'. There was to be a massive march on London and a huge demonstration on Kennington Common, and then a monster Petition to be presented defiantly to Parliament. The threat was taken seriously, and the Duke of Wellington assumed command of the defence of the capital. Major possible objectives of attack were surrounded by troops and artillery. One or two wise heads maintained that there was actually nothing to fear. George Eliot, aged 28 at the time, was utterly dismissive.

> Our working classes are eminently inferior to the mass of the French people [she wrote in a letter to John Sibree]. Here there is so much larger a proportion of selfish radicalism and unsatisfied brute sensuality ... that a revolutionary movement would be simply destructive – not constructive. Besides, it would be put down.[25]

Michelet, the veteran French historian, hurried over from France and stayed with Benjamin Jowett at Balliol College, Oxford, where they were joined by A.P. Stanley. Michelet was confident that the Chartists would succeed. Jowett knew better. 'It will be of little consequence,' he predicted. Stanley then made the wisest observation of all: 'Ireland will be our revolution,' he said.[26]

The revolution never came; and Chartism never recovered from what turned out to be a fiasco. Many reasons have been advanced to explain its failure. It might reasonably have been supposed that Manchester would turn out to be the really effective trouble-centre, but the loyalties of the disaffected elements in the capital of the north were divided. Some chose to agitate for the repeal of the Corn Laws under the banner of Richard Cobden and John Bright, both far better organizers of a streamlined campaign than Fergus O'Connor and his associates. More to the point, perhaps, was the fact that the Chartists themselves could never display a completely united front. Any alliance between the advocates of 'moral force' and those of 'physical force' was bound to be an uneasy one; and there were tensions, too, over the issue of teetotalism. Whereas the respectable wing wished to demonstrate their moral superiority within the country at large by canvassing Chartists to sign the pledge, O'Connor was shrewd enough to perceive that this would end by causing an irretrievable split.[27] Here he showed perception. Actually, however, he was a poor leader: an effective braggart, but with no stomach for fighting when it came to the crunch. 'O'Connor's greatest service to the cause of working-class suffrage', Harold Perkin has written, 'was his cowardice on Kennington Common on 10 April 1848, when he obeyed Police Commissioner Maine and called off the march to the Houses of Parliament.'[28] The police also, to their credit, were restrained and did not provoke conflict. Although they were empowered to use cutlasses, they were seen by the demonstrators to be carrying only truncheons.[29]

A deeper reason for the failure of 1848, however, was the fact that London was not really a centre of Chartism – not, at least, of the physical force variety. Its very size 'militated against organization';[30] and, as Francis Place observed at the time, 'London differs very widely from Manchester, and, indeed, from every other place on the face of the earth. It has no local or particular interest as a town, not even as to politics.'[31] A few decades later, when the London dockers had acquired a strong union, they were to become a potent force. But this was not so in 1848. Those who had strong Radical leanings, as well as the marchers who had come down from the north, felt betrayed by the average Londoner's apathy. It would not be quite true to say that Queen Victoria was apathetic, but she was certainly not unduly dismayed by the Chartist threats. After all, she had unshakeable faith in the Duke of Wellington. In March 1848 she was confident enough to write to her uncle, the King of the Belgians, to express her sympathy for the other crowned heads of Europe, compared to whose plight 'our little riots are mere nothing'.[32]

All this leads to a wider question: was there ever a moment during the Queen's reign that a revolution actually could have succeeded? Dr Kitson Clark thought not. An undisciplined crowd, however angry and whatever makeshift arms they might have amassed, could never prevail against a trained, loyal body of soldiers. The Newport rising in 1839 was a case in point. Three thousand miners rushed into the town to storm the gaol and release the Chartist prisoners held there. They were quelled and dispersed by a tiny detachment of twenty-two soldiers, who opened fire on the insurgents, killing eleven in all.[33] The moment that crowned heads should consider packing their bags comes when troops switch allegiance to the mob; the only occasion on which something like this threatened was in 1797 when there was a Naval mutiny at Spithead and the Nore. A further danger comes when the authorities panic and fail to take action, as happened during the Gordon Riots and the Bristol riot of 1831. There was no repetition of this during the Chartist troubles. On the whole, right through Victoria's reign, successive governments were wily enough never to allow class conflict to harden to the point where wide-scale violence was inevitable. Concessions might come late, but some measure of conciliation was usually offered before the dam burst. Perhaps, too, Walter Bagehot was not wrong when he described the attitude of the English people towards authority as fundamentally 'deferential'.[34]

This, at least, is how the situation appears in retrospect. But what a historian can discern by looking backwards is not necessarily what contemporaries are able to appreciate by looking inwards. Bertrand Russell knew enough of his grandfather Lord John Russell's anxieties to write:

> It is not always easy to realise in reading history that the actors in any period, unlike ouselves, did not know the future. We know that Victorian England developed peaceably, but the contemporaries of the Chartists did not know this.[35]

By 1851 Macaulay's genuine anxieties had subsided. As he watched the crowds at the Great Exhibition, he wrote in his diary: 'I saw none of the men of action with whom the Socialists were threatening us ... There is just as much chance of a revolution in England as of the falling of the moon.'[36] The corner had been turned, or so it seemed. Certainly the statistics of violent crime, recently examined by V.A.C. Gatrell, reveal a general decline in the incidence of violence, both in London and elsewhere, from the mid 1860s onwards.[37] No single reason can be advanced, although the evidence suggests that better policing and more effective surveillance of the known criminal classes played an effective part in reducing street crime, especially pick-pocketing and mugging.[38] Nevertheless the spectre of the mob on the rampage continued to haunt urban property-owners, and with good reason. Another major crisis occurred in 1866, with a downturn in the economy, bad harvests, unemployment and bankruptcies as a result of the collapse of the great financial house Overend and Gurney, all coinciding with political agitation for a further extension of the franchise. The troubles began with the defeat of a moderate Reform Bill introduced by Earl Russell and Gladstone in June of that year. A huge rally was organized in Hyde Park to put pressure on the new Conservative government of the Earl of Derby and Disraeli and, at the last minute, was banned by the Home Secretary and the Commissioner of Police. For a few ugly hours the propertied classes of London trembled as the park railings were uprooted and a crowd of nearly 200,000 ran amok.

Order was restored, but it was a near thing. It needed only the conversion of those railings into spears and lances for the watching troops to retaliate with force. To Karl Marx, who was an observer of the incident, it was all an anticlimax. His hoped-for 'bloody encounter' never took place; he had been counting on the prospect that 'there would have been some fun'.[39] Matthew Arnold, on the other hand, was outraged by the feebleness of the authorities. His father had had a recipe for dealing with a rabble like the Hyde Park 'roughs' of 1866: 'Flog the rank and file, and fling the ringleaders from the Tarpeian rock!'[40]

The events of 'Bloody Sunday', 13 November 1887, provoked the confrontation that Arnold felt such a situation demanded. A huge demonstration by socialists, radicals and Irish, most of them unemployed, erupted into violence in the Strand, and the police, supplemented by the Life Guards, had no option but to intervene. They left a trail of a hundred wounded, two of whom died from their injuries. William Morris had nursed the same hopes as Karl Marx; and after the failure of the uprising he came to the conclusion that the revolution which one day must surely come could only be achieved by prior organization and with the populace adequately armed. In his futuristic dream *News from Nowhere*, published three years later, he described in detail the various stages which would be necessary for the establishment of his highly idiosyncratic late-medieval Utopia, once the existing government had been overthrown.[41]

It seems that Victorian England never felt really safe from some such catastrophe. Tennyson, for instance, never forgot something he had heard as a boy. 'Our country coachman,' he recalled shortly before his death, had looked to the day when he could go up to London 'in order to be there when the poor cut the throats of the quality.'[42] George Gissing, at the close of the century, described the potentially explosive character of the London mob in words which take one straight back into the world of Dickens in the 1840s. 'As a force, by which the terror of the time is conditioned,' he wrote, 'they, the crowd, inspire me with distrust, with fear; as a visible multitude, they make me shrink aloof, and often move me to abhorrence.'[43] And Gissing knew the London slums, portrayed so graphically in *The Nether World* in 1889. During his marriage to an alcoholic prostitute, he had been forced to live there.

Fear of the mob, then, and distrust of the poor in a lump, cast some shadow over every decade of the Queen's reign; and at least one symbol of that fear has survived, in most of its detail, until the present day. One grand London house built for occupation by the 'quality' is very much like another. They are little fortresses in their way: heavy shutters on the windows; a deep drop into the basement area to create a sort of waterless moat between the residence and the thoroughfare; just a single flight of steps or narrow causeway to the stoutly-built front door, which is therefore easily defended; and in front of the moat, huge cast-iron railings to keep the crowd at bay. From many of these town houses an essential part of the fortification has now disappeared: those forbidding railings have gone, melted down to make munitions during the Second World War.

IV

'And what is the Spirit of the Age?' asked Coningsby.
'The Spirit of Utility,' said Lord Everingham.

Disraeli, *Coningsby*

Suppose a 'man had gone to sleep in 1846', Mark Pattison wrote in his *Memoirs*, 'and had woke up again in 1850, he would have found himself in a totally new world.' He was actually writing of Oxford and the change 'as if by the wand of a magician'[1] which took place after the collapse of the Oxford Movement following Newman's secession to Rome, when theological conflict ceased and the university returned to its proper business. The sentiment expressed, however, could have applied equally to the country as a whole. Victorian England was about to enter into that phase of nearly twenty years which has been labelled 'the age of equipoise'. Awakened from the nightmare of the Chartist riots and the grievous problems of a starving Ireland, people came suddenly to realize that their country truly led the world, not only in its maintenance of political stability while governments were crashing all over Europe, but also in its commercial and industrial supremacy and – what affected the population generally and most immediately – in its unrivalled prosperity. So it was that G.M. Young could declare that 'of all decades in our history, a wise man would choose the eighteen-fifties to be young in'[2].

The truth of their privileged situation really struck home throughout the nation when thousands, pouring into London by train after train, were able to view Joseph Paxton's gigantic and glittering palace of glass in Hyde Park in which was housed the Great Exhibition of 1851. It was officially opened by the Queen on 1 May: a magnificent ceremony, watched by 25,000 spectators and attended by the whole royal family and dignitaries and ambassadors from all over the world. There were massed choirs, two great organs, bands augmented by trumpeters, all of whom combined in a climactic rendering of Handel's 'Hallelujah Chorus'. This was 'the *greatest* day in our history', the Queen reported to her uncle in Belgium. 'It was the *happiest, proudest* day in my life.'[3] It passed without a hitch, too; or perhaps with only one slight embarrassment. The Archbishop of Canterbury (J.B. Sumner) led in the great procession, but was so amazed at the splendour of the exhibits confronting him in his stately progress that he kept stopping to gaze at them, with the result that his chaplains had to pull up sharply to avoid stumbling into him. The Lords in Waiting, next in line, were walking backwards before the royal party, and therefore kept colliding with the clergy, causing them great discomfort by grazing their heels.[4]

Prince Albert's dream had come true. There it stood as a moving symbol of 'a new era, when commerce and discovery were to bind the nations of the earth together, and enlightened industry was to succeed in making an end of war after Christianity had tried and failed.'[5] Tennyson captured the mood of the times in *Locksley Hall*:

> When I dipt into the future, far as human eye could see,
> Saw the Vision of the world, and all the wonder that would be.

This was a new and stirring world picture. How had it come about? Free trade was the answer of the economists. The abandonment of protectionism by the Repeal of the Corn Laws in 1846 seemed of momentous significance. The landed interest who had resisted this so vehemently had not suffered as they had feared. In fact, the years between 1852 and 1862 have been described as 'probably the most prosperous decade ever enjoyed' by British farmers.[6] A diary entry by Absolom Watkin at the end of Whitsun week in 1853 noted a sense of unusual well-being among the Manchester work force. 'Our country', he wrote, 'is, no doubt, in a most happy and prosperous state. Free trade, peace, freedom. Oh, happy England!'[7]

Macaulay rejoiced to see his optimistic prediction of 1848 fulfilled. His own answer to the question 'why?' was that the nation was profiting from the triumphs of applied science by 'the greatest and most highly civilised people that ever the world saw'.[8] In his essay on Lord Bacon he equated all the manifestations of the 'progress' of the times with the extent to which Baconian induction had become the dominant force in British intellectual life.[9] John Stuart Mill had no doubt that the nation had to thank Jeremy Bentham and the Utilitarians for this new emphasis on the inductive approach to problems. Bentham, according to Mill in an essay of 1838 in the *Westminster Review*, was the supreme inductive thinker of his day.[10]

Macaulay was never a Benthamite. Indeed, in 1829, in three articles in *The Edinburgh Review* on James Mill's *Essay on Government*, he had launched a forthright attack in which he actually criticized Bentham *inter alia* for confusing induction with deduction;[11] so powerful was Macaulay's onslaught that he gave the younger Mill furiously to think, and even to question some of the fundamentals of the Benthamite approach on which he had been nurtured by his father.[12] Nevertheless the principle of 'Utility', as underlying so much of the thinking and actions of the Victorians, became almost a watchword to them – hotly debated, frequently caricatured – and indisputably constituted a feature within their world picture. Since Utilitarianism and Benthamism are so often employed as synonymous terms, and Mill himself was to give the classic exposition of his own understanding of the meaning of the doctrine in his treatise on *Utilitarianism* in 1861, revised two years later, some explanation is clearly called for.

Who reads the novels of John Galt nowadays? John Stuart Mill, at least, read one of them, *Annals of the Parish* (1821), in a rare moment of light relief for one who was by nature so burdensomely over-serious. His attention was caught by a word he had never encountered before – 'utilitarian' – and, immediately seeing its applicability to the philosophy of Bentham, he borrowed it for that purpose, thereby endowing John Galt with a rarely-acknowledged immortality.[13] The only knowledge that Bentham regarded as worth having was 'useful knowledge'; the whole purpose of government was to serve a 'useful' end; and Bentham had defined that end as the promotion of the greatest happiness of the greatest number. As Mill explained, in his treatise:

> Utility or the Greatest Happiness Principle, holds that actions are right in proportion as they tend to promote happiness, wrong as they tend to produce the reverse of happiness. By happiness is intended pleasure … by unhappiness, pain.[14]

So much was well-known of Bentham's teaching. One of the reasons for Mill's later exposition was to try to render less contentious the hedonism implicit in Bentham's unwillingness to distinguish between types of pleasure – between poetry and push-pin, as the notorious example.

Bentham himself was one of history's great originals. This does not quite mean – as he himself liked to maintain – that he had no intellectual progenitors. The Greatest Happiness principle, for instance, was first enunciated by the French philosopher Helvétius;[15] and in the development of Bentham's ideas and schemes, it is not always clear from his relationship with his disciples who really influenced whom. There seems little doubt, for instance, that he was converted to the principle of universal suffrage by James Mill in 1808; and the affinity of his educational philosophy with that of Robert Owen also suggests that their influence on each other was mutual and reciprocal. But what set Bentham apart from all other philosophers was his determination, until the end of his long life (he died aged 85 in 1832), to transform society by the practical application of his plans and projects, all worked out in the minutest detail.

Many of them read like so many futuristic fantasies. His particular obsession was his new model prison, the *Panopticon*, in the prosecution of which he spent some twenty years of his life (and the best part of his fortune) making importunate overtures to the crowned heads of Europe, in the conviction that this nightmare of a penal institution, with its never-blinking, all-seeing eyes, would effect the moral reformation of society. He had detailed plans for a model unsectarian day-school, the *Chrestomathia*, so wedded to the inculcation of Useful Knowledge, to the exclusion of everything else, that it would have been the delight of Dickens' Thomas Gradgrind – all 'facts, facts, facts'. It hardly helped to advance his cause that his exposition of the *Chrestomathia* was rendered at times almost unintelligible by his employment of neologisms such as 'catastatico-chrestic physiurgics' and 'coenonesioscopic noology'.[16] He devised a programme of law reform and an extraordinary scheme for creating a truly representative legislature. He even pioneered the exercise of jogging in the interests of good health, causing his friends some embarrassment by occasionally practising it in their company, to the amusement of passers-by in St James's Park.[17] He had plans for almost everything, while succeeding in practically none of them, at least in his own lifetime. To the credit of this strange visionary, however, his influence can be detected in almost all the essential reforms that took place in the fifty or sixty years after his death.

Perhaps because his vision of future society was so wide-ranging and his recipes were such a mixture of the perceptive and the eccentric, both the understanding and the application of his teaching by his disciples – call them Benthamites, Utilitarians or Philosophical Radicals – differed in various particulars. As John Clive has put it:

> Like Marx, like Coleridge, Bentham was the kind of seminal thinker who attracted fanatical disciples, but whose ideas reached far beyond those disciples to a much wider public, which often accepted them only in part or saw something sound in them without going all the way.[18]

In Bentham's own lifetime, for instance, he had a passionate disciple at Cambridge in Charles Austin, a future eminent QC whose advocacy even – for a while – struck awe in the heart of the young Macaulay, not usually given to such feelings, except sometimes when admiring his own rhetorical accomplishments. But Austin would have nothing to do with Bentham's concept of democracy.[19] James Bowring, the devotee *par excellence*, who accepted the task shunned by other disciples of editing Bentham's posthumous *Deontology*, went north to Lancashire, where – not unreasonably – he applied the Greatest Happiness Principle to the ardent advocacy of Free Trade.[20]

In London, largely through the proselytism of James Mill and the parliamentary support of the law-reformer Samuel Romilly, Benthamism and Philosophical Radicalism became one, with the objective of refashioning the whole basis of English law and society. Francis Place, Joseph Lancaster (pioneer of the monitorial system of education of the poor) and Robert Owen (whose model cotton-mill at New Lanark was based entirely on Benthamite principles) were all active participants. There was to be a complete reappraisal of the nature and methods of education, based on the philosophy of Associationism, whereby children would be taught according to the principle of scientific experimentation, associating everything they learnt with its bearing on moral and social behaviour. The end result – so they confidently predicted – would be such a sense of social obligation that a child would never 'separate his personal happiness from the happiness of his fellows'.[21]

This is what 'Useful Knowledge' really meant; and this was how 'Utility' was to be ultimately achieved. Edward Bulwer deplored the fact that people who quoted Bentham's name had rarely bothered to study his works. He deserved to be read:

> He combined what had not been yet done, the spirit of the Philanthropic with that of the Practical. He did not declaim about abuses: he went at once to their roots; he did not idly penetrate the sophistries of Corruption; he smote Corruption herself. He was the very Theseus of legislative reform, – he not only pierced the labyrinth – he destroyed the monster.[22]

In the London circle of the Mills, and the London Debating Society, where Macaulay delighted in taking issue with James Mill's son, the Utilitarian ideals were freely discussed and, as C.R. Fay has pointed out, they left a deep impression on figures like Grote, Roebuck, Gibbon Wakefield, Charles Buller, and Lord Durham of the famous Durham Report on colonial administration in Canada.[23] But it was in India that the Benthamites found an ideal field for implementation of both their doctrines and their methods. Legislation towards the end of the eighteenth century had effectively wrested control of the British possessions

in India from the East India Company, the various provinces thereafter
to be ruled by a Governor-General and a government-appointed Board
of Control. James Mill's nine-volume *History of India* appeared in 1817,
and became a sort of weighty *vade mecum* for tackling the new administration of what Mill had represented as a culturally and politically backward people. Mill's authority could hardly be questioned after he
became chief examiner for the East India Company (in 1830), and his
recommendations were treated with the utmost respect by Lord William
Bentinck, the Governor-General, and also – rather surprisingly, in view
of his previous attacks on Mill – by Macaulay, on his appointment as
Legal Member of Council for India in 1833.

In assessing 'the Utilitarian strain amid the the new forces making for
dynamic change in India', John Clive has written:

> Where India was concerned, it was the authoritarian rather than the
> libertarian potential of Utilitarianism that was in the ascendant. The happi-
> ness of the greatest number of Indians mattered more than their freedom;
> and that, in terms of governance, meant, if possible, an all-powerful leg-
> islative and executive authority.[24]

It also meant that the educational system – on Mill's recommendation
– should not be based on the indigenous culture. 'The great end', James
Mill wrote, should be directed to 'useful learning'.[25]

A note of caution should, however, be sounded here. Research in
recent years has tended to question the extent to which the influence of
Benthamite ideology went beyond a respectful lip-service paid to it by
politicians and administrators in order to endow measures taken for
simple pragmatic reasons with a philosophical rationale. According to
Boyd Hilton, on occasions when governments acted 'the main purpose
of theory was to justify not originate measures'.[26] The background to
the repeal of the Corn Laws was a case in point. While Cobden and
Bright were convinced opponents of protectionism, 'the ultimate conversion of Whig ministers to free trade measures in 1841 came not
through the logical forces of economic theory but through a series of
budgetary deficits which persuaded ministers that a higher revenue was
obtainable through lower tariffs.'[27] Professor Eric Stokes has observed
that the Benthamite influence on the administration of British rule in
India also provides an example of ideology tempered with pragmatism.
The ideology, in this instance, came first; but 'the men who were respon-

sible for the subsequent elaboration of the structure were conscious pragmatists largely innocent of theory.'[28]

Bentham wrote so much on so many different subjects during the course of a long life that it is not surprising that elements of paradox appear in any attempt to summarize the essence of his teaching. One sometimes could wish that the phrase *laissez-faire* had never been invented, productive as it is of so much misunderstanding. There were *laissez-faire* principles such as the dominant economic theory of the time that growth and prosperity are enhanced by free trade and unrestricted economic competition. In theory, at least, the Benthamite formula of the Greatest Happiness of the Greatest Number suggests that if everyone were allowed freely to pursue their own goal of personal happiness, without direction or governmental interference, then general happiness would prevail. But Bentham was well aware that without the aid of education to establish that some 'pleasures' were of a higher quality than others, and ultimately more gratifying, the principle was valueless. At the same time, he would not accept that what the majority might believe the pursuit of happiness to entail should be imposed upon a dissentient minority. When John Stuart Mill delivered his most famous dictum on the nature of Liberty – the need for society to protect itself from the tyranny of the majority[29] – he was echoing his master's voice: 'Surely when any power has been made the strongest power, enough has been done for it; care is therefore wanted rather to prevent that strongest power from swallowing up all others.'[30]

The paradox amounts to this: in theory, Bentham would have wished to see individuals left to their own devices; in practice, they could not be; and given the circumstances of the times, which cried out for sweeping reforms of the whole political and social system, they must not be. Utilitarianism, therefore, became a programme of legislative reform in direct opposition to the principle of *laissez-faire*. The Poor Law Amendment Act of 1834 is a classic example of the paradox, aimed at eradicating the ill-advised interference in the balance of nature through the artificial means of doling out poor relief, which was seen as wasting public money as well as encouraging idleness and over-population. The only way it could be curtailed, however, was by legislation; and the procedure devised to ensure that the legislation was effective was a perfect exhibition of 'applied Benthamism', too. Edwin Chadwick, the architect of the new Poor Law, followed the Benthamite model to the letter.

First, one must establish the facts (by a Special Commission); secondly, legislate on the basis of the facts, collated in an official report; and finally, create a machinery to enforce the law by appointing an inspectorate. This was a new experience for all parties, but it was a procedure which has since become the blueprint for modern legislation.

The forces arraigned against Bentham, Chadwick and the Utilitarians generally were formidable. The leading writers of the time were almost solidly antagonistic. Coleridge poured scorn on the Greatest Happiness Principle. 'But *what* happiness?' he scoffed; '... Your mode of happiness would make *me* miserable.'[31] Carlyle abhorred the doctrines root and branch. 'I call this gross, steam-engine Utilitarianism an approach towards new Faith,' he wrote in his essay 'On Heroes'; '... you may call it Heroic, though a Heroism with its *eyes* put out!'[32] In *Sartor Resartus* he made play with the word 'Mill', although whether it was father or son (probably both) he was deriding is not clear. There is an 'Arithmetic Mill', the 'Mill of Death', the 'Motive-Millwrights', and all are clearly servants of 'the monster UTILITARIA'.[33] Decades later, Ruskin in *Unto This Last* indulged in a parody of Mill's 'economic man', and in his celebrated assertion that 'there is no wealth but life' set his own convictions against 'all political economy founded on self-interest'.[34]

Utilitarianism lent itself to parody, ridicule and outright repudiation. Bentham was personally a benevolent man. But sometimes his conception of human beings made them appear like automatons and his schemes for reform gave the impression of cold, analytical calculation. Carlyle dismissed Mill's *Autobiography* as 'the life of a logic-chopping engine, little more of human in it than if it had been done by a thing of mechanized iron'.[35] Disraeli put his finger on what was lacking. The Utilitarians resembled the 'Unitarians in Religion. Both omit Imagination in their system, and Imagination governs mankind.'[36] After the new Poor Law of 1834, he devised a new name for their doctrine: 'Brutilitarianism'.[37]

Not surprisingly, all those nervous of change, and the Tories therefore most of all, were vehemently opposed to the Utilitarian influence. The principle of 'Utility', when applied to long-established institutions, raised uncomfortable thoughts; and none more uncomfortable than with regard to the unreformed Church of England, whose defenders raised the cry of 'the Church in danger' when the Whigs at last secured power under Lord Grey in 1830. An Oxford Movement, with Newman,

Keble and Pusey at its head, determined to reassert the Catholicity of the Anglican Church, might have come at any time in the 1830s, but its militant shape was unquestionably precipitated by the Whig government's intention to place church reform at the top of its legislative agenda.

Could any Christian view the menacing influence of Utilitarianism with equanimity? Bentham himself regarded Christianity as an irrelevance. It seduced gullible people into vain supernatural hopes, stunted their pleasures and clogged their minds with incomprehensible mysteries. Mill, in his *Autobiography*, observed that he had never had any Christianity to discard.[38] He had never even entered a church.[39] Occasionally, however, for conflicting reasons, Utilitarians and Evangelicals found themselves fighting the same battles. There was, for instance, a shared conviction of the principle of *laissez-faire* as an economic doctrine and the undesirability of misguided governmental paternalism such as indiscriminate distribution of poor relief. The 'main exemplar of Evangelical economics', Boyd Hilton has shown, was the Scottish divine Thomas Chalmers.[40] 'Bibles before bread' was his declared priority. As Hilton has put it, 'God runs the world on *laissez-faire* lines, in the sense that he does not meddle with his own mechanism, and so man should not meddle either.'[41] This was also the standpoint of the celebrated Evangelical philanthropists of the Clapham Sect – William Wilberforce, Henry Thornton, Zachary Macaulay and others – who, despite their merited acclaim for securing the abolition of the Slave Trade, were in total sympathy with the Utilitarian thinking behind the new Poor Law. Private benevolence was one thing, but charitable largesse which failed to distinguish between the deserving and the undeserving poor was another. The poor needed to be taught that the world is beset with temptations and sufferings, and that mankind is on trial awaiting judgement. It was therefore through 'self-help' and the virtues of moral restraint that salvation could be achieved both in this world and the next.

A Utilitarian would not have shared this last sentiment. But sometimes he could speak in similar language. Walter Houghton once challenged his readers to identify the Evangelical author of the following words: 'to abstain from the enjoyment which is in our power, or to seek distant rather than immediate results, are among the most painful (and necessary) exertions of the human will.' The answer is: not an

Evangelical at all. This is the Benthamite economist Nassau Senior, advocating the means to attain commercial success.[42]

Nassau Senior was that singular hybrid, a secular Evangelical. Examples of the inversion of the oxymoron a 'Christian Utilitarian' can also be found. Lord William Bentinck, in India, was a moderate Evangelical while also an admirer of James Mill.[43] At a certain point, however, the paths had to diverge, because the moralism that united the two opposites had such a different ultimate end. Nevertheless it was this common moralism that enabled the French historian Elie Halévy to propound his much-debated thesis that the two movements, Utilitarianism and Evangelicalism, taken together, constituted the primary force which ensured the stability of society in early and mid-Victorian England. After all, if one can improve the morals of the underprivileged and teach them to be respectable citizens, weaning them away from drunkenness and vice, then one reduces the number of potential troublemakers and useless drifters, and society must gain in stability.

The stance of an ardent Evangelical like Antony Ashley Cooper, seventh Earl of Shaftesbury, differed from that of Chalmers and the Clapham Sect. He was a genuine humanitarian in his protest against the working conditions of factory employees and miners and in his efforts to put an end to the exploitation of child labour. These were reforms which were part of the Utilitarian programme, and despite his abhorrence of the secularity of their doctrines, Shaftesbury was prepared to co-operate with every ally he could obtain. On the humanitarian issue, Broad churchmen like Charles Kingsley and F.D. Maurice were equally prepared to join forces in fighting governmental apathy and non-intervention.

The strongest force of all against which the Utilitarians had to battle was what Oliver MacDonagh has described as the prevailing mood of Victorian England until well into the 1870s – its 'positive and aggressive individualism'.[44] England was a free country. It hated Boards, Commissions, Inspectorates. They all smacked too much of France and of centralization, bureaucracy and the Napoleonic Codes. Even if a particular administration felt itself compelled to listen to the reformers, there was always the House of Lords to contend with. In July 1850, for instance, Lord Londonderry rose to give his considered opinion on a very moderate Bill to introduce an advisory inspectorate to ensure that crucial safety measures were being observed in coal mines. He would oppose, he said, every dot and comma 'of the most mischievous and unjust measure that could possibly be imagined'. Why should a pit-owner allow an outsider to pry into his affairs, thereby exhibiting to all and sundry 'the interior concerns of his work, all his wealth, all his property?'[45] It is not without significance that reforming activity was at its lowest ebb in the period between 1851 and 1868, and that for nine of these years Palmerston, John Bull personified, was Prime Minister.

By contrast, it was during these same years that John Stuart Mill's influence was at its height. Leslie Stephen recalled the vogue for Mill in Cambridge: 'The young men who graduated in 1850 and the following ten years found their philosophical teaching in Mill's *Logic*, and only a few daring heretics were beginning to pick holes in his system.'[46] It should be remembered, however, that Mill wore his Benthamism with a difference. If one were to plot a graph of his adherence to classic Utilitarianism it would display occasional peaks and troughs, according to the influences of the moment. Unlike Bentham he had a receptive mind. As is well known, his father had done his best to inoculate his son from contaminating influences. So relentless had been his pressure to reproduce his own kind in his offspring (the boy was studying Greek at the age of three), it is a wonder that so over-fertilized a young plant did not intellectually wither and die. Although he never acquired a sense of humour, displaying a 'monotonous joylessness' (as R.H. Hutton put it) to the end,[47] Mill learnt from reading Wordsworth that there was such a thing as 'feeling'; and this led him to a study and a new appreciation of Coleridge. He also found himself drawing closer in sympathy with the Positivist philosophy of Auguste Comte. How much actual influence Harriet Taylor exercised over him is a debatable point, but it seems that his own lavish tributes after her death in 1858 'were extravagant even by the most uxorious standards'.[48] Certainly Harriet Taylor's growing attachment to socialism and communism in her last years is not reflected in Mill's own work.

We have a vignette of Mill, three years before Harriet's death, recorded by Kate Amberley, which suggests a much more rounded personality than his father had intended to produce. Mill and his step-daughter, Helen Taylor, were staying with the Amberleys at their new home, Ravenscroft, in Chepstow.

After dinner Mr Mill read us Shelley's Ode to Liberty and he got quite excited and moved over it rocking backwards and forwards and nearly choking with emotion; he said himself: 'it is almost too much for one.' Miss Taylor read the Hymn to Intellectual Beauty but in rather a theatrical voice not as pleasant as Mill's. He also read some of his favourite bits of Wordsworth which he admires very much. I read them Lowell's Present Crisis which they did not know and some of Emerson's poems.[49]

In these last years Mill was coming more and more to put his faith in the influence of education and in his long-held belief that the best form of government was meritocracy. As early as 1821 he had expressed his distaste for majority rule.

The majority must either have wrong opinions, or no fixed opinions, or must place the degree of reliance warranted by reason, in the authority of those who have made moral and social philosophy their peculiar study ... In the last resort they must fall back upon the authority of still more cultivated minds.[50]

It is not, then, surprising that he approved of Coleridge and his notion of the 'clerisy', his ideal of the 'national church' which should comprehend 'the learned of all denominations ..., all the so-called liberal arts and sciences, the possession and application of which constitute the civilization of a country, as well as the theological.'[51] No priests, no theology, however, for Mill; philosophers, rather; a leisured class, with an opportunity for solitude so that they could 'cultivate freely the grace of life'.[52] There is almost a suggestion of Matthew Arnold in this. Mill found the same aspiration in Comte. In the final stage of the development of mankind, the ideal would be 'not the blind submission of dunces to men of knowledge, but the intelligent deference of those who know much to those who know still more.'[53]

By the 1870s Mill's qualified Utilitarianism was beginning to look more like the Positivism of Herbert Spencer and Comte. After his death, new moral philosophers were coming to the fore to inspire the next generation. In Cambridge, Henry Sidgwick; in Oxford – even more influential – T.H. Green. The days of Utilitarianism might seem to be over. But actually, almost unnoticed, changes had been taking place – quietly and undramatically – which were fulfilling Bentham's vision of an England in which all the remnants of feudalism should be extirpated. By the late 1880s – as will be seen in due course – both government and administration had assumed the essential features of Collectivism; and once set on that path, there could be no return.

When Lord Everingham, in Disraeli's *Coningsby*, defined the 'Spirit of the Age' as 'the Spirit of Utility', he was pooh-poohing the medieval play-acting of the young aristocrats who thought that the peasantry would be entertained and rendered happy by dancing round the maypole.[54] 'Utility' meant getting rid of all that was useless. When, however, one tries to find any single attribute common to the Utilitarians, almost every definition invites a contradiction. They advocated *laissez-faire* as sound economic policy; but they were compulsive interventionists when it came to rectifying the social problems of their day. They were admirably humanitarian in intention, and yet were the architects in 1834 of one of the most inhumane pieces of legislation in the statute book. They had a noble concept of the nature of liberty, while seeming to pose an intrusive and authoritarian threat to their countrymen's love of individualism. It might seem safe to say that at least all genuine Benthamites were indifferent to the claims of the Christian religion. But what does one make of James Bowring? Scrupulously faithful to his revered master, Bentham, and then becoming a sort of general factotum within his circle after Bentham's death in 1832, he yet spent his leisure moments in writing hymns.[55]

V

'What is it to be a gentleman?'

W.M. Thackeray in 1861

'I shall be a gen'l'm'n myself one of these days, with a pipe in my mouth, and a summer house in the back garden.'

Sam Weller in Dickens, *Pickwick Papers*

Why was Thackeray never quite at ease in society? It was in attempting to answer this question, in a review in 1864 of a recent biography of the author of *Vanity Fair*, that Walter Bagehot propounded his celebrated theory about the uniqueness of English society compared to the caste system of the East and the passion for equality in France and the USA. In England, he wrote, there had come about a system of *removable inequalities*, where many people are inferior to and worse off than the others, but in which each may *in theory* hope to be on the level with the highest below the throne, and in which each may reasonably, and without sanguine impracticability, hope to gain one step in social elevation, to be at least on a level with those who at first were just above them.

So eager were all classes in society to advance that one step higher, to be in a position of having inferiors, that 'some poison of snobbishness' was inevitable.[1]

Thirty years earlier, Edward Bulwer had made a similar observation. Everybody seemed to be aspiring to be on the move – upwards; and each stage of the advance was associated with the acquisition of money. In the higher echelons, the rich trader looked 'to obtain the alliance of nobles', and since

> wealth is the greatest of all levellers ... the highest of the English nobles willingly repair the fortunes of hereditary extravagance by intermarrying with the families of the banker, the lawyer, and the merchant.

So arises 'that eternal vying with each other, that spirit of show', and 'wealth is affected even when not possessed'. It is a 'contagion' which 'extends from the highest towards the verge of the lowest'.[2]

England in Victorian times was not a closed society, but it was certainly acutely class-conscious. Within the traditional divisions of upper, middle and lower (or, as an Irish judge in 1798 defined the social scale, 'noblemen, baronets, knights, esquires, gentlemen, yeomen, tradesmen and artificers'),[3] there had developed a host of subtle yet generally acknowledged gradations. Within the lower class, the fundamental distinction was between the artisan who, as a skilled operative, had every incentive to hope for better things, and the unskilled labourer. Within both these groups, aspirations were likely to differ according to the degree of acquiescence in remaining a poor man at the gate of the rich man's castle, or to the amount of determination, if not to better one's own prospects, at least to work and save in the hope that one's children might advance in the world. As late as 1873, Thomas Wright was anxious to dispel the error of supposing that the working-classes constituted

> a single-acting, single-idea'd body. They are practically and plurally *classes*, distinct classes, classes between which there are as decisively marked differences as there are between any one of them and the upper or middle classes.[4]

Always, however, it was that next step above which marked the practicable, and perhaps the only ultimate, objective. The literate might read in the pages of Samuel Smiles the stories of humble men who made good through 'self-help', and thereby moved up to become wealthy members of the middle classes; but for most working men the highest aspiration they could nourish was to rise out of the ranks of wage-earners: to run a little business of their own – a corner-shop, perhaps; and – who knows? – trade might be good enough to enable you to employ an assistant whose wages you could yourself then determine. This was a pipe-dream for the many, probably; but it had been known to happen.[5]

Such a fulfilment of working-class ambition would technically mean a move into the middle class, in so far as that large amorphous grouping admits of definition, containing as it did all sorts and conditions of men below the landed gentry and above the 'workers', and therefore embracing even more subtle distinctions of gradation. Dr Kitson Clark has accordingly warned historians to proceed with caution when employing a term which has 'done more to stultify thought about Victorian England than anything else'.[6] Nevertheless Victorians were very well aware of what they meant when they used the term themselves.

As early as 1831, Lord Grey reminded a ministerial colleague that 'the middle classes ... form the real and efficient mass of public opinions ... without whom the power of the gentry is nothing.'[7] In the same year, Lord Brougham warned the House of Lords against supposing that they represented the nation in their attempts to frustrate the passing of the Reform Bill. The world had moved on. The middle classes had become the nation, representing 'the wealth and intelligence of the country, the glory of the British name'.[8] By 1857 Thackeray had convinced himself of the social status of a successful novelist within a specific gradation of the middle class, when he declared in an after-dinner speech:

> I belong to the class that I see around me here, the class of lawyers and merchants and scholars, of men who are striving on in the world, of men of the educated middle classes of the country.[9]

Even Matthew Arnold was bold enough to make a similar declaration, although the context suggests a touch of insincerity, if not mock modesty. In the Preface to the first series of *Essays in Criticism*, he confessed that his 'avocations led me to travel almost daily on one of the

Great Eastern Lines – the Woodford Branch'. In modern parlance, he had become a commuter. 'The English middle class, of which I am myself a feeble unit, travel on the Woodford Branch in large numbers.' Whether or not he really believed himself to be a 'feeble unit', he was emphatically identifying himself with that class which 'has done all the great things which have ever been done in England'.[10]

Social distinctions within the middle classes were, because of their many gradations, more pronounced than within the classes above and below them. They can be seen, for instance, in religious affiliation. The Establishment held the advantage all along the line, partly because until late in the century the prestigious universities of Oxford and Cambridge were their exclusive preserve. A Nonconformist might, through business success, amass considerably more wealth, but he had a serious handicap to overcome if he were to be accorded the same social status. In his own particular domain, this might not greatly bother him. The man who rose to prominence, having no rivals in the particular 'trade of the town' – a steel king in Sheffield, for instance, or the leading manufacturer of hardware in Birmingham – exercised a power not significantly weaker than that of a feudal lord of old.[11] In the lesser provincial world – the world that George Eliot knew so well – it was very different. Recalling the days before the 'Catholic Question' had begun to agitate Protestants of all denominations, she wrote, in *The Mill on the Floss*:

> Dissent was an inheritance along with a superior pew and a business connection; and Churchmanship only wondered contemptuously at Dissent as a foolish habit that clung greatly to families in the grocery and chandlering lines, though not incompatible with prosperous wholesale dealing.[12]

The setting of *Middlemarch* was different. According to Mrs Fairbrother, theological conflict had lowered the tone of the Establishment. She assured Dr Lydgate that

> It was not so in my youth: a Churchman was a Churchman, and a clergyman, you might be pretty sure, was a gentleman, if nothing else. But now he may be no better than a Dissenter, and want to push aside my son on pretence of doctrine.[13]

Within Dissent itself, however, there were social distinctions. At the top of the scale, and very definitely above the lower middle class, came the Unitarians, mainly because of their intellectual standing. The Methodists were not far below them, but the split branches of the

Methodists veered towards the lower end; and the lowest rung of all was occupied by the Congregationalists and the Baptists. The Roman Catholics formed an entity apart: in their indigenous strongholds, proudly and aloofly aristocratic; among the rank and file (mainly immigrant Irish), the lowest of the labouring class, with many destitute. Until the influx of the Anglican converts in the 1840s and 50s, English Catholicism was a social anomaly. It had no middle.

Dr Johnson once said that 'it is the essence of a gentleman's character to bear the visible mark of no profession whatever.'[14] This was the eighteenth century speaking. But it raised at once the nerve-jangling question for those engaged in the professions, all therefore within the middle class, whether their particular calling warranted the additional status of 'gentleman' – the most coveted cachet of all. The nerves hardly ceased to jangle during Victoria's reign. Echoes of the eighteenth-century definition could still be heard. Macaulay's criterion of a gentleman presupposed scholarly leisure: reading Plato with one's feet on the fender (actually the only comfortable way in which Macaulay could cope with his edition of Plato: a seventeenth-century folio, sixteen inches long by ten inches broad, weighing twelve pounds).[15] This brought little joy to most professional men; neither did Coleridge's definition: 'a man with an indifference to money matters'.[16]

But were there not outward and visible signs of gentlemanly status which could only be the consequence of a healthy income? Sam Weller's little fantasy of days that could never be for him were material symbols of leisure – 'a pipe in my mouth, and a summer house in the back garden'.[17] Thackeray supplied a more generally acknowledged status symbol in *Vanity Fair*. The scene is Dr Swishtail's famous school, and two boys are conversing:

> 'Your father's only a merchant, Osborne,' Dobbin said in private to the little boy … At which the latter replied haughtily. 'My father's a gentleman, and keeps his carriage.'[18]

Nineteenth-century society, however, required more than outward and visible signs. There had to be some inner graces as well. *John Halifax, Gentleman*, in Mrs Dinah Craik's novel of 1856, rose from humble beginnings to sufficient affluence to keep his carriage, and his son's reaction was the same as young Osborne's. 'We are gentlefolks now,' he exclaimed. His father knew better. 'We always were, my son,' he said.[19]

He meant by that not the gift of education; not what Magwitch in *Great Expectations* believed would convert Pip into a gentleman – 'money and education' – but something akin to moral graces: one's behaviour to other people, the possession of a Christian manly spirit.

This was the ideal of Arnold at Rugby: 'to make it a place of Christian education ... to form Christian men'.[20] He therefore exhorted his essentially middle-class clientele not to ape the arrogant ways of the aristocracy, but to be exemplars of the Christian virtues; to be truth-loving, pure and manly. It is interesting that Thackeray, who – like John Halifax – was no product of Rugby, gave this ideal its fullest expression in his lectures on 'The Four Georges' in 1861.

> What is it to be a gentleman? Is it to have lofty aims, to lead a pure life, to keep your honour virgin; to have the esteem of your fellow-citizens and the love of your fireside; to suffer evil with constancy; and through evil or good to maintain truth always?[21]

A counsel for perfection, indeed. Perhaps Thackeray, so unsure of his own social status, set the terms of reference so high that no one except a saint could aspire to them. Trollope shared Thackeray's anxieties over where he stood in the social scale, but in *The Duke's Children*, published in 1880, when the word 'gentleman' crops up, he goes to the opposite extreme, setting the terms of reference so low that practically anybody could claim the title. At least, so the Duke of Omnium maintains. His private secretary regarded himself as a gentleman; so did the local curate. 'The word is too vague to carry any meaning that ought to be serviceable.'[22]

Trollope's personal agonizing over status was genuine enough. It might have been otherwise had his family fortunes not failed. As a result, he was miserable at Harrow as a day boy (also for a short time at Winchester), and was taunted and teased as a charity boy by his patrician schoolfellows. He never forgot the sense of shame. 'There are places in life which can only be well-filled by "gentlemen",' he wrote in his *Autobiography*. 'The word is one the use of which almost subjects one to ignominy.'[23] A clerkship in the London Post Office at a salary of £90 a year was not likely to make good his earlier deficiencies. He could not let the word 'gentleman' alone in his novels. In *The Last Chronicle of Barset* even a poor parson who cannot provide his daughter with a dowry is assured by Archdeacon Grantly that 'we stand ... on the only perfect level on which such men can meet each other. We are both gentlemen.'[24] Samuel Prong in *Rachel Ray*, a vulgar Evangelical, was not so favoured. He lacked that quality which is

> recognisable but not definable ... It is caught at a word, it is seen at a glance, it is appreciated unconsciously at a touch by those who have none of it themselves ... Now Mr Prong was not a gentleman.[25]

Had it all started at Arnold's Rugby? T.H. Green, who was himself a Rugbeian, but under A.C. Tait, not Arnold, thought not, as he explained in a lecture on the foundation of a new Oxford High School for Boys. The public schools had, however, taken over the manufacture of that 'kind of manner and tone of feeling' which was exacerbating unhealthy class distinction. He admired the qualities, but looked to the day when liberal education was open to all.[26]

Liberal education, as provided by the traditional public schools and the many new foundations of the 1840s and 1850s, almost without exception inspired by Arnoldian ideals, meant an education based on the Classics. All other subjects were considered to be little more than luxurious optional extras. As Gladstone once put it in defending his own Eton background, science, modern languages – even history – should never be regarded as occupying a parallel position to Classical studies: 'their true position is ancillary, and as ancillary it ought to be limited and restrained without scruples.'[27] Within those ancillary subjects, science was accorded the lowest place of all. Liberal education was also respected as the most fitting requirement in the nurturing of a 'gentleman'; and therefore middle-class families, anxious to ensure that social cachet for their sons, patronized the public schools in ever-increasing numbers during the second half of the nineteenth century. The consequence, although barely perceived at the time, was to prove detrimental to the nation's economy. The persistent refusal to recognize the role of science and technology in the schools that were setting the pattern of all secondary education in the country, together with the stigma increasingly attached to careers in industry and trade, did absolutely nothing to encourage the future generations of these aspirants to gentlemanly status to bear the torch of Britain's industrial prosperity onwards to meet the challenges that lay ahead from foreign competitors.

In a recent study on the decline of the industrial spirit during the second half of the nineteenth century, Martin Wiener has observed that during this time 'industry' had come to mean 'an uncomfortable close-ness to working with one's hands, not to mention an all-too-direct earning of money'.[28] Similar criteria had for long been applied in deter-mining the social distinctions within the various professions. When Joseph Toplady (a very old man at the time) remarked to Lord Rosebery that he always considered Sir Robert Peel was 'not quite a gentleman because he corresponded with Under-Secretaries direct',[29] he was pitch-ing it rather strongly. Nevertheless there was an acknowledged distinc-tion between the man who distanced himself from pecuniary dealings with his clients and those to whom fees were paid without an intermedi-ary. A barrister was higher in the social scale than a solicitor, who included the barrister's fees in his own. An author, who was reimbursed by his publisher, was superior to an artist.[30] Trollope's Dr Thorne failed to show proper embarrassment when taking money from his patients, so relegating his status to that of an apothecary.[31] Even a very distinguished physician, expected to receive a peerage, was denied it, so an informant told Hippolyte Taine, because 'a man who held out his hand to receive his guinea could not properly be a peer of the realm.'[32] For the same reason, it was impossible for a man engaged in the retail trade to be acknowledged a gentleman. Perhaps this is why somebody who put on the airs of a gentleman when he was manifestly nothing of the sort was contemptuously described as a 'grocer'. Apparently the same derogatory term was used in France. Montalembert so described Louis Philippe.[33]

The clergy of the Established Church (apart from the unfortunate Samuel Prong) claimed the accolade of gentleman as of right, partly as graduates of Oxford and Cambridge, and partly also because – for the very few highly-favoured – there was a natural passage, on becoming a bishop, into the House of Lords. This amused Arthur Benson, whose father rose from the humbler ranks of the middle class to become Archbishop of Canterbury, presiding over his fellows in lawn sleeves, all conscious of a similar origin. 'We have a middle class taint about us,' Arthur Benson wrote. 'We are none of us aristocrats in any way.' It turned the heads of some of their wives. He was thinking particularly of Mrs Creighton, who – when her husband was translated from the See of Peterborough to become Bishop of London – begged the wife of his successor 'to *insist* that the clergy should call the Bishop "My Lord" ... It seems to me due to the position.'[34]

Who were these bishops? A fair proportion of them had previously been headmasters of public schools. The last four Archbishops of Canterbury in Victoria's reign had all had that honour – C.T. Longley, Headmaster of Harrow, A.C. Tait, Headmaster of Rugby, E.W. Benson, Master of Wellington, and Frederick Temple, yet another who had sat in Arnold's chair. The public schools not only manufactured gentlemen; those who taught in them enjoyed an unprecedented boost in social prestige. As early as 1847, Brooke Foss Westcott, recently ordained, considered his 'future course of life'.

> A schoolmaster or a clergyman? I am fearful, if once I embrace the former profession, I shall be again absorbed in all the schemes of ambition and selfish destination which used continually to haunt me.[35]

He accepted a post at Harrow, and was not actually a very good schoolmaster; but he ended as Bishop of Durham.

Such openings would not, of course, have been available to any of Dickens' schoolmasters – a Bradley Headstone, or even a Dr Blimber. It was the prestige of certain public schools that mattered. The most prestigious of all was Eton, where Arthur Benson became a housemaster. He too had occasional soul-searchings about his position in society. He confessed in 1903 to a glow of pleasure when, at a dinnerparty at Terling, the country residence of Lord and Lady Rayleigh, his neighbour – Lady Alice Archer-Houblon – turned to him and said 'we in *our* class', obviously including himself. At a similar gathering in the company of another Eton housemaster, Stuart Donaldson, his neighbour (Lady Helen Boyle) remarked that when staying in New Zealand with her brother, Lord Glasgow, she could not help feeling rather vexed at finding 'Doctors and Dentists' also invited to dine, 'though I don't think I am proud'. Arthur Benson observed that '50 years ago she wd have been offended by sitting between two schoolmasters.'[36]

Academic distinction conferred a certain prestige, but this was not reflected in its material rewards. The standard annual dividend of a Fellow of an Oxford or Cambridge college was £200 in the middle of the century. All but Heads of Houses were bachelors in Orders, and therefore board and residence were 'found'. A senior Classical master at a major public school was decidedly better off. E.W. Benson, when teaching the Classical Sixth at Rugby in the early 1850s, earned £900 a year. Edmond Warre, as Head Master of Eton in the closing decades of the century, earned £4,000 annually (a hundred times more than the pitiful salary – mid-century – of Benjamin Jowett as Regius Professor of Greek at Oxford; admittedly, this was regarded as a scandal). When T.H. Huxley became an FRS in 1851, his remuneration was so poor that he could not contemplate marriage until he had collected a plurality of academic posts: Professor of Natural History in the Government School of Mines, Curator of Palaeontological Collections and Naturalist to the Geological Survey, and Fullerian Professor of Physiology to the Royal Institution. He deplored the priorities of a world that could pay Sir Richard Owen, Hunterian Professor and probably the second greatest scholar in his field, only £300 a year. 'A man who chooses a life of science', Huxley wrote, 'chooses not a life of poverty, but so far as I can see, a life of *nothing*, and the art of living upon nothing at all has yet to be discovered.'[37]

He would have done better to become an engineer. There were fair chances of making a fortune, especially if you belonged to the acknowledged aristocracy of the profession – the civil engineers. They were among the earliest to form their own professional association, in 1818. As the century progressed more and more of the professions saw the advantage of fostering their corporate interests and giving proof of their high credentials by following suit: the Law Society in 1825, the British Medical Association in 1856, the Ship Masters in 1857, Chartered Surveyors in 1868, with many more to follow.

A further way to advance one's interests was to create unofficial circles of self-conscious élitism by shrewd alliances within a particular profession or calling, cemented by intermarriage. The City of London was not slow to appreciate this. Here was a world of its own. In the Square Mile, dominated by the Royal Exchange and the network of coffee-houses surrounding it, rose the giants of finance on whom much of the prosperity of Victorian England came to be based. A man like Nathan Rothschild had no worries at all about his social rank. He could live like a lord. His particular field was the negotiation of foreign loans. He had twice intervened to save the country (and the Duke of Wellington in particular), by obtaining the bullion, and making it available, to pay the Duke's army in Spain in the Peninsular War, and by intervening to save the Bank of England during the run on the banks in the financial crisis of 1825. He knew that 'ultimately it was money, not legislation, that made the world go round'.[38] He died in 1836, but by that time something of a financial aristocracy had come into being, and some of its prominent members had been elevated to the peerage. Pitt found the financial advice of the banker Robert Smith so crucial during the 1790s that he gave him the title of Lord Carrington. The House of Baring, the most diversified of the merchant banks, was honoured when Alexander Baring became Lord Ashburton in 1836. Within the world of stock-broking, interesting alliances were forming: a complex of uncles, cousins, brothers-in-law with names such as Capel, Cazenove, Marjoribanks, Coutts and Wagg. Many of this City fraternity were Jews (the Montefiores and the Roths-childs were related, to their mutual advantage), some were Quakers, notably Samuel Gurney. Some would rise, and some would fall; but the power in their hands was vast.

There were clerical oligarchies, too. One such has recently been analysed by Clive Dewey in his fascinating study, *The Passing of Barchester*. This was the circle of High Church clergy centred on the figure of William Lyall, Dean of Canterbury from 1845 to 1857. He was 'a broker in a hierarchy of patronage. He obtained preferment from patrons above him and distributed preferment to his relatives below';[39] and, through his alliance with the High Church ginger-group known as the Hackney Phalanx, with its own network of influential personal contacts, he exercised a powerful influence in protecting the Anglican Church against real threats of disestablishment and disendowment. This may sound like ruthless nepotism. In fact the patronage was conducted in such a way as to ensure that the ablest men occupied positions of influence.

There was deliberate contrivance here. But a potential élite can also come about rather more naturally from the circumstance of intermarriage between families of similar social standing within a circle of common intellectual, religious or cultural affinities. If one traces, as Noel Annan has,[40] the marriages of the offspring of certain members of the Clapham Sect – the Venns, Stephens, Macaulays in particular – and also those from the alliance of the Wedgwoods and the Darwins, with their link with the Arnolds, the circle both widens and, in another sense, contracts (through becoming increasingly close-knit in the intellectual force that it represents). This was primarily a Cambridge circle, and while developing from an Evangelical base, its religious affiliation diminished with each generation, in many instances into agnosticism. A circle that counted within it such names as Darwin, Macaulay, Trevelyan, Stephen, Vaughan, Butler, Sidgwick, Balfour, Dicey and Maitland, had become by the close of the century a genuine intellectual aristocracy.

Middle class in origin, it did not have to trouble itself about social standing. If power meant influence, then effectively it recognized no power higher than itself.

E.E. Kellett recalled hearing in the 1880s – the exact date is not certain – the shortest prize-giving speech ever delivered. It was by Lord Cromer, and it is here given in full: 'I have only three things to say to you: love your country, tell the truth, and *don't dawdle.*'[41] The Victorians felt that they had a call to be 'up and doing'. As their acknowledged recipe for bettering one's prospects in life, they offered the one word – 'work'.

> For there is a perennial nobleness, and even sacredness, in Work [Carlyle wrote in *Past and Present*] ... There is always hope in a man that actually and earnestly works; in Idleness alone is there perpetual despair.[42]

Thomas Arnold had dinned the same lesson into the heads of his pupils, both at Laleham and at Rugby. With his 'intense earnestness to life', Bonamy Price wrote, he taught that 'Work is the appointed calling of man on earth, the end for which his various faculties were given.'[43] One can hardly find a dissentient voice throughout the Queen's reign. 'Habitual exertion is the greatest of all invigorators', was how Fitzjames Stephen put it.[44] In 1871, in *Sesame and Lilies*, Ruskin reminded an assemblage of girls that 'God dislikes idle and cruel people more than others; that His first order is "Work while you have light".'[45]

Whether God actually said anything of the sort, it pleased Ruskin to think so; and he was at one with even the humblest of preceptors. Mary Garth, in George Eliot's *Middlemarch*, echoed Carlyle when she told Fred Vincey that 'my father says that an idle man ought not to exist, much less be married.'[46] There were sound enough reasons. In terms of pure self-interest, it would not do to be left behind in the race for success. Mr Pancks in *Little Dorrit* expressed his philosophy thus:

> Keep always at it, and I'll keep you always at it, and you keep somebody else always at it. There you are with the Whole Duty of Man in a commercial country.[47]

But there was a moral glory in work, too. It gave a man not only self-respect and dignity, but something else besides. Jowett did not mince words when remonstrating with an idle Balliol undergraduate. 'You are a fool,' he said. 'You must be sick of idling. It is too late for you to do much. But the class matters nothing. What does matter is the sense of power which comes from steady working.'[48]

The work ethic was translated for the edification of the lower classes into the phrase 'Self-Help'. This was the gospel of Samuel Smiles, whose book of that title was published in 1859. An 'old-fashioned' lesson, he called it; it had served him, personally, well; and it had served hundreds of others. It also served the nation well. 'National progress is the sum of individual industry, energy and uprightness as national decay is of individual idleness, selfishness, and vice.'[49] It proved to be a phenomenal best-seller: 20,000 copies were sold in the year of publication; 55,000 in the first five years; by 1905, over a quarter of a million. How did one set about the process of self-advancement? Three things above all were necessary: first, diligence; second, self-improvement (or 'character', as Smiles put it); third, thrift. Thrift meant prudent saving by taking advantage of Friendly Societies, contributing to funds for sickness benefit and death benefit. The middle years of the century saw a burgeoning of mutual benefit societies of one form or another, and they were a classic example of effective voluntary associations and the doctrine of *laissez-faire* at its most productive. Lancashire was the birthplace of the largest of them. By the 1870s, the three Friendly Societies – the Oddfellows, the Manchester Unity and the Ancient Order of Foresters – had 800,000 members between them.[50] But thrift also meant not wasting your money on the demon drink.

The Temperance Movement, in its early days, derived its impetus from the working class. There were pre-Victorian Radicals, like Francis Place and Orator Hunt, who enjoined sobriety for the purpose of countering accusations of disorderliness in their demonstrations; and the Temperance Movement itself was founded as early as 1829, confining its strictures then to the drinking of spirits. It was in the late 1840s that the 'Seven Men of Preston' – artisans for the most part – initiated the Pledge. History does not tell us whether they were surprised or gratified by the response, but they should not have been disappointed. As Brian Harrison has pointed out, 'the teetotal movement appealed strongly to the working-class desire for self-dependence, self-education and respectability.'[51]

'Respectability' was the key word. Even by 1833, Edward Bulwer observed, it had become the favourite description of the leading virtue of the age.[52] That Evangelicalism, both within and without the Establishment, played the largest part in disseminating the ideal cannot be doubted. Respectability harmonized well with the puritan virtues; it was an end achievable by moral restraint. More than that, church-going or attendance at chapel, the holding of family prayers, the desire to read edifying literature and to observe Sunday as a day of pious rest – all were accepted manifestations of respectability. The Methodists in particular were insistent on the duty of self-scrutiny, and members of their congregations were encouraged to monitor the behaviour of their fellows. Radical influences also often served to work for the same end. It was a common feature of mass meetings and demonstrations to exhibit orderliness and respectability by being conducted almost as if they were religious services. In August 1858, the Chief Constable of Staffordshire recorded some notes on a mass meeting of colliers at Horsley Heath, assembled to agree strike action (there was therefore a considerable police presence). It began with a hymn. The speaker then assured his audience that he was both 'a teetotaller and a Sunday school teacher'.[53] Richard Cobden maintained that if you wanted to gain a hearing from a crowd, it was good policy to find 'a moral issue enforced by biblical illustration'. You rarely failed to gain a response.[54] And this tells its tale. Religious issues had permeated deeply enough for them to be respected; even, perhaps, at times, exploited.

When it came to finding opportunities for self-improvement, attendance at church or chapel (and more likely chapel for a labouring man) would be an obvious start. There were also the Mechanics' Institutes. The evidence of their efficacy at providing education for working men has been examined in depth by Edward Royle. They made some impact, he concludes, but – on the whole – they failed to fulfil the high expectations of the pioneers. 'The banquet was prepared for guests who did not come', wrote Richard Elliott in 1861.[55] Those who attended were largely from the lower middle classes. It may be that the Institutes aimed too high, assuming a basic knowledge that the working classes lacked. Perhaps there was also a suspicion of indoctrination, aimed at weaning the workers away from Radicalism.

Respectability was essentially a middle-class virtue. Many of the great landed families, those belonging to the sporting set of the aristocracy or to the dissolute rakish element (like Sir Mulberry Hawke in *Nicholas Nickleby*) regarded it with disdain. But if you aimed to rise in the world, it was an indispensable requirement in Victorian times. Appearances counted. There were ways of demonstrating your rise in status: how you furnished your house, for instance; the number of servants you employed; how you spent your money; how you dressed. The lower down you were in the social scale, the more little things counted. The day would come when the possession of a piano in the front room would signify lower middle class. Not yet, however; but a watch and chain, or a clock on the mantelpiece, were little badges of superiority in working-class communities.[56] In the rows of terraced houses, the front doorstep that had not been scrubbed clean and thoroughly stoned was an immediate occasion for down-grading. 'Keep the front doorstep clean. There's more passes by than comes inside' was a maxim of Lancashire working-class women.[57]

You could not always hope to deceive others and one little slip could let you down. 'The real tyranny' of modern society, Mill once wrote, 'is the tyranny of your nextdoor neighbour';[58] the fear of being found out to be not really what you are pretending to be. Trollope gave himself away – according to John Bright – at a dinner-party in 1876, given by Sir Charles Trevelyan. Bright noted in his diary: 'Trollope, the author of many novels, was there. He is rather loud and boisterous in his manner of speaking.'[59] Charles Dickens sometimes, unconsciously, betrayed his origins. In 1843 he paid a visit to Manchester in order to preside at the opening soirée of the new city Athenaeum. He was in the midst of writing *Martin Chuzzlewit* at the time, and had recently returned from America, full of reflections from his *American Notes*. As the evening wore on, he relaxed. When he was occasionally interrupted by a question, he let fall from his lips a very common expression – 'oh Lord no'. But worse was to come – a genuine cockneyism: 'Oh, lor', no,' he said.[60] It did not pass unnoticed.

VI

'God preserve me from being poor.'

Diary of Absolom Watkin

'There's no knocker here, sir, to be hammered at by creditors and bring a man's heart into his mouth ... It's freedom, sir, it's freedom.'

Dr Haggage in the Marshalsea in Dickens, *Little Dorrit*

The trouble with Mr Bulstrode, for all his pious airs, old Mr Featherstone told Fred Vincey in George Eliot's *Middlemarch*, was that he was 'a speckilating fellow! He may come down any day, when the devil leaves off backing him.'[1] There were more serious troubles with Bulstrode than this, as the story was to unfold: nevertheless, if speculation was one of his temptations, he was in good (and sometimes bad) company in Victorian England. Walter Bagehot, author of *Lombard Street* (1873) among other perceptive studies of his times, knew the financial world through and through. 'One thing is certain,' he wrote, '... at particular times a great many stupid people have a great deal of stupid money.'[2]

At a time of an abundance of surplus capital and phenomenal industrial development, the temptation to make a financial killing if one could was, for many, almost irresistible. Until the railway boom of the 1840s the most propitious area for fortune-making was foreign loans, offering considerably higher rates of return than British government stock, especially loans to the newly-liberated countries of Latin America – Colombia, Chile and Peru. The year 1824 was one of those 'particular times' which Bagehot had in mind. Baring's and Rothschild's negotiated reasonably secure loans with Buenos Aires and Brazil. More speculative was a Mexican loan in the hands of Goldschmidt and Company, who had already netted a tidy profit of a quarter of a million pounds. By 1825 a sort of loan fever had developed. Richard Rush, the resident American minister, recorded that

> Nothing was ever like it before, not even the days of the South Sea scheme ... Shares in some of the companies have advanced to seventeen hundred per cent within a few months, and are bought with avidity at this price.[3]

The crash soon followed. The young Benjamin Disraeli was one of the first to burn his fingers (and nearly bankrupted his publisher, John Murray) by rash speculation in South American mining shares. During the second half of the year, disillusionment turned to panic, hundreds faced bankruptcy and there was a run on the banks, the Bank of England being saved in the nick of time by the personal intervention of Nathan Rothschild. Years later, Mark Pattison commented on how the blessings of a nation can also be its bane. 'The English industrial development', he wrote, 'is big with the threatening evils of pauperism, fraud, and bankruptcy, of which none can yet foresee the issues.'[4]

A collapse in the American market occurred in 1837, involving disastrous losses for those who had invested in unsecured loans. The most devastating reversal of fortunes, however, came in 1847 when, as has been noted earlier, millions of pounds were lost in the aftermath of almost manic speculation in railway shares. At the centre of the crash was the Merdle-like figure of George Hudson, a Yorkshireman of humble origins, the promoter of grandiose schemes of railway expansion – as G.M. Young described him, 'one of those not uncommon characters who persuade themselves that an aptitude for business carries with it a genius for fraud.'[5] He became an MP, with a magnificent residence in Albert Gate – until he was found out and forced to flee the country, leaving a trail of misery behind him. Many of his backers were left penniless. Charles Brookfield, the self-appointed wit of the Sterling Club, was obliged to surrender his London house.[6] Another member of the club, Richard Monckton Milnes – rather handsomely, in the circumstances, and perhaps a little out of character for a man regarded as a tuft-hunter – went out of his way to offer protection to Hudson's shattered family, whom he had left behind in his flight.[7]

Dickens' famous fraudster Merdle, in *Little Dorrit*, was not actually based on Hudson. The date of publication – 1857 – gives the clue. This was the year of yet another financial crash, at the heart of which was the swindler John Sadleir, a Tipperary banker. Like Merdle and that other fictional fraudster, Melmotte in Trollope's *The Way We Live Now*, Sadleir committed suicide in 1856 when his malpractices came to light: an easier way out than the degradation that the courts were prepared to inflict upon a man convicted of fraud. In October 1856 Sir John Dean Paul, the banker, and his partners – Messrs Strahan and Bates – were sentenced to fourteen years' transportation, the known horrors of which, for an eminent man – Monckton Milnes told his wife – so 'haunted' him that 'he could think of nothing else' for days.[8]

What could be done to protect the gullible or the greedy? In 1844, Peel's Bank Act was a measure to prevent banks issuing notes beyond their gold reserves (a return to the gold standard dated from 1821), but on three occasions during financial panic the Act was suspended. In 1855 and 1862, two Limited Liability Acts were passed, protecting investors from liability beyond the nominal value of their holdings, the intention being to offer 'safe investments for small capitalists'.[9] H.A. Shannon's researches into their efficacy suggest, however, that 'fraud, ignorance and misjudgment'[10] continued much the same as before. In an indirect way, the legislation actually contributed to the sad demise of the most prestigious firm of bill-brokers and discount bankers, Overend and Gurney, in 1866 – a tragedy that sent shock waves throughout the country. It would never have happened under the wise stewardship of Samuel Gurney, who died in 1856. The chief responsibility appears to lie at the door of David Ward Chapman, who became a partner with Samuel's successor, Henry Edmund Gurney. He persuaded the firm to diversify beyond their traditional activities; and they over-diversified. By taking the step, in 1865, of registering as a public limited company, they were compelled to publish their accounts. The prospectus, however, deliberately concealed the extent of their indebtedness: they were effectively bankrupt. The immediate consequence of discovery was a financial panic that recalled the frenzy of 1825 ('a complete collapse of credit in Lombard St.', Bagehot warned Gladstone, 'and a greater amount of anxiety than I have ever seen'). Lady Downshire was holding a ball on the evening of what came to be called 'Black Friday'. It was not a success. There was only one subject on people's minds. 'Everybody spoke of the immense City failures.'[11] In due course, the partners were taken to court.

'Stupid people with stupid money.' Gladstone miscalculated more than once. His losses in Metropolitan District Railway stock in 1884 have already been mentioned. But he also lost thousands in the late 1840s by his purchase of Oak Farm, near Stourbridge, in the expectation of gaining large yields from its supposedly rich mineral deposits. Tennyson was apt to go wild investing in cranky ventures. In 1842 he sank the whole of his capital in an invention called the 'Pyroglyph' – a patented system to carve furniture by machine rather than by hand. This was the brain-child of a friend, William Allen, who ran a private lunatic asylum. Tennyson lost every penny.[12] If investment was a precarious undertaking, so – of course – was any trade or industry dependent upon volatile market forces. To a self-made man, like Absolom Watkin, who was totally dependent upon the state of the cotton trade, the fear of a reversal of fortune was a private nightmare. 'God preserve me from being poor' was his constant prayer.[13] There seemed to be no safety nets to catch you when you fell.

The sanctimonious had a reply to this: you should not expect otherwise. A Malthus-minded, 'moral restraint' Evangelical like Thomas Chalmers had no hesitation in pointing out that failure in business or misfortune in investment was God's way of teaching men not to be greedy. If famine was His chastening instrument for the benefit of the poor, bankruptcy was His providential method of forcing go-getters and the well-to-do to turn their minds to contemplation of their souls.[14] At least two of the most prominent members of the Clapham Sect accepted uncomplainingly the loss of their considerable fortunes: William Wilberforce through the profligacy of his eldest son, and Zachary Macaulay through the mismanagement of the family business by a nephew. Four of the major religious figures of the Victorian age had to come face to face, in boyhood or early manhood, with the collapse of their family fortunes through the bankruptcy of their fathers: the future Cardinals, Manning and Newman; an Archbishop of Canterbury, in Edward White Benson; and James Martineau, the acknowledged and almost universally respected leader of the Unitarians.

At least one can say that their faith was strengthened rather than weakened by misfortune; and they do not appear to have suffered the nagging anxieties which scarred the lives of both Trollope and Dickens, whose fathers had suffered the same fate. Both these men felt thereafter somehow cheated, deprived of advantages that they had had every reason to expect. Dickens had seen his father consigned to the Marshalsea and his own educational prospects so abruptly curtailed that, for a while, he had to eat his heart out in bitter resentment, working in foul conditions in a blacking factory. Life for both of them was a precarious condition. They could never be sure, whatever success they obtained, that they were sufficiently safe to withstand a sudden onset of adversity. The only answer was keep on writing; keep on earning; because you never know.

The sense of precariousness was experienced quite as agonizingly lower down the scale. In Dickens' monthly chronicle *The Household Narrative of Current Events*, a gold-mine of revealing facts and figures for the short period of its life, there appeared on the back page of each issue a doleful column containing the names and occupations of those registered as bankrupts during the month. An interesting picture emerges. During the first six months of 1852, the total number of bankrupts registered was 448 (a monthly average of 74.6). They cover the whole gamut of businesses and occupations, but two categories in particular predominate: shopkeepers and merchants (a total of 156 shopkeepers and 67 merchants). Of the shopkeepers, tailors and drapers figure at the top of the list (55 in total), and next come grocers (43), constituting between them 63 per cent of all shopkeepers who failed during those six months.[15] Statistics supplied by V. Markham Lester in a recent detailed study of Victorian insolvency, covering the closing decades of the century, show that the situation hardly changed over the years. The number of builders declared bankrupt increased, but among the shopkeepers the same two categories topped the lists by far, the only significant difference being that grocers overtook the tailors, drapers and haberdashers (in the year 1885, for instance, a total of 317, compared to 248).[16]

Perhaps, after all, that summit of the ambition of a working-man to own a little corner-shop was only to move from one state of precariousness to another. Dickens' fictional shopkeepers never seemed to do a very good trade. Solomon Gills in *Dombey and Son* put it down to:

> competition, competition – new invention, new invention – alteration, alteration – the world's gone past me. I hardly know where I am myself; much less where my customers are.[17]

As for Mr Venus in *Our Mutual Friend*, he only seemed to have one customer – Silas Wegg. Grocers were, of course, the largest single group of retailers, and therefore might be expected to figure high on the list of failures. But Thackeray had some sympathy for tailors, because they were so vulnerable to exploitation by wealthy (or allegedly wealthy) clients. As he reflected in *Vanity Fair*:

> Who pities the poor devil of a tailor whom the steward patronizes, and who has pledged all he is worth, and more, to get the liveries ready which my lord has done him the honour to bespeak? When the great house tumbles down, these miserable wretches fall under it unnoticed: as they say in the old legends, before a man goes to the devil himself, he sends plenty of other souls thither.[18]

The labouring man had no compensation if he was 'slack of work'; no redress if he suffered an industrial accident, which was more than an occupational hazard for a mineworker. There was no safety-net to cushion the visitation of illness, or the death of a bread-winner. An article by Maria Trench that appeared in *The Nineteenth Century* in January 1883 makes grim reading. She had visited five sisters in a workhouse in the north of England. Their father had risen by his own exertions to be a supervisor in a blast-furnace works; but he fell ill and died. Everything of value in their house had to be pawned to buy food. In the end, mother and children had to take refuge in the workhouse, where the mother soon died. The children recounted their sufferings under a new Governess – 'a thorough, bad cruel one' – and the pitiful tale turned into a horror story.[19]

The workhouse was the dreaded symbol of the precariousness of a poor family's existence. Betty Higden, in *Our Mutual Friend*, reduced to abject poverty, was still too proud to accept charity from rich benefactors, and too independent to contemplate the institutional alternative. She would not have the word 'Poorhouse' mentioned. 'Kill me sooner than take me there ... I'll die without that disgrace.'[20] There were many Betty Higdens in real life. In the course of her interviews with elderly women whose memories went back to working-class life in late nineteenth-century Lancashire, Elizabeth Roberts met a Mrs Burns, who recalled being one of a family of five children when her mother died at the age of 32, leaving them in charge of a drunkard father. A neighbour called on the grandmother:

> 'Rosie, you'll have to put all the children in the workhouse.' M'grandma said 'Our Margaret Jane's children in the workhouse? Never. Not while I draw breath.'[21]

The only alternative available to them was help from the 'extended family', the hope that they would rally round to keep them solvent. The Burns family were saved by the determination of the grandparents to keep on working long after retirement age. The grandmother was true to her word.

The fear of illness and its possible consequences was not, of course, confined to the working classes. The poor, certainly, had a dread of hospitals, second only to that of the workhouse. Everybody, however, flinched from the thought of the surgeon's knife, applied without anaesthetic. Charles Darwin, whose original scientific intentions were to study medicine at Edinburgh, changed his mind rapidly after witnessing 'two very bad operations, one on a child ... The two cases fairly haunted me for many a long year,' he wrote.[22] Marianne Thornton recalled a dreadful day at their house, Battersea Rise, when Harriet Melville was operated upon for cancer, and 'those awful screams which sent Lucy into hysterics and drove Melville out of the house as they penetrated even into his room. I never believed before that the human voice had such strength.'[23] Not until 1852 was chloroform first used ('what a blessed discovery', Darwin noted).[24] Queen Victoria was one of the first beneficiaries (to ease her pain during a confinement); George Eliot, too, who had a tooth extracted under chloroform in June 1853.[25] The fear of hospitals would seem to have been amply justified by the disturbing death rate of patients, mainly through post-operational sepsis. As late as 1874, a death rate of 25 per cent for University College Hospital was deemed 'very satisfactory'. Compared with Edinburgh Infirmary (43 per cent), perhaps it was.[26]

Recommended medical 'cures' may seem somewhat grotesque to modern minds. The poor stricken daughters of A.C. Tait – all five died from scarlet fever at the Deanery in Carlisle in the space of six weeks in 1856 – were treated with frequent hot baths, shaven heads and potions of champagne and water.[27] James Martineau's daughter was treated for sleeplessness in 1848, while in Germany, with hot medicinal baths, followed by an ice-cold douche from a great height on the crown of her head.[28] This sounds rather like the so-called Priessnitzen therapy which Tennyson underwent at a hydropathic institution in Prestbury in 1843: a two-month cure to extract poison from his system, involving 'no reading by candlelight, no going near a fire, no tea, no coffee, perpetual wet sheet, and cold bath and alternation from hot to cold ... I have much faith in it,' Tennyson added.[29]

The most vulnerable to fatality were infants in the age group from birth to five years; and those born to working-class families, especially those living in industrial urban areas, had the worst chance of survival. It is difficult to believe, when faced with some of the available statistics, that there had been a marked improvement since the eighteenth century. Edwin Chadwick's *Report on the Sanitary Condition of the Labouring Population* in 1842 produced similar figures for the poorer districts of two northern cities: Manchester and Leeds. Out of every 1,000 children born, 570 died before the age of five.[30] Statistics for Sheffield covering the five years 1837 to 42, supplied from another independent survey, reveal almost the same rate of infant mortality: there were 11,944 deaths (of all ages) recorded, of which 6,038 were infants under five.[31] Figures are not so readily available for rural areas, but one random sample – the little Cumbrian village of Thornthwaite – does not support the contention that chances of survival were markedly higher. The burial registers of the parish church record a total of 20 deaths between 1860 and 1862. Of these, nine were infants under five. The year 1871 presents an even worse picture. Seven out of the ten deaths recorded were infants in that same age group.

Some families were obviously luckier than others. Mrs Mulholland, a Lancashire working-class wife, was one of the unlucky ones. Between 1878 and 1896 she bore sixteen children, but only three survived to adulthood.[32] The one safe deduction to be made is that Victorians who set about raising a family had to steel themselves to expect the worst. Clearly they did. Thomas Arnold expressed the hope, in a letter, that his sons would learn to love the truth, 'if they live to manhood'.[33] He was fortunate: they did. Isaac Williams wrote his *Autobiography* in 1851, recounting his experiences within the Oxford Movement. His prefatory note began as follows:

> My dear children, If any of you should live to manhood, you will be glad to know something of the history of my life.[34]

Killer epidemics added to the sense of precariousness. *Timor mortis* was never very far from the minds of the Victorians. It might be scarlet fever, or TB (euphemistically described as a 'mischief on the chest');[35] or typhus, or smallpox, of which there was a virulent epidemic in 1871–2; or diphtheria (a notorious killer of infants). But by far the worst threat was cholera. 'The very name spread panic,' S.E. Finer has written. 'Its symptoms were frightful, its suddenness appalling. Attacked by violent stomach pains, vomiting and diarrhoea, the victim rapidly sank into collapse.'[36] It came somehow from India, where the disease is endemic, hitting Exeter first of all, towards the end of 1831. It reached London during the following year, claiming 18,000 victims. Since the bacterium (technically, a *vibrio*) is transmitted through a carrier's excrement, the infection speedily became a pestilence in crowded urban areas, with filthy open sewers, the more deadly in hot weather when a single fly, making contact with food, could cause instant transmission. Because the bacterium cannot survive long in water, however, a period of heavy rain could bring relief, and this was probably why the epidemic ceased almost as suddenly as it had appeared.

But when would it strike again? It came in two waves, in 1848 and 1849, the first a relatively minor epidemic in Scotland, the second – during the hot months of June, July and August 1849 – a devastating visitation upon London, via Manchester, Hull, Leeds and Liverpool. The next outbreak came in 1853–4, Newcastle, in particular, suffering horribly; but again, London bore the brunt of it. Twelve years passed before the next (and final) epidemic, in 1866–7. For no explicable reason, it never returned. Of all the visitations, the severest was the epidemic in the mid 1850s – 'three times as deadly as in 1848–9', according to Professor Finer.[37] The Church clamoured for a national fast day, in the hope that the wrath of God might be averted. Lord Palmerston refused, and Charles Kingsley rejoiced at this rebuff to the foolish clergy who were indulging in 'lazy and selfish Manichaeism', instead of supporting every effort to 'abolish pestilence by sanitary reform'.[38] This was totally in character of the man whom Chichester Fortescue (later Lord Carlingford) visited in 1858, when he was told that, while diphtheria was raging in his parish at Eversley, Kingsley took to his horse 'with two great stone bottles of gargle each side of his saddle, making all the children gargle & gargling himself to show them how'.[39]

The creator of *The Water-Babies* was also almost neurotic about the therapeutic qualities of clean water. A cold bath first thing in the morning was his recipe for preventing drunkenness. 'With a clean skin in healthy action, and nerves and muscles braced by a sudden shock, men do not crave for artificial stimulants.'[40] This was Kingsley in one of his frequent muscular Christian moods. He could be neither faulted nor ridiculed, however, for his answer to the problem of cholera. He nodded knowingly when, as a further outbreak of the disease threatened in 1860, incessant rain flushed the potentially pestilential sewers and drains of London. Again his fellow clergy had incurred his wrath for suggesting that the nation should pray for dry weather.[41]

Hippolyte Taine once observed that the English 'spend one fifth of their lives at a wash-basin'.[42] This was all very well; but the water that Londoners washed in was full of impurities. Only Birmingham, of the large cities, prided itself on plentiful supplies of clean water; probably one of the reasons why the city practically escaped from all the cholera epidemics.[43] While most of the medical profession seemed to be at a loss how to cope – their remedies for cholera ranging from doses of chalk and laudanum to induce constipation, to filling a man's stomach with olive oil to achieve the opposite effect[44] – there were a few notable exceptions. Dr Kay (later Sir James Kay-Shuttleworth) was one. He had submitted a horrific report on the health hazards arising from the filthy urban condition of Manchester in 1832. Dr Southwood Smith was another, a working-colleague, if no particular friend, of the most ardent sanitary reformer of all: Edwin Chadwick, the author of two sensational reports in 1842 and 1843 on London's sanitation and the appalling state of the metropolitan cemeteries. In 1847, Chadwick moved from the Poor Law office to chair the Royal Commission on Public Health, which resulted in his becoming the leading spirit of the Board of Health, set up a year later.

Chadwick's answer to cholera was this: remove everything with a bad smell; get rid of open sewers and exposed rotting corpses. He was unquestionably right, if for the wrong reasons. He had no understanding of bacteria, and adhered to the long-standing 'miasma theory' of infection, the notion that cholera was 'atmospheric', transmitted by poisonous exhalations from rotting organic matter. All his efforts met resistance. Here and there he won a battle to improve water supply and to encourage the disposal of sewage through underground pipes, but few of his victories were in London. His schemes were adjudged too costly. Worst of all, he had to fight against vested interests in the hopeless complex of parish councils, vestries and independent commissions, all determined to retain their autonomous authority; and the Board of Health had very restricted powers of enforcement. In the provinces he frequently encountered a similar problem. The Municipal Corporation Act of 1835 had been merely an enabling measure to encourage greater efficiency in local government; and many of the unfranchised boroughs clung to their traditional pattern of inert parochialism.[45] Opposition to anything that smacked of centralization was still deeply rooted. Chadwick himself was very sensitive to accusations that he had learnt his methods from France.[46] In the end, it was these combined forces of resentment, especially in London, that led to the demise of the Board of Health and to Chadwick's less than golden handshake in 1854. He did, however, receive a knighthood. Sir John Simon was left to continue the battle, but not until C.T. Ritchie's Local Government Act of 1888, when London – apart from the City – was made a county under the control of the LCC, were the worst of the anomalies eradicated.

The twilight years of a frustrated reformer whose occupation had gone saw Chadwick becoming more and more unhinged. He became fanatical about the need to introduce military drill into schools. Water continued to be a fixation. Schoolchildren, he maintained, should be compulsorily and regularly washed, because research showed that 'a pig that is regularly washed would put on a fifth more flesh, and that flesh was of better quality than a pig that is unwashed.' He was elected to the Political Economy Club, but was not a social success. 'He babbled too much,' one member recalled, 'not of green fields, but of sewage.'[47]

It is a strange feature of the England of the Victorians that, while the sense of the precarious was so omnipresent, they seemed almost to revel in a good disaster. Perhaps this is simply human nature, and as true of the twentieth century as it was of the nineteenth. Disasters are, after all, the meat and drink of the press. Nevertheless there is a difference between the present century and the Victorian age, difficult to define and equally difficult to explain. Every monthly issue of *The Household Narrative* contained several pages under the enticing heading 'Accidents and Disasters'. A twentieth-century reader would find the uninhibited revelations of the goriest details, almost as if the writer were savouring the degree of suffering inflicted on the victim, very difficult to take. Similarly, when *The Illustrated London News* first appeared in 1842, the highly successful brain-child of Herbert Ingram, the artists commissioned to portray the plight of passengers on a sinking ship or the agonizing fate of foundry-workers blown to fragments in an explosion left nothing to the imagination in the horrors they depicted. By contrast, the need to prevent a blush on the cheek of any young person restrained, to the point of prudery, the depiction of anything that might be sexually embarrassing. A reviewer of Tom Hughes's *Tom Brown at Oxford*, for instance, was so offended by the mere fact that the hero of the story carried a girl with a broken ankle in his arms, that he protested: 'If this be muscular Christianity, the less we hear of it the better.'[48]

Can this be explained? The Victorians lived very much closer to pain, disaster and death than the generations that followed them. There were nauseating sights to be seen daily in the Manchester slums or in the alleys of Whitechapel, almost beyond the nightmare imaginings of modern minds. Perhaps, too, there was a sort of dreadful thrill, amounting to titillation of the fear of precariousness, in witnessing, or reading about, the worst that could actually happen. The Victorians were not only conscious of the precariousness of their lives; they seemed also to be endlessly fascinated by it.

They certainly had a whole host of cares to trouble their minds; and it must not be supposed that the particular anxieties examined so far constitute the sum total of the darker areas of their world picture. The darkest area of all, for many of them, was the threat posed to their faith by the twin forces of Darwinian evolutionary science and German biblical criticism. Since, however, the disturbing questions thrown up by the phenomenon of 'unbelief' belong to the heart-searching perplexity of what may lie for mortal man beyond the grave – and whether, indeed, eternal hope was nothing more than wishful thinking – discussion of these problems must be deferred until consideration is given to that part of the Victorian world picture which was formed by 'looking beyond'.

Add all these anxieties together, and one might well wonder whether the Victorians ever enjoyed a moment's peace of mind. Of course they did. They were not all worriers; and those that worried did not worry about the same things; nor did they worry all the time. The process of 'looking inwards', like any form of introspection, tends to magnify inadequacies rather than strengths. When the Victorians 'looked outwards', however, they found their spirits lifting and felt a sense of self-congratulation as they compared their standing in the world with that of their less fortunate neighbours. They could then feel buoyant, confident, even complacent. This was particularly so during the mid-Victorian period; less so in the closing decades of the century, when their observation of the world outside raised uneasy doubts whether their nation was quite as strong, quite as unassailable in its commercial and industrial supremacy, as they had supposed. The fear of loss of status then began to appear within a national context; and the phrase 'the Great Depression', the label given by historians and contemporaries alike to the decline of the British economy, could be said to acquire a certain relevance to the state of mind of many of the country's leading intellectuals.

W.G. Ward, the *enfant terrible* of the Oxford Movement, was once told by his doctor that 'the chief causes of insanity in England are the pressure of the commercial system and the uncertainty of religious opinion.'[49] The remark is undated. But in 1878 an American doctor by the name of George Miller Beard came up with the diagnosis of a particular condition of mental illness that he described as 'neurasthenia', prevalent among the middle classes of society, which takes the form of nervous debility; a type of accidie, or physical and mental torpor, causing its victim to lose all appetite for life, in the conviction that he has nothing more to give. This is undoubtedly what took possession of

Ruskin in 1878, and he was rarely free from it until his death in 1900. It practically immobilized T.H. Huxley from 1884 onwards.[50] It crippled Leslie Stephen in his last years, exacerbated by the death of his second wife (but – as Noel Annan has observed – 'all the Stephen family ruined their health through overwork, a symptom of a deep-rooted family neurosis').[51] It may also explain the black years suffered by Carlyle, Kingsley, Bulwer Lytton, J.A. Symonds, and Mill.

Ruskin himself repudiated any suggestion that his own illness had been caused by overwork. It had been brought on, he said, 'by grief at the course of public affairs'.[52] This may be technically described as neurasthenia. But Sainte-Beuve in 1833 had coined a phrase which exactly fits Ruskin's condition, and that of many others who had become disillusioned by observation of their times. They had fallen victim to *mal du siècle*.

CHAPTER 2

Looking Outwards

I

'Clemency is the brightest jewel in the crown of a Briton's head, for which you'll overhaul the constitution as laid down in Rule Britannia, and, when found, *that* is the charter as them garden angels was a singing of, so many times over.'

Captain Cuttle in Dickens, *Dombey and Son*

TWO OF J.M. Turner's paintings from the early 1830s speak more subtly than words in their perhaps unconscious exhibition of the peculiar virtue of the British people, which their continental neighbours, and the Latin nations in particular, could neither understand nor emulate. Allen McLaurin, who was the first to perceive their significance, has pointed out that in Turner's depiction of *Venice* (in 1834), the beautiful city appears bathed in sunlight; and while a sort of bustle is conveyed, the mood of the scene is of 'indolent Southern civilization in decline'. In the following year, Turner produced his *Keelmen hauling coals by moonlight*, and the mood is totally different. It is a strong painting of hard, purposeful work on a busy English river, redolent of muscularity, prosperity and power.[1] The message is clear. England built up her position of industrial and commercial supremacy by the essentially Northern, Teutonic, qualities of honest hard work and the determination to be 'up and doing' while other nations were drowsing in the sun.

When Archbishop Sumner led the prayers at the opening of the Great Exhibition of 1851 he sounded a note which was to be repeated many times in the decade that followed. This was all God's doing. The British had become His chosen people.

> While we survey the works of art and industry which surround us [he said], let not our hearts be lifted up that we forget the Lord our God, as if our own power and the might of our hands had gotten in this wealth.[2]

This was a foretaste of Rudyard Kipling's 'Not unto us, O Lord, The praise or glory be, Of any deed or word'; or A.C. Benson's 'God who made thee mighty, make thee mightier yet'. God be thanked. But there was history to thank as well.

The English were freeborn men of Anglo-Saxon stock, and that indigenous love of freedom embodied in Anglo-Saxon institutions withstood and survived the Norman yoke, successfully resisted incipient despotism by the Great Charter, and yet again curbed the pretensions of the Stuarts in the 1640s and in 1688. But this was not all. God's favour had fallen upon the British people because of their religion, their repudiation of papal tyranny in the sixteenth century, vindicated for the whole world to see in their humiliation of Spain in 1588, when the huge armada of the strongest Catholic power, notorious for its priest-ridden oppression, was put to flight by good, honest, sturdy English sea-dogs, the bravest and the best of men who became the glory of the Protestant world. And was it not significant that wherever enterprise, energy, enlightenment, material and intellectual progress were to be found in Europe, it was in Protestant countries; while, conversely, in the centres of Catholicism – obvious for all to see – were the contrasting features of stagnation, superstition, obscurantism and sloth?

Finally – a special providential blessing – came the simple circumstance of geography. Britain was an island nation. No foreign power could threaten her shores without braving the Channel and the formidable maritime resources enlisted to defend it. In the words of the 'Tory member's elder son' in Tennyson's *The Princess*:

> God bless the narrow sea which . . .
> Keeps our Britain, whole within herself,
> . . . God bless the narrow seas!
> I wish they were a whole Atlantic broad.[3]

Geography also determined England's blessed climate. Educated Victorians knew their Aristotle well; and Aristotle had extolled the virtues of Greece, in both culture and political organization, because its climate was the mean between the chills of the north (which made the people who dwelt there high-spirited but unintelligent) and the excessive heat endured by Asians (intelligent but wanting in energy). Was not this equally true of Britain? Matthew Arnold quoted the words of Sir Charles Adderley, addressing some Warwickshire farmers: 'The old Anglo-Saxon race are the best breed in the world ... The absence of a too enervating climate, too unclouded skies, and a too luxurious nature ... has rendered us so superior to all the world.'[4]

Providences are not lightly bestowed by God. So Thomas Arnold mused, while touring in the south of France in 1839: 'The English are a greater people than these – more like, that is, one of the chosen people of history, who are appointed to do a great work for mankind.'[5] With Charles Kingsley this destiny became a sort of divine mission, arising from the God-given blessing of our superiority in the scientific conquest of nature. In a lecture on 'How to study Natural History', he had this solemn injunction to give:

> Do you not see, then, that by following these studies ... you are training in yourselves that habit of mind which God has approved as the one which He has ordained for Englishmen, and are doing what in you lies toward carrying out, in after life, the glorious work which God seems to have laid on the English race, to replenish the earth and subdue it.[6]

The same message filtered through to the less-privileged Pip in *Great Expectations*, as he entered London for the first time to seek Mr Jaggers' office in Little Britain, turning over in his mind – as Dickens put it, with a pleasing touch of irony:

> [that] we Britons had at that time particularly settled that it was treasonable to doubt our having and our being the best of everything: otherwise, while I was scared by the immensity of London, I think I might have had some faint doubts whether it was not rather ugly, crooked, narrow, and dirty.[7]

One might justify one's chauvinism by endowing it with a theological imprimatur; equally, if God were replaced by Darwin's theory of 'natural selection', a rather reassuring scientific basis for racial superiority could be advanced. Certainly, when Darwin came to write *The Descent of Man* in 1871, much under the influence of Herbert Spencer, his social evolutionism was not one whit less chauvinistic than that of the providential school. This is the conclusion of Sheelagh Strewbridge, who writes: 'For Darwin there was simply no question that the western nations of Europe stand "at the summit of civilization" and that amongst these nations the Anglo-Saxons excel.'[8] Indeed, from the opinions of many Victorians, looking outwards from their vantage point of undeniable superiority, a sort of pecking order within the various races and nations of the world can be devised.

Backward coloured races, through no fault of their own, would have to occupy a very low status. Macaulay, in 1834, scoffed at a friend's predilection for dabbling in ethnology. 'Your talents are too great, and your leisure time too small,' he wrote, 'to be wasted in inquiries so frivolous.' What did it matter 'whether the Cherokees are of the same race with the Chickesaw?' He would do better to study Herodotus.[9] Sir Henry Maine's endeavours to earn respect for the institutions of India proved an uphill struggle. It comes as a surprise to find a philosopher of the integrity of Henry Sidgwick – but he was only 27 at the time – admitting to a friend that 'we don't want to know what particular black stones the aborigines adored – at least I don't.'[10] The ancient cultures of the Far East were not accorded a much higher rank in the racial scale. When Richard Cobden (supported by John Roebuck and Gladstone) censured Palmerston's bombardment of Canton in 1857, Roebuck's tribute to Chinese civilization, especially their natural courtesy compared with the truculence of the West, caused an eruption of ironical laughter in the House.[11] At least the vote of censure was obtained by a majority of sixteen votes, but Palmerston chose to make this a resignation issue and won the ensuing election resoundingly.

It was the French who first opened the eyes of Europeans, and eventually of the British, to what has been described as 'the uncanny delicacy' of oriental art.[12] A Japanese woodcut spotted by a French painter, Felix Bracquemond, was to prove the beginning of a new vogue in aesthetic taste, passing in time via Baudelaire and Manet to Whistler and D.G. Rossetti. In the closing decades of the century, at the height of the Aesthetic Movement, caricatured in W.S. Gilbert's *Patience*, collectors vied passionately with each other for the acquisition of Japanese screens, fans and prints, and the so-called 'Blue' or 'Blue and White' seventeenth- and eighteenth-century porcelain of China.

When George Eliot came to write *Daniel Deronda*, however, in 1876, the traditional prejudices were still in the ascendant. She had become sickened by her fellow-countrymen's small-minded anti-Semitism and dismissive superiority in their treatment of orientals:

> Not only towards the Jews [she wrote to Harriet Beecher Stowe], but towards all oriental peoples with whom we English come in contact, a spirit of arrogance and contemptuous dictatorialness is observable which has become a national disgrace to us. There is nothing I should care more to do, if it were possible, than to rouse the imagination of men and women to a vision of human claims in those races of their fellow-men who most differ from them in customs and beliefs ... It is a sign of the intellectual arrogance – in plain English, the stupidity, which is still the average mark of our culture.[13]

The Victorians had a national pecking order for European countries, too. Germany, because of the kinship of a common stock, was unquestionably at the top; Switzerland and the Low Countries were in the second rank, with the Latin nations coming at the bottom. Although chauvinism suggests complacent insularity, continental travel was in fact a much-favoured occupation of the Victorians, ranging from the affluent to the reasonably well-to-do. For the educated classes, at least one continental tour was deemed an essential. Spain tended to be avoided, being considered too hazardous. Russia, too, was rarely visited, until a through railway link had been established. In 1867 two Oxford dons, Students of Christ Church, namely H.P. Liddon and Charles Dodgson, made the trip together by train, via Calais, Brussels, Cologne, Berlin, Danzig, St Petersburg and thence to Moscow: an improbable pairing, the highest of Anglican High Churchmen and the shy and retiring author of *Alice in Wonderland*.[14] One wonders what they found to talk about together.

France, despite the lofty disdain with which the English regarded it as a nation, was almost always the first country to be visited because the majority of the Channel crossings were to French ports. Paris had a magnetic attraction for two good reasons. The restaurants and cafés were intriguing novelties – both French inventions, as the later universality of their descriptive titles bears witness. If the Revolution had achieved nothing else, at least it created this abundance of eating-houses, established by the displaced cooks of the noblesse, who were 'obliged to turn their hands to feeding the democracy'.[15] The second reason was that Paris was the assembly-point for the engagement of couriers, practically a necessity for an English party travelling beyond France, and especially if crossing the Alps into Italy, as a protection against exploitation and to assist with language difficulties. That such help was so often necessary casts doubt on the astonishing statement that appeared in an article in *The Illustrated London News* in May 1851, to the effect that it was 'rare to find an Englishman who did not speak French, or perhaps German and Italian, more or less perfectly',[16] as compared with the average foreigner's ignorance of English.

The evidence would seem to point quite the other way. After all, both Pusey and Robert Wilberforce were Oxford scholars of the highest eminence; and the only way they could acquire a knowledge of German was to study in that country. Wilberforce never succeeded in following a lecture delivered in German. The future Cardinal Manning was considered a rarity among his contemporaries in acquiring fluency in Italian, but there is no evidence that he ever mastered German. Newman had even greater difficulties with foreign languages: very hesitant French, even less Italian, and no knowledge of German at all. An educated Englishman abroad was much more likely to look to his wife or daughter for help in linguistic difficulties. According to Mr Bingley, in Jane Austen's *Pride and Prejudice*, 'a thorough knowledge ... of modern languages' (so he assured Elizabeth Bennett) was among his friend Darcy's requirements for an 'accomplished woman'.[17]

Too often, Mark Pattison complained, the English traveller disgraced his country.

> See our worthy countryman [he wrote] when he is travelling on the Continent. How strange, and awkward, and uncomfortable he is! What foreigners call our 'pride' is only the result of ignorance and *gaucherie*. We have not been to the great school of the world, and learnt there how to behave. We feel this, and try to carry it off by swell and swagger.[18]

It would be seen at its worst in Italy and France. A visit to Italy was often the climactic experience of the Grand Tour; and many who made the journey felt as Shelley once expressed it:

> There are two Italies: one composed of the green earth & transparent sea and the mighty ruins of antient times ... The other consists of the Italians of the present day, their work and their ways. The one is the most sublime and lovely contemplation that can be conceived by the imagination of man: the other the most degraded disgusting & odious.[19]

Ruskin felt very much the same. So did Newman. When he went to Rome to study for the Roman priesthood in 1846, he likened the Italians to the Irish: a people of dirty habits, offensive to those who came from a nation that valued cleanliness.[20] The English were, however, prepared to make certain exceptions. Freedom-fighters like Mazzini and Garibaldi were lionized in liberal circles and by the public at large. In Garibaldi, after all, there were just those virtues which they liked to think were peculiarly their own: a love of liberty, contempt for papal pretensions and – above all – sturdy, defiant manliness.

Sooner or later the Eternal City had to be visited, not only for its antiquities but also to satisfy a compulsive curiosity to witness the very heart and soul of the most powerful Christian communion in the world, which so many Englishmen had been taught from their cradles to abhor. Prejudices at one moment evaporated at the grandeur of the spectacle and the immensity of the historic claims, which somehow – in a Roman setting – seemed breathtakingly irresistible. Then, after sober reflection, their Protestant consciences began to nag. As the young Edward White Benson expressed it in a letter from Rome to his future wife, Mary Sidgwick: 'One felt there must be a truer fulfilment somewhere ... How strangely are good and evil mixed in this complicated earth.'[21]

Whereas the attitude of the English to Italy was one of love of the country and dislike of its inhabitants, their response to a visit to France tended to be rather the opposite. They felt no particular repugnance towards the French people, but France as a country sometimes made them shudder. It is true that the French were disconcertingly un-English. They were often thought of as somewhat effete. They were overfond of dancing, for instance; and their preferred method of set-tling a dispute was by duelling rather than manly fisticuffs. This, at least, was how Pierce Egan expressed it in his popular *Book of Sports* in 1832.[22] They prided themselves in over-subtlety and cleverness rather than down-to-earth English honesty and bluntness, Trollope sug-gested, and were therefore inclined to dismiss the English as dull. 'Dullness is our line,' he wrote, 'as cleverness is that of the French. Woe to the English if they ever forget that.'[23] According to Henry Sidgwick, the French observation of English boys (in 1865) was rather different. Compared to themselves, they were '*beaucoup plus sages; mais moins intelligents*'.[24]

When it came to England's opinion of France as a country, however, chauvinism – especially in the middle years of the century – began to look more like xenophobia. France was a country of systems rather than associations. Its education was intolerably systematized, constant surveillance of the young resulting in the stifling of individuality. Its whole administrative structure was a complex of systems – petty officialdom, soulless bureaucracy and intrusive police – all constituting a standing indictment of centralization.

The very word 'police' was liable to excite accusations of insidious infiltration of French methods. In 1839, one of Edwin Chadwick's measures to introduce municipal police forces aroused a fury of opposition throughout the country. When Lord John Russell introduced modified proposals into the Commons, handbills appeared in Manchester protesting against the importation of 'Bourbon Police'.[25] The same cry was raised in 1856 when Sir George Grey proposed to establish police forces in every county and the appointment of Inspectors of Constabulary. The member for Walsall moved for rejection, on the grounds that 'the system of centralization ... however it might suit the Governments of the Continent, was repugnant to the feelings and habits of Englishmen.'[26] Years later, when state organization and collectivism were clearly winning the long-standing battle, critics still pointed to the dreadful example of France. Herbert Spencer, in *The Man versus the State*, put forward the questionable historical judgement that centralized government had been the cause of the French Revolution.[27] It all went back to what Mr Podsnap, in *Our Mutual Friend*, had sententiously declared to 'the stray personage of a meek demeanour': 'Centralization. No. Never without my Consent. Not English.'[28]

The same reservations might well have been expressed about Prussian bureaucracy, but somehow the Prussians could be forgiven on the ground that they were Germans (and Protestants as well).[29] The English had plenty of opportunity to sample German life. Tours of the Rhineland were very popular. The few who appreciated the giant strides being made in historical, philological and theological scholarship in Germany were eager to meet, or to sit at the feet of, the acknowledged Titans themselves, and they seemed to have no difficulty in gratifying their wishes. Between them, Julius Hare and the ubiquitous Baron Bunsen (Prussian minister at Rome, and then ambassador in London) acted as ever-willing go-betweens. Connop Thirlwall had already met Schleiermacher in London, in 1829, and ten years later went to Dresden to meet the poet Ludwig Tieck, co-editor of the works of one of the leading German Romantics, Novalis.[30] In 1830, both Thomas Arnold and Richard Monckton Milnes were in Bonn, the one to hold converse with Niebuhr, and the other to meet the brother of the recently-deceased Friedrich Schlegel. Milnes was rather disillusioned by Schlegel: 'he is insufferably vain of his person, though over seventy,' he wrote, 'and arranges his wig from a little looking-glass in his snuff-box, and ill-natured people say he rouges.'[31] James Martineau was also much disappointed by his experience of attending a lecture by Neander in Berlin in 1849: all fidgets and mannerisms, pulling his pen to pieces and rocking backwards and forwards, and then 'finishing every clause by spitting, in a quiet dropping way upon the floor'. After a while, Martineau decided to slink out of the room.[32]

George Eliot, by contrast, was more favourably impressed by her encounter with German worthies. She was an accomplished German-ist, having published a translation of Strauss's *Das Leben Jesu* in 1846, and then – in 1854 – beginning work on Feuerbach's *Essence of Christianity*. While in Berlin she was admitted to the prestigious literary salon of Fräulein von Solmar, and duly recorded her impressions:

> It is amusing to see how very comfortable the Germans are without many of the things which England considers the safeguards of society ... I think them immensely inferior to us in creative intellect and in possession of the *means* of life, but they know better how to use the means they have for the end of enjoyment. One sees everywhere in Germany what is the rarest of all things in England – thorough *bien-être*, freedom from gnawing cares and ambitions, contentment in inexpensive pleasures with no suspicion that happiness is a vice which we must not only not indulge in ourselves but as far as possible restrain others from giving way to.[33]

The peculiar virtues of Germany were expressed rather differently by J.A. Froude. He had become sickened in the late 1860s by the way in which his fellow-countrymen equated progress with materialism, and by the trivial dissensions which were sapping the vitality of both the Establishment and the Dissenting churches. 'Only the Germans', he wrote, '... have carried out boldly the spirit as well as the letter of the Reformation', and only they 'are meeting the future with courage and manliness'.[34] England must therefore look to her laurels. Her primacy in the pecking order was giving way to Germany's.

Where did America fit in the pecking order? This was less easy to define because, for the most part, Americans had once been ourselves: men and women of mixed Anglo-Saxon and Celtic stock who had, either from choice or compulsion, sailed away to distant shores, there to establish over the years their own culture and their own way of life. In the nineteenth century, the cultural interaction became steadily closer: in the first instance, through the poems and writings of R.W. Emerson, 'that clear and pure voice', as Matthew Arnold expounded to an audience of Bostonians in 1883, 'which, for my ear, at any rate, brought a strain as new, and moving, and unforgettable, as the strain of Newman, or Carlyle, or Goethe.'[35] The poems of Longfellow, Mrs Harriet Beecher Stowe's *Uncle Tom's Cabin* (near the top of the list of nineteenth-century best-sellers) and Fenimore Cooper's *Last of the Mohicans* intensified interest in American life. R.H. Hutton awarded the crown, however, to Nathaniel Hawthorne – 'almost the first, and quite the highest, fruit of American culture'.[36]

Those who actually made the journey to America, especially if they travelled steerage, rarely returned, however; unless, like Martin Chuzzlewit and Mark Tapley, their expectations of making their fortune there were dashed. Writers and *savants* occasionally went to see for themselves or to engage in lecture tours. Dickens was one such, in 1842, and he liked it not at all: 'business and money, money and business, coarseness of manner and a dismal concern with commerce ... No laughter.'[37] He let Mark Tapley express his views:

> I should want to draw it like a Bat, for its short-sightedness: like a Bantam, for its bragging: like a Magpie, for its honesty: like a Peacock, for its vanity: like an Ostrich, for its putting its head in the mud, and thinking nobody sees it.

Young Martin Chuzzlewit conceded a virtue, however: 'And like a Phoenix, for its power of springing from the ashes of its faults and vices, and soaring up anew into the sky.'[38]

Richard Cobden and John Bright, so often at one in their political and social views, begged to differ over America. Bright, who never set foot in the country, constantly sang its praises, and – in his admiration for Lincoln – became, in the 1860s, 'of all Englishmen ... the most admired and revered by the American people'.[39] Cobden, on the other hand, after a visit in 1835, declared that 'their inordinate vanity' made his blood boil.[40] The trouble with America, Matthew Arnold once observed, was that '[it is] just ourselves, with the Barbarians quite left out, and the Populace nearly'.[41] That is to say, it was a country populated by Philistines. He had to be a little more prudent in his expressions, if not markedly less condescending, when he came to address an American audience in 1883. They *did* have one virtue which they shared with the English people. They were fifty millions mainly sprung from German stock.

Of the German stock it is, I think, true as my father said more than fifty years ago, that it has been a stock 'of the most moral races of men that the world has yet seen, with the soundest laws, the least violent passions, the fairest domestic and civil virtues.'[42]

Powerful voices within England itself expressed despair at times at the insularity of their fellow-countrymen, especially when travelling abroad. They so often shut their eyes to the merits of countries other than their own. In Germany they would notice, with a sense of self-satisfaction, Matthew Arnold complained, 'the eternal beer, sausages and bad tobacco', while not perceiving 'the industry, the well-doing, the patient steady elaboration of things, the idea of science governing all departments of human activity'.[43] The result would be immeasurable loss in the long run, as England declined 'into a sort of greater Holland, for want of ... perceiving how the world is going and must go, and preparing herself accordingly'.[44] The same accusation came from J.S. Mill and Benjamin Jowett. Englishmen were failing, through complacency, and undue preoccupation with petty religious disputes, to keep up with the European movement of thought, Mill complained.[45] In Jowett's words: through the narrowness of our chosen fields of study, 'we are so far below the level of the German Ocean that I fear one day we shall be utterly deluged.'[46] Sooner or later, Jowett was saying, English historians and theologians had to face up to the undoubted superiority of German scholarship in its refined critical methodology. To George Eliot, this blinkered adhesion to outmoded methods of study was the pathetic plight of Edward Casaubon in *Middlemarch*. As Will Ladislaw explained to Dorothea:

The Germans have taken the lead in historical enquiries, and they laugh at results which are got by groping about in the woods with a pocket-compass while they have made good roads.[47]

Was there nothing to be learnt from France? Later in the century, a great deal, because the Aesthetic Movement was virtually imported from Paris; and – in the 1860s – Renan's *Vie de Jésus* was more widely read than Strauss's earlier quest for the historical Jesus. Above all, the positivist philosophy of Auguste Comte was gaining a profound influence on leading British thinkers, notably Herbert Spencer and Mill. But the real Francophile among English *savants* was Matthew Arnold. As early as 1843, when witnessing the riots in Trafalgar Square in March of that year, he had written to his mother: 'In a few years people will understand better why the French are the most civilised of European peoples, when they see how fictitious our manners and civility have been.'[48] Wearing his hat as a somewhat disenchanted inspector of schools in 1859, following eight years of dreary inspections, mainly of Dissenters' schools, which had only served to confirm his distaste for English provincialism, he went to France to see what could be learnt from their very different approach to education. He returned with an admiration for the *lycée* system, and took a perverse delight in his exposition of its merits in his 'provocatively-titled' *A French Eton*, published in 1864.[49]

When he changed his role to that of literary critic, Arnold posed the question: where – within Europe – might the ethos of 'sweetness and light', in which both the Barbarians and the Philistines were so sadly deficient, be truly found? He had no doubt himself that one needed to look no further than France, probably well aware that such an answer would irritate and offend his readers. For the very essence of 'sweetness and light', his fellow-countrymen needed to steep themselves in the writings of Senancour, or Maurice de Guérin and his sister, Eugénie. Alas, Arnold sang their praises in vain. The vast majority of English readers had never even heard of them.

II

'We are entering upon most dangerous times.'
Prince Albert to Lord John Russell, December, 1851

Chauvinism and xenophobia are not quite the same thing. One can harbour chauvinistic feelings towards races or nations that one supposes to be inferior, rather as the average Victorian looked down upon the

Chinese: if they presumed to be a nuisance, they could be swept aside, flicked off one's coat sleeve like an irritating fly. Xenophobia, however, is a deeper emotion altogether because it is engendered by the fear that the object of one's intense dislike poses a definite threat. Tsarist Russia was so regarded, not only for its despotic regime – the symbol of 'old corruption' on a European scale, and hated as such by all liberals of whatever nationality – but also because it was suspected of expansionist designs, deeply injurious to British interests. Closer at hand, however, was the threat posed by France, especially during the middle years of the century. After all, she was Britain's historic foe and rival; and there was a lurking fear that the overthrow of Napoleon at Waterloo in 1815 was – in French eyes – the unforgivable sin that one day must be avenged.

This was how Thackeray put it in *Vanity Fair*:

> You and I, who were children when the great battle was won and lost, are never tired of hearing and recounting the history of that famous action. Its remembrance rankles still in the bosoms of millions of the countrymen of those brave men who lost the day. They pant for an opportunity of revenging that humiliation; and if a contest, ending in a victory on their part, should ensue, elating them in their turn, and leaving its cursed legacy of hatred and rage behind to us, there is no end to the so-called glory and shame ... in which two high-spirited nations might engage. Centuries hence, we Frenchmen and Englishmen might be boasting and killing each other still, carrying out bravely the Devil's code of honour.[1]

On 2 December 1851, Britain's worst fears seemed to be confirmed. Bonaparte's nephew, bearing the same dreaded name, seized absolute power in France by a sudden and successful *coup d'état*. It was the very anniversary of the battle of Austerlitz. Just over a year later he had himself crowned Emperor of France, with the title Napoleon III. Things boded ill for England. Only three months before, the Duke of Wellington had died, and although the new master of France had publicly declared, at Bordeaux, that 'L'Empire c'est la Paix', there was something sinister to English ears in the words that followed: 'I have, like the Emperor [his uncle], conquests to make ... We have everywhere ruins to restore, false gods to overthrow, truths to establish in triumph.'[2] Shortly after his coronation he admitted to Lord Cowley that 'he was determined not to fall as Louis-Philippe had done by an ultra-pacific policy; that he knew well that the instincts of France were military and domineering, and that he resolved to gratify them.'[3]

There was an immediate invasion panic in England; but within a year Napoleon III embarked upon his policy of gratifying the bellicose sentiments of his people in a totally unlooked-for alliance with France's traditional enemy. That England and France should find themselves as allies was improbable enough; even more so was their third ally: Turkey, a nation that both countries despised for its cruel and corrupt regime. Only the threat of Russian designs on Constantinople, upsetting the balance of power in Europe, could have created such a situation. It was Russia who precipitated hostilities by claiming the protectorate of all Orthodox Christians in Turkish dominions, and then occupying the principalities of Wallachia and Moldavia on the west of the Black Sea as a provocative bargaining point. Not unexpectedly, the response was an ultimatum from Turkey demanding the evacuation of the occupied territories, which was predictably refused.

In retrospect, it would seem that a dreadful and costly war could have been avoided. Lord Aberdeen, titular head of a precarious Whig–Peelite coalition, had no wish for it, nor had his Foreign Secretary, Lord Clarendon. But the Cabinet was divided, and very soon the worst fears of a convinced non-interventionist like Richard Cobden were to be confirmed. Cobden had had personal experience of the corrupt Turkish regime during a tour of Turkish dominions in 1835–6, and had forcibly expressed his anxiety that fear of Russia – to his mind, exaggerated, if not illusory – would prove a more powerful emotion than contempt for the iniquitous tyranny of the Turks.[4] Furthermore, the concept of 'balance of power', which he regarded as a diplomat's abstraction – a pure 'chimera'[5] – was only too easily exploited by warmongers. If France were seen successfully to preserve it, all the credit would go to Napoleon III; and that would never do.

Nearly forty years had elapsed since Waterloo; and in the intervening years British forces, both on land and at sea, had not exactly been inactive. There had been military engagements in Burma, Afghanistan, Sind and China, and expeditions to quell risings by the Sikhs, the Maoris, and the Kaffirs, some of them very costly in lives. The Navy had been in action against the Turks (at Navarino), bombarding Algiers and policing the seas against pirates and slave-traders. As far as the nation was concerned, however, these were necessary operations in faraway places, to extend and maintain British imperial possessions. The Crimean War was something very different.

There were several reasons why. Despite the pious protestations of an endless vista of peace at the Great Exhibition, the popular mood was becoming more and more belligerent, partly from fear of France, which could easily turn to Russophobia, given provocation; partly also because the notion was becoming current that if Britain really was the supreme power of the Western world, as undeniably exhibited in her commercial and industrial predominance, the time was now ripe for her to prove this to the world by some manifestation of military glory. Too long a period of peace slackens the muscles. Once John Delane of *The Times* got the bit between his teeth, he could command a circulation sufficient to exploit this mood. The most articulate of the Russophobes were – with a few exceptions – the Radicals. They had listened with sympathy to the appeals of Louis Kossuth and other exiles from the oppressed countries of Hungary, Poland and Italy, and were eager to join any 'crusade against the arch-tyrant of Russia, in the interests of the subject peoples of Europe'.[6] They found a powerful spokesman, too, in John Arthur Roebuck, whose change of constituency from Bath to Sheffield coincided with an infusion of radical zeal, allied to his natural predilection for blunt speaking.

Warmongers require and expect instant success. A victory over the Russians at the river Alma in the Crimea in September 1854 seemed a promising beginning; Balaclava and Inkerman in the following months uplifted many hearts. But the objective insisted upon at home was the mighty Russian stronghold of Sebastopol. An entry in Greville's *Memoirs* on 31 December 1854 reflects the descent into disillusionment:

> The last day of one of the most melancholy and disastrous years I ever recollect. Almost everybody is in mourning, and grief and despair overspread the land. At the beginning of the year we sent forth an army amidst a tumult of joyous and triumphant anticipation ... and the end of this year sees us deploring the deaths of friends and relations without number, and our army perishing before the walls of Sebastopol, which we are unable to take, and, after bloody victories and prodigies of valour, the Russian power hardly as yet diminished or impaired.[7]

Who was to blame? Highly disturbing news was being fed from the front in the regular bulletins of *The Times* correspondent, W.H. Russell. More and more evidence came through of bungling and incompetence, both by the commanders in the field and by those responsible for the commissariat at home: reports of the pitiful inadequacy of medical supplies, incomprehensible delays in meeting urgent and desperate requests from the front; bad generalship, displaying profligate disregard for the lives of the soldiers. Some of it was highly-coloured; but a good deal was true. Prince Albert had been deeply concerned by the lack of experience and training of the military commanders (all but two of the six divisional commanders were over sixty, and the Duke of Cambridge had never seen action before).[8] He had noted, too, the grievous deficiencies in the whole mechanism of ensuring supplies for a large military force operating at a long distance from home, and had written a typically prudent and measured memorandum on the subject.[9] All this came as grist to Roebuck's mill, and he was fully prepared to launch an attack upon the government in much less measured terms.

The Whig–Peelite coalition of Aberdeen was damaged beyond repair. In the confusion that followed Aberdeen's resignation, eventually the public secured the man they most hoped would be able to restore confidence and to turn the tide of Britain's fortunes: Lord Palmerston. John Bright, who had deplored the war from the very beginning, wrung his hands in despair. 'What a hoax!' he wrote in his diary. 'The aged charlatan has at length attained the great object of his long and unscrupulous ambition.'[10] Palmerston had one price to pay, however. The only way in which Roebuck could be silenced was to appoint him chairman of a Select Committee to investigate the alleged abuses in the conduct of the war, in the full knowledge that Roebuck's main object of attack would be the whole system of purchase of commissions in the army – an obvious invitation to indulge in nepotism, especially by the aristocracy.

If there were any heroes in the unhappy story of the Crimean War, Palmerston was not one of them. Sebastopol was taken in September 1855, but the elation at the news was somewhat dampened by the fact that the French forces in the final engagement greatly outnumbered the British. This was one reason why Palmerston was reluctant to enter into peace negotiations in March 1856. He would have preferred to continue hostilities until an outright and indisputable British victory could be celebrated. There were individual heroes in plenty among the fighting men; and one celebrated heroine in Florence Nightingale, in her courageous determination to surmount every obstacle – professional, military, bureaucratic and denominational – in order to effect a transformation of the hospital and nursing facilities at Scutari and other hospitals in Balaclava.

There were some heroic stands in the tiny ranks of the anti-war party. Both Cobden and Bright, united once more in their non-interventionist stance as they had been in the Anti-Corn Law League, endured public obloquy for speaking out, estranged even from their old 'Manchester School' allies. Cobden, for a while, thought that this marked the end of their political effectiveness. 'The Radicals have turned out more warlike than the Tories,' he wrote to Bright in September 1856. 'So you will see that I am desponding. The world will I suppose come right in the end, but we don't stand now where we did 8 years ago.'[11] Both had to pay the penalty, losing their parliamentary seats in the election of 1857 (a dissolution caused by Cobden's attack on Palmerston over the bombardment of Canton). Bright's effigy was publicly burnt in the streets of Manchester. Birmingham forgave him, however, immediately electing him as their member; and both men surfaced with dramatic effect during the American Civil War.

It would be an exaggeration to say that the Crimean War compelled the Victorians to look out upon the world with different eyes; but at least it obliged them to make some adjustments in the perspective of their world picture. Their complacency had received a severe jolt. Foreign policy had begun to take precedence over home issues almost from the moment that Palmerston became Foreign Secretary under Lord John Russell and Aberdeen. With Palmerston effectively at the head of the administration for the next ten years, this shift in priority was now to be confirmed. Both the organization and the status of the Army underwent fundamental changes. The War Office was restructured so that all aspects of military operations came under its control; and the ordinary British soldier, hitherto – in the popular image – an 'idle, drunken, hard-swearing fighting man', gained greatly in respect, largely through the testimony of Florence Nightingale.[12] Finally, a process of great social and political consequence had been set in motion. Roebuck's Select Committee had not laboured in vain. Although it must have seemed to its leading spirit an unconscionable time before its recommendations took effect, the purchase of Army commissions was abolished in 1871. The nature of entry to the Civil Service was undergoing a similar change. The Northcote–Trevelyan enquiry, set up by Gladstone in 1854, had recommended the introduction of entry by competitive examination. The Indian Civil Service took the first step; and by 1870 most of the posts in the home Civil Service had become exclusively competitive.

The days of aristocratic patronage were passing, giving way to the principle of meritocracy. Principle – as far as commissions in the Army were concerned – was not quite the same as practice, however. The Duke of Cambridge was never shaken in his conviction that 'the British officer should be a gentleman first and an officer second';[13] and, as Correlli Barnett has shown, British military leadership remained for decades to come predominantly aristocratic.[14]

Any retrospective assumption that the mid-Victorian period was a tranquil age of peace was not shared by those living at the time. In February 1864 J.A. Froude lectured at the Royal Institution on 'The Science of History', in the course of which he looked back to the sanguine expectations enunciated at the Crystal Palace in 1851. What had been the result? he asked. 'Battles, bloody as Napoleon's, are now the familiar tale of every day.'[15] What had taken place in India between 1857 and 1859, however, was even bloodier, in the perpetration of ghastly atrocities, than anything that had happened in living memory.

The English public in general had hardly given a thought to the potentially explosive situation in a distant outpost of Empire, populated by heathen who presumably bowed down to wood and stone. Within India itself, the notion that British government and administration backed by a military presence which was largely dependent upon native troops could hold in indefinite subjection a vast complex of annexed territories was based on certain very questionable assumptions. The first was that the Hindus and the Moslems were so jealous of their respective religious beliefs that never the twain would combine in resistance. This did not prevent the British authorities, however, from trampling on their religious susceptibilities, justifiably in some cases – such as the practice of widow-burning (suttee) and the ritualized killings of the Thugs; in others – such as the insistence that troops should tear open with their teeth cartridges greased with tallow made from beef or pork – needlessly inflammatory.

A second assumption was that subject peoples would speedily appreciate the advantages of British justice and the privilege of being ruled by the most civilized nation of the Western world. This brought no joy to Nana Sahib, self-styled Maharajah at Bithur, who steadfastly maintained that British justice had deprived him of his pension, titles and inherited rights; and induced nothing but contempt from his more sinister agent, Azimullah Khan, whose fruitless visit to England in 1854–5 to plead his master's cause merely served to arouse the suspicion that the vaunted claims of British power were illusory. This suspicion turned into a conviction when on a visit to the Crimea in 1855 he witnessed, through the good offices of W.H. Russell of *The Times*, the desperate plight of the English forces at Sebastopol.[16] He reported back to his master that the British hold on India was 'merely a hollow serpent's skin' which could be shaken off 'with a shrug of the shoulders'.[17]

It needed just a single uprising for a jihad to be called; and a mutiny of the native garrison of Sepoy troops at Meerut in May 1857 provided the occasion. The revolt then spread with the force of some massive conflagration to Delhi and to twenty-two different military stations in Bengal, Oudh and the North-Western provinces. The European forces were hopelessly outnumbered; and the ensuing carnage, especially the massacres and the torments inflicted upon the Europeans of all ages and both sexes at Lucknow, Allahabad and – worst of all – at Cawnpore, stunned the English public. Shock was succeeded by outraged fury.

Macaulay recorded the mood of the country in his diary:

> The cruelties of the Sepoy natives have inflamed the Nation to a degree unprecedented within my memory ... There is one terrible cry of revenge. The account of that dreadful military execution at Peshawar, forty men blown at once from the mouths of cannon, heads, legs, arms, flying in all directions, was read with delight by people who, three weeks ago, were against all capital punishment. Bright himself declared for the vigorous suppression of the Mutiny. The almost universal feeling is that not a single Sepoy within the walls of Delhi should be spared, and I own that is a feeling with which I cannot help sympathizing.[18]

If Bright allowed his Quaker pacifism to be overruled by his emotions, Cobden drew a lesson from it all to confirm his distaste for imperial pretensions and the supposition that peoples of a different culture can be elevated either to Christian faith or to the higher civilization of the Western world. He issued a prophecy: 'Indians will prefer to be ruled badly, according to our notions, by their own coloured kith and kin, than to submit to the humiliation of being better governed by a succession of transient intruders from the Antipodes.'[19]

This was not a warning heeded by Cobden's posterity. Gradually the Mutiny was suppressed, at great loss of life, the British cripplingly disadvantaged in having to fight campaigns in a heat so intense that thermometers could not register the temperature but burst above their highest range of 130 degrees.[20] Even before the last remnants of resistance had been crushed, steps were taken to avert the possibility of a recurrence of the catastrophe. Tighter controls were imposed on the native troops who, after 1857, were denied the possession of artillery. The East India Company's authority, already greatly eroded, was officially transferred to the Crown. 'Amazingly Anglicisation survived the shock of the Mutiny,' Clive Dewey has written. '... The most serious insurrection in the history of the raj had ... few long-term effects on British policy.'[21] There can be little doubt, however, that the attitude of government hardened, and relations between the British and her subject peoples were never to be quite the same again.

Wars and rumours of wars punctuated the next ten years of the Queen's reign: a punitive expedition to China in 1859, culminating in the burning down of the Emperor's palaces in Peking as retribution for outrages against British shipping involved in the illicit opium trade; a long series of actions in New Zealand against the rebellious Maoris; and a highly hazardous campaign launched from India against Abyssinia in 1867. But the war which everybody dreaded – the long-awaited conflict with France – was the one which was never actually fought. All had seemed very well in 1855, at least to the Queen, when she and Prince Albert visited Paris as the guests of Napoleon III, to witness the dazzling Paris Exhibition of that year: the first occasion that a British sovereign had entered the French capital since the coronation of the infant Henry VI in 1431. Victoria was entranced by the spectacle of the 'gayest town imaginable', and also by the almost flirtatious welcome by the Emperor himself, who had recently been entertained at Windsor. Her earlier suspicions of bellicose designs evaporated. 'I should not fear saying anything to him,' she wrote. 'I felt – I do not know how to express it – safe with him.'[22]

But for how long? She herself had become – as Lord Clarendon put it – consumed by a sort of 'military mania' since the ending of the Crimean War,[23] having persuaded herself that the Navy was under strength and that there were insufficient military contingents based at home to defend the country's shores. By 1858, although reluctant to change her opinion of Napoleon III, she feared the evidence of the alarming build-up of the military and naval forces of France.

The extraordinary exertions which France is making in her Naval Department [she wrote to Lord Derby in January 1859] oblige us to exercise the utmost vigour to keep up a superiority at sea, upon which our very existence may be said to depend ... The war in India has drained us of every available Battalion ... England will not be listened to in Europe, and be powerless for the preservation of the general peace ... if she is known to be despicably weak in her military resources ... For peace and for war, an available Army is a necessity to her.[24]

War fever had again gripped the country in response to menacing protests from France, following the assassination attempt by members of the Italian Carbonari society led by Felice Orsini, whose grenades hurled (in vain) at the imperial coach outside the Paris Opera were discovered to have been manufactured in England. Tension mounted during 1859 when Napoleon, in conjunction with Cavour of Piedmont, precipitated war with Austria, ostensibly to strike a blow for the unification of Italy. The predominant liberal mood in Britain was to support unification, but Napoleon's decision to fish in these troubled waters without consultation with the other European powers made the British people deeply suspicious. He had engineered the quarrel with Austria presumably for his own ends. As Gladstone put it: 'The relief of Italy is an honourable end, but it must not be sought by unholy means.'[25]

The Queen was furious. She wrote to her uncle, the King of the Belgians, on 8 May 1860:

Really it is too bad! No country, no human being would ever dream of *disturbing* or *attacking* France; every one would be glad to see her prosperous: but *she* must needs disturb every quarter of the Globe and try to make mischief and set every one by the ears; and, of course, it will end some day in a *regular crusade* against *the universal disturber* of the world! It is really monstrous![26]

She had not forgotten – nor was she likely to forget – the words of Pope Pius IX to Odo Russell the previous July, duly reported to her: 'I will give you some advice. Prepare and take care of yourselves in England, for I am quite certain the French Emperor intends sooner or later to attack you.' Lord John Russell endorsed this report with a pencilled comment: 'Very curious,' he wrote.[27]

Already, however, on 12 May 1859, the War Office had given its official sanction to the formation of the Volunteer Rifle Club Movement; and so eager was the country to respond to the appeal to rush to its defence that by February 1860, 60,000 men had been enrolled. Tennyson added his voice to the recruitment campaign:

Be not deaf to the sound that warns!
Be not gulled by a despot's plea!
Are figs of thistles, or grapes of thorns?
How should a despot set men free?
Form! Form! Riflemen form!
Ready, be ready to meet the storm!
Riflemen, riflemen, riflemen, form![28]

Palmerston and his Chancellor of the Exchequer, Gladstone, went through – not for the first time – a period of strained relations. Gladstone begrudged the expenditure of some ten million pounds (especially if financed, as Palmerston had suggested, by negotiating a loan) in order to provide adequate coastal fortifications. 'However great the loss to the Government by the retirement of Mr Gladstone,' Palmerston wrote to the Queen, 'it would be better to lose Mr Gladstone than to run the risk of losing Plymouth or Portsmouth.'[29] Gladstone did not resign; and he successfully resisted all pressure upon him to raise a loan.

There was no invasion. Napoleon III's attentions in the early 1860s turned to Mexico, and plans to extend French influence in Central America by the installation of a puppet emperor. At the same time, Britain's attentions turned westward, to North America, when civil war broke out in January 1861, following the secession of South Carolina, and then other southern states, from the Union. The riposte of the newly-elected President, Abraham Lincoln, was to proclaim a blockade of all the southern ports. British sympathies promptly polarized. Commercial interests dictated strong support for the South and intense resentment against the blockade. Cotton, after all, was the economic lifeline of the Lancashire mill towns. Humanitarian issues, however, predisposed the many readers of *Uncle Tom's Cabin* to favour the North and to support any action that could lead to the extirpation of slavery. The initial reaction of the government was to avoid involvement. 'For God's sake', Russell, Foreign Secretary at the time, exhorted the Commons, 'let us, if possible, keep out of it.'[30]

For a time this looked easier said than done. The southern states, determined to enlist British support, despatched two envoys who attempted to avoid the blockade by sailing from Havana on a British ship, the *Trent*. It was stopped by an American warship and the envoys taken prisoner. The British sense of outrage on this occasion was later equalled by the anger of the American North when a blockade-runner – the *Alabama* – was built at a Liverpool shipyard and allowed to slip its moorings and to harry the ships enforcing the blockade (an act of 'supine folly', John Bright recorded in his diary).[31] On the whole, educated opinion was firmly on the side of Lincoln and the North. Lord Bryce recalled the mood at Oxford at the time, where Goldwin Smith acted as the leading spokesman for the North, securing 'three-fourths of the best talent' of the university. One young disciple, T.H. Green, declared that 'the whole future of humanity was involved in the triumph of the Federal arms'.[32] It was a different matter in London. In the Commons and London society in general, according to Monckton Milnes, supporters of the North were a tiny minority.[33] Gladstone's stance was curiously equivocal. He was anxious to dissociate himself from any suggestion of sympathy with the iniquitous system of slavery, but he doubted the justice of the Union's attempt to impose its will upon the seceders by force. Unfortunately, in a speech at a banquet in Newcastle in October 1862 he 'let fall a sentence about the American war', John Morley wrote, 'of which he was destined never to hear the last', when he acknowledged that the 'leaders of the South have made an army; they have made, it appears, a navy; and they have made what is more than either, they have made a nation.'[34]

But one voice was more vehement, and ultimately more effective, than any other, in determining not only the stance that the British people should take in the conflict, but also the significance that they should read into the fundamental principles of the cause for which Lincoln was prepared to fight to the death. This was John Bright's. Not only did he succeed in persuading a reluctant Cobden to swallow his dislike of Americans and join him in his crusade, but he also successfully appealed to those whose livelihoods were hardest hit by the blockade to subordinate their commercial interests to the much more important moral issues. The Civil War, to Bright, was essentially a conflict between an old, oppressive, aristocratic order, clinging to its property rights – both in land and in human beings – and the emerging American people. When Roebuck attempted in June 1863 to persuade the Commons to accord official recognition to the southern states as an independent nation, Bright's oratory was so powerful that he won the day and 'shook Roebuck as a terrier shakes a rat'.[35]

The ultimate success of Lincoln and the North, together with the lessons that Bright drew from the whole issue, paved the way for significant consequences on the domestic front. What could Britain learn from what had happened across the Atlantic? At the beginning of the conflict, Mill had mused over the possibility of separatist movements in Wales and Scotland, taking heart from the action of the American South.[36] What was much more to the point was the boost given to those who, inspired by the later disintegration of the rich land-owning class of the South, sought to move in the same direction in England by an urgent extension of the franchise; and, once again, through the reputation that he had gained as the spokesman of the working classes, Bright's influence was paramount.

Certain events had to come to pass before the second Reform Bill of 1867, with its proposed doubling of the number of the electorate in England and Wales, had any hope of reaching the statute book. The death of Palmerston in October 1865 was one. The conversion to the cause of parliamentary reform of the one man capable of leading an administration – Gladstone, by this time firmly established as a Liberal – was another. Most important of all, however, was the creation within the country at large of a mood so resolutely determined to extend the franchise that no government could hope to survive without meeting the popular demand. Both Gladstone and Bright applied the full force of their oratorical skills to the achievement of this end, Bright unashamedly recalling, in the Commons debate, the debt that the nation owed to him in putting an end to the Corn Laws: 'If we do not find ourselves', he said, 'surrounded by hungry and exasperated multitudes ... have I not as much as any living man some claim to partake of the glory?'[37]

Neither Gladstone nor Bright was a member of the government that passed the second Reform Bill. This was Disraeli's privilege, coming into office on the defeat of its first draft and realizing – despite his initial reluctance – that the mood of the country was forcing his hand.[38] But the electorate had no doubt as to who were the true architects of the measure, as the return of the Liberals under Gladstone in 1868, with Bright in his cabinet, testified.

In the meantime, what had Napoleon III been up to? The answer is that he had been consistently and skilfully outmanoeuvred by the formidable figure of Otto von Bismarck, who in 1862 had become Minister–President of Prussia. During the 1860s the Victorians, when they looked outwards, looked West, with just occasional glances at Italy, where the ultimate triumph of Victor Emmanuel of Piedmont seemed assured. They still distrusted Napoleon, however. When France attacked Austria in 1859, the reaction had been 'Riflemen form!' as has been seen. But when Bismarck defeated Austria at Sadowa in 1866, not a ripple of anxiety was felt. The number of ironclads being built by France was watched with mounting apprehension, but the enormous military strength which Bismarck was amassing in Prussia was hardly noticed, nor the fact that Prussia was now the leader of the German-speaking people.

Why should it be cause for concern? Britain and Germany were natural allies. The Crown Prince of Prussia, later to become in 1888, if only for a short time, the second German Emperor, was the Queen's son-in-law; his heir, Kaiser William II, was her grandson. If the British did not discern the subtlety of Bismarck's master-plan, they were not alone. Bismarck knew precisely what he wanted: France isolated, and then France decisively humiliated by German arms. The suitable moment of provocation was a vacancy on the throne of Spain in 1868, followed by the proposal to put forward a member of the Prussian royal family as a candidate, which was certain to be anathema to the French. The plan nearly failed when the King of Prussia acceded to French pressure to abandon the scheme. But the wish of the French to turn a diplomatic victory into a triumph, by demanding a guarantee that the issue would never be raised again, gave Bismarck the opportunity he had been waiting for. The King was bound to object to having his given word questioned; but the despatch from Ems signifying his displeasure was carefully edited by Bismarck to read like an insolent and peremptory rebuff. France took the bait. She declared war on Germany, and therefore appeared in the eyes of Europe as the aggressor.

English sympathy was pro-Prussian almost to a man, and the national press did its best to ensure that it remained so. British journalists were regularly supplied with up-to-date bulletins by the Prussians, and W.H. Russell of *The Times* was accorded the privilege of membership of the Crown Prince's immediate entourage.[39] A letter from T.H. Huxley to a scientific colleague in Germany captured the mood exactly:

> If you Germans do not give that crowned swindler, whose fall I have been looking for ever since the *coup d'état*, such a blow as he will never recover from, I will never forgive you. Public opinion in England is not worth much, but at present, it is entirely against France.[40]

'This dreadful war is vile and unforgivable!', the Queen wrote to Queen Augusta of Prussia on 10 July 1870. 'May God protect our dear, beloved Germany! My heart is indeed heavy and bleeds for you!'[41]

The defeat of France was swift and almost clinical in the face of the efficiency of the German war machine. The Second Empire effectively collapsed after the defeat of the French army at Sedan early in September 1870. The Prince Imperial and the Empress Eugénie took refuge in England, soon followed by the Emperor himself. The *coup de grâce* was delivered at Metz in October. Paris was then encircled. Only at that point did some begin to wonder at the might of Germany, and to feel sympathy for the appalling sufferings of those trapped in the beleaguered city. Even Victoria switched allegiance after the seizure by the Prussians of Alsace-Lorraine. 'Odious people the Prussians are,' she wrote, '*that I must say.*'[42] For nearly twenty years, almost every move of Napoleon had been observed in England with distrustful eyes. For the first time it occurred to some of these observers that they might have been watching the wrong man.

III

'Our approaching decrepitude.'

J.A. Froude in 1870

'I sometimes fear that with all our great wealth and commerce we are only an orange going to be sucked by France and America.'

Benjamin Jowett to Lady Amberley, 7 January 1866

Bismarck was well worth watching closely, too; and not only because of his formidable build-up of military strength which one day might threaten Britain's security. He, and the unified Germany which he had done so much to create, could teach Britain some valuable lessons which she seemed to be perilously failing to heed. Such was the opinion of James Anthony Froude in an article entitled 'England's War', written in 1870. Fifty-five years on from Waterloo, and what had happened to the country that had been 'indisputably the first Power in the world'?

English officers tell us that they can scarcely show their faces at a table d'hôte in Germany without danger of affront. English opinion is without weight. English power is ridiculed. Our influence in the councils of Europe is a thing of the past. We are told, half officially, that it is time for us to withdraw altogether from the concerns of the Continent: while, on the other side of the Atlantic, Mr Emerson calmly intimates to an approving audience, that the time is not far off when the Union must throw its protecting shield over us in our approaching decrepitude.[1]

One should never take Froude's jeremiads too seriously. He had learnt from his master, Carlyle, that if you want to make a point to your fellow-countrymen, you must bark and splutter at them with a mixture of insult and hyperbole. But Froude's was not a lone voice. As early as 1847 Richard Cobden had complained bitterly of the consistent misdirection of British foreign policy. We should be looking westwards, not to the Continent. He had for years been convinced 'that the United States, and not any Continental power, was the quarter from whence rivalry for England was to be apprehended'.[2]

That the Prince Consort – yet another warning voice – should choose to point to Germany was, however, only to be expected. In September 1859, in the course of his presidential address to the British Association for the Advancement of Science, at their meeting in Aberdeen, he had deplored the neglect of the claims of science and technology by governments, educationists and the public at large. The Continental universities were putting us to shame. In Britain, science depended upon 'the begging bowl' for its funding, when it ought to be speaking 'to the State like a favoured child to its parent, sure of his parental solicitude for its welfare'.[3] In the same year Wellington College in Berkshire – the national memorial to the Great Duke – opened its doors to its first pupils. The Prince Consort was both the founder and its first President. He had despatched the College's first Master, Edward White Benson, to Prussia to visit certain chosen schools, especially in Potsdam, in order to observe their methods and their curriculum, believing both to be superior to what was traditionally offered in English public schools. It was his plain intention, as recorded in the College's prospectus, to provide instruction in 'those branches of scientific knowledge which have a special application to the Arts, Commerce and Industry of the Country'.[4]

It was not to be. Benson was a Cambridge Classicist who had served as an assistant master under Frederick Temple at Rugby. A German *Realschule* made him shudder; and – because of the untimely death of the Prince Consort in 1861 – Benson's determination to model Wellington on Rugby was to prevail. A promising opportunity had been lost. Looking back with understandable bitterness and regret, Sir Richard Gregory, the editor of *Nature*, wrote in 1928: 'How vastly different the course of British history might have been had the Prince Consort lived, say, another twenty-five years.'[5]

A tremor of disquiet was felt in 1867 by those from Britain who visited the Paris Exhibition of that year. There they saw machinery, applications of chemical and scientific research, even – God forbid! – textiles, from other countries, which in invention and quality were as good as, if not superior to, anything exhibited by Great Britain. They came away with the feeling that British goods 'were beaten in everything'.[6] The *Annual Register* of that year had a sorry tale to tell, and some robust advice to give:

> It is a favourite argument with those who consider no precautions necessary, that England shows no sign of decay at present. To this argument there are two answers: the first, that when the signs become clearly visible, the catastrophe will perhaps have ceased to be avertible; the other, that there may be signs already ... She [England] ... owes her great influence, not to military successes, but to her commanding position in the arena of industry and commerce. If she forgets this, she is lost: not perhaps to the extent of being conquered and reduced to a province, but undoubtedly to the extent of having to give up the lead, and ceasing to be a first-rate power. The signs, for those who can read, are present, and can be plainly seen.[7]

Economic cycles are not easy to date precisely, and the period of the so-called 'Great Depression' in industry, commerce and agriculture is no exception. Some historians date its beginning from the writing on the walls in the late 1860s; some question whether the economy was quite as depressed as has been commonly accepted. Some date its ending in 1886 (the year of the final report of the Royal Commission on the Depression of Trade and Industry), while others believe that no significant recovery can be established until the middle years of the 1890s. The answer to such questions must depend on the chosen index by which prosperity, or the lack of it, is to be determined. If, however, that index is taken to be falling prices and the elusiveness of profits, then a period from 1873 to 1895, admittedly with occasional intermissions, would seem to be the least controversial dating of the phenomenon.

Certain features of the downturn in the economy are incontestable.

In the first place, there were these odd moments of intermission. According to the analysis of H.L. Beales, the slumps in industry and commerce were actually three in number, which he dates as 1873 to 1876, 1882 to 1886, and 1890 to 1895, partial recoveries taking place in the intervening years.[8] Secondly, whereas many descriptive titles given to a period, or to significant social or cultural movements – such as 'the Renaissance' or 'the Rise of the Gentry' – are retrospective labels invented by historians, the phrase 'the Great Depression' is not one of them. 'Depression' was the chosen word on the lips of contemporaries. This does not, of course, necessarily mean that they were right. Historians are able to supply a perspective which is denied to those living at the time. E.J. Hobsbawm, for instance, poses the question: if one reserves the word 'depression' for the 1870s and 1880s, what word is left to describe the far worse calamities, for at least the working-classes, in the 1830s and 1840s? Nevertheless he concedes that if 'depression indicates a pervasive – and for the generations since 1850 a new – state of mind of uneasiness and gloom about the prospects of the British economy, the word is accurate. After its glorious advance, the economy stagnated.'[9] It is also true that a nation can sometimes talk itself into a depression, when statesmen and journalists bandy the word around indiscriminately. This is what exasperated one of the leading statisticians of the time, Sir Robert Giffen.

> To anyone who has ever glanced at the economic history of England during the present century [he wrote], the common talk now about the 'unusual' depression of our trade appears simply ludicrous. The people who indulge in it have simply never thought of what depression in trade is.[10]

He was speaking of trade, let it be noted. A third incontestable feature of the state of the economy during these years is not only that agriculture was hardest hit, but that the effects of the blows sustained turned out to be irreversible. A whole combination of adverse circumstances contrived to make the twenty years between 1875 and 1895 a nightmare period for British farmers, and especially grain producers. A series of wet summers, culminating in the wettest season in living memory in 1879, meant an alarmingly low yield in successive harvests. The normal option in such a contingency – that of raising prices – was not open to them, for the simple reason that they were being consistently undersold by the importation of cheap grain from the New World. The major corn-growing areas (the counties of the east and south-east) were unable to compete against the produce of the American prairies, where mechanical reapers – the invention of an American, Cyrus McCormick – were in widescale use, thereby cutting labour costs. By the 1870s American technology had advanced to the use of self-binders, while the new railroads and steamships were cutting transport costs. Just at the moment when the farmer needed to increase his prices in order to make any sort of profit at all, he was compelled to lower them: from 50 shillings a bushel in 1877 to under 40 shillings in 1884, gradually dropping to 22 shillings. In the drought year of 1894 he was lucky to sell at 19 shillings.[11]

This spelled ruin, especially since the only other option, of cutting labour costs by reducing wages, was bound to provoke organized resistance from the recently-formed National Union of Agricultural Labourers, under the leadership of Joseph Arch. Indeed, the first notable success of the Union was the raising of wages over wide areas, together with improved hours of work. After 1877, however, as many farmers faced bankruptcy, wages had to be cut, notwithstanding the Union. If the farmers nourished hopes that the Conservative victory at the polls in 1874 would lead to measures of protection or compensation, such hopes were vain. The Corn Laws once repealed were never to be restored. Disraeli was well aware that this would have been political suicide. Nevertheless, the failure of his administration to devise any effective measure of relief was to cost his party dear at the next election in 1880. When the appeal was renewed between 1885 and 1891, Salisbury's reply was 'not practical politics'.[12]

Some farmers switched from arable farming to grazing and the production of livestock; but a cruel fate continued to pursue them. A virulent epidemic of liver-rot in 1879 led to the mass slaughter of sheep, followed in 1883 by widespread foot-and-mouth disease, requiring a similar conflagration of cattle. By this time, the introduction of cold storage by refrigeration had led to large quantities of meat being imported from Australia and New Zealand, and the inevitable consequence of falling prices. What was there left to do? Some turned to market-gardening and orchards; others, taking advantage of the relatively new passion for golf in England,[13] sold their land for golf-courses.

In 1895 a Royal Commission on the Agricultural Depression had this to say about the grievous situation in Essex:

Between 1880 and 1884 the number of farms given up either in despair or for reasons over which the occupiers had no control was stated to have been enormous. On poor estates no attempt was made to bring the land round; it was left alone and gradually 'tumbled down' to such coarse and inferior herbage as nature produced ... A regular panic set in; some tenants who had hitherto weathered the storm refused to renew their leases upon any terms, while others continued from year to year at large reductions ... Rents were reduced between 1880 and 1886 from 25 to as much as 80%.[14]

On the whole the great landowners suffered less than the small agricultural squires. They had diversified their resources and investments, and derived the maximum amount of profit from industrialization. As F.M.L. Thompson has shown, when the disasters of the 1870s hit British farming,

Many landowners were shielded from the full effects ... because they had profited directly from the great industrial expansion of the times, and were by no means wholly dependent upon their farm rents. For some, though not for all, mines, railways, docks or urban ground rents helped to provide the money which was poured into their farms.[15]

Some, however, pulled out of agricultural property altogether. Lord Monson, as early as 1851, had come to the conclusion that it was 'an infernal bore' because of the uncertain returns. One would do better to put one's money in Consols.[16] The name of a peer looked very well among the list of directors published in a company's prospectus, a fact fully appreciated by the third Earl of Verulam, who set about collecting directorships in African and American mines, and profited greatly from the operation.[17] This was all very well; and for a time the long-term consequences of the depression might not have too much bothered those who could cushion themselves against financial loss. But from time immemorial, the wealth, status and power of the British aristocracy had rested firmly on its territorial base. In David Cannadine's words:

Land was wealth: the most secure, reliable and permanent asset; land was status: its ownership conferred unique and unrivalled celebrity. And land was power: over the locality, the county and the nation.[18]

When tumbling prices and rentals obliged the aristocracy to try to preserve their fortunes elsewhere, they discarded their strongest source of influence. 'The whole territorial basis of patrician existence was undermined.'[19]

As for those below the very great, few escaped the necessity for substantial retrenchment and a lowering of the quality of life. L.E. Jones's account of his Victorian boyhood on a prosperous Norfolk farm, where the name of Joseph Arch (elected MP for the neighbouring constituency) was never uttered except in tones which had 'a sinister ring for us', tells of his puzzlement, because the events were never really explained by his parents, as both farm and household underwent disturbing changes in the early 1890s. There was

> talk of low rents, and of rents remitted, and of the losses of the Home Farm. One by one, the laundry was closed, the footman left, and after him the groom; Mr Bashan retired from the garden and was not replaced; my father's riding-horse was sold. We were partly aware, in short, of the economic conditions of the nineties as they touched ourselves; we knew nothing of the cottager's, nothing of the tenant-farmer's distress.[20]

Not everybody shed tears for the farmers' plight. Henry Sidgwick, for instance, in 1885, expressed the view in his diary that they, like everybody else in the modern business world, had to learn to adjust to market forces and not to demand of the state the provision of safety-nets every time they suffered a reverse. 'I look with satisfaction', he wrote, 'on the changes of a different and more truly modern kind which are forcibly modernising the traditional ways of these landed people – the cheapness of corn which is driving them all to look into ways and means as any man of business would.'[21]

The fact remains, however, that land was changing hands. And the closing decades of the nineteenth century saw the arrival into grand country houses of a new breed of landowner – the successful manufacturer or financier, happy perhaps to employ an army of gardeners to embellish his surroundings and of gamekeepers to rear his pheasants, and so to provide ostentatious evidence of his wealth and standing, while failing, however hard he tried, to disguise his origins and to command the deference naturally accorded to heredity and a time-honoured association with the land. British agriculture would never be quite the same again. The major casualty was cereal farming, and a single statistic tells the story. In the sixty years between 1870 and 1930 the area in Britain under cereal crops halved.[22] Put the question 'why?' to a grain producer in the 1880s, and his answer would come back without hesitation: 'Look across the Atlantic to the USA.'

Industry, too, had good cause to look with concern in the same direction. Even as early as 1851, British engineers had noted at the Great Exhibition three inventions capable in time of mass-production, all of them products of American engineering: the sewing-machine, the Colt revolver and the mechanical reaper. They were not slow to observe, either, a few years later, that the USA, following the German pattern, had introduced a national system of education, and that the emphasis was practical and technical rather than the traditional liberal curriculum of English schools.[23] It also became clear that, when necessary, America was prepared to invoke protectionism. The McKinley Tariff of 1890, for instance, delivered a body blow to the British export of textiles.

The most serious threat to British industry and commerce, however, was posed by the phenomenal progress in industrialization on the Continent, notably in Germany, Belgium and France. This did not mean that suddenly the rate of industrialization in Britain slackened, or that the ingenuity of British inventiveness somehow dried up. In 1872 there seemed no cause for alarm, and little reason for paying heed to the warnings of the pessimists. The year saw record export and import figures; coal-production was booming; all seemed very well in the ship-building industry, the textile trade and all the metallurgical industries. What was happening at the same time, however, was that other countries were catching up at a rate of acceleration that meant they would soon exceed the productivity of the once-acknowledged 'workshop of the world'. The traditional strength of British exports had for long been in manufactured goods (with the single exception of coal), textiles consistently topping the list. But there would be no call to buy British once other countries could produce goods of the same quality, and therefore the export demand was bound to dwindle as the market world-wide became increasingly more competitive.

It was Britain's misfortune, or perhaps short-sightedness, that she did not always take full advantage of the fruits of her own technology. In the field of metallurgy, iron was giving way to steel. Britain initially led the way. The Bessemer process of conversion (as well as the 'open-hearth' method) required the use of iron obtained from non-phosphoric ores. Britain was ideally placed to exploit this. The appropriate ore was shipped easily to Middlesbrough from Sweden, and to South Wales and Barrow-in-Furness from Spain. While that situation continued, the

Continent was largely dependent upon British steel, and the industry was booming as steel replaced iron both in the railway system and in ship-building. In 1877, however, Sidney Gilchrist Thomas discovered a process of converting phosphoric iron into steel, and Germany leapt in to take advantage of it.[24] By the 1890s Germany had built up a gigantic steel industry which not only threatened to cut Britain out of the market, but also supplied herself with the wherewithal to enhance her already frightening military and naval strength.

It was not that Britain's rivals, by some miracle, made themselves invulnerable to slumps. The constant cry during the period of the Great Depression was that prices were falling; but they were also falling world-wide. Dynamic expansion tends to lead to over-speculation, as had happened during the British railway boom of the 1840s. The United States experienced something very similar during their railway boom of the 1870s. A post-war building mania in Germany during the same decade brought financial crashes in its wake. In Britain the only banking house to be seriously affected in the 1870s was the City of Glasgow Bank, which was compelled to stop payments in 1878. Then, in 1882, the great French bank, the Union-Générale, paid the penalty of over-speculation, causing panic and a general fall in prices all over Europe.

In 1890, however, the unthinkable occurred in England: the collapse of the House of Baring, the 'Sixth Great Power in Europe' as the Duc de Richelieu described it in 1818.[25] This was again a case of over-speculation, and of the folly of Lord Revelstoke ('Ned' Baring), the senior partner, in floating a huge loan to the Buenos Aires Water Supply and Drainage Company without ensuring that the issue was fully underwritten. At the last moment, the reluctant Governor of the Bank of England – William Lidderdale – and an even more reluctant Lord Salisbury and George Goschen (the Chancellor of the Exchequer), with the help of other London bankers, agreed to bail Baring's out by meeting liabilities of 10 million pounds.[26] The final figure proved to be in excess of 17 million.[27] Had they not done so, the fall of Baring's would have brought down most of the great London banking houses with it, and Britain would have had to face not only the loss of its position as the workshop of the world, but also so complete a loss of confidence in its financial integrity that it would have ceased to maintain its reputation as the acknowledged centre of world finance. The Great Depression would have been immeasurably greater still.

One contemporary observer of the British industrial and commercial scene in the late 1870s, T.H.S. Escott, linked the failure to outpace her rivals with a sort of nervousness at the volatility of the money market.

> The trade of the United Kingdom dragged along with heaviness [he wrote]. Enterprise, that wholesome energy of speculation which is the soul of prosperous business, was wanting. Those who had means were afraid to risk it out of their sight, and most of those who had little or none failed to obtain the necessary credit. They could no longer borrow.[28]

Apathy would be too strong a word to apply to the mood. But it is difficult to resist the impression that an element of complacency at what had been achieved engendered the inclination to sit back and enjoy the fruits of success, and served to deaden awareness that it is in the nature of technology to develop into more sophisticated forms, provided that the incentives to continue experimenting, and investing capital, are there. Benjamin Jowett was shrewd enough to observe this as early as 1866, when he vouchsafed certain qualms to Lady Amberley:

> I sometimes fear [he wrote] that with all our great wealth and commerce we are only an orange going to be sucked by France and America. John Bull has certainly grown very fat; he can sit in his counting-house but he can't walk about as well as he used to do.[29]

He wrote this letter four years before the Franco-Prussian war. Otherwise he would have substituted Germany for France.

Although British agriculture and industry both experienced a depression at roughly the same time, precipitated to a large extent by the pressure of foreign competition, their respective predicaments differed in significant ways. Whereas loss of profits compelled many landowners either to abandon their properties or to turn the land to other uses, British industry struggled as best it could to weather the storm. But it also had to contend with either indifference to its plight, or actual deliberate disparagement from the most influential sections of the country's 'clerisy'. During the first half of the century, the powerful voices of William Cobbett and Coleridge had inveighed against industrialization, and Carlyle had added derision to their detestation of the dark satanic mills. During the 1850s, however, the nation as a whole felt justifiable pride in the achievements of its engineers, exhibited for the whole world to see in 1851; Samuel Smiles had added his voice, at the end of the decade, to the tributes to self-made men, whom others had every cause to try to emulate. Robert Stephenson, the son of the pioneer of the 'Rocket', was honoured, on his death in October 1859, by burial in Westminster Abbey. But in the decades that followed, at the moment when industry had every cause to look for support, the clerisy conspicuously failed to give it them. Even Jowett, who accurately discerned the dangers from foreign competition, went no further than to express his concern. Balliol, under his Mastership, was more in the business of nurturing pro-consuls than of supplying captains of industry. Edward Thring, Headmaster of Uppingham, founder of the Headmasters' Conference and arguably the most influential figure in publicschool history since Arnold, emphatically rejected any attempt to modify the traditional liberal curriculum by introducing elements of vocational training; he was not in favour of it for the professions, and certainly not for careers in industry and commerce.[30]

The sages and the savants, moreover, in their different ways, combined to represent the image of industry as somehow alien to the nation's cultural heritage and way of life. Matthew Arnold's plea for 'sweetness and light', for instance, was hardly a recipe for thrusting industrial enterprise. To his mind, as Richard Jenkyns has written, 'wealth and industry were *necessarily* the enemies of culture: in his vocabulary, coal, railroads and machinery are words as automatically pejorative as incense or chalice in the literature of the Protestant Truth Society.'[31] Mill actually declared that the cessation of economic growth and the competitive spirit would turn out to be a 'very considerable improvement on our present condition';[32] and he chose the occasion of his Rectorial address at St Andrews in 1867 to deplore the influence of 'commercial money-getting business' (as well as 'religious Puritanism').[33] John Ruskin and William Morris both detested the degradation of the concept of work by the factory system, looking to the day when factories would be no more, the dignity of labour restored by a revival of the medieval craft guilds.

The true heart of England, they all seemed to be saying, was not to be found in a nation of cotton mills, blast-furnaces and factories. It lay rather in the 'adorable dreamer ... home of lost causes', which was Matthew Arnold's romanticized picture of Oxford;[34] or in the peaceful – if occasionally catty – Cathedral Close of Trollope's Barchester; or in the rustic world of Thomas Hardy's Wessex, the popularity of which caused its author some surprise.[35] All these seductively attractive scenarios, with their nostalgic appeal, served – in many cases quite deliberately – to tarnish the image of British industry.

Those actively engaged in industrial and commercial battles would not have been much impressed or influenced by the element of fantasy in writings such as these. But they would not have been unaware of the seriousness of the two lessons that Britain had failed to learn or – at least – was coming to learn too late in the day. One was the crucial importance of linking science and technology within a national educational system. The other was the comparative weakness of a nation which adhered to a structure of industrial firms, in the same line of business, failing to co-operate with each other or to consider amalgamation, as a way of increasing capital for investment. Germany with its huge cartels, and the USA with its trusts and combines, thought differently and ultimately more profitably. The British people were thoroughly shaken in 1901, for instance, on discovering that the United States Steel Corporation had acquired a capital of a billion dollars.[36] With massive capital resources such as this, the scope for pioneering new inventions or developing existing technology seemed limitless; and the development of the chemical industry in Germany and of the electrical industry in the USA saw Great Britain lagging badly behind. And how dearly Britain would have wished to be the pioneer of the high-speed internal combustion engine, patented by Gottfried Daimler in Germany.

In 1896 there appeared a book by E.E. Williams entitled *Made in Germany*. It went through several editions and gave the British people some uncomfortable moments just at a time when the country saw the clouds lifting, as prices began to rise again, partly as the result of the influx of South African gold.

> Take observation in your own surroundings [so the book enjoined]. You will find that the material of some of your own clothes was probably woven in Germany. Still more probable is it that some of your wife's garments are German importations; while it is practically beyond a doubt that the magnificent mantles and jackets wherein her maids array themselves on their Sundays out are German-made and German-sold, for only so could they be done at the figure.

This hit hard: *textiles* imported, and disturbingly cheap. But then, as H.L. Beales has commented, from his own perusal of further pages of the book, we come to 'toys and the dolls and the fairy books ... and the piano, and the mug inscribed "A Present from Margate", the drain-pipes, the poker, the opera and its singers, the texts on the wall, and the German band that rouses you from sleep in the morning – all made in Germany.'[37]

The markets, even one's own home market, were being flooded by German products. What was the answer? One had already been thought of. Looking outwards to the Continent and to the USA brought little comfort, so the sensible course was to look further afield. Create new markets. This meant the Empire, whose bounds might yet be made wider still.

IV

'The British Empire ... divinely ordained.'
                    J.E.C. Welldon, Bishop of Calcutta

'If we can only open the interior of Africa a little further, we can get everything that is wanted.'
                    Lady Carbury in Trollope, *The Way We Live Now*

The word 'imperialism', with its connotation of a deliberate policy to extend a nation's subject possessions, in the interests of commerce, pres-tige or simple power-politics, is – according to the *Oxford Dictionary* – of relatively recent currency, at least as applied to Britain. She had been an imperial power long before Victoria came to the throne, but her acquisi-tions had been built up 'on the strength of a rather crude and blind instinct', in J.R. Seeley's famous phrase: 'in a fit of absence of mind'.[1] As the century progressed, however, and most notably in its closing decades, the whole mood changed. The Empire became part of a polit-ical programme, and imperialism was born.

An atlas of the world studded with territories coloured in red to denote British possessions can give a misleading picture of imperial unity, failing to distinguish between colonies, dependencies, and areas of direct as opposed to indirect rule. The anomalous position of Ireland may be taken as an illustration; and since Irish problems dogged British politics throughout the Queen's reign, some consideration of the nature of the anomaly is clearly called for.

In 1800 Ireland officially became part of the United Kingdom. In effect this meant that, following an unsuccessful rebellion at the end of the eighteenth century, Ireland ceased to have its own (somewhat restricted) Parliament, its interests thereafter being represented by the Irish members elected directly to Westminster. But she was never an integral part of the United Kingdom in the sense that Scotland and Wales were, her subject status being confirmed by the executive authority reposing in the person of the Viceroy and his entourage in Dublin.

The marriage of the two nations had never been a happy one, mainly because they were hopelessly unequal partners. As far as the British people were concerned, when they observed Ireland in the context of their times, they saw different things depending upon whether they looked inwards or looked outwards. When they looked inwards they saw the Irish, and found the sight distinctly unpleasing. They failed to appreciate the debt they owed to the gangs of Irish navvies who were playing such a large part in the construction of the railways. Instead they looked with repugnance at their ghetto-mentality (almost as bad as the Jews, people thought), and the revolting squalor of the urban dens and 'rookeries' which housed them. They were poor, dirty, bug-ridden, intemperate, and – above all – Roman Catholic. Even their fellow workers in the labouring class regarded them with distrust. They constituted a threat to the labour market by their acquiescence in lower wages; and in the event of a strike, they had been known to act as 'knobsticks' – the north-country term for strike-breakers.[2] All in all, England would have been happier without them.

When, however, the British looked outwards to Ireland itself, it was rarely to sympathize with the grievances of that unhappy land, but more often to deplore its lawlessness and its nuisance-value within the general setting of British politics. It is woefully significant, in comparing the standing of the two countries, that nobody in their right mind chose to emigrate *to* Ireland. All the movement was the other way – or from Ireland westwards, to the United States. Furthermore, although the land of Ireland was largely the property of English landowners, the bulk of them chose to be absentees, and almost every conceivable disadvantage was imposed upon their tenants: no security of tenure, no protection against arbitrary raising of rents, and no compensation for any improvements they might make in their holdings.

Indeed, it is difficult to find a single advantage that Ireland gained from its union with Great Britain. England offered no help to relieve the intractable problem of a desperately poor country in which the mass of the people were living barely at subsistence level at a time when population was increasing and the amount of land under cultivation was not. The staple diet of the Irish poor was the potato. If the crop failed, they faced starvation. Except in Ulster, where the bulk of the non-Catholic (Presbyterian) population lived and a reasonably thriving linen industry was conducted, there were neither natural resources such as coal and minerals nor the means – such as steam-power – to enable industry to be established. The country as a whole was required to pay two-seventeenths of the taxation of the United Kingdom, which was beyond its capacity, and the population, the vast majority of whom were Roman Catholics, was required to support an Anglican Established Church which was both an affront to their faith and a constant reminder of their inferior citizenship.

Advantage might have accrued from the Union only if the rest of the United Kingdom had been prepared to pour capital into Ireland to improve its communications and to invest in industrial enterprises. Here, perhaps, Ireland itself had to share part of the blame for the refusal of investors to show the remotest interest in helping the country out of its plight. The Irish resentment against their grievances encouraged violence, vandalism, and sometimes blood-curdling reprisals by members of secret societies, forcing successive governments to pass Coercion Acts and the executive to invoke the power of martial law to counteract insurrection. Every move somewhat grudgingly taken to rectify some of these grievances was in danger of frustration by the violence of extremists who demanded more. Daniel O'Connell, who had been the prime mover in gaining Catholic Emancipation in 1829, found that his further efforts to obtain the abolition of the payment of tithe by Catholics, and ultimately to secure the repeal of the Union, were continually hampered by lawlessness and the belligerent 'Young Ireland Movement'.

And so the sad story continued through Victoria's reign: small gestures, such as a grant to the Catholic College of Maynooth in 1845 (hotly contested by its opponents in England); then acts of terrorism, at their most serious in 1867, committed by the Fenians, an American–Irish organization pledged to recover Ireland for the Irish. Could nothing be done to heal the country's wounds? When Henry Edward Manning, one of the most distinguished of the Anglican converts to Rome (in

1851), became Archbishop of Westminster in 1865 he joined forces with his friend of Anglican days, Gladstone (who in December 1868 became Prime Minister for the first time), determined to work with him to secure the first priority in tackling Ireland's grievances – the disestablishment of the Irish Church. Manning provided Gladstone with appropriate ammunition in his published 'Letter to Earl Grey' in March 1868, in which he marshalled unanswerable arguments to show that 'England treats its colonies, in education as well as in religious equality, better than it treats Ireland.'[3] Not without a fierce fight, that battle was won; but it was only the first step. A year later Gladstone secured the passage of his Irish Land Act, which at last introduced protection for tenants against indiscriminate eviction. Manning – and Ireland – hoped for more, but they had to wait until 1881 (Gladstone's second Land Act) to achieve the three most important concessions, the so-called 'three Fs': Fixity of tenure, Fair rents and Free sale.

The extremists soon returned to the offensive. Michael Davitt's Land League and the Plan of Campaign (to 'boycott' any person rash enough to take possession of the land of an evicted tenant) threatened anarchy, and yet again the government was forced into the position of taking away with its left hand what it had given with its right. The tragic murder of Lord Frederick Cavendish, the new Chief Secretary for Ireland, in Phoenix Park in May 1882, by a group of Irish terrorists called the 'Invincibles', lost Ireland such sympathy as Gladstone and the dynamic leader of the Irish MPs, Charles Stuart Parnell, had been doing their utmost to enlist.

Gladstone never gave up. His efforts from the early 1880s until the end of his life were concentrated on securing Home Rule for Ireland. Both his Home Rule Bills, in 1886 and 1893, were defeated. It seemed impossible to find an agreed formula among his allies, some wanting the restoration of a separate parliament, others insisting on the retention of Irish members at Westminster, voting only on Irish affairs. Both Manning and Parnell switched allegiance to the Conservatives in 1885, believing – as it happened, in vain – that they could obtain a better deal.[4] Joseph Chamberlain devised a formula of his own and eventually broke with Gladstone, becoming his fiercest opponent; and when Parnell incurred public disgrace over his liaison with Kitty O'Shea in 1890, Gladstone was forced to disown him, and thereby – as Roy Jenkins has put it – 'to stultify the end of his own political life as well as to turn

Parnell from a (superficially at least) disciplined and dedicated ally into a wild destructive force'.[5] The one person in the realm who clapped her hands in not particularly secret glee was the Queen. No Home Rule for Ireland, as far as she was concerned; and she had regarded Gladstone's persistence in vainly trying to convert her as the ravings of a 'dangerous old fanatic'. Betty Ponsonby, the daughter of the Queen's private secretary, happened to be dining with her at Osborne in August 1892, when Gladstone, who had just been returned to power for his last administration, was also present. She sat next to him at dinner.

> After dinner [Betty Ponsonby recalled], the Queen came straight up to me and asked: 'What did Mr Gladstone talk to you about?' 'Home Rule, ma'am!' She shrugged her shoulders and said, 'I know ... he always will!'[6]

Why did it matter so much to retain Ireland within the Union? She could not add a penny to Britain's prosperity; she was only a drain on public expenditure and a recurring source of political tension. Perhaps memories of the landing of a French army in County Mayo in August 1798 died hard. An Ireland released from bondage to England was a country in which bitter memories might fester into open hostility, and she might prove an ideal base from which a foreign invader could launch an attack upon England's relatively defenceless west coast.

Until Britain fell victim to a sort of Empire-fever in the 1870s, she was probably more conscious of the nagging problem of Ireland than of the concerns and interests of other portions of her Empire (with the exception of India during and after the Mutiny). The phrase 'the white man's burden' had not yet been coined, but many adhered to the view of Adam Smith that 'Great Britain derived nothing but loss from the dominion over her colonies'.[7] Even Disraeli in the 1850s was dismissive, describing 'those wretched colonies' as 'a millstone round our necks'.[8] In economic terms, the expenditure on their defence was barely worth the balance accrued by the export trade. In 1846 the cost of colonial defence amounted to £4,000,000, while the total value of their export trade was £8,000,000. 'For every £1 worth of goods sold the country was finding 10/– for defence'.[9] During the mid-Victorian period, the need to create protective markets seemed outmoded. Goldwin Smith expressed it thus:

> The time was when the universal prevalence of commercial monopoly made it well worth our while to hold colonies in dependence for the sake of

commanding their trade. But that time is gone. Trade is everywhere free, or becoming free.[10]

But there could be other advantages, depending in part on whether the overseas possession was strictly speaking a 'colony', like Australia and Canada, where Europeans had settled and were in the process of making their home a country, or whether it was a genuine dependency, a non-European country with a native coloured population over whom the English had established a domination by force of arms – like India, Ceylon or the West Indies. The European colonies were certainly valuable markets, but they were also – quite literally – 'plantations':[11] havens for white emigrants. It is true that many of the emigrants to New South Wales and Van Dieman's Land were unwilling wretches, despatched in atrocious conditions at the rate of 4,000 a year as convicts to penal settlements. Many obtained their 'tickets of leave' after a few years and settled there permanently. But there were as many emigrants who sailed to the Antipodes freely in the hope of making their fortunes, especially after the Gold Rush of the early 1850s.

This could only be to the advantage of the mother country, J.A. Froude vigorously maintained:

> Here at home we have no room to grow [he wrote in 1870] ... We want land on which to plant English families where they may thrive and multiply without ceasing to be Englishmen ... Each husband and wife as they establish themselves will be a fresh root for the old tree, struck into a new soil.[12]

This was the philosophy of 'Greater Britain' – the title of a best-seller by Charles Dilke – whereby new societies which in time would acquire their own form of responsible government would continue to be tied by bonds of kinship to Great Britain. As Dilke put it: 'it would bring us a step nearer to the virtual confederation of the English race'.[13] Lord Durham and Edward Gibbon Wakefield had been pioneers in the 1830s and 1840s in charting such a future for Canada, if not envisaging complete independence. It was actually granted Dominion status in 1867. The acquisition of New Zealand in 1840, in which Wakefield again played a major part, was a very different story. Here was a land on which even the most intrepid missionary hardly dared to tread because of the ferocity of the Maoris. The British government was loath to encourage settlement there. The decision to send an armed force to annex the country and place it under British rule was taken almost on the spur of the moment, on receiving intelligence that France had just such an intention with a view to establishing a penal settlement there. Once it fell into British hands, it became immediately the richest soil for another plantation of Greater Britain.

The non-European possessions in India, the Far East, the West Indies and West Africa presented a different problem. These were initially the field of missionaries and traders, sometimes trade following the Cross, sometimes the Cross following trade; and the British flag following (or sometimes preceding) both. Motives were often so intermingled as to be indistinguishable. The career of Stamford Raffles, the creator of Singapore, illustrates this well. His first mission to the Far East, on behalf of the East India Company during the Napoleonic wars, was both commercial and political – to safeguard British interests against Dutch competition in the area of Java and Malacca, and to take preventive measures in the event of Napoleon going ahead with his stated aim to encircle India. After the war was over, trading priorities came first. Raffles had already conceived the plan to create a great entrepôt in the region of the Straits of Malacca, partly to frustrate Dutch ambitions to control the gateway to the East, but also because he had developed a genuine affection for the people of the Malay states, whose whole standard of life he was striving to raise.

Just before returning to England in November 1823 – a tragic voyage, as it turned out, because his ship caught fire and his priceless specimens and papers were destroyed – he wrote of his work in Singapore to a friend in the East India Company:

> Schools have been set on foot on a very respectable scale, and I trust these moral and religious institutions will be a sufficient counterpoise for the commercial character of the People – and at any rate prevent them from becoming too exclusively commercial ... We shall require more aid from Europe – a dozen good and zealous missionaries would find abundant employment in extending the objects of the Institution ... The Public at Singapore were inclined to entertain a flattering opinion of my Administration there, the Address which was unexpectedly delivered to me ... on the eve of my departure will be a sufficient proof ... At Bencoolen our Schools have succeeded admirably – the Parent School contains upwards of 200 Boys who are trained on the plan of the British and Foreign School Society – and if we do not advance the intellect we shall at any rate teach them discipline and

good habits. If we have no great chance of mending the present generation, we may entertain hopes of doing something for the next, and while I am doing the most I can in sowing the seed I must be content to leave to others the satisfaction of reaping the harvest.[14]

Despite the conviction of cultural superiority, Raffles writes with a moving sincerity. Thirty years later, in 1853, Samuel Wilberforce, Bishop of Oxford, delivered a speech on the link between the Indian Civil Service and the universities. The peroration was duly reported in the papers. Its tone of lofty condescension makes it somewhat uncomfortable to read:

It was not much in the habit of the British people ... to raise magnificent structures as emblems of their power and greatness. It was rather their vocation – and he thought it a higher one – to leave as the impress of their intercourse with inferior nations, marks of moral teaching and religious training, to have made a nation of children see what it was to be men – to have trained mankind in the habits of truth, morality and justice, instead of leaving them in the imbecility of falsehood and perpetual childhood; and above all, to have been instrumental in communicating to them ... that moral superiority, that greatest gift bestowed by God upon ourselves, true faith in His word and true belief in the revelation of His Son.[15]

The Victorians had a very strong sense of mission: not only to proclaim the Christian gospel, but also to civilize peoples of a totally different culture by the inculcation of Western standards and ethics. Much of this was admirably high-minded. Even the much-quoted, and sometimes abused, linking of Christianity and commerce by David Livingstone was totally altruistic, in that he had the specific evil of the slave trade in Central Africa to combat, and there is no evidence that his heroic efforts were directed to anything other than the ultimate good of the Africans themselves. The language of the missionaries and the pioneers can sometimes sound more patronizing and condescending than was actually intended. But moral issues are raised, none the less. It can hardly be condemned as morally indefensible for a missionary to appeal to peoples of a different religion in the hope that he can – following St Paul – 'show them a still more excellent way', provided his motives are sincerely humanitarian and that he is prepared to take the consequences of failure. Equally, it is difficult to condemn an administrator of a subject district if he endeavours to eliminate corruption, however generally accepted it may be among the native people.

Macaulay, for instance, insisted against much opposition on establishing in Bengal an equal system of justice for Indians and Englishmen. Years later, Lord Elgin, as Viceroy, refused to reprieve an English soldier who had murdered an Indian, on the incontestable ground that he would not have reprieved an Indian for the same offence against an Englishman.[16] The law can have no favourites.

Not all British governors of subject peoples will go down in history as models of even-handed justice, however. The accusations against Sir James Brooke, Rajah of Sarawak, who was compelled to face a Commission of Enquiry over his seemingly indiscriminate slaughter of Dyack pirates in 1849, were probably misdirected, as Charles Kingsley always stoutly maintained.[17] The notorious Governor Eyre of Jamaica, who in 1865 ordered a mass execution of demonstrating native peasants, cannot be so easily exonerated. The other side of the picture is that exemplar of sensitivity to the feelings of his subjects, Sir Arthur Gordon, Governor of Fiji, who in 1875 drew up a constitution for responsible government in close co-operation with native representatives. To Gordon it seemed that a dependency should be, as far as possible, treated like a colony. 'The people must be given responsibility, and their institutions must be in accord with their own ideas. Changes must come about in response to local demand, not to the whim of a European Governor or his home government.'[18]

During the 1870s the idea of Empire began to grip the imagination of the British public. It is customary to date the change of mood from the speech delivered by Disraeli at the Crystal Palace on 24 June 1872, two years before he defeated Gladstone at the polls. Disraeli was making an appeal to the working-classes, asserting that they were 'proud of belonging to a great country, and wish to maintain its greatness – that they are proud of belonging to an Imperial country, and are resolved to maintain, if they can, their empire.' But as Robert Blake has pointed out, the references to the Empire appear 'to have been thrown out more or less casually and without any special appreciation of their significance. He barely mentioned India.'[19] Nevertheless he had struck the right note. There were two things above all that the British people wanted in the decades that coincided with the Great Depression: something to feel proud about, and new markets for their goods. Once in office, Disraeli very soon played to this yearning for national pride, especially in his *coup de théâtre* in obtaining for the British government the controlling interest in the French-inspired, and largely French-financed, Suez Canal in 1875 (although Gladstone at once perceived the dangerous aftermath of inevitable entanglements in Egypt). A year later, Disraeli flattered the Queen's own imperialist aspirations by bestowing upon her the title of Empress of India. In 1878 he played a highly risky game by ordering Indian troops to the Mediterranean, not to punish the Turks for the Bulgarian atrocities which had become Gladstone's main preoccupation while out of office, but to threaten war with Russia in order to dissuade the old enemy from another attempt to gain control of Constantinople. At the Congress of Berlin and by the treaty of San Stefano, he seemed to have succeeded in calling everyone's bluff. In the same year, Cyprus was annexed, and British troops were engaged in action in Afghanistan and against the Zulus.

The British public seemed to love it all. As T.H.S. Escott observed in 1885, it pleased the working classes, whose disposition was to favour 'a big England rather than a small',[20] while serving to unite all classes in heady enthusiasm for sabre-rattling.

> An imperial policy not only means abundance of civilian, but regularity of military employment. At the same time that it commends itself to the English mind as a policy worthy of a race which has made its greatness by the sword, it is recognized also as stamped with the more or less avowed approval of the upper classes of English society.[21]

As for the attraction of new markets, H.M. Stanley, who seemed to personify an almost Romantic element in the thrill of exploration in the Dark Continent, knew exactly how to appeal to the commercial interests of the north, while linking his enticements with appropriate moral and religious sentiments. He addressed the Manchester Chamber of Commerce in the following words:

> There are forty millions of people beyond the gateway of the Congo, and the cotton spinners of Manchester are waiting to clothe them. Birmingham foundries are gleaming with the red metal that will presently be made into ironwork for them, and the trinkets that shall adorn those dusky bosoms, and the ministers of Christ are zealous to bring them, the poor benighted heathen, into the Christian fold.[22]

Such language would have driven Cobden into a fit of apoplexy; but before his death he had formed a disciple in his own image: Sir Louis Mallet, who employed an invective as powerful as his master's to warn his countrymen of the folly of 'the attempt to civilise the better part of Africa by missionaries, breech-loaders, and brandy'; and of allowing the intoxication of the acquisition of the Khedive Ismail's Suez Canal shares to drive Britain into the occupation of Egypt.[23]

It was Gladstone's ironical fate that, after his successful onslaught on 'Beaconsfieldism' in his Midlothian campaign and his subsequent return to power in 1880, he was forced by his imperialistic inheritance to initiate or to endorse actions which, in Opposition, he would have hotly denounced. He lost the services of his cabinet colleague John Bright over his decision to bombard Alexandria, an action which was followed by the invasion and occupation of Egypt. He was committed to continued warfare in Afghanistan and to fighting the Boers in the Transvaal, where his forces suffered a disastrous reversal at the battle of Majuba Hill. Mallet's prediction had proved correct. A policy of annexation once embarked upon is carried forward by its own momentum. The bloody insurrection of the Mahdi in the Sudan in 1883 could not be ignored, although it was Gladstone's misfortune that the commander sent out to advise on the military position, General Charles Gordon, chose to ignore his specific instructions, refusing to withdraw from Khartoum. He was killed there after a siege of 320 days, just before the relieving force arrived. Gladstone had to carry the public odium and the unrelenting anger of the Queen. He did not live to see Kitchener's revenge, when he reconquered the Sudan and defeated the Dervish army at Omdurman in 1898.

Africa had, indeed, become the stage of a new imperialism conducted for specific overriding motives: the acquisition of territory, the demonstration of power, the determination to get there first; the so-called 'scramble for Africa', in fact. Some of it was achieved by an agreed shuffling of the available pack by the interested, competing powers of Britain, Germany and France. Britain gained a protectorate over the Niger territories; a special company was chartered to extend British rule in Kenya and Uganda; and again, with Cecil Rhodes as chairman, the British South Africa Company was formed in 1889 to acquire control of Rhodesia. But there were problems not so easily overcome by diplomacy; one of them was the known abundance of gold and diamonds, and – as G.M. Young expressed it – the presence of 'fifty thousand Dutchmen in possession of the land where the gold and diamonds were to be had'.[24]

Full-scale war nearly developed in 1895 after the foolhardy Jameson Raid, a plot hastily conceived by Cecil Rhodes to overturn the rule of the Boers in the Transvaal, and most particularly to secure the gold-mines of the Rand in the area of Johannesburg. The most ominous feature of its failure was the worsening of feelings between Britain and Germany, when it became known that the Kaiser had sent the leader of the Boers, Kruger, a telegram to congratulate him on his victory. Four years elapsed before the Boer War began in earnest, the result of British demands for concessions to the non-Dutch mining settlers in the Transvaal.

What had Britain to show for it all? A vast accumulation of territory had been added to the Queen's dominions – something approaching five million square miles.[25] A degree of national pride had been fostered, which spawned a new descriptive term – 'Jingoism'. It left its mark on the literature of the period, creating almost a new genre, saluted in a review entitled 'The Present State of the Novel' in 1887, by George Saintsbury, in which the writer credited Rider Haggard and Robert Louis Stevenson with the return to 'the pure romance', as distinguished from 'the more complicated kind of novel' of Eliot and her contemporaries with its 'minute manners-painting and refined character analysis'.[26] Here were stirring adventure stories, written by men, to be read by men. G.A. Henty came into his own with titles like *With Clive in India* (1884) and *Through the Sikh Wars* (1894). It is no coincidence that *The Boy's Own Paper* came into being in 1879, the creation of the Religious Tract Society, subtly combining wholesome, manly tales of adventure with barely concealed moral didacticism.

It was not only the Evangelicals, however, who took over the muscular Christianity of Kingsley and Thomas Hughes in order to present it in the guise of highly readable manuals for aspiring Christian empire-builders. Notwithstanding the diminution of the missionary element in 'Jingoism', the same pious conviction that Britain was engaged in a godly work was reiterated by many of the most prominent churchmen of the period. J.E.C. Welldon, Bishop of Calcutta, paid tribute to the imperial spirit as 'a strong and solemn consciousness that the British Empire has been divinely ordered as an instrument of freedom, justice and righteousness'.[27] Brooke Foss Westcott, Bishop of Durham, went even further in expressing the same sentiment. On the South African war, he wrote:

An imperial call has been met by an imperial temper ... God has called us to reign, who welcome the conditions of royalty and reign in Him who reigned from the Cross ... We hold our Empire in the name of Christ.[28]

Maisie Ward recalls the out-and-out 'Jingoism' of Baron von Hügel during the Boer war, and how he wrote to her father, Wilfrid Ward, to assure him that:

I utterly fail to see even a little cloud on the horizon, of a race and empire coming, more favourable to a decent, manly, healthy standard of morality.

The Empire was such a strong power for good, he continued, that the day would surely come when the world would see 'justice and fair play done and shown to all, the Church included'.[29]

Rudyard Kipling seems, by contrast, more measured and temperate in his understanding of the role of the Empire. As Noel Annan has shown, Kipling's shrewd assessment of the behaviour and mores of social groups in India revealed a depth of sociological analysis almost approaching the new methodology of a Weber or a Durkheim. Indians and the English in India were two totally different worlds, so cemented into the conventions and mentality of their groups that inter-communication between them could only be at the most superficial level.[30] India might have been the 'white man's burden', but the real weight of the burden was the inability of the British to do other than patronize those over whom they were set to rule. One exception, as Clive Dewey has shown, belongs to the twentieth century: Sir Malcolm Darling, who rose to distinction in the Indian Civil Service. Like so many before him, he was a product of the public schools (educated at Eton, and King's), but unlike the mass of them, he was convinced that racial misunderstanding amounting to racial hatred lay at the root of the problems of the British Raj. 'He believed ... the Indians yearned for affection, only Englishmen were too inhibited to respond to their longing.'[31]

A passage from Lady Wilson's *Letters from India* (1911) makes the same point from her own observation:

An Indian said to me once, 'If the Sahibs would only talk to us about them-selves. We are a sentimental people. We could be so easily influenced, if they would only tell us what they think and feel, and let us understand their ideal.' 'That will never do,' I assured him. 'You may guess what they think by what you see them do. They will work for you and die for you, and if you were to cut them up, you would certainly find India written on their hearts. But they won't talk about it, and if they were more emotional and did, they would have different natures and lose something by the exchange.'[32]

John Robert Seeley, Charles Kingsley's successor as Regius Professor of History at Cambridge, has not received much attention from his posterity. He is chiefly remembered for his attempt to write a life of Christ in the book *Ecce Homo*, published anonymously in 1865, which caused much affront to Evangelicals but was so admired by Gladstone that he secured Seeley's appointment to the Regius chair. In 1883 he published his *Expansion of England*, which became a best-seller – 80,000 copies were sold within two years. It claimed that England's history pointed clearly to an exhilarating destiny, hers for the taking if she would only discard the outdated parochialism of looking inwards at the superior virtues of her constitution – a palpable hit at Macaulay – and resolve instead to look outwards to the 'extension of the English name into the other countries of the globe, the foundation of Greater Britain'. India hardly came at all into his reckoning. He looked rather to the white colonies – to Canada, South Africa and Australasia – as the future 'United States of Greater Britain'.[33] If she failed to follow the direction in which her past history was clearly pointing, Britain would sink into the position of Sweden or Spain, once great powers, but left now with only dim memories of what glory had meant.

Lord Rosebery swallowed this whole; and so did Joseph Chamberlain, who became Colonial Secretary under Lord Salisbury in 1895, interpreting Seeley's vision as the eventual apotheosis of Anglo-Saxon virtues:

> I believe in this race [he proclaimed], the greatest governing race the world
> has ever seen; in this Anglo-Saxon race, so proud, tenacious, self-confident
> and determined, this race which neither climate nor change can degener-
> ate, which will infallibly be the predominant force of future history and uni-
> versal civilisation.

Alfred Cobban, who quotes this passage, sees in it a touch of pseudo-Darwinism;[34] it is certainly a glorification of power-politics which could never again be so stridently proclaimed after the reversals and frustrations of the Boer war.

To give Seeley his due: however one might question his conclusions, he was saying to his generation that if they wanted to comprehend their role in the wider world – to be able to discern their position in the world picture – it was not sufficient to confine their observation to looking inwards or to looking outwards. A historian should look before in order to be able to look after. The formation of a world picture, then, required a reading of the past.

CHAPTER 3

Looking Before and After

I

'We went to a free library ... By reference to the records I was able to see that *Lives* of Nelson and Wellington, and works of theology, are the favourite reading.'

Hippolyte Taine, *Notes on England*

How can an informed picture of the world one lives in be acquired without some understanding of what has gone before? Any investigation into the reading habits of Victorians of almost every degree of literacy suggests that J.R. Seeley was preaching to the converted. Commenting on the popularity of Charles Kingsley's lectures in Cambridge in the 1850s and of Thomas Arnold's at Oxford in the early 1840s (in their respective roles as Regius Professors of History), John Kenyon has concluded that 'there was an enormous appetite for history in Victorian England, and a new belief in its significance.'[1] As early as 1832, *Chambers's Edinburgh Journal* published its first issue, claiming that it had been brought into being by the spirit of the age which seemed to be clamouring to know more about the world in all its aspects.

The grand leading principle of this paper [the Editor wrote] is to take advantage of the universal appetite for instruction which at present exists: to supply to that appetite food of the best kind, and in such form and at such a price, as must suit the convenience of *every man in the British dominions*.[2]

The enquiring spirit, then, was by no means confined to history. There was, for instance, a burgeoning curiosity in all matters scientific, little gratified by formal education except in Dissenting academies and the medical schools of Scotland; and, what may seem surprising to a more secular age, an insatiable yearning for edification through religious and theological instruction. The Victorians seemed to thrive on sermons: at second best, through reading them, but best of all by drinking in the eloquence of the spoken word.

The stamina of the Victorians in their absorption of pulpit oratory almost defies belief. Gladstone in 1837 recalled a dinner with Sir Robert Peel when a church bookseller, by the name of Collins, assured him that 'no sermon ought ever to fall short of an hour, for in less time than that it was not possible to explain any text of the Holy Scripture'.[3] That this was regarded as par for the course is confirmed by an occurrence one Sunday morning on the Marquess of Bute's yacht *Ladybird*, when the passengers found that there was no minister present to preach a sermon. They therefore agreed that, instead, there should be read 'some immense bit of Scripture, e.g. the whole Epistle to the Romans'.[4] But a popular preacher could safely exceed an hour. In 1824 Edward Irving preached the annual sermon of the London Missionary Society. He allowed two pauses for hymn-singing, to enable him to rest his voice, because the whole sermon lasted three and a half hours. R.W. Dale's predecessor at Carr's Lane Independent Meeting House in Birmingham (John Angell Jones) emulated this feat of oratory, revived at times by oranges pelted into the pulpit to provide necessary lubrication. The 210–minute sermon was delivered from memory, with occasional promptings from his brother who sat beside the preacher in the capacious pulpit with the manuscript on his knee.[5]

What is even more extraordinary is the stamina of the preacher himself, and his ability to cope with the strain of projecting his voice (there being no efficient means of amplification) to ensure that his words were heard by a vast congregation. The capacity of the new Pomona Hall in Manchester, for instance – built for just such occasions – was said to be 20,000.[6] The celebrated Baptist preacher C.H. Spurgeon was prepared to address huge audiences, numbering as many as eight thousand, in the open air in Vauxhall Gardens. Young Lord Amberley, aged 13, was present on one of these occasions, and reported in his diary: 'A very wonderful preacher. He is a dissenter of some kind ... His sermon was very good, and very curious.'[7] It did not, however, protect Amberley from his declension into agnosticism in later life.

There seemed to be no inhibitions about eclecticism in either attending or reading sermons. Gladstone, while an undergraduate at Christ Church, with his friend Francis Doyle risked rustication in order to hear Thomas Chalmers preach at Dissenting chapels on two separate occasions. They also broke bounds to hear Rowland Hill. 'The most adventurous thing I ever did at Oxford,' Doyle recalled.[8] It was no unusual thing to find copies of Newman's *Parochial and Plain Sermons* on the shelves of Nonconformist ministers, or the Broad Church sermons of F.W. Robertson in Evangelical households. High Churchmen and Evangelicals alike studied with profit the work of the leading Unitarian of his day, James Martineau – *Hours of Thought on Sacred Things*.[9] Walter Bagehot, the son of a Unitarian, took a volume of F.D. Maurice's sermons with him on his honeymoon to read aloud to his wife of an evening.[10]

Public lectures were considered a popular form of entertainment as well as instruction. When one embarked upon a series of such lectures for the first time, it was customary to ensure a large and, if possible, prestigious audience by soliciting for subscriptions in advance. In 1837 Carlyle made his first appearance on a public platform in London with a course on German literature. Even though he had just published his *French Revolution*, he still felt it necessary to advertise for subscribers some time beforehand.[11] Again, an audience required substantial length for their money's-worth. It is almost refreshing, however, to learn from the diary of Kate Stanley (Lady Amberley) that when she and her husband went to Manchester in January 1867 to hear Goldwin Smith give a lecture on Cromwell which lasted an hour and forty-five minutes, she found her patience sorely tried. 'I could hardly keep my eyes open,' she admitted.[12]

What does this all tell us? It speaks of a need felt by people at the time; and once a need is identified or articulated, literature will be produced to gratify it. Mark Pattison expressed it thus: 'Literature is simply the form in which the existing opinions of a country are registered. It is palpably a product and measure of the intellectual attainment of a people, not its source.'[13]

This is a generalization and, as such, will not always serve. Thomas Carlyle, for instance, delighted to shock his public and to shake it out of its complacency with works like *Past and Present* and *Chartism*; rather less successfully with *Sartor Resartus*, because the book's idiosyncratic clothes symbolism was beyond the comprehension of most readers. Kingsley, however, while intending to awaken social consciences with his *Alton Locke* and *Yeast*, was deliberately addressing a constituency which he knew was waiting for its own anxieties to be articulated. As he expressed it in *Yeast*: 'In the following pages, I have attempted to show what some at least of the young in these days are really thinking and feeling.'[14] Harriet Beecher Stowe had a definite purpose in her *Uncle Tom's Cabin*, but its sensational impact suggests that practically none of her English readers had previously given any thought to the plight of the slaves on the cotton plantations of America's southern states.

If Pattison had confined his observation to the relatively new phenomenon of the periodical or magazine, there would be less cause to quibble. Each publication tended to have a well-defined constituency to foster and nourish, according to its political colour or prejudice. *The Edinburgh Review*, the oldest, served the Whig–Liberal interest; *The Quarterly Review*, the Tory and Anglican; the *Westminster Review* was the organ of the Philosophical Radicals. Each religious denomination, too, had its own particular mouthpiece; and then there were those aimed at a less intellectual clientele, with a definite emphasis on entertainment, like *Bentley's Magazine*, *Once a Week* and Dickens' *Household Words*. But in the 1850s and 1860s – as John Gross has shown – 'an unprecedented number of serious journals of opinion managed to strike root and prosper.'[15] *The Saturday Review* (launched in 1855) led the way, with such distinguished writers and scholars as Henry Maine and Fitzjames Stephen as regular contributors. In the same decade *The Spectator* was transformed under the editorship of R.H. Hutton and Meredith Townsend. These were organs of literary significance, if not without their particular prejudices. *The Saturday Review* was no friend to Disraeli or to John Bright; and 'their pet victims were hot-gospellers, demagogues, sentimental novelists.'[16]

Major developments in printing technology – especially the introduction of the rotary press in the 1860s – and the gradual abolition of such taxes as advertisement duty (removed in 1853), stamp duty (in 1855) and the paper duty (in 1861), led to a vastly-increased range, as well as circulation, of newspapers, again directed to particular sections of the community. The number of provincial papers increased from 200 in 1846 to 750 in 1865; and the quality of some of the older-established provincial papers, like *The Scotsman*, the *Manchester Guardian*, the *Liverpool*

Daily Post, and the *Birmingham Daily Post* was such that it was an ill-founded concept of Londoners to suppose that the nation's opinions were manufactured or registered in the metropolis.[17] The literate among the working class might have had neither time nor money to spend on a 'daily' but there is evidence that, at least by the 1840s, many were regular readers of the Sunday papers.[18]

Opinion-forming, they were; but also opinion-confirming. As Owen Chadwick has written: 'To articulate opinion is not to create it. Nor is it to leave it as it was. Men understand their opinions better when they articulate them ... But newspapers also followed opinion.'[19] This meant that, while controversy and criticism were (and still are) the life-blood of the press, there was always a point beyond which it was dangerous to proceed if a paper were to retain its particular reading public. It had to be sensitive to Christian susceptibilities; and when it revealed public scandals and indulged in forthright invective (the Victorian press was never mealy-mouthed), it had to choose objects of derision that appealed to the prejudices of its clientele. The tendency, however, was to disparage rather than to praise. The Queen therefore hated the press. Journalists were not to be received at Court. They had been known to leak confidential information passed between herself and her ministers.[20] *The Times* had dared in 1861 to vilify Germany, and her even more beloved Prussia.[21] The stock-in-trade of the press, she told her uncle in 1854, was abuse. 'Abuse is somewhat the *staff of life in England,* everything, everybody is to be abused; it is a pity, as nothing more unproductive as this everlasting abuse can well be imagined.'[22] It was to get no better as the century progressed. In *New Grub Street* (1891), George Gissing deplored the first manifestations of the 'gutter press', feeding the uncultivated and jejune sentiments of the barely literate, 'the great new generation that is being turned out by the Board Schools, the young men and women who can just read, but are incapable of sustained attention.'[23]

Actually the illiteracy rate among the working classes was falling fast, even before W.E. Forster's 1870 Education Act. According to the Registrar-General's returns, it was calculated that in 1845, 33 per cent of the male population of the United Kingdom were illiterate and 49 per cent of the female. The 1851 Census revealed a slight drop to 31 per cent and 45 per cent respectively (although it also revealed that out of 29,425 private schoolmasters and mistresses, 708 were unable to sign their names). In 1871 the illiteracy figures had fallen to 19 per cent of males and 26 per cent of females.[24] R.K. Webb's researches, confined to England, present a rather less gloomy picture. There was considerable variation in the statistics, depending upon both geographical and economic factors. Railway workers, for instance, in the 1840s, had one of the highest illiteracy rates, compared to the handloom weavers with one of the lowest. Not surprisingly, many more could read than could both read and write. The normal test of literacy was the ability to read a passage from the Bible. On the basis of this test, Webb writes, 'the commonest figure of literacy for the forties would seem to hover about two-thirds to three-quarters of the working classes, perhaps nearer the latter than the former.' He therefore concluded:

> Some degree of literacy must have been nearly universally diffused in the portion of the working classes which made up the great political potential in English society – that terrifying unknown quantity which was to be educated for political life, or, in another view, to be educated to be quiet.[25]

What, then, did the literate working classes read? At the lowest level, a man who could just stumble through a passage in the Bible could cope with broadsheets and popular ballads. There were sensational penny weeklies, like the *People's Police Gazette*, and a whole host of penny novelettes, intended to be 'elevated and impassioned', with titles such as *Alice Horne, or the Revenge of the Blighted One*, and *Ada the Betrayed*.[26] In a respectable working-class house, where books were precious and there was a genuine desire to advance through self-education, the standard works to be seen on the shelf would be the Bible, Shakespeare, Milton and Bunyan.[27] Moving up the social scale, one might find a bookcase rather than a shelf, and Dickens would be there, Tennyson and Longfellow, perhaps some Bulwer Lytton and Macaulay.[28] One self-educated Mancunian read the five volumes of Macaulay's history aloud to his neighbours, and sent the author a vote of thanks 'for having written a history which working men can understand'.[29]

The autodidact was by no means a rarity in Victorian England. Books were written to help him in his quest for knowledge: Cassells' *Popular Educator*, for instance, or *The Pursuit of Knowledge under Difficulties*. If one wanted further guidance, a sort of unofficial preceptor might be found in the local secondhand bookseller.[30] A particularly popular manual of curiosities to satisfy interest in some of the amazing and wonderful phenomena of the universe was John Timbs' *Things not Generally Known*, published in 1859. Its instant success prompted Timbs to produce a sequel. Clearly John Stuart Mill was sufficiently aware of a thirst for serious reading among the humbler elements of society for him to resolve not to take royalties from the cheaper editions of his works, so that they could be priced within the reach of the working classes.[31]

E.E. Kellett recalled, as a young man in the 1880s, meeting an auto-didact face to face. He was travelling by train in a crowded compart-ment. As another passenger attempted to find a seat, his neighbour – a pork-butcher by trade – called out: 'There's no room except on the rack.' Kellett could not resist an apposite Shakespearean quotation, feeling a little pompous as he voiced it: 'I fear you speak upon the rack, where men enforced do speak anything.' The pork-butcher's face lit up. 'That's Portia,' he said.[32]

With the steady increase of literacy during the century, the Victorian consumption of books reached a peak never even contemplated before and probably never exceeded since. After all, there was little else to do of an evening, before the advent of radio and television; and with dinner as early as five o'clock, the evenings were long. While the ladies of the house were knitting or sewing, they would listen to a book being read aloud. Publishers and authors clearly bore this in mind. *The Spectator* was launched in 1828 for family reading in the upper middle class. Pious households would share the daily (including Sundays) instalments of John Kitto's *Daily Bible Illustrations*. Examples of the range of literature mutually enjoyed or absorbed can be easily cited because so often recorded in diaries and journals. John Bright, shortly after his marriage to his second wife, Elizabeth Leatham, read her the whole of *The Merchant of Venice* one evening, taking all the parts himself.[33] Ruskin, in *Praeterita*, recalled evening readings from Byron by his parents.[34] The young Arthur Stanley, staying with Augustus and Julius Hare at Hurstmonceux Rectory, shortly after leaving Rugby, was enchanted by having read to him each evening 'things which I should not be likely to read – Wordsworth, Charles Lamb, Coleridge, Milton's prose etc., and (oh, tell it not in the streets of Gath!) Alfred Tennyson.'[35]

Kate Stanley's reading was severely monitored by her mother. She begged to be allowed to read *The Mill on the Floss* ('an odious book,' her mother rejoined), and eventually was permitted to read the first two volumes only, so that she should remain in ignorance of Maggie Tulliver's fall from grace. When she married Lord Amberley, however, she was introduced to more demanding fare. He read aloud to her Goethe's *Wilhelm Meister* – in German.[36] Charles Darwin preferred to be read to, rather than read aloud himself. When the day's work was over, he listened to novels. There was one stipulation, however. They had to have a happy ending.[37]

Among the highly-educated, literary and political circles, intellectual debate was a favourite occupation in a variety of *conversazioni*, more or less formal as the case might be, but often tending to command an exclusiveness which made membership a greatly coveted mark of social prestige. One of the earliest of these closed societies was 'The Apostles', founded in Cambridge in the 1830s, the leading lights being F.D. Maurice, John Sterling, Tennyson, Connop Thirlwall and Richard Monckton Milnes. As many of these men gravitated to London they formed a rather larger circle, although still exclusive, dating from 1838, first called the Anonymous Club – later, the Sterling Club – in which the Cambridge nucleus was augmented by notables such as Carlyle, Julius Hare, Thomas Arnold and Samuel Wilberforce, pretentiously describing themselves as 'the witty, the wise, and the inspired'.[38] Holland House became the successor to Lansdowne House as the regular headquarters of literary soirées, to which groups of interesting and witty talkers were invited – Sydney Smith, the wittiest of them all, being the particularly favoured guest.

'Breakfast parties', pioneered by Samuel Rogers at his house in St James's Place and soon followed by Monckton Milnes in his chambers at 26 Pall Mall, became the vogue. These usually began at ten and continued until noon, and were often the preferred conversational relaxation of politicians, who – when the House was sitting – could less easily escape for an evening engagement. Milnes especially rejoiced in his selection of guests to ensure both acknowledged distinction and stimulating discussion. The mistake was to invite Macaulay and Carlyle to the same party, because both expected to monopolize the conversation, and tempers could become frayed. The same names of allegedly scintillating talkers would crop up among the guests at the salons of Lady Ashburton or the soirées of Charles Brookfield and his wife (where Thackeray was a favourite, eventually becoming Mrs Brookfield's lover).

'Talking-shops' of one sort or another seemed to proliferate in the middle and late years of the century: sometimes radiating around a literary figure of distinction, like the cosmopolitan gatherings hosted by George Eliot and G.H. Lewes; sometimes new élitist bands of intellectuals, like the Old Mortality Society at Oxford with T.H. Green, Swinburne, A.V. Dicey, James Bryce and Walter Pater prominent members. The 'Sunday Tramps', who met together to discuss questions of the day over formidably strenuous walks in the London area, were a group of largely like-minded lawyers and agnostics (F.W. Maitland, Frederick Pollock, Leslie Stephen and others). The short-lived Metaphysical Society, founded by James Knowles, was very definitely not for the like-minded, its intention being to bring together for intellectual debate the most distinguished representatives of different cultural and religious traditions.

Almost all these talking-shops died with the century that had brought them into being. G.W.E. Russell dated the end of breakfast parties to the disappearance from the political scene of Gladstone.[39] Certainly the Grand Old Man took great pleasure in bringing to Hawarden, for weekend parties, an interesting assortment of guests. In 1878, for instance, determined to make the acquaintance of Ruskin, who had written some disparaging comments about him in *Fors Clavigera*, Gladstone succeeded in persuading him to stay for a weekend in the company of – among others – Henry Scott Holland, Lord Acton and Alfred Lyttelton. If one were to choose this as a test case to discover what significant results accrued from the meeting of great minds on social occasions, it has to be conceded that they failed to put the world to rights. All those present at this eagerly-awaited confrontation recorded their impressions subsequently. Many controversial topics were discussed, and – in the end – Gladstone and Ruskin parted on amicable terms, Ruskin even agreeing to expunge the offending passage in *Fors*. They had found themselves in total agreement, however, on one issue only: they both strongly disapproved of competitive rowing at Oxford.[40]

Gladstone, we are told, read some 20,000 books in the course of his life:[41] an incredible feat, even if he had had nothing else to do. Of the non-Classical authors, he derived most profit – he said – from Joseph Butler and Dante.[42] He was in good company here, among the Victorian *literati*. Dante, largely through Coleridge's proselytism, was

virtually rediscovered in the nineteenth century, and by their own testimony proved a source of inspiration to prominent figures in church
and state of very different leanings. Macaulay's respect for Dante
bordered on adulation;[43] F.D. Maurice,[44] R.W. Church[45] and D.G.
Rossetti[46] felt the same. Tennyson – according to Michael Wheeler –
derived his understanding of the nature of divine love, as expressed in
In Memoriam, from his reading of Dante.[47] F.W. Robertson was so moved
by the *Inferno*, which he read in 1845, that he committed the whole of
it to memory.[48]

That Gladstone and Tennyson shared the same enthusiasm comes as
no surprise; but it is interesting that when John Morley once asked
Gladstone to select his favourite line in poetry, he chose nothing of
Tennyson's. He toyed with Wordsworth's 'Or hear old Triton blow his
wreathed horn', but eventually gave the palm to Milton. Unfortunately
when Morley came to record the conversation he had forgotten the line
in question, so posterity will never know.[49] Nevertheless, among the
literary luminaries of the mid-Victorian period Tennyson was beginning to displace Wordsworth, who died in 1850, the year of the publication of *In Memoriam*. His rating slightly slipped in 1855 when *Maud*
appeared, causing many furrowed brows. The young Robert Browning
was much more difficult to fathom, however. *Sordello* was practically
incomprehensible. What possible meaning, asked R.H. Hutton, could
be attached to the 'curious mob of pronouns and verbs' in the
parenthetical lines 'To be by him themselves made act/ Nor watch
Sordello acting each of them'?[50] Browning had to wait until 1868 (the
year of publication of *The Ring and the Book*) for his reputation to tran-
scend that of his wife, who died in 1861. Thereafter Browning Societies
began to spring up like mushrooms in the night. The most widely
reprinted poem in the English language, however, while belonging to
this period, was neither Tennyson's nor Browning's: it was Matthew
Arnold's *Dover Beach*.[51]

This may cause one to hesitate over producing a ranking for mid-
Victorian novelists – the golden age for that genre, as it surely was. Amy
Cruse has offered one, although it is not entirely clear on what basis she
made the assessment. In the first rank come Dickens, Thackeray,
Charlotte Brontë and George Eliot; in the second, Trollope, Kingsley
and Elizabeth Gaskell.[52] This is a difficult and dubious game to play. If
one takes immediate popular impact, where does one put the works of

a prolific writer whose books have not stood the test of time, like Charlotte Yonge? *The Daisy Chain* and *The Heir of Redclyffe* attracted an enormous following. How does one rate a writer like Thomas Hughes, who produced very little, yet scored a sensational success with *Tom Brown's Schooldays*?

There would seem to be little doubt, however, that Dickens had no rival in popularity. As Walter Bagehot put it, 'there is no contemporary writer whose works are read so generally through the whole house, who can give pleasure to the servants as well as the mistress, to the children as well as to the master.'[53] The approbation was not universal. Gladstone, for instance, disapproved of *Nicholas Nickleby* because 'there is no Church in the book, and the motives are not those of religion'.[54] He thought more kindly of Dickens after reading *Dombey and Son*. Perhaps it was the death of young Paul Dombey that did the trick. As Thackeray said, after reading that poignant passage: 'There's no writing against this ... It's stupendous.'[55] Sarah Gamp in *Martin Chuzzlewit* and Sam Weller in *Pickwick* were the Victorians' favourite characters. William Morris and a group of friends played a game of 'Twenty Questions' while on an excursion on the Thames. A vociferous dispute broke out when the question 'is it abstract or concrete?' was put to one of their number who had elected to be Sarah Gamp's 'friend, Mrs Harris'.[56] The result of the argument is not known.

The reading market was immeasurably enlarged by the business perspicacity of the shrewd pioneer of the subscription lending library, Charles Edward Mudie, who in 1840 opened a little shop in King Street, Bloomsbury, charging a guinea for an annual subscription to borrow books, limited to one book at a time. He was forced to move to larger premises in New Oxford Street in 1852, when his list of subscribers had risen to 25,000. By 1861, because of the huge turnover of books, he moved yet again, to a specially constructed edifice with a capacity for holding 800,000 volumes. W.H. Smith made a fortune for himself by appreciating the need of railway passengers for recreational or purposeful reading matter to while away the tedium of their journeys. He began the experiment in 1846; and by 1862 he had bookstalls operating on almost every important line, passengers borrowing a book at their station of departure, on payment of a deposit which would be repaid, less a small deduction, on the book's return. Both Mudie (a strong Evangelical) and W.H. Smith (a Methodist) imposed their own censorship to ensure that nothing on offer could offend their public's sense of decency or religious susceptibilities.[57]

Mudie bought in bulk: two thousand copies of Livingstone's *Travels* in 1857, for instance; five hundred copies of *Adam Bede* in 1859. Some of his chosen authors had a sensational turnover, especially Wilkie Collins with *A Woman in White* and *The Moonstone*. Ouida was boosted to fame and prosperity by Mudie, her books sometimes read by the most improbable borrowers. Burne-Jones recalled with amusement the sight of Cardinal Manning and John Ruskin 'routing on their knees amongst some books' to find a copy of Ouida's *The Dog of Flanders*.[58]

The distribution of Mudie's titles is interesting. Among the new acquisitions of 1859 fiction predominated, as one might expect, accounting for 44 per cent of the total. History and biography followed in second place, at 28 per cent. Travel and adventure came third, at 13 per cent.[59] The withdrawals from Free Libraries (a useful indication of the tastes of studious working men) also confirm the high rating of history, and of historical biography in particular. In 1862, Hippolyte Taine visited the Free Library in Manchester. 'By reference to the records', he wrote, 'I was able to see that *Lives* of Nelson and Wellington, and works of theology, are the favourite reading.'[60] The particular choice of historical biography is significant. Two years earlier, an undergraduate giving evidence before a Royal Commission was asked the question, 'What books did you read at school?' His answer was 'Scott, Dickens, Macaulay, Tennyson; Kingsley, of course.'[61] This gives a score of three out of five for historians or writers of historical romances. Kingsley came last in the list, but the 'of course' signified that he really should have come first. The young man had been inspired by *Westward Ho!*

One conclusion, at least, can be drawn from all this. While the Victorians formed a picture of the world they lived in by their observation of their times, that picture was inevitably coloured by the sort of books that they chose to read. They wanted to know what had gone before them, and also what the future might bring. There seems, however, to have been a particular yearning for the heroic. Fashions and attitudes change over the years. The opening verses of the forty-fourth chapter of Ecclesiasticus are not read at church services today as often as they used to be; the Victorians, by contrast, had no reservations at all in declaiming 'Let us now praise famous men'.

II

'Great men are profitable company.'

Carlyle, *On Heroes*

One day in 1803 the young Edward Hawkins (he was only 14 at the time) took a walk up Holborn, and suddenly became aware of an excited crowd in the streets. Hearing a ripple of applause, he looked round about him to discover the reason. Then he saw on the opposite pavement an officer in naval uniform, whose features were vaguely familiar. He had only one arm. It was none other than Lord Nelson. Not unnaturally, the youngster felt a thrill of excitement. And then something spoilt it for him. 'I saw', he said, 'that he liked it.'[1]

Many of that crowd doubtless lived into the Victorian age to tell the tale, although few perhaps were as shrewdly observant as the future Provost of Oriel. They had seen a hero of history. Since the Duke of Wellington survived until September 1852, there will have been many more with cherished memories of seeing the victor of Waterloo walking or riding in the street, sharing the opinion of their Queen that they had lived to see 'the GREATEST MAN this country ever produced'.[2] There were good grounds for a feeling of exhilaration at the consciousness that one was living at a time when one did not have to wait for the judgement of posterity to know that the world was peopled with great men; and that greatness was not confined to warriors who had achieved notable victories on land or sea.

> Young men in 1850 [G.M. Young wrote in an essay on 'The Victorian Noontime'], reading with the proper avidity of youth, could have found most of their tastes, and most of their curiosities, satisfied by masterpieces published, since their birth, by men who had been pointed out to them in the streets. To watch Mr Macaulay threading his way through the Piccadilly traffic, book in hand; to see Mr Dickens running up the steps of the Athenaeum; to recognize the Laureate by his cloak and Mr Carlyle by his shawl, were the peculiar joys of that time. The stone-cutter by the Tiber, chipping out 'Carmen composuit Q. Horatius Flaccus' on the memorial of the Secular Games, must have had the same feeling that he too was living in a great age, peopled with Immortals.[3]

There was more to this than mere acknowledgement of the status of certain individual men of genius, who happened to be living at the time.

It was as if the age, and especially the early decades of the nineteenth century, still so powerfully influenced by the spirit of Romanticism, both yearned for hero-worship and sought the evidence of the titanic wherever it might be found. Contemporaries were viewed and described in terms larger than life. The prevailing mood in the 1820s and 1830s at Oxford and Cambridge, for instance, was one of vibrant expectation. Theirs was a chosen generation in whose hands lay the opportunity and the talent to achieve momentous things. This was partly the result of the introduction of class lists, which enabled the evidence of superior intellect to be publicly displayed, thereby fostering a fierce competitive spirit the like of which had never been seen before.

The will to succeed, and to be seen to have succeeded, was manifested in areas other than the academic. Oratorical feats in the newly-founded Oxford and Cambridge Unions would establish one's credentials as a budding statesman (the future Cardinal Manning was heralded as a Prime Minister in the making after his first sensational triumph in the Oxford Union in 1829). Superior physical prowess could be publicly demonstrated at Lord's, where Oxford and Cambridge met for the first time at a cricket match in 1827, or at Henley, for the first Boat Race in 1828. Those who recalled those stirring days described the achievements of their fellows in titanic terms. There was J.B. Mozley's triumph in the Oriel Fellowship examination, for instance, when – during the essay paper – he sat motionless for hours while other candidates scribbled busily away. Then, at the last moment, he flung himself down on the floor to catch the light from the dying embers of the fire, to write an essay of only ten lines. Those 'ten lines were such as no other man in Oxford could have written', it was said; at any rate, he duly received the prize.[4]

Perhaps this was a favoured generation. William Tuckwell had no doubts. Writing of Oxford at the beginning of the 1830s, he observed:

> Never in the history of the University has a decade opened and progressed amid a group so brilliant. In 1830 we have Gladstone, Liddell, Charles Wordsworth, Hope, T. Acland, Manning, Church, Halford Vaughan, William Adams, Walter Hamilton, Lords Dalhousie, Elgin, Lincoln, Canning, to take names almost at random ... At Cambridge in the very same year gathered ... Spedding, Thompson, Brookfield, Trench, Tennyson, Monckton Milnes, Charles Buller, Merivale, Arthur Hallam.[5]

The point to be made is that they sensed that they had a power to shape the future. J.E. Baker has suggested a parallel with fifth-century Athens.[6]

Dean Church compared the atmosphere of Oxford in the 1830s to the period of the Florentine Renaissance.[7] Both, however, in their analogies, were perceiving features which those earlier periods of cultural dynamism had in common with the Romantic movement: especially the cult of personality, the sense of release from the blinkered vision of the generations that had preceded them, and an intense faith in the power of the human will, ministering to the spirit of jubilant individualism. How else can one explain the self-conscious attitudinizing and unashamed self-dramatization of so many of this generation? They could not resist writing about themselves. When Wordsworth completed the first draft of *The Prelude* in 1805, he conceded that it was 'a thing unprecedented in literary history that a man should talk so much about himself'.[8]

A whole host of autobiographies were to follow. Quite the most self-important was Charles Wordsworth's *Annals of my Early Life* (1891), written – at his own admission – 'to renew and deepen my thankfulness for the numberless mercies I have received from the Giver of all good'.[9] The text, however, suggests that his unremitting catalogue of early achievements was published in order to establish that he deserved better in later life than the modest distinction of becoming Bishop of St Andrew's, Dunkeld and Dunblane. J.S. Mill's *Autobiography* and Ruskin's *Praeterita* were attempts to chart the subject's mental history, although it could be said of both that the studied omissions aroused more interest than the chosen revelations. At least one of these public soul-searchings achieved the status of a classic of the English language: Newman's *Apologia pro Vita Sua;* and although it is not without an element of self-indulgence, Newman had a perfect excuse for writing about himself, having had the motives for his conversion to Rome so viciously challenged by Charles Kingsley. Ruskin's account in *Praeterita* of his successive 'conversions' – the sight of the aspen-tree at Fontainebleau in 1842, and of a picture by Veronese in Turin in 1858 – have a characteristic period quality about them: the Romantic compulsion to see episodes in one's life as scenes of intense dramatic moment leading to a sort of rebirth; almost as if providence, or the hand of God, had intervened to give to this or that man of genius an experience equivalent to what once had happened on the Damascus road.

It was not only the great and famous who were given to self-dramatization. Found on the body of a young cabinet maker, killed in the

Chartist rising in Newport in 1839, was a letter to be delivered to his mother. It read:

> I shall this night be engaged in a struggle for freedom and if it pleases God to spare my life I shall see you soon but if not do not grieve for me. I shall fall in a noble cause.[10]

Poor young hero, whose praises were unsung. Not so, however, the revered Headmaster of Rugby, whose sudden death in June 1842 endowed Thomas Arnold with heroic stature even before Arthur Stanley's biography elevated him to sainthood. A.C. Tait was so overcome by the thought of succeeding him that he wrote to Stanley: 'The responsibility of such a situation seems to me every day more awful'; and when he heard of his election, he wrote in his diary: 'When entering on this situation, let no worldly thoughts deceive me. The sudden death of him whom I succeed should be enough to prevent this.' Stanley's letter of congratulation to Tait began with the words, 'The awful intelligence of your election has just reached me ... '[11]

When the Brookfields heard of the death of Thackeray in December 1863, the hallowed tone of their tribute failed to suppress a possibly unintended acknowledgement of a trace of greatness in themselves:

> The great men of these days were wonderful, not merely in their works, but in their lives and their friendships. It was not a pose of the time to stand alone in solitary grandeur, or to turn aside to centres where they perforce must shine; they preferred and received the society of the talented; they lived surrounded by intellect and were plied and fed upon it, and if that in which they became steeped had not always the nature or the calibre of their own genius, it still had something in it that stimulated, and even sometimes assisted to polish their own thoughts.[12]

The Victorians were brought up to reverence heroes. As 'the stranger' observed to Coningsby in Disraeli's novel, 'To believe in the heroic makes heroes.'[13] Carlyle put it thus: 'Universal History, the history of what man has accomplished in this world, is at bottom the History of the Great Men who have worked here ... Great Men ... are profitable company.'[14] He then supplied a curious bede-roll. Having asserted that hero-worship is 'the germ of Christianity itself',[15] he offered the names of David (not faultless but given to repentance), followed by Mahomet (because of his freedom from cant). Then came Dante, because of his intensity; Shakespeare, the model of 'joyful tranquillity'; Luther, a man of 'unsubduable granite'; John Knox, because he was 'honest-hearted and brotherly'; Dr Johnson, Rousseau and Robert Burns, for reasons not quite clear; and Napoleon and Cromwell, the first because he was the ideal 'strong man' as king, and the second because 'he grappled like a giant, face to face, heart to heart, with the naked truth of things'.[16]

In 1849, the Pre-Raphaelite Brotherhood drew up a list of its heroes: 'The Immortals'. It was pyramid-shaped, with Christ at the apex, and Shakespeare and the author of the Book of Job immediately below. A strange assortment followed: Dante was there, as one might expect, and many contemporary men of letters along with historical figures like King Alfred and George Washington. Interestingly, heroines were not included. Charlotte Yonge offered a bede-roll of her own in her *Book of Golden Deeds*, written to encourage young people to emulate acts of heroism and self-sacrifice. John Ruskin, in *The Crown of Wild Olive*, gave the following advice to the officer cadets at the Royal Artillery Institution at Woolwich in 1869:

> Exactly in the degree in which you can find creatures greater then yourself, to look up to, in that degree you are ennobled yourself, and, in that degree, happy. If you could live always in the presence of archangels, you would be happier than in that of men. .... Thus all real joy and power of progress in humanity depend on finding something to reverence, and all the baseness and misery of humanity begin in a habit of disdain.[17]

Of all the Victorian didactic writers, the most forceful and the most emphatic in their understanding of the nature of the heroic ideal were Thomas Carlyle and Charles Kingsley. Both had a predilection for strong men – the hero-king, the great man who appeared in times of darkness to deliver the people from chaos; and as each of them advanced in age, so their heroes tended to become more robust, physical and even brutal. Walter Houghton has suggested that the chief lesson both absorbed from Darwin was the law of the survival of the fittest. 'That the stronger should push the weaker to the wall was not only a cosmic fact, it was a beneficent process by which the nation got rid of its liabilities.'[18]

Carlyle's hatred of democracy and his increasing conviction that he was living in degenerate times led him in his old age to become 'madder and madder, shriller and shriller', as John Kenyon has put it, in his adulation for despotic regimes.[19] Cromwell was therefore eulogized for his massacre of the Irish at Drogheda and Wexford; Frederick the Great for his out-and-out militarism; and in his *Latter-Day Pamphlets* and his 'Occasional Discourse on the Nigger Question', he anticipated his defence of Governor Eyre's brutality in Jamaica, by his scant sympathy for 'our beautiful Black darlings' in the West Indies.'[20] All the compassion that he had shown earlier for the victims of the new Poor Law in *Past and Present* had soured into open contempt both for weakness and for those who dared to resist the rule of the strong. 'If people would not behave well, put collars round their necks. Find a hero, and let them be his slaves' was his message to Mazzini on his meeting the acknowledged European champion of democracy one evening. Margaret Fuller, who was present at the occasion, felt both embarrassed and ashamed.[21]

Kingsley had infinite compassion for the downtrodden, but he had a genuine horror of the mob and could sometimes echo Carlyle on the need for savage measures against insurgents. Perhaps he had right on his side in publicly defending Rajah Brooke by dedicating *Westward Ho!* to him; but he, too, refused to censure Governor Eyre. Again, like Carlyle, he believed that history was essentially the unfolding of the great deeds of courageous people who had changed the fortunes of their times. His history lectures at Cambridge were more like sermons. One who attended them has left this description:

> He loved men and women, you felt that. He never sneered at their faults ...
> Again, he had such a warm, passionate admiration for fine deeds. His eyes
> used to glisten, his voice in its remarkable sea-like modulations to swell like
> an organ as he recounted something great, till his audience listened – quiet,
> spell-bound, fixed, till the climax came, and then rushed into a cheer before
> they were well aware of it.[22]

But he had his preferences, both in character and in the type of deed. To use an expression much appreciated in his day, he liked his great men to 'have bottom':[23] to have both physical and moral courage, and – above all – to be manly. Norman Vance has noted Kingsley's attraction to Esau rather than to Jacob; the one 'a wild man like himself' but good at heart, the other 'smoothly plausible' and therefore not to be trusted.[24] And in Kingsley's gallery of heroes, the Esaus of history were good Protestants (preferably married) as opposed to Catholic celibates (the Jacobs). They were Teutons rather than Romans; ready with their fists to defend a good cause or to help a fellow-being in distress, rather than wielders of facile pens which could distort honest truth into casuistry. Like his brother-in-law, J.A. Froude (also an admirer of history's strong men), he rejoiced in the exploits of the Elizabethan sea-dogs. Amyas Leigh in *Westward Ho!* is very definitely an Esau, as wild as they come, but the 'symbol ... of brave young England longing to wing its way out of its island prison'. After all, 'no wind can sweep the earth which does not bear the echos of an English voice'.[25] Hereward the Wake, the eponymous hero of Kingsley's last novel, was an Esau-hero too. From its very first page, the reader is promised a 'tale of doughty deeds', set in the Fens, a land 'hard, yet cheerful; rearing a race of hard and cheerful men'[26] – Esaus, every one of them. The linking of the two adjectives is significant. Hereward is a fearsome warrior, but he can laugh as he slays. The essence of the Kingsley hero of his later books is, in Norman Vance's phrase, a sort of 'good-natured brutality'.[27]

Kingsley's heroes conformed much more to the popular image of John Bull than Carlyle's. John Bull was tough and manly, but he had a sense of humour. Carlyle's *Cromwell* depicted a tight-lipped disciplinarian whom John Bull would have wanted to punch on the nose. And Carlyle lost his public with *Frederick the Great* and the *Latter-Day Pamphlets*. After all, from the beginning of the century, and even before, the public liked to invest their historical heroes with a romantic colouring. This was one of the reasons why Walter Scott was so avidly read. His novels had adventure, with historical figures of flesh and blood, plenty of great deeds, but also a heroism tinged with pathos; and – perhaps the most appealing feature of all – evocations of nostalgia, taking his readers' minds away from contemporary industrial society. He did not create the historical novel, but he succeeded in so firmly establishing the genre that he gave – at least until the 1850s – writers like Bulwer Lytton and Harrison Ainsworth an easy public. Trollope, however, discovered in 1857 that the public taste had changed. When he approached a publisher with a proposal, he was told: 'I hope it's not historical, Mr Trollope! Whatever you do, don't be historical.'[28] This did not deter the leading poets from choosing rousing historical themes: Tennyson and Browning, even Swinburne with his Mary Stuart trilogy. Byron had not lost a reading public, even though Felix Holt, in George Eliot's novel, scoffed at continuing adulation for the Byronic hero: what was Byron but 'a misanthropic debauchee ... whose notion of a hero was that he should disorder his stomach and despise mankind?'[29]

Historical subjects were still eagerly espoused by painters into the closing years of the century. Some themes were more popular than others: heroic deeds of the Middle Ages (G.F. Watts's *Alfred inciting the English to resist the Danes*); the heroes of the Civil War – both Charles the Martyr and Cromwell, to suit rival tastes. Roy Strong has noted that between 1820 and 1900, something of the order of 175 paintings on a Civil War theme were exhibited at the National Gallery.[30] The sixteenth century proved a propitious field, too, with Millais' *The Boyhood of Raleigh* (1870) perhaps the most celebrated. The tragic heroine proved a favourite subject. Between 1827 and 1877, a total of twenty-four representations of the unhappy fate of Lady Jane Grey were exhibited in the National Gallery (Maria Callcott's description of her in her *Little Arthur's History of England* suggests a model Victorian heroine: 'she was beautiful, virtuous and wise, and, above all, a Protestant'.)[31] But Mary Queen of Scots was also highly favoured. 'She was cast in the right mould for the romantic age,' Roy Strong writes. 'She was young, beautiful and accomplished', and then subjected to barbarism and finally execution.[32]

The three most widely-read historians of the Victorian age were Macaulay, J.A. Froude and J.R. Green. Of the three, Green was the least preoccupied with drawing out the tales of doughty deeds and the heroism of individuals, mainly because of his emphasis on social history and his determination not 'to sink into a "drum and trumpet" history'.[33] Certainly he was as concerned as Macaulay to demonstrate that the past was essentially a success story, but he was not seduced by the glamour of great names and stressed the role played by ordinary people who, while struggling towards the goal of freedom, never aspired to be the 'strong men' so eulogized by Carlyle and Kingsley. Froude's heroes were the Tudors, true benevolent despots, and those who gave them loyal service.

> My own work [he wrote] had brought home the same convictions to me which Cromwell had brought to Carlyle. I regarded the Reformation as the grandest achievement in English history ... the work of two powerful sovereigns, Henry VIII and Elizabeth, backed by the strongest and bravest of their subjects. To the last up to the defeat of the Armada, manhood suffrage in England would at any moment have brought back the Pope.

Therefore history, as Froude conceived it, taught one crucial lesson: to give the unlettered and the foolish the same voice in government as the wise and worthy was 'a delusion, and the demand for it ... one of those epidemics of passion which at various periods have swept over the human race'.[34]

Macaulay admired strength, and he had his heroes, but he had no time for fanatics. While he was undoubtedly a Whig in politics, and – not without good reason – taken to be the quintessential Whig historian, his chosen heroes were very rarely Whigs themselves. His accolades tended to be reserved for men like William of Orange and the Marquis of Halifax, and emphatically not for the Duke of Marlborough.[35] His admiration for Napoleon seems to have been a personal quirk,[36] because it does not fit with his usual criterion for a hero, described by John Burrow as a man who was 'energetic, vast-conceiving, above all stoical'. Warren Hastings was just such a man, displaying 'heroic equanimity' in the midst of adversity and danger.[37] By comparison with the stridency of Carlyle, Macaulay's admiration for great men was temperately expressed. But he never for one moment doubted the didactic responsibility of the historian. It served a people ill to ignore the past or to disparage the achievements of those who had gone before. As he expressed it memorably in words which deserve to be embossed in gold:

> A people which takes no pride in the noble achievements of remote ancestors will never achieve anything worthy to be remembered with pride by remote descendants.[38]

This precept was not lost on Victorian society – at all levels. Samuel Smiles made precisely the same appeal to his readers, if they wished to acquire the means of self-advancement. Learn from good examples, he reiterated time and time again in *Self-Help*. Heroes need not necessarily be eminent men and women.

> Though only the generals' names may be remembered in the history of any great campaign, it has been mainly through the individual valour and heroism of the privates that victories have been won.

Nevertheless, 'biographies of great, but especially of good men, are ... most instructive and useful, as helps, guides and incentives to others.' What were the lessons to be learnt from the Indian Mutiny? It demonstrated:

> the unflinching self-reliance and dormant heroism of the English race. In that terrible trial all proved almost equally great – women, civilians, and sol-

diers ... Indeed in no age of England have the finest qualities of men been so brilliantly displayed.[39]

This was the lesson that the Victorian young were exhorted to take to heart, both at school and in the home. G.M. Young recalled coming across a little sixpenny encyclopaedia, written to assist young schoolboys on the eve of examinations. 'It contained, with other useful matter, a list of the Hundred Greatest Men: "to know their deeds is to know the history of civilization".'[40] In 1871, a fourteen-year-old schoolboy at Wellington College was given a devotional manual as a confirmation present. He treasured it greatly, and wrote, in the end-papers, lists of those whom he intended to remember in his prayers. One list contained the names of his own particular historical heroes, compiled without regard for chronology: Alfred the Great, Marcus Aurelius, St Paul, Joan of Arc, Edward I, Cromwell, Shakespeare, Alexander the Great, Caesar, Nelson, Martin of Tours and John Bunyan. On the fly-leaf, before the title page, he inscribed the following text from Shakespeare's *Henry VIII*:

> It is a sort of good to say well,
> And yet words are not deeds.[41]

There is a touching sincerity about this; the more so when one appreciates that when the boy became a man, he continued to add the names of friends to his bede-roll, and that he clearly continued to use the manual for devotional purposes until his death in 1934. By that time hero-worship had become unfashionable. During the later decades of the nineteenth century the emphasis laid by historians on the significance of Great Men in history had begun to shift, too. William Stubbs led the way in his researches into the medieval chronicles and his studies of early constitutional history. The first verse of the forty-fourth chapter of Ecclesiasticus gave way to the ninth: 'And some there be, which have no memorial: who are perished as though they had not been.' Stubbs's contemporary E.A. Freeman, however, still gloried in worthies, preferably Teutonic ones – Earl Godwin, for instance, a sort of Simon de Montfort before his time, and Harold, the archetype of the 'patriotic and tragic hero' who died defending England against the Norman invader.[42]

As late as 1888 Benjamin Gregory, the Wesleyan Methodist who had been an ardent disciple of the 'Methodist Pope', Jabez Bunting, brought out his *Handbook of Scriptural Church Principles and of Wesleyan Methodist Polity and History,* a sort of manual in catechetical form for the instruction of the younger members of that denomination. One of the questions in the catechism reads as follows: 'Is there any great name in English history of which you are reminded by the genius and career of Jabez Bunting?' The correct reply was: 'William Pitt and the greatest of American statesmen, Alexander Hamilton.' In 1898, Gregory thought of a possible third name to add: 'Pericles'.[43]

It goes without saying that if you cherish heroes as ardently as the Victorians were inclined to do, you will also be very much aware of anti-heroes or villains in the drama of the past. There is no shortage of them in Carlyle. They are paraded in the fullness of their iniquities in *Past and Present*: Benthamites, Mammon-lovers of the business world, idle aristocrats, mealy-mouthed politicians, all given fanciful names like Sir Jabez Windbag and Plugson of Undershot. Kingsley's villains were, as has been seen, the smooth-tongued Jacobs, unnatural celibates, Papists all. It is surprising to find, however, that Napoleon is almost consistently regarded as a hero. Macaulay's admiration for him is strange, but Lord Acton's – bearing in mind his obsession with the historian's duty to mete out justice, especially to those in high places – seems even stranger.[44]

The admiration was not extended to his nephew, Napoleon III. But what of his wife? Goldwin Smith, to his delight, discovered an extraordinary instance of a Kentish squire who hero-worshipped the Empress Eugénie. On the occasion of her visit to England with her husband in 1854, this ardent devotee bribed the chambermaid at the inn at Dover, where they broke their journey, to procure for him the contents of the Empress's chamber-pot 'to preserve in a bottle as a sacred relic'.[45] The story was passed to Carlyle to include in his book *On Hero Worship*. Not even Carlyle dared to put that into print.

III

'For was, and is, and will be, are but is:
And all creation is one act at once.'
                            Tennyson, *The Princess*

When Alice was posed a riddle to which there was no answer, she sighed wearily and said to the Mad Hatter: 'I think you might do better with the time ... than waste it.' 'If you knew Time as well as I do,' said the Hatter, 'you wouldn't talk about wasting *it*. It's *him*.'[1] Charles Dodgson, no doubt, knew well what he was about when he put these words into the Hatter's mouth. So preoccupied had the historians of his day become with the concept of Time that they had practically invested it with a personality. The word most favoured by the Germans was *Zeitgeist*. If time had not exactly been personalized, at least it was conceived as some sort of controlling spirit or force which shaped the destiny of men and nations.

Time, after all, is something that almost defies definition. In one sense, it is an abstraction, a concept whereby human beings measure the movement of their lives and create a dimension in which they can understand what has gone before and what may come hereafter. In another sense, it is a reality which, in relation to eternity, presumably had a beginning and is therefore likely to have an end. But between those two termini its motion is inexorable, because the one certain thing about time is that it can never be made to stand still. During the nineteenth century, however, the whole concept of time dimension was revolutionized by researches into archaeology, anthropology, geology and the various branches of the natural sciences, in that it was discovered to have acquired an elasticity inconceivable to earlier generations. The origin of man, confidently believed to have been dated from the Creation in 4004 BC, had to be pushed back so far into some dark unknown that the emergence of *Homo sapiens*, whether by chance or by design, had to be relocated almost within a new cosmology: a mind-blowing experience for those who first grappled with its implications. The concept of the end of time, equally confidently predicted by millennialists from eccentric calculations of scriptural mathematics, also acquired both a new dimension and a hitherto unexpected source, towards the end of the century, in the discovery of the second law of thermodynamics, leading to what the physicists described as entropy, or – effectively – the end of life on earth.

These were revelations which were to come in due course. Even during the eighteenth century, however, primarily in Germany but also in France, historians and philosophers were beginning to discern within the time-process, as manifested in history, patterns which forced them to question the extent to which mankind, at any given moment, was entirely the master of its fate. Largely through continental influences,

English historians began to toy with the same idea, some more emphatically than others. Great men and noble deeds were still the stuff of history, but might there not be some higher force – call it Providence or the *Zeitgeist* – which determined the rise and fall of nations and ordained that the most-favoured nation of today should become, tomorrow, the least, as the mantle of domination was passed on to another?

Carlyle drank copious draughts from the fount of German Romanticism – from Goethe, Fichte, Herder and Novalis; and the first enunciation of his Germanic approach to history came with the publication of *Sartor Resartus* in *Fraser's Magazine* during 1833 and 1834. The English public had encountered nothing like it before. Time is the ruler of man; not man the master of time. So his character Professor Teufelsdrockh declaims:

> It continues ever true ... that Saturn, or Chronos, or what we call TIME, devours all his Children: only by incessant Running, by incessant Working, may you (for some threescore-and-ten years) escape him: and you too he devours at last. Can any Sovereign, or Holy Alliance of Sovereigns, bid Time stand still; even in thought, shake themselves free of Time? Our whole terrestrial being is based on Time, and built of Time; it is wholly a Movement, a Time-impulse: Time is the author of it, the material of it ... O Time-Spirit, how hast thou environed and imprisoned us.[2]

In 1837 appeared Carlyle's *The French Revolution*: one of the most extraordinary histories ever written. It did not purport to be a narrative history; it is a series of graphic scenes, character sketches, savagely evocative descriptions of individual dramas and of the rise and fall of heroes of the moment, compiled – as Carlyle himself admitted – 'by a *wild man*, a man disunited from the fellowship of the world he lives in: looking king and beggar in the face with an indifference of brotherhood, an indifference of contempt.'[3] But it had a very definite didactic purpose. In the first place, Carlyle presents the movement of history through time as cyclical (an idea probably derived from the Saint-Simonian school in France).[4] Organic eras of growth are inevitably followed by critical eras of decay. Vitality gives way to sloth, genuine idealism to affectations and imposture. Carlyle was a moralist, first and foremost, and the virtues contributing to growth, as opposed to the vices which signify decay, are precisely the virtues which posterity has come to regard as quintessentially Victorian and which Carlyle

1. Uncontrolled industrialization: the Black Country near Wolverhampton (1865)

2. The Great Exhibition of 1851, and crowded London streets (Cruikshank): one of a pair of drawings; the other depicted the empty streets of Manchester whose inhabitants had all gone to London

3. *The Last Judgement*: detail from a painting by John Martin, 1853. The Pope can be seen scrabbling among the damned, as well as a railway train plunging into the abyss

4. The Chartist demonstration on Kennington Common, April 1848:
this is one of the first 'news' photographs ever taken

5. Brain workers: F. D. Maurice and Thomas Carlyle. Detail from Ford Madox Brown's *Work*. This painting was begun in 1852, but not completed until 1863. Carlyle (in hat) was too impatient to sit for Brown, who was compelled to use a photograph (adding the grimace)

6. The Gentleman: Chichester Fortescue, by James Tissot, 1872. Fortescue, who later became Lord Carlingford, was the model for Trollope's political hero, Phineas Finn

7. Uniformed guard on the South-Eastern Railway (1885)

8. Black Friday, 11 May 1866: the bank of Overend and Gurney closes its doors on its creditors

9. Volunteers at the Firing Point on Wimbledon Common, 1866, by H. T. Wells

10. 'Barbarous cruelties' from Illustrated Police News, 1888: a typical piece of Victorian sensationalism; the top half of the page is devoted to Jack the Ripper's gory exploits in Whitechapel

11. Colonial life: a memsahib's house, Simla, 1867: Simla, in the Himalayan foothills, was a refuge for the British from the heat of the Indian plains. Even there the only way to keep plants alive was in easily watered pots

"ALLURED TO BRIGHTER WORLDS AND LED THE WAY."

12. Victoria and Albert in Anglo-Saxon costume
(W. Theed): commissioned in 1868 as a present
for her mother by Vicky, the Queen's eldest
daughter and wife of the Crown Prince of
Prussia; a bizarre offering to underline
Anglo-Germanic ties

13. *The Doubt: Can these dry bones live?* (H. Bowler): a painting (1856)
full of symbolism. On the tombstone inscribed '*Resurgam*', a horse chestnut
conker is sprouting, while a butterfly – a symbol of the resurrected human soul –
sits on the skull

14. The Gladstone family picnic in Scotland, 1893: a tired 84-year-old Prime Minister relaxes after a summer spent debating Home Rule. He has just swept off his hat for the photographer. Mrs Gladstone sits on his left

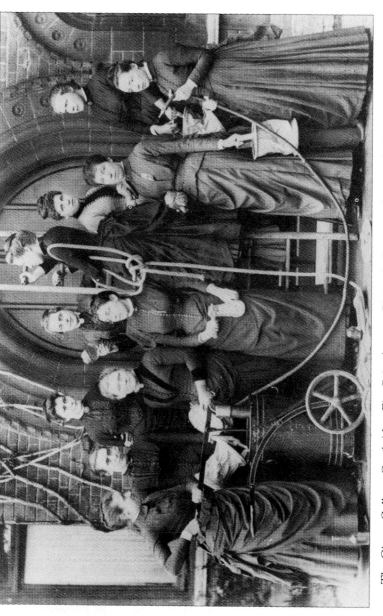

15. The Girton College, Cambridge, Fire Brigade, 1887: Girton, built purposely at a safe distance from the men's colleges, was obliged to supply its own fire-fighting arrangements

16. 'John Bull: Decadent' (Aubrey Beardsley): this rendition of John Bull
(and his bulldog – bottom left) appeared in the first issue of *The Savoy*
in 1895. One is reminded of Jowett's concern in 1866 that
'John Bull has certainly grown very fat'

preached so forcefully in *Past and Present*: 'work, discipline, thrift, self-help'.[5]

This moralism supplies the second major significance of his history. *The French Revolution* is a vast essay about the judgement of providence. Carlyle was not passing the expected judgement on the wickedness of radicals and revolutionaries. He was writing a cautionary tale to reveal how providence will use these instruments of brutality to punish a ruling class that has abdicated its responsibilities. These things will happen in England if the aristocracy and greedy manufacturers do not heed the rightful, providential retribution that took place in France. This explains a third unique feature of his history. It is written entirely in the present tense: not only to heighten the sense of drama, so that the reader feels that these terrible events are happening now; but also to show that, in a sense, this is history about to repeat itself unless the wrath of providence can be averted.

Massively influential as Carlyle was within his generation, his later historical works never matched the power and the impact of his *French Revolution*. Fitzjames Stephen read with interest his

> odd book about Cromwell. A good book, because it has all his genuine letters and speeches ... But that poor jargon, that conjuring with words, is a flimsy business ... a mere veil to hide from Carlyle himself the essential poverty of his thoughts.[6]

This was a view shared by Jowett[7] and Matthew Arnold.[8] He was 'never seriously listened to by thinking men', R.H. Hutton concluded.[9] Perhaps Hutton had been influenced by James Martineau, who sent him his own opinion of Carlyle's work in May 1852. His religion was a sort of 'pantheism', so

> wholly unsystematic, illogical, wild and fantastic, that thought finds nothing in it to grapple with ... His power over intellectual men appears to me not unlike that of Joe Smith the prophet over the Mormons, dependent on strength of will and massive effrontery of dogma.[10]

Carlyle's most faithful disciple, as a historian, was J.A. Froude. In Froude, although one finds a healthy scepticism about treating history as a science, there is a strong affinity with Carlyle in his belief that history teaches that 'the world is built somehow on moral foundations; that, in the long run, it is well with the good; in the long run, it is ill with the wicked.' Therefore history has a firm didactic purpose. 'We learn in it to sympathize with what is great and good; we learn to hate what is base.'[11]

Edward Bulwer maintained in 1833 that historical writing in England was at a low ebb. 'We have surely not even secondary names: we have commentators on history, rather than historians.'[12] This may seem a harsh judgement on scholars like Henry Hallam and John Lingard. Bulwer would certainly have had cause to reconsider these words, had he written ten years later. Within that time Thomas Arnold had produced his edition of Thucydides and the first two volumes on the history of the Punic Wars; Carlyle had exploded his bombshell on the French Revolution; and Macaulay started work on his *History of England from the accession of James II* in 1839. With Arnold, the influence of German historical scholarship, and of Niebuhr in particular, is most evident. For this he had to thank Julius Hare who, in 1824, had persuaded him that a knowledge of German was essential if he were to make his mark as an historian.[13] Arnold also acknowledged his debt to Coleridge. 'I think with all his faults', he wrote in 1836, 'old Sam was more of a great man than any one who has lived within the four seas in my memory.'[14]

This requires some explanation. In so far as Arnold was, in his religious standpoint, one of the pioneers of the Broad Church movement ('latitudinarian', his critics were inclined to label him), there is no doubt that Coleridge influenced him profoundly. It was from him that Arnold learnt that a fundamentalist approach to the study of the Scriptures was misconceived, that the text of the Old Testament needed to be read with an informed understanding of both the context of the events described and the moral code of the times in which they were written. Furthermore, all the Scriptures should be scientifically studied on the same principles and methods as one would employ in an analysis of the text of Thucydides. But Coleridge was a philosopher, not an historian; at least not an historian in the sense of a Carlyle or a Macaulay. He himself admitted that he was totally insensitive to historical context.

> Dear Walter Scott and myself [he once said] were exact, but harmonious, opposites in this; – that every old ruin, hill, river or tree called up in his mind a host of historical or biographical associations, ... whereas for myself ... I believe I should walk over the plain of Marathon without taking more interest in it than any other plain of similar features.[15]

To Coleridge, history was a 'process governed by the presence of ideas';[16] as Owen Barfield has put it: 'all real history was history of thought'.[17] He believed that much could be profitably learnt from its study, provided one looked for the moral pointers that are of universal applicability. In *The Statesman's Manual* (which – to Coleridge – was none other than the Bible itself), he insisted that the facts are always less important than 'the general principles, which are to the facts as the root and sap of a tree to its leaves'.[18] He shared with Carlyle the conviction that calamitous events, like the French Revolution, arise from neglect of the moral laws, as enunciated in the Bible. There is a passage in Coleridge's essay *On the Constitution of the Church and State* which could almost have been written by Carlyle himself:

> The reading of history may dispose a man to satire; but the science of history, history studied in the light of philosophy, as the great drama of an ever unfolding Providence, has a very different effect. It infuses hope and reverential thoughts of man and his destination.[19]

This is also what Arnold profoundly believed. As an historian, he learnt from two masters. From Coleridge, faith in the ultimate control and guidance of divine providence. From Niebuhr (and, later, a reading of Vico's *Scienza Nova*), he became convinced that the foolish conceit born of the French enlightenment and exemplified in Condorcet, that reason and the march of mind were leading civilization into a condition of ultimate perfectability, was fundamentally 'wrong-headed' and perilous.[20] History, Niebuhr had taught, followed a cyclical pattern. Nations go through similar stages of development – from childhood to manhood; and history provided plenty of examples of decreasing vitality into a relatively impotent old age. These examples should be studied in order that the right lessons be absorbed. In his teaching at Rugby, Arnold was for ever posing the question to his pupils – 'What does this remind you of?'[21]

The conviction that Classical learning was the basis of all sound education, arising from a deep respect amounting to veneration for the wisdom of the ancient world, was part of the inheritance of the nineteenth century, and by no means a discovery made by the Victorians. Nevertheless, the focus of Classical studies shifted significantly as the spirit of Romanticism began to prevail over the Augustan culture and ethos of the first half of the eighteenth century. Rome was gradually giving way to Athens. What Horace had been to the Augustans, Robert Ogilvie has suggested, Plato and Thucydides were to the Victorians.[22] The process of transition owed much to both Coleridge and Thomas Arnold. All the Romantic writers, to a greater or lesser extent, were influenced by the Platonic dialogues and the writings of the Neo-platonists, but none more so than Coleridge; and the Platonic foundation of his philosophy inspired his successors of the Broad Church School, Julius Hare and F.D. Maurice, and eventually led – through the proselytism of Jowett – to Plato gaining equal rank with Aristotle in the Oxford school of *literae humaniores* ('Greats') by the late Victorian period.[23] If the rediscovery of Plato was largely Coleridge's gift to his posterity, the intensification of interest in Thucydides was Arnold's enduring legacy. Although his attention had been directed by Niebuhr to the history of Rome, Arnold never had any doubt about the superiority of the Greek historians or the greater value to be obtained by a study of Greek history. Stanley recalled how his headmaster dismissed 'half of the Roman history' as 'totally false, at least scandalously exaggerated'; but 'how far different are the ... impartial narratives of Herodotus, Thucydides, and Xenophon.'[24]

What fascinated him was the peculiar relevance of the circumstances of Athens at the time when Thucydides was writing to the condition of England in the 1830s. He concluded his preface to the third edition of Thucydides with the following words:

> The history of Greece and of Rome is not an idle inquiry about remote ages and forgotten institutions, but a living picture of things present, fitted not so much for the curiosity of the scholar, as for the instruction of the statesman and citizen.[25]

In his heart, however, he nursed deep forebodings about his country's destiny, as he looked about him in the 1830s. There was a real danger that the all-too-rapid changes he was witnessing, accompanied by a sort of restless impatience to realize objectives that might come in the orderly process of time – the wild talk about 'democracy' was one such – were subjecting his generation to an overdose of oxygen.[26]

Arnold was never a millennialist; but his language sometimes suggested the approach of Armageddon. 'The Church as it now stands, no human power can save' (in 1832).[27] 'I cannot, I am sure, be mistaken as to this, that the state of society in England at this moment was never yet paralleled in history' (in a letter to Carlyle in 1840).[28] 'If there be any signs, however uncertain, that we are living in the latest period of the world's history, ... the importance of not wasting the time still left to us may well be called incalculable' (in his inaugural lecture at Oxford in 1841).[29] This is why Duncan Forbes came to the conclusion that Arnold, and the Liberal Anglican school of historians of which he was the leading force, presented to their contemporaries a world picture that was essentially cataclysmic. Connop Thirlwall echoed Arnold's misgivings. 'The moment of highest prosperity [of a nation]', he wrote, 'is often that which immediately precedes the most ruinous disaster.'[30] In 1848, Dean Milman stated his own adherence to the Arnoldian concept of history's cyclical nature, and this conjured up in his mind an uncomfortable prospect. 'The fatal cycle will continue to revolve with more intense force and rapidity – speculation, prosperity, over-production, glut, distress.'[31] When will a nation ever learn?

Such Cassandra-like wailings made no sort of sense to Macaulay; they belied the evidence both of modern history and of one's own eyes. Nor had he the remotest sympathy for those who talked pompously about 'the dignity of history', as if it were some kind of mystery, intelligible only to initiates, or a science which elevated its practitioners far above their proper station. As Andrew Browning has noted:

> History in his view is not dignified: it is real, and anything real is appropriate material for it ... Complete impartiality ... led nowhere. The business of a historian was to set forth his own honest opinions, whatever these might be.[32]

An early essay on 'History', written in 1828, gave promise of what was to come. Macaulay challenged the contemporary fashion of regarding ancient history as a profitable study for gullible schoolboys, for the simple reason that it led them to admire the wrong things. 'We have classical associations and great names of our own which we can confidently oppose to the most splendid of ancient times ... Our liberty is neither Greek nor Roman; but essentially English.' He offered a few examples.

> The dying thanksgiving of Sidney is as noble as the libation which Thrasea poured to Liberating Jove; and we think with less pleasure of Cato tearing out his entrails than of Russell saying, as he turned away from his wife, that the bitterness of death was past.

Then, how did the English deal with the enemies of liberty? Charles I 'was not murdered by men whom he had pardoned and loaded with benefits. He was not stabbed in the back by those who smiled and cringed before his face. He was vanquished on fields of stricken battle; he was arraigned, sentenced and executed in the face of heaven and earth.'[33]

Two essays which he wrote while in Calcutta – one on Sir James Mackintosh and the other on Francis Bacon – set the tone of his most famous historical masterpiece. One's judgement of figures of the past, while always mindful of the changed situation and different mores and traditions, must be based – he argued in the Mackintosh essay – on the all-important questions which their posterity has the right to ask:

> Were their faces set in the right or the wrong direction? Were they in the front or in the rear of their generation? Did they exert themselves to help onward the great movement of the human race, or to stop it? [34]

On the basis of these questions, he could unreservedly praise the controversial figure of Bacon. What Bacon perceived was the necessity to aim philosophy at realizing 'the practical benefits to be enjoyed by all mankind', to produce what he called 'fruit'. And who can deny that – over the centuries, although not necessarily uninterruptedly – these benefits have rendered the lot of human kind infinitely superior, more civilized and happier than what was experienced in the distant past? Bacon's gift to his posterity was to proclaim a philosophy borne out by events since his day: 'a philosophy which never rests, which has never attained, which is never perfect. Its law is progress.'[35]

Although Macaulay's *History of England* – for reasons of his ill-health – covered only a fragment of time, its popularity was immense. The first two volumes, published in 1848–9, sold 22,000 copies within a year. By 1875, the total copies sold had risen to 133,000.[36] The two features which especially appealed to his readers were, firstly, the intense patriotism – the belief that the liberties that were achieved through the Glorious Revolution of 1688, and the peculiar virtues of English parliamentary government, set this country apart from all other nations, making her the envy of those less fortunate. Secondly, in his celebrated third chapter, describing the economic and social state of England in 1685, he provided a picture of what life for ordinary men and women must actually have been like. There was a clear message of hope here. From the progress that had been accomplished since that day it was difficult to conceive how that forward momentum could ever cease, so that it held out the prospect that 'numerous comforts and luxuries which are now unknown or confined to a few may be within the reach of every diligent and thrifty working man'.[37] Even more heartening was Macaulay's conviction that all these blessings were thoroughly deserved. English probity and integrity were receiving, and would continue to receive, their just reward.[38]

Macaulay died in 1859, too soon to appreciate that posterity would credit him as the leading founding-father of the 'Whig interpretation of history'. He was well aware, however, that his exposition of the onward march of Progress was not only a message that many of his contemporaries wanted to hear; it was also shared by others whose opinions were of weight. John Stuart Mill was firmly on his side. Before a word of his *History* had been written, Mill had stated:

> The conviction is already not far from being universal, that the times are pregnant with change; and that the nineteenth century will be known to posterity as the era of the greatest revolutions of which history has preserved the remembrance, in the human mind, and in the whole constitution of human society.

That being so, Mill declared himself converted to 'the doctrine of the indefinite progressiveness of the human mind'.[39] Carlyle might think that the world was going to the dogs, but Trollope's Bishop of Elmham in *The Way We Live Now* (1873) felt that such pessimism warranted a mild rebuke. 'I think that men on the whole do live better lives than they did a hundred years ago,' he said.[40]

The date is significant. Men were beginning to express reservations in the 1870s. The high-water mark of Victorian optimism, Owen Chadwick has suggested, may be seen in W.E.H. Lecky's *History of the Rise and Influence of the Spirit of Rationalism in Europe* of 1865, which charted the triumph of reason over the ages, ousting magic, superstition and obscurantism in its all-conquering advance. But when, in 1913, J.B. Bury published his *History of Freedom of Thought*, it was regarded as an extraordinary anachronism – 'a ghost ... out of the dead years', Scott Holland observed.[41] So had opinion changed. After all, Tennyson in 1886 thought it necessary to produce his famous sequel *Locksley Hall Sixty Years After*, with the lines, 'Let us hush this cry of "Forward" till ten thousand years have gone'. A decade later, Conrad could write: 'If you believe in improvement you must weep.'[42]

Germany was still obsessed with the *Zeitgeist*, however. Hegel's influence had been steadily growing since his death in 1831. In the tradition of German polymaths, he had written on many things, among them a theory of progressive historical development on the pattern of some irresistible dialectic, in which the interaction of antithetical forces unceasingly operated to shape the course of history. What the source of this transcendant impulse might be was not definable – *Zeitgeist*, perhaps; Fichte preferred to say 'God' – but behind it all lay some moral purpose. Hegel's understanding of this dialectic had an uncomfortable contemporary twist to it. The interacting forces making for conflict were conceived in terms of nations and states, and not of the individuals that composed them, all of which seemed to be disturbingly confirmed by the actual wars and tensions between European countries, especially in the mid nineteenth century. Hegel had expressly intimated that the state of war was a mark of a nation's moral strength, preserving it from the stagnation induced by 'enduring peace'.[43]

As the notion of historical dialectic passed from Hegel to his most famous pupil, Karl Marx, it acquired a very different twist: the concept of an equally irreversible process of class conflict, whereby a truly socialist order would achieve its inevitable fulfilment. All this was beginning to look very much like a sort of historical determinism; and during the 1850s such a view of the subordination of human agency in the shaping of the course of history was gaining currency through the researches of social scientists. To praise the acts of famous men was a pleasing fancy. If the pioneers of sociology – Durkheim and his disciples – were correct in their conclusions, all the major revolutions or convulsions of the world would have taken place at some time or another, with or without the particular human agent whom history had chosen to honour.

This is a million miles away from Macaulay; and – on the whole – from most English historians of the nineteenth century. J.R. Seeley might have said to his pupils, 'Most good books are in German',[44] an opinion shared by Maitland, at least in his appreciation of German medieval scholarship,[45] but only in one aspect did the German influence evoke a significant response. This was in the appreciation of the techniques of German scholars like Niebuhr and Ranke in the critical study of sources. Even the excessively Germanic Carlyle probably owed less to Novalis and Fichte than is sometimes suggested. He was, as Noel Annan observed, too much of an original, too self-consciously 'his own man', to follow any master, and in the writing of history he relied rather on his overactive imagination than on any critical historical method.[46]

The influence of Hegel was late in coming. George Eliot, probably one of the ablest Germanists of her day, knew something of his writings and encouraged her friend John Sibree to embark on a translation.[47] But not until J.H. Stirling's *The Secret of Hegel*, published in 1865, were most English scholars even aware of him. Benjamin Jowett became his chief advocate in Oxford, although he admitted that Hegel's writings were so difficult to understand that each page had to be read as if tackling a problem in mathematics.[48] It almost looks as if Hegel became the property of Balliol, and – once lodged there – found it difficult to penetrate beyond. T.H. Green went through a phase of Hegelianism, but conceived a profound dislike of Hegel's subordination of the individual to the state.[49] Then Edward Caird took over the advocacy, and through Caird the influence of his philosophical writings, rather than the historical, began to percolate through to other scholars; but that story belongs to the twentieth century. T.H. Green mused over the comparative neglect of Hegel by his fellow-countrymen:

> Hegel's doctrine [he wrote] has been before the world now for half a century, and though it has affected the current science and philosophy to a degree which those who disparage it seem curiously to ignore, yet as a doctrine it has not made way. It may be doubted whether it has thoroughly satisfied even those among us who regard it as the last word of philosophy.[50]

The chief continental influence on English historical writing and philosophy came rather from France. It was Mill, in his *System of Logic* (1843), and George Henry Lewes, in his *Biographical History of Philosophy* (1845–6), who introduced the Positivism of Auguste Comte to English thinkers. Here again was a confident interpretation of the time-process, fitting neatly into the dominant idea of Progess, which itself owed its origin to the French enlightenment. History did, indeed, seem to confirm that civilization (or at least Western civilization) passed through successive phases in man's understanding of the world around him. In its childhood, it needed dogmatic instruction, as supplied by theologians; in its adolescence, the questioning speculation over what lay beyond the easily demonstrable saw the world advancing into metaphysical enquiries. The stage of manhood coincided with the realization that the seemingly unknowable lay within the grasp of man through the triumphs of experimental science. Herbert Spencer was deeply influenced by this teaching. He had exhibited his total acceptance of the idea of Progress in his *Social Statics* in 1851; but the moment when he saw the means of establishing Positivism on an unassailable basis came with the publication of Darwin's *Origin of Species* in 1859, which seemed so surely to confirm through the theory of evolution everything that Comte and his disciples had taught. As Robert Young has expressed it: 'Out of the belief in progess through struggle there grew the ideology of so-called "Social Darwinism".'[51]

Not everyone was convinced. 'Of all the sickening humbugs in the world, the sham pietism of the Positivists is to me the most offensive,' T.H. Huxley complained in 1889.[52] Henry Sidgwick had come to the same conclusion, accusing Comte and Spencer of 'fatuous self-confidence'.[53] W.H. Mallock in his fictitious dialogue *The New Republic* satirized their dogmatic effrontery in the person of 'Mr Saunders':

> The main use of history ... is of course, as Comte has so well established, to teach us his philosophy of it – to show us, in other words, how entirely *non compos mentis* the world was till our time, and that it is only in the present century that it has acquired the power of passing a reasonable judgement.[54]

In Frederic Harrison, Spencer found his staunchest ally. Not even Macaulay at his most rhapsodic could equal Harrison's unbounded confidence that perfectability was just around the corner.

> Take it all in all [he wrote in the early 1880s], the merely material, physical, mechanical change in human life in the hundred years, from the days of Watt and Arkwright to our own, is greater than occurred in the thousand years that preceded, perhaps even in the two thousand years or twenty thousand years.[55]

One other name deserves mention, because more strictly an historian than either Spencer or Harrison: H.T. Buckle, whose *History of Civilization in England* actually antedated Darwin's *Origin of Species* by two years. It was the one serious attempt to demonstrate that the history of a nation can only be fully understood if one accepts that the actions of men 'have the same uniformity of connexion which physical events have, and no other; and the law, or laws, of these uniformities can be inductively ascertained in the same way as the laws of the material world.'[56] It was Mark Pattison who said the last word on this approach to history. He was no believer in Positivism, and actually preached against it – one of his very rare appearances in a pulpit – in 1865.[57] But Buckle's approach was sheer nonsense: a classic example of the truism that 'when we can leave out what we don't like, we can demonstrate most things.'[58]

Towards the end of the nineteenth century, the lead in historical studies in England had passed to the medievalists. They had interpretations of their own, but at least they resisted playing games with Time, and with external forces determining the actions of human kind. During the century, history had been interpreted as providential, cyclical, cataclysmic, progressive, positivist, dialectical and determinist – most of these variants on the theme of the *Zeitgeist*. Few of them actually survived the end of the century; perhaps only the sociological-determinist interpretation and the dialectical materialism of Marx. When Tennyson wrote the fifth verse of his introduction to *In Memoriam* in 1850, was he making a prophecy or just indulging in wishful thinking, one may wonder? 'Our little systems have their day … And Thou, O Lord, art more than they.'

IV

Mrs Skewton, with a faded little scream of rapture: 'Don't you doat upon the Middle Ages, Mr Carker?' 'Very much indeed,' said Mr Carker.

Dickens, *Dombey and Son*

Thomas Arnold had one serious blind spot as an historian. He had no time for the Middle Ages. He confessed to A.P. Stanley in 1841 that 'I could not bear to plunge myself into the very depths of that noisome cavern, and to have to toil through centuries of dirt and darkness.'[1] Macaulay seems to have agreed with him. In the unfolding drama of England's rise to greatness, the Middle Ages constituted an irrelevance lasting some twelve hundred years. James Anthony Froude, in a beautiful passage of emotive historical prose in the first volume of his *History of England,* expressed the conviction that the old world that died with the advent of modern times in the sixteenth century was lost for ever.

> Between us and the old England there lies a gulf of mystery which the power of the historian will never adequately bridge. They cannot come to us, and our imagination can but feebly penetrate to them. Only among the aisles of the cathedral, only as we gaze upon those silent figures sleeping on their tombs, some faint conceptions float before us of what these men were when they were alive; and perhaps in the sound of church bells, that peculiar creation of medieval age, which falls upon the ear like the echo of a vanished world.[2]

Yet at the time that all three were writing, 'medievalism' (which is not quite the same thing as medieval historical scholarship) was fast becoming almost a cult among many of their contemporaries, expressed in a variety of forms; so much so that it is almost true to say that the nineteenth century rediscovered the Middle Ages.

This will not quite do. The fascination with all things 'Gothic' was one of the earliest manifestations of the revolt of Romanticism against the excessively rational, ordered, mechanistic tone of eighteenth-century thought and culture. Great movements of the mind may start with seemingly bizarre and trivial attempts to meet a generation's yearnings for nourishment to feed the imaginative faculties and to stir the emotions. Horace Walpole's *The Castle of Otranto* (1765) and Ann Radcliffe's *The Mysteries of Udolpho* (1794) can never be described as literary masterpieces, but they were read avidly by a public who felt starved of the sort of escapism offered by a harking-back to a distant world in which mysterious, irrational forces were at work; a bit ghoulish and creepy, too. Even creepier was the new genre of so-called 'Graveyard Poetry', sombre and melancholy, but also spine-chilling. Banal to the point of absurdity were some of the German mystery dramas which took London by storm towards the end of the century. But they did not seem so to Coleridge. He wrote a review of Matthew Gregory Lewis's grotesque extravaganza, entitled *The Monk*, in tones of unstinting praise. 'The tale of the bleeding nun is truly terrific,' he wrote.[3]

There is, of course, far more to Romanticism, far more to Coleridge too, than this. His indiscriminate ransacking of the wisdom of the past was prompted in part by his desire to rescue his generation from the barren rationalism of John Locke and the 'Age of Reason'; partly also to discover some principle of unity (or 'Oneness'), some common hidden truth perceived, cherished and guarded by the Neoplatonists and representatives of the Hermetic tradition through the ages, which – he was convinced – lay at the root of all knowledge. Wordsworth described this same yearning in the memorable lines of the 1805 edition of *The Prelude*: 'There is a dark/ Invisible workmanship that reconciles/ Discordant elements, and makes them move/ In one society.'[4]

Such a quest supplies the clue to other essential attributes of the Romantics – the vibrant individualism striving to emancipate itself from the false conventions of the age; the belief in the higher perception afforded by imagination; the certainty that the ultimate truths belonged more to the heart than to the head. As Keats expressed it in *Endymion*:

> Feel we these things? that moment we have stept
> Into a sort of oneness, and our state
> Is like a fleeting spirit's.[5]

This was a European phenomenon; and the affinity between the thinkers of the German Romantic Movement and the English is very striking. Some of it was partly derivative: Coleridge learnt much from the seventeenth-century Platonist Jacob Boehme and from Kant, Carlyle from Goethe; but some of it was also an example of how minds working independently at any one time can arrive at similar conclusions. A notable instance is the similarity between Wordsworth and Schelling.[6] The Romantics themselves were more inclined to argue that the truths they stood for had, in a sense, no actual origins which could be dated. They had always been there, if – at various points in history, like the eighteenth century – they had belonged to the underground of thought, waiting for the moment to rise to the surface. As Newman once put it:

> It is not here or there: really it has no progress, no causes, no fortunes; it is not a movement, it is a spirit afloat ... everywhere. It is within us, rising up in the heart where it was least expected.[7]

It was to take various forms; and the impulse to explore the fascination of the medieval past was one of them. This acquired a particularly popular appeal through the genius of one writer: Walter Scott. As Alice Chandler observed, he may have been the 'populariser', but the appeal that his historical novels made 'came out of the air in which he wrote'.[8] His success can also be explained by the care that he took to endow his medievalism with genuine authority. He had steeped himself in Bishop

Percy's *Reliques of Ancient English Poetry* (1765) and Sharon Turner's *History of England to the Norman Conquest* (1799–1805); and his evocations of an age of chivalry, high personal honour and altruistic courage, and of the protective benevolence of the ideal feudal relationship, seen especially in *Ivanhoe*, stirred the imagination of a generation only too anxious to avert their eyes from the uglier features of their own society in a state of transition from a rural to an industrial economy.

The nostalgic element is strong; but Graham Hough points to something more:

> Perhaps the most striking characteristic of nineteenth-century romantic medievalism [he writes] is that what began as a fashionable antiquarian pastime developed into a comprehensive and determined set of beliefs with serious social and religious consequences.[9]

With William Cobbett, for instance, there was a very definite social message that he intended to deliver, combined with nostalgia for a saner, better-ordered, more natural and happier world than the England he witnessed in the course of his rural rides. The moment when all went wrong was the Reformation, bringing with it the dissolution of the monasteries, which had been – in Cobbett's view – both the agents of selfless caring for the poor and the symbol of the pre-Reformation Church's priority in always putting the interests of the ordinary people first. The destruction of the manor and the erosion of the yeoman class came next, converting a paternalistic system into the rapacious, competitive, inhumane society created by commercialism.

Cobbett pined for a return to what he described as the 'cottage economy': small units in which there was a genuine mutual sense of obligation and respect between the farmer and his labourers, eating together at the common table. He had no time for Evangelical philanthropists and for charity bestowed in a spirit of condescension. But Cobbett was not just a dreamer. Granted the changed conditions, and the disposition of the new manufacturing class to exploit the workers, he was prepared to take his stand as a tribune of the people to assert their rights, and above all to sell their labour in a free market. He was therefore a vehement opponent of the Combination Acts. Conflict between employer and labour was never Cobbett's ideal. But if the Middle Ages were gone never to return, then resistance to inhumane oppression was both necessary and inevitable.

In this respect Cobbett differed from Carlyle, who also, in *Past and Present*, offered a medieval scenario in admiring terms. Quite apart from the fact that a tribune of the people was the last role that Carlyle would ever have chosen for himself, nostalgia was not an emotion that ever beat within his breast. His picture of twelfth-century England presented a model, certainly. But his survey purported to be an 'authentic image of a Time now wholly swallowed'.[10] There were lessons to be learnt from it. Abbot Samson is a Carlyle hero-figure, who personified all the virtues most necessary for the healing of England's present wounds – strength, tempered with humility; diligence, with forcefulness to require the same response from his monks; a sense of duty towards those in his charge, with a healthy respect for the stern discipline to be meted out to backsliders. Nevertheless the bond that binds him to them is a personal one, not the 'cash-nexus' of the nineteenth century. Furthermore, religion is a pure and working one:

> Alas, compared with any of the *Isms* current in these poor days, what a thing! Compared with the respectablest, morbid, struggling Methodism, never so earnest; with the respectablest, ghastly, dead or galvanised Dilettantism [by which he meant 'Puseyism'], never so spasmodic.[11]

The element of nostalgia is most marked in the Young England group, the circle that surrounded Lord John Manners, George Smythe and Disraeli in his younger days, a group whom Carlyle would certainly include among his Dilettantes and Dandies. Their recipe for the 'condition of England' question was a reconciliation of The Two Nations (the sub-title of Disraeli's *Sybil*) by a reforging of the natural alliance between the aristocracy and the underprivileged poor, of which the finest example that history had to show was the principle and practice of medieval feudalism.

> The principle of the feudal system [Disraeli declared in one of his most florid speeches on the hustings] ... was the noblest principle, the grandest, the most magnificent that was ever conceived by sage or ever produced by patriot.[12]

Their understanding of its glories was derived from a reading of Scott and their admiration for Cobbett (who appears in *Sybil* in the character of Walter Gerard), coloured by the highly-romanticized picture of courtly, chivalrous protection of the weak and the less-favoured in Kenelm Digby's *The Broad Stone of Honour*, which became to them almost their 'breviary'.[13] Disraeli's trilogy of 'silver-fork' novels (*Coningsby*, *Sybil*, and *Tancred*) was completed between 1844 and 1847. *Coningsby* had a definite political propaganda purpose, as Disraeli freely admitted in his dedicatory note to Henry Hope. All the major figures of the Young England party appear in the book under different names. The sincerity of Disraeli's political convictions is not to be doubted, nor his belief that England's troubles could only be set to rights by the enthusiasm and ideals of the best of the country's youth. 'It is a holy thing', said Coningsby, 'to see a state saved by its youth.'[14] The image of a future with people dancing together round the maypole[15] – the realization of Lord John Manners' dream of the revival of national holy-days and recreations – is, one suspects, a touch of tongue-in-cheek.

Perhaps not. In *Sybil*, a more powerful book altogether, with a purpose more avowedly social than political, the nostalgic yearning for times long gone, expressed by Sybil herself, has a poignant quality beside which Cobbett's prose sounds shrill.

> When I remember what the English people once was: the truest, the freest, and the bravest, the best-natured and the best looking, the happiest and most religious race upon the surface of the globe, and think of them now ... [16]

Romantic medievalism, uttered in such superlatives, invited derision and mockery. Queen Victoria thought the whole Young England group were a party of fools.[17] Trollope satirized the re-enactment of medieval games and joustings in the party given by the Ullathornes in *Barchester Towers*. Dickens had some fun at their expense in *Dombey and Son*, when Mrs Skewton puts the question to Mr Carker (the bad one of the two brothers):

> 'Don't you doat upon the Middle Ages, Mr Carker?' 'Very much indeed,' said Mr Carker. 'Such charming ideas!' cried Cleopatra, 'so full of faith! so vigorous amd forcible! so picturesque! so perfectly removed from common-place!'[18]

Ten years earlier, in *Nicholas Nickleby*, Dickens made play with the silver-fork novel. The poor long-suffering Kate Nickleby was required to relieve the boredom of the impossible Mrs Wititterly by reading aloud to her a book entitled *The Lady Flabella*.[19] On the other hand, in 1860 in *Great Expectations*, Wemmick and the 'Aged P' are sympathetic characters living in their queer little Gothic house – 'Wemmick's Castle'

– a welcome and relaxing contrast to the heartless atmosphere of Mr Jaggers' office.[20] Outside fiction, however, the question posed by more practical minds was: what purpose could be served by trying to put the clock back? 'You might as well sow a husk!' snorted Julius Hare.[21]

Were the Tractarians, under Newman's leadership at Oxford in the 1830s, trying to put the clock back? The answer must surely be, yes; although not all the major figures of the Oxford Movement would have agreed on how far back it was necessary to go in order to recover the Catholic ethos of the Anglican Church. John Keble would have been satisfied to return to the days of the Caroline divines in the seventeenth century, in whose hands the fearful errors of the Protestant Reformation had been corrected. Newman's heart, on the other hand, lay with the early Church, the age of the Fathers and of the saints and martyrs of the first five centuries of Christianity. The Gothic and the period of the high Middle Ages, during which 'Romish' error had departed from the purity of the primitive Church, never had any attraction for him. Nevertheless he identified among his generation the sense of a sort of devotional void which could only satisfactorily be filled by recovering what had been lost or destroyed in the sixteenth century: 'a growing tendency', as he put it in 1838, 'towards the character of mind and feeling of which Catholic doctrines are the just expression.'[22] Walter Scott had done much to awaken this consciousness of a 'mental thirst'; and John Keble, in his volume of devotional poems, *The Christian Year*, published in 1827, had – somewhat to the surprise of the author himself – supplied exactly the spiritual nourishment for which so many of his contemporaries were craving – evocations of past ages of sanctity, a sense of mystery heightened by some of the recondite imagery of the poems; and above all, a tone throughout which exuded the beauty of holiness. Newman again, years later in the *Apologia*, recalled its phenomenal appeal. 'It woke up in the hearts of thousands a new music, the music of a school, long unknown in England.'[23]

The Catholic movement in the Church of England ('Puseyism' to its critics) prospered in the climate of Victorian medievalism, even if the Oxford pioneers had tended to seek their inspiration elsewhere. At Cambridge, for instance, John Mason Neale and Benjamin Webb, in 1839, while still undergraduates, founded the Cambridge Camden Society, later to be called the Ecclesiological Society. They had no inhibitions at all over acknowledging their reverence for all things

Gothic. Nor had another young man, still in his twenties, Augustus Welby Pugin, a Roman Catholic convert who – quite independently – resolved to dedicate his life to the transformation of English ecclesiastical architecture from its almost pagan predilection for Classicism to, as he conceived it, the only possible style in which worship could realize the beauty of holiness: the Gothic of the great medieval cathedrals.

Young men of ardour like to think of themselves as pioneers, and it is indeed questionable, as Giles Worsley has shown in his examination of the long tradition of Gothic architecture stretching far beyond Horace Walpole's villa at Strawberry Hill, whether 'the Gothic Revival' was anything more than a fresh phase in a continuing tradition.[24] What cannot be disputed, however, is the sensational impact made by the virulence of Pugin's language in his first publication, in 1836, *Contrasts: or a Parallel between the Noble Edifices of the Fourteenth and Fifteenth Centuries, and Similar Buildings of the Present Day: showing the Present Decay of Taste: Accompanied by Appropriate Text.* Although he acquired a wealthy patron in Lord Shrewsbury and was appointed Professor of Architecture at Oscott College, his influence on church building was far more powerful within the Anglican Church than in his own communion. This may be in part because Pugin was gratuitously rude about the architecture of Roman Catholic churches, but mainly because his writings coincided with an unprecedented spate of church building during and immediately after his lifetime, short as it was. He died at the age of 48. In the thirty-six years between 1840 and 1876, a parliamentary return revealed that 1,727 new churches had been built and 7,144 had been restored.[25] The Ecclesiologists were not slow to jump upon this band-wagon too, although they steadfastly maintained that, while staunchly supportive to Pugin, they had never at any time been his disciples. It is interesting that they, too, traced the origin of their medieval enthusiasm to Walter Scott. He had been the first, an article in *The Ecclesiologist* claimed, to portray 'truthful and attractive' pictures of medieval times 'which the grossness of a later age had treated with unmixed contempt'.[26]

That the medieval influence on Victorian architecture should soon have been reflected in pictorial art was almost inevitable. The formation of the Pre-Raphaelite Brotherhood dates from 1848, its leading spirits being D.G. Rossetti, Holman Hunt, John Millais, Ford Madox Brown and Edward Burne-Jones. Their avowed aim was defined by their chief champion, John Ruskin, in 1851:

Pre-Raphaelitism has but one principle, that of absolute, uncompromising truth in all that it does, obtained by working everything, down to the most minute detail, from nature, and from nature only ... Every Pre-Raphaelite figure ... is a true portrait of some living person.[27]

The medievalism of their respective undertakings consisted of a studied emulation of the vividness of colour, as well as the sharp definition of detail, which had been the glory of pre-Renaissance Italian painting. From the subjects that they chose to paint – simple people hard at work, nature in all its wildness and minutest detail, evocations of joy and freedom, but never drabness – may be seen the mingling of romanticism and medievalism, with a touch of typical Victorian didacticism. It almost seems as if they were trying to depict Sybil's idealized notion of 'what the English people once was'.

All these things, with the addition of a definite social message, describe the medievalism of Ruskin himself. He longed for colour.

At first [he wrote], it is evident that the title 'Dark Ages' given to the medieval centuries, is, respecting art, wholly inapplicable. They were, on the contrary, the bright ages; ours are the dark ones ... We build brown brick walls, and wear brown coats, because we have been blunderingly taught to do so ... There is, however, also some cause for the change in our tempers. On the whole, these are much *sadder* ages than the early ones; not sadder in a noble and deep way, but in a dim wearied way, – the way of ennui, and jaded intellect, and uncomfortableness of soul and body.[28]

What had gone wrong, and how could our terrible mistakes be rectified? We need, Ruskin told the young cadets at Woolwich, to recover the medieval sense of knighthood: 'to subdue the wicked, and aid the weak'.[29] He returned to the theme in *Unto This Last*: we have lost the fair method of trading that was enshrined in the medieval concept of the 'just price'.[30] In an essay on 'The Nature of Gothic', he deplored the way in which the worker was deprived of his pride in using his craft freely to produce what he knew to be worth while, so that we have degraded 'the operative into a machine'.[31] He himself tried to recreate, by setting aside a tithe of his income, his own model of a medieval guild – the Guild of St George – probably aware that such quixotic gestures would be doomed to failure. But at least it would show that he was prepared to teach by example.

Was he living in a fantasy world? A reviewer in *The Athenaeum*, assessing an exhibition of Pre-Raphaelite art, dismissed the whole attempt of these sentimental medievalists to speak to their age:

> They will labour in vain – for the incredulity, scepticism and science of the nineteenth century are not to be contented with the pictorial pap and panada that satisfied the simple faith and ignorance of mankind's medieval infancy.[32]

William Morris, the most incurably nostalgic of all Victorian thinkers, had been brought up in a fantasy world, where he imbibed medievalism with his mother's milk. The family home (Woodford Hall) was a moated grange, where ancient festivities were still actually observed. As a boy, he was presented with a tiny suit of armour to wear as he rode about the park. In his youth he became a devotee of Pugin and a disciple of Ruskin, whose revelations on the nature of medieval craftmanship provided Morris with the inspiration for his life's work. Unlike the unhappy factory worker of their own day, the medieval craftsman was not fettered to a single, soulless task, like some cog in a machine. The stone mason, for instance, worked on a design of his own conceiving, and chipped away and carved and moulded until he saw his work completed.

This was the principle on which, in time, the workmanship of the firm of Morris, Marshall, Faulkner and Company would be based. As for himself, Morris was prepared to turn his hand to a whole range of creative ventures, all Gothic-inspired. From architecture, as an apprentice of G.E. Street, he turned briefly to painting, under the tutelage of D.G. Rossetti. He experimented with furniture design, and constructed a settle of such mammoth proportions for the flat in Red Lion Square (which he shared with Burne-Jones) that it defied all efforts to convey it upstairs. It was obliged to squat on the pavement until tackle had been procured to hoist it through a window.[33] When he moved to the Red House at Bexleyheath, he designed a medieval garden. But more ventures were to come in his Kelmscott days – interior decoration, intricately patterned textile and carpet designs, poetry, translating Icelandic sagas, calligraphy. In his later days some of the joyous abandon drained away as he became more and more involved in left-wing politics.

But his concept of Utopia never changed. *News from Nowhere* was the dream of a time-traveller who sees an England of the future – a recreation of the fourteenth century, following a violent revolution. There is only one significant difference from the later Middle Ages: there were no churches to be seen; no Christianity. The question was put to the time-traveller:

> Where is the difficulty in accepting the religion of humanity, when the men and women who go to make up humanity are free, happy, and energetic at least, and most commonly beautiful of body also, and surrounded by beautiful things of their own fashioning, with a nature bettered and not worsened by contact with mankind? This is what this age of the world has reserved for us.[34]

By 1890, the year of the publication of *News from Nowhere*, English historical scholarship had virtually passed into the hands of the medievalists: William Stubbs, Edward Augustus Freeman, F.W. Maitland, J.H. Round, Mandell Creighton, Frederick Seebohm, Mary Bateson, and the great Russian scholar Paul Vinogradoff, who settled permanently in England in 1895. With the exception of Creighton, they were all at work on different aspects of the pre-Conquest period and its immediate aftermath, tracing the origins of legal and political institutions and systems of medieval land tenure. None would have disputed the debt owed to Sharon Turner and to J.M. Kemble, pioneers of Anglo-Saxon scholarship. Kemble, in particular, had directed all subsequent workers in the field to the crucial lessons to be learnt from Germany. The Germans had every reason to study early English history. Through the laws and institutions of England's Saxon invaders could be traced the evolution of their own legal systems – which had escaped from the pervasive influence of Roman law – helping them, therefore, to understand the better their own national identity.[35]

The notion that English liberties and her unique parliamentary institutions could be traced back to Anglo-Saxon times, and that the imposition of the 'Norman yoke' in 1066 had been a temporary hiatus – after all, the Conqueror had felt himself obliged to reaffirm the laws of Edward the Confessor – had become almost a part of English folk-lore. Christopher Hill has traced it from the late Middle Ages to the writings of Sir Edward Coke in the seventeenth century, after which the tradition became firmly embedded in the national culture.[36] E.P. Thompson has provided several instances of English Radicals invoking their fundamental Saxon 'liberties' to confound such continental excrescences as the

use of *agents provocateurs* (the notorious spy, 'Oliver') and repressive legislation like the Combination Acts.[37]

This was just the sort of noble, patriotic and manly conception that
would fire Charles Kingsley's enthusiasm. In his pro-Chartist days, he
composed a placard to be posted up in London in April 1848 to deter
the demonstrators from resorting to violence. It was addressed to
'Workmen of England':

> Englishmen! Saxons! Workers of the great cool-headed, strong-handed
> nation of England, the workshop of the world, the leader of freedom for
> 700 years, men say you have common sense! Then do not humbug your-
> selves into meaning 'licence', when you cry for 'liberty'; who would dare
> refuse your freedom?[38]

His countrymen's pride in their Saxon ancestry was not lost upon
Dickens. When Daniel Doyce, in *Little Dorrit*, left England's shores for
his foreign travels, he was cheered on his departure; and 'in truth, no
man on earth can cheer like Englishmen, who do so rally one another's
blood and spirit ... that the stir is like the rush of their whole history,
with all its standards flying, from Saxon Alfred's downward!'[39] Mortimer
Lightwood, in *Our Mutual Friend*, saluted Mrs Boffin's ancestors:
'Vigorous Saxon spirit ... bowmen, Agincourt and Cressy.'[40]

It was this theme that Stubbs and Freeman, in particular, set out to
explore in their different ways, in order to establish the validity of the
claim to continuity from Saxon times to Magna Carta and beyond.
Freeman's Whiggish, democratic enthusiasm led him to conclusions
little less triumphal than Kingsley's. 'As far at least as our race is concerned,' he wrote, 'freedom is everywhere older than bondage.'[41] To him
the Germanic community of the mark – the free village community –
came with the Saxons into England, and therefore the folk-moot of pre-
Conquest times was essentially a populist institution. Ever echoing in
Freeman's ears, and bringing inspiring pictures to his mind, was – as
John Burrow has put it – 'the approbatory clashing of spear on shield
and the most spirit-stirring of earthly sounds, when a sovereign people
binds itself to obey the laws which it has itself decreed.'[42]

Stubbs was more cautious, and immeasurably more scholarly. His
understanding of the spirit and institutions of the Saxons was much
influenced by the description in the *Germania* of Tacitus. Although, like
Freeman, he did not dispute the connection between the Anglo-Saxon

witana-gemot and the later Great Council, he tended to stress 'the vigour of the humbler institutions of local government',[43] and the way in which custom over the years gradually established itself as law. Maitland, the greatest scholar of the three, was even more cautious. In the first place, his approach to the study of pre-Conquest England was totally different. In tracing the origins of the manor, he told Frederick Pollock in 1888 that he had come to the conclusion that one had to work backwards from the known into the unknown.[44] Accordingly his classic exposition, in *Domesday Book and Beyond*, was based on the assumption that 'the doctrine that our remote forefathers being simple people had simple law' was an error. 'Simplicity is the outcome of technical subtlety: it is the goal not the starting point.'[45] Hence his conclusion that the tendency to romanticize the free village community of Saxon times was perilous. 'We are among guesses and little has as yet been proved.'[46]

The golden age of late Victorian medieval scholarship hardly survived the century. Mary Bateson, Maitland's protégée, of whom he had such great expectations, died in November 1906. 'Where's our Medieval History now?' he lamented.[47] Maitland himself died a month later. Stubbs, who died in 1901, was at the height of his powers when, in 1884, Gladstone made him a Bishop (of Chester first; he was translated to Oxford in 1887). He had a host of absorbing historical projects before him, but they were all abandoned. He must have felt as Richard Whately did, years before, after becoming Archbishop of Dublin, when plucking ruefully at his lawn sleeves he said, 'I don't know how it is; but when we have these things on, we never do anything more.'[48]

Throughout the Queen's reign, however, the looking-back to medieval times, either out of nostalgia or for a definite social, cultural or political purpose, never seemed to slacken, and certainly never lacked a powerful spokesman. Indeed, in the closing decades of the century, with the relentless acceleration of all the processes that were to transform Victorian society into the Edwardian age, the element of nostalgia began to assume an almost spiritual dimension. As Owen Chadwick has observed, there seemed in those closing years a wistful longing for a return to simplicity. 'Why', he asks, 'did the reputation of St Francis of Assisi rise so rapidly during the last forty years of the nineteenth century, among Protestants and unbelievers as well as Catholics?'[49]

Twentieth-century nostalgia has tended to express itself in the creation of fantasy worlds, or in quite deeply significant analogies cast within the fortunes of the animal kingdom. But at least there still exists one gratifyingly solid and therefore, one hopes, imperishable monument to Victorian medievalism and its looking-back to Alfred and his kingdom of free-born men. It is a felicitously incongruous tableau of Victoria and Albert, executed by William Theed in 1868. They are draped in Anglo-Saxon garb.[50]

CHAPTER 4

Looking Beyond

I

'An Englishman would be very upset if he could not believe in an after-life ... In every great crisis ... his thoughts become solemn and tend towards ideas of the *Beyond*.'

Hippolyte Taine, *Notes on England*

IF SOMEONE were asked to select a scene which was quintessentially Victorian, strange if not unknown to the eighteenth century and utterly alien to the mores of the twentieth, a picture of a household assembled for family prayers could hardly be improved upon. It would speak of the centrality of the home, the social unit that admitted no rival, and of the pattern of domestic piety which had spread both upwards and downwards in the social scale from the example of middle-class families whose lives had been transformed by the spiritual awakening of the Evangelical Revival. The practice was not, therefore, of Victorian origin. The old Puritan spirit, which had lain dormant for over a century, had only been slumbering. Like the underground of Neo-platonism, which had come to the surface again in the closing years of the eighteenth century to give birth to Romanticism, so pietism, a few decades earlier, had reawakened with John Wesley and George Whitfield, and – mainly through Wesley's influence – had set in motion perhaps the most powerful and pervasive religious revival in the history of England.

By the turn of the century, although Wesley had reluctantly abandoned the Church of England to found Methodism, Evangelicalism had injected the Establishment with a new vitality; and if to any one circle of influence the dissemination of its characteristic piety can be ascribed, it would surely be to the members of the Clapham Sect. William Wilberforce was its central figure, with his Clapham friends – Henry Thornton, Charles Grant, Zachary Macaulay and James Stephen. In close alliance with them were prominent Evangelical clergy, like Charles Simeon, John Venn, Isaac and Joseph Milner and Daniel Wilson.

Methodism would never have influenced the upper classes of English society. But men like Wilberforce and Thornton, while upper middle-class in origin, were both affluent and conspicuous in public life: Members of Parliament with friends in the government. Wilberforce will always be remembered as the Great Emancipator, but the abolition of the slave trade was to him and his friends very much the means to an end. By identifying themselves, and eventually the nation at large, with a great humanitarian cause, they hoped to spread the gospel of 'vital religion', and thereby to raise the whole tone of the country's morals and manners. What followed has been aptly described as the 'democratizing effect of Evangelicalism',[1] not in the sense of a political objective but in the extent to which every class of society was touched by its moralizing influence. Hannah More, at Barleywood, a close friend of the Wilberforces, targeted the lower classes by producing and distributing her *Cheap Repository* tracts, full of pious moralisms and cautionary tales about those who failed to absorb them. Thomas Bowdler made his objective the moral regeneration of the whole nation by purging the texts of Shakespeare and Gibbon of anything remotely improper. To invade the citadels of the aristocracy and the upper classes with reminders that 'nominal Christianity' was not enough was the main task of Wilberforce and his friends. At the very least they required the example of a high moral tone to be set from the top. 'It was nearly always through wives and daughters that seriousness was introduced into aristocratic households,' Ian Bradley has noted. 'At the time of Queen Victoria's succession at least twenty noble houses had Evangelical ladies at their head.' One of the doughtiest fighters for vital religion was the Duchess of Beaufort, who brought up all her eight daughters as committed Evangelicals. She was less successful with 'the unpromising figure of Charles Greville, the worldly diarist and wit, whom she forced into reading the whole of Thomas Chalmers' lectures on the Book of Romans in 1842.'[2]

It has to be said that their influence stopped short at the pre-Victorian Court. But with the accession of a young Queen in 1837 the atmosphere changed markedly for the better, for her own personal reasons rather than from any specific Evangelical influence. After her marriage, for the first time in living memory the nation could look to their sovereign for a pattern of domesticity accompanied by strict moral decorum. By this time, however, even contemporaries acknowledged that the golden age of Evangelicalism had seemed to die with the passing of its major figures. As a party within the Church it was still numerically strong, but the joyousness and buoyancy of old were no longer the properties of the second generation. Less attractive notes of mean-mindedness and aggressiveness came to the fore, mainly because it felt threatened by a new source of spiritual vitality from a very different tradition.

This was the reassertion of High Church principles in a rejuvenated spirit, emanating from Oxford in the widely-publicized *Tracts for the Times*, the majority of which were the work of one man – John Henry Newman. If anything, the influence of Newman, Keble, Hurrell Froude and Pusey reinforced the high moral tone of Victorian religion, but the whole emphasis was different. Evangelicalism, because of its highly personal nature and its Bible-centred Christianity, was essentially the religion of the home. Tractarianism, by contrast, was a religion of the Church. Its emphasis on the priestly function, respect for liturgy and the centrality of the sacraments seemed to invert the priorities of the Evangelicals. Newman had the deepest and most reverential appreciation of the role of the Scriptures, but his insistence that the Scriptures must be understood in accordance with the teaching of the Church was an assertion that no Evangelical, in his heart of hearts, could really accept. Furthermore, Newman's teaching on the nature of justification, together with Pusey's severe strictures on post-baptismal sin, made Evangelicals seriously question whether the cherished Protestant doctrine of 'justification by faith alone' was being subtly transformed into the totally unacceptable Catholic notion that 'good works' might be adjudged as meritorious within the economy of grace. It was in this respect that Newman's teaching seemed to impose frighteningly severe moral imperatives. In one of his early sermons, he reminded his congregation that 'heaven would be hell to an irreligious man',[3] and this was by no means the only occasion when Newman gave the impression – as Michael Wheeler has observed – that heaven would turn out to be a sort of church.[4]

It seemed that a Victorian could not escape from moral teaching wherever he might turn. Exhortations to live an upright life, and to be seen to do so, were dinned into his ears whether at chapel or in church, whether by high churchmen or low. If he eschewed Christianity altogether and went for guidance to the Benthamites, he exchanged only one taskmaster for another. Even the most sceptical, like Bentham himself, or atheistical, like James Mill, were fierce moralists. Harold Perkin has written:

> The principle of utility, the universal test of the greatest happiness of the greatest number, was a moral imperative more categorical than the Evangelical version of the Christian ethic, in that it was pursued for its own sake, as good in itself, and not motivated by supernatural reward and punishment.[5]

It is true that some of the most persistent and strident moralists of the Victorian age did not always in their private lives succeed in living up to the standards set by the Queen. At least three of the most celebrated (and possibly a fourth, in John Stuart Mill) failed to fulfil the injunctions in the Book of Common Prayer on the blessed function of the marriage bed. With Carlyle and Ruskin, for instance, it was a case of marriage and no bed; with George Eliot, in her relations with G.H. Lewes, a case of bed and no marriage. This does not seem to have diminished their influence. George Eliot resolutely divorced her didacticism from any suggestion of religious teaching. To her, *duty* was the primary ethic of this life; and she did a service, G.M. Young has suggested, to those who, like her, abandoned faith in Christianity. 'Grave and wise men', he wrote, 'thought that George Eliot had, single-handed, by her ethical teaching, saved us from the moral catastrophe which might have been expected to follow upon the waning of religious conviction.'[6]

Those who took the same path as George Eliot seemed almost to go out of their way to insist that the abandonment of Christianity did not mean a lowering of their ethical standards. Frederic Harrison, the Positivist, had a very straight answer to give to his son, who put to him the question 'What is a fellow to do who cannot marry and falls in love?' His reply was: 'A man who cannot learn self-control is a cad ... A loose man is a foul man ... He is a beast.'[7] Leslie Stephen asserted, on his decision to become an agnostic: 'I now believe in nothing, to put it shortly; but I do not the less believe in morality ... I mean to live and die like a gentleman if possible.'[8] Perhaps the most remarkable testimony of all was Lord Amberley's declaration to Kate Stanley just before their marriage. He reminded her that it would be her duty 'to prove by daily constant example, that Christian virtues in their purest, their most perfect, form may exist quite apart from the remotest tincture of Christian doctrine.'[9] Amberley subsequently, in 1876, published his reasons for a total repudiation of Christian dogma in his *The Analysis of Religious Belief.* Yet he continued to pray to some 'Infinite and mysterious Power';[10] and Kate recorded how, on New Year's eve, in 1871, in the company of their friend T.J. Sanderson, they spent the evening reading some of 'their favourite bits' to each other, including Matthew Arnold's *Rugby Chapel* and Thomas à Kempis' *Imitation of Christ.* Amberley 'sang 3 hymns just before midnight; then we all 3 knelt together and prayed – and so saw in the New Year 1872 in silent prayer and love.'[11] Matthew Arnold's predicament, when he lost his faith in orthodox Christian dogma, was not dissimilar. But, as he explained at length in *Literature and Dogma*, he clung to the moral content of Christian teaching, in his conviction that 'conduct, not culture, is three-fourths of human life'. So the 'God of the Bible' – for him – was 'as Israel made him ... simply and solely "the Eternal Power, not ourselves, that makes for *righteousness*".'[12]

The Victorians were unquestionably moralists. Whether one can be equally confident in describing them as a religious people must, however, take into account the fact that both 'honest doubt' and the spread of religious indifference were a constant source of anxiety throughout Victoria's reign. For the first time in English history the phenomenon of 'Unbelief' emerged as so evident an intellectual and emotional problem that the whole question of what lay beyond one's life on earth, hardly ever before considered to be a matter for speculation or debate, became the subject of fierce and bitter dispute. Doubt is a Cross that thinking people may have to carry; religious indifference, on the other hand, is a more tacit and facile assumption that the Church, and all it stands for, is an irrelevance and can simply be ignored. Since doubts tend to be articulated, they can be identified, and attempts made, effective or otherwise, to answer them. Religious indifference, by being muted, is correspondingly difficult to locate and therefore to counter.

The Establishment, and – indeed – all the Christian denominations, received a nasty jolt in 1851 when, for the first and last time, Census returns required details of attendance at religious worship at all services on a particular Sunday (30 March of that year). The statistics revealed that out of a total population of nearly 18 million, only 7,261,032 had attended some service in church or chapel; and what was particularly galling to the Establishment was that only a little more than half of these attended Church of England services. Over 5 million – an estimate based on calculations of those too young or too sick or too otherwise engaged in public employment to be able to attend – were unaccounted for. Since the official report, innumerable revised estimates and analyses of these figures have been made, with not very significant adjustments.[13] The cry went up from the churches that the census should have been taken on Easter Sunday or at Christmas. But there was no disguising the fact that – in the words of the report – 'a sadly formidable portion of the English people are habitual neglecters of the public ordinances of religion.'[14]

Such figures would be a matter for rejoicing in the late twentieth century. At the time they caused gloom and despondency. To make matters worse, although contemporaries could not be aware of it the world had but eight years to wait before the publication of Charles Darwin's *The Origin of Species*, at which point, as Owen Chadwick has put it, religious doubts came to be represented as 'Doubt, in the singular and with a capital D'.[15] It appears, too, that religious indifference in the 1850s was not the preserve of the inarticulate working classes alone. After the secession of Newman to the Roman Church in 1845 the atmosphere in Oxford changed almost overnight, as Mark Pattison recorded in a memorable passage of his *Memoir*. Religious fervour and unprofitable theological discussion – 'the nightmare which had oppressed Oxford for fifteen years' – faded almost out of memory.[16] J.R. Green noted the same transformation, in a letter to A.P. Stanley: 'High Churchmen fell with a great crash and left nothing behind.'[17] Cambridge soon went the same way. When Kingsley returned there as Regius Professor of History in 1861, he too reported to Stanley. This time it was the Evangelical influence, once so dominating in Charles Simeon's day, that had almost completely evaporated, leaving nothing but a 'cool indifferentism'.[18]

These observations should, however, be understood within their context. Both Pattison and Kingsley were contrasting a temporary period of religious quiescence with their memories of a particular phase of intense spiritual vitality. As far as foreign visitors were concerned, a peculiar English religiosity, so different from what they encountered at home, still pervaded the national life.

> Even grown men here [Taine wrote] believe in God, the Trinity, and Hell, although without fervour. Protestant dogma is very well suited to the serious, poetic and moral instincts of the people. They do not have to make an effort to maintain their faith in it ... An Englishman would be very upset if he could not believe in an after-life ... In every great crisis of his life his thoughts become solemn and tend towards ideas of the *Beyond*.[19]

De Tocqueville, thirty years earlier, had raised the question of religious indifference with a Catholic priest in Portsmouth. The priest conceded that it was probably on the increase; but – he said – 'the English are a naturally religious people. With them religion is seldom a passion engendering enthusiasm. But it is a deep, personal feeling which does not easily slacken its hold.'[20]

When religious passions *were* aroused, however, it was as well to steer clear of the line of fire. John Bull could be exceedingly pugnacious if his Protestant susceptibilities were affronted, and he was no lover of Roman Catholics. Time and again statesmen and governments found themselves under threat when they ventured to make even the most moderate concessions to their loyal Catholic subjects. Peel lost his university seat at Oxford on the issue of Catholic emancipation. In the fierce conflicts in 1845 over a small grant to the Irish Catholic seminary at Maynooth, Gladstone felt compelled to resign on a matter of principle. A major constitutional crisis was only narrowly averted in 1869 on the issue of the Disestablishment of the Irish Church. Sometimes the temptation to let loose the dogs of war with the cry of 'No Popery' could rebound against the rabble-rouser. Lord John Russell's Ecclesiastical Titles Act of 1851, prompted by the restoration of the Catholic hierarchy in England, while appealing to the prejudices of the mob, 'kindled the just resentment of Ireland' and lost him the crucial support of the Irish Members in the Commons. Richard Cobden's prophecy that Russell's 'disgusting display ... bids fair to close his political career' was entirely accurate.[21] Within a matter of months he was voted out of office. All these instances substantiate the judgement of George Kitson Clark, that 'probably in no other century ... did the claims of religion occupy so large a part in the nation's life, or did men speaking in the name of religion continue to exercise so much power.'[22]

'Honest Doubt' leading to unbelief, however, posed a grievous problem to all the churches for two good reasons. The doubters were, for
the most part, men or women of considerable intellectual standing
and influence, and many of the questions that they raised proved
exceedingly difficult to answer. Secondly, the clergy themselves were not
immune to the same heart-searchings. If the impact of Darwinism after
1859 was to rock the boat of orthodoxy more alarmingly than anything
encountered before, it was because the revelations of the *Origin of Species*
came at a time when the accepted authority of the Scriptures was
already being challenged – ironically, by the calling into question of that
very aspect of Victorian religious teaching that had been so confidently
regarded as the most essential message to be absorbed and put into
practice by all Christians: the moral content of the Word of God in the
Scriptures.

James Anthony Froude, in his *The Nemesis of Faith*, written in 1849,
soon after his disillusionment with his early Tractarian enthusiasms, was
one of the first to publish his rejection of a moral code which, in the Old
Testament, represented God too often in the guise of a 'fiend'. How
could anyone worship a God who sanctioned the massacre of the
Canaanites?

> That the unchanging God should have directly prompted, should have
> interfered to assist in what humanity shudders at while it reads – oh, I would
> sooner perish for ever than stoop down before a Being who may have power
> to crush me, but whom my heart forbids me to reverence.[23]

Put the two Testaments together, and what could one honestly make of
a Creator who deliberately tempts his own creation to sin, and then
visits that sin upon their children and their children's children, and
appears content to see the largest portion of mankind – the many 'not
chosen' – sentenced to 'a retribution so infinitely dreadful that our whole
soul shrinks horror-struck before the very imagination of it'?[24]

The problem of the wretched Canaanites became a popular stum-
bling-block. Tom Mozley recalled being stopped by a journeyman-tailor
and his friend, early one morning, in Bell Yard, when he was on his way
to deliver some proofs to an office in Fleet Street. Since he was conspicuously a parson, he was immediately called upon to explain the moral
implications of the command to Joshua to slay all the Canaanites. 'The
women and children too? What harm had they done?' He struggled in-

effectively to find an answer.[25] Connop Thirlwall, Bishop of St David's, also had his qualms about the Old Testament. He admitted to his friend Canon Perowne, in 1871, that the command to Abraham to slay his son Isaac troubled him greatly. 'I wish I could propose any view of the narrative which would bring it more into harmony with the genuine principles of Christian ethics,' he wrote.[26]

But the Christian doctrines drawn from the text of the New Testament also raised grave moral problems. William Blake was one of the first to express horror at the whole notion of the Atonement. 'It is a horrible doctrine!' he said. How could it be right for God to be content to punish the innocent in place of the guilty?[27] Coleridge, too, rebelled against the notion that it was consistent with God's nature to require a sacrifice to appease his wrath.[28] But by far the most intense disquiet concerned attempts to reconcile a God of love with a God who could countenance punishing sinners by the everlasting torments of the fires of Hell. This was sufficient, as far as John Stuart Mill was concerned, to render the feeble defence of the goodness of God on the ground that his goodness must be qualitatively different from that of men so futile that he declared:

> I will call no being good, who is not what I mean when I apply that epithet to my fellow-creatures; and if such a being can sentence me to Hell for not so calling him, to Hell I will go.'[29]

The debate over the meaning of 'eternal punishment' and the literal or metaphorical concept of Hell-fire lasted throughout the century. Coleridge – brave spirit as ever – was one of the first to question the literal meaning; and in the 1870s, the clergy were still hotly divided over the retention of the damnatory clauses in the Athanasian Creed. The battle was fought on two issues. The first was textual and linguistic. Had the actual words in the relevant texts (especially Matthew, 25,v.46) been misinterpreted? This was the powerful argument of F.D. Maurice in his *Theological Essays* in 1853, when he maintained that the word 'eternal' had a qualitative meaning, and was not therefore synonymous with 'everlasting'.

> What, then, is Death eternal, but to be without God? ... What dread can I have – ought I to have – beside this? What other can equal this? Mix up with this, the consideration of days and years and millenniums, you add nothing either to my comfort or my fears.[30]

This was not an insight that had occurred to Maurice alone. F.W. Robertson, also of the so-called Broad Church school, had raised the same queries.[31] But Maurice, holding a professorial chair at King's College, London, had to pay the penalty for his boldness: he was dismissed for heretical teaching. He had made, however, a crucial distinction between physical torments and the sense of loss ('What is Perdition but a loss?' were his words),[32] and his repudiation of the lurid imagery of the horrors of what a never-ending torture must involve was soon echoed by other Broad Churchmen like Charles Kingsley, A.P. Stanley and – most explicitly – F.W. Farrar, whose series of sermons published in 1878, entitled *Eternal Hope*, was the most forceful exposition of Maurice's convictions. Not surprisingly, the defenders of the orthodox doctrine were equally forceful in their condemnation of such teaching. H.L. Mansel dismissed Maurice's conclusions as anthropomorphic, in supposing that man's concept of justice could be attributed to his omnipotent Creator. J.B. Mozley accused Maurice of inventing 'a new subtlety and a crotchet as impalpable as the air'.[33]

The second issue to which this controversy gave rise was a moral one. As stated by Mozley, in his review of Maurice's *Theological Essays*, once people were released from the fear of eternal punishment, they would 'plunge into self-indulgence without hesitation'.[34] 'The fear of Hell drives people back to God', Pusey maintained in 1864, in support of his part in organizing a petition signed by 11,000 clergy in defence of the traditional doctrine.[35] Terror tactics had had a long history. In the eighteenth century Isaac Watts, the writer of some of the most beautiful hymns in the English language, had not hesitated to resort to them in his *Divine Songs for Children*, in which the following unfortunate verse appears:

> There's not a sin that we commit,
> Nor wicked word we say,
> But in Thy dreadful book 'tis writ,
> Against the judgement-day.[36]

Children, because so impressionable, were the obvious, vulnerable targets for indoctrination by fear. William Carus-Wilson (Charlotte Brontë's 'Mr Brocklehurst' in *Jane Eyre*) offered the following sobering food for thought in his cautionary tale 'The Bad Boy', included among his *The Child's First Tales*:

> There is an hour when I must die,
> Nor do I know how soon 'twill be;
> A thousand children, young as I,
> Are called by death to hear their doom.[37]

But quite the worst offender, in the nineteenth century, was the Catholic Redemptorist priest by the singularly appropriate name of Father Joseph Furniss, who took delight in terrifying young children by describing in graphic detail the torments of Hell, which – it seems – he had somehow been privileged to witness:

> The little child is in the red-hot oven. Hear how it screams to come out; see how it turns and twists itself about in the fire ... God was very good to this little child. Very likely God saw it would get worse and worse and never repent and so it would have been punished more severely in hell. So God in His mercy called it out of the world in early childhood.[38]

Could a God of love possibly be party to cruelty such as this? And what sort of discipleship could he possibly be asking from those who responded to threats such as these? In fact, Maurice maintained, such morally repugnant teaching was causing thinking and feeling people to leave a Church that could spread such nonsense. Years later, Charles Gore expressed his own conviction that mid-Victorian unbelief had chiefly arisen from 'a very widespread rebellion of conscience against everything in the current religious teaching which described the action of God as tyrannical, arbitrary and cruel'.[39]

The sort of misinterpretation of scriptural texts which could lead to an unacceptable literalism, as Maurice had argued, was one problem. Another – and a grievously disturbing one – was, how authentic were the texts on which so much religious teaching was based? Even as early as the late 1820s, Thomas Arnold expressed concern over the fact that the majority of his clerical colleagues were hopelessly unprepared for the shocks that were about to come from Germany.[40] His son, Matthew, shook his head sadly when he saw that prophecy fulfilled. He wrote to his mother in 1869:

> In papa's time the exploding of the old notions of literal inspiration in Scripture, and the introducing of a truer method of interpretation, were the changes for which, here in England, the moment had come. Stiff people could not receive this change.[41]

Howls of execration had greeted Thirlwall's translation of Schleiermacher's *Critical Essay on the Gospel of St Luke* in 1825, which cast doubts on the historical accuracy of this gospel and posed awkward questions on the authenticity of Matthew's. Potentially more dangerous were the researches of Schleiermacher's pupil, F.C. Baur, the founder of the Tübingen school of biblical criticism. Baur's method was Hegelian, tracing the emergence of Christian doctrine as a synthesis of a series of antitheses, originating from his theory of a fundamental conflict between St Paul and the original disciples. If one refused to accept the Hegelian premiss, then Baur's conclusions might be discounted. But the meticulousness of his historical scholarship was impressive, and not until the emergence of scholars with a comparable critical apparatus could some of his disturbing conclusions be answered. The Old Testament posed problems too. Should the Book of Daniel, written at a much later date than that conventionally accepted, properly belong to the Apocrypha with other Maccabaean literature? Even more worrying, later in the century, was the formidable Old Testament scholarship of J.C. Wellhausen, giving the first hints of what, in the twentieth century, came to be described as Form Criticism.

Inevitably, once historical accuracy was seriously questioned, scepticism began to spread about the validity of the gospel miracles. At the same time, it became almost the fashion to attempt to write biographies of the founder of Christianity, stressing Jesus' humanity as opposed to his divinity. Strauss's *Leben Jesu* was the first, translated by George Eliot in 1848. Then came Renan's *Vie de Jésus* in 1863, and J.R. Seeley's *Ecce Homo* in 1865. More substantial and more reverential was F.W. Farrar's two-volume *Life of Christ* in 1874. It was acknowledgedly the most popular and the least offensive, but it was not received well by all. W.H. Mallock gleefully retold the story of Farrar, at a dinner party, ruefully complaining that although his sales had been prodigious, he had received only £300 in royalties. A neighbour was heard to mutter: 'In the good old days the same job was done for thirty pieces of silver.'[42]

Many were the clergy who sighed for those good old days to return. The Catholic Church was less bothered. When, in 1861, the attempt was made by a group of liberal churchmen to assimilate some of the aspects of critical scholarship in *Essays and Reviews*, leading to the prosecution of two of the contributors, Newman observed: 'Plenary inspiration of

Scripture is peculiarly a Protestant question; not a Catholic.'[43] Evangelicals, on the whole, were reluctant to concede that the good old days were no more. Dean Close firmly asserted that 'the cultivation of the intellectual powers can of itself have no tendency towards moral and spiritual good.'[44] But there was a genuine Protestant dilemma, as Mark Pattison was quick to point out:

> It must either give up Scripture, or put a veto on its interpretation. If the principle of 'Scripture the only source' was to be maintained, it could only be maintained by applying the recognized laws of interpretation. To veto interpretation was to reduce Scripture to silence.[45]

As far as the 'man in the pew' was concerned, the dilemma was less grievous. The whole matter was too technical for the majority to understand. A conscientious young priest, however, might have to try to answer the question posed by Mr Langham to Robert Elsmere, in Mrs Humphry Ward's best-selling novel:

> 'I don't understand you,' said Robert, flushing ... 'Christian theology is a system of ideas indeed, but of ideas realised, made manifest in facts.'
>   Langham looked at him for a moment, undecided ... 'How do you know they are facts?' he said drily.[46]

II

'Mr Darwin's theory *need* not then be atheistical.'
                              John Henry Newman in 1868

'I see no good reason why the views given in this volume should shock the religious feelings of any one.'
                              Charles Darwin, *The Origin of Species*

The early careers of Charles Darwin and T.H. Huxley reveal remarkable similarities. They both began their scientific education as medical students, a calling which they soon discovered not to be to their taste. They both established their credentials in the fields of geology and natural history by obtaining appointments on surveying ships engaged in voyages of exploration to the Tropics, Darwin on the *Beagle* and Huxley on the *Rattlesnake*. Both based their subsequent researches on a foundation of the whole range of scientific studies, in days when special-ization was almost unheard-of; and they reacted in similar ways to books which young scientists could hardly have failed to read during the first half of the nineteenth century: Charles Lyell's *Principles of Geology* (1830–3), read with mutual admiration, and the sensational *Vestiges of the Natural History of Creation* (by Robert Chambers, but published anony-mously in 1844), in which the theory of evolution and the transmutation of species was first propounded at a popular level. This they both deplored. As Huxley expressed it, 'the book simply irritated by the pro-digious ignorance and thoroughly unscientific habit of mind manifested by the writer.'[1]

As their respective researches advanced, they both found themselves out of sympathy with the group of scientists and natural philosophers who, contributing to the eleven-volume encyclopaedia of natural theol-ogy entitled the *Bridgewater Treatises* (1833–6), reiterated the earlier notion of William Paley that the universe constantly exhibited the evidence of Design and the handiwork of a benevolent divine creator. In their uneasiness at such an assumption, much influenced by Lyell, they found themselves drawn into closer fellowship with, while working entirely independently of, other rising figures in the scientific world, notably J.D. Hooker and John Tyndall. In two other respects their later careers fol-lowed a parallel course. Such early attachment as they may have had to orthodox Christianity faded into an indefinite sort of Theism, and thence into – to use Huxley's own term – 'agnosticism',[2] Huxley tending, in his abandonment of religious convictions, to be always slightly one step ahead of his friend. Darwin described himself as a 'theist' in the year that the *Origin of Species* was published (1859);[3] twenty years later, he wrote: 'I have never been an Atheist ... an Agnostic would be the more correct description of my state of mind.'[4] Finally, both men were fre-quently incapacitated by ill-health. Darwin was forced to rest for hours each day; the cause of his condition is not clear. Huxley suffered fre-quently from dyspepsia, but – more seriously, in terms of his ultimate output – he was also dogged by what his son described as 'hypo-chondriacal depression'.[5] At one stage, shortly after becoming an FRS, he was so borne down by depression that he seriously contemplated giving up scientific resarch altogether in order to become – of all improbable alternatives – a brewer.[6]

On The Origin of Species by means of Natural Selection did not burst upon a world wholly unprepared for cosmic revelations. *The Vestiges of Creation* had become something of a best-seller, 25,000 copies having been bought in Britain before Darwin's work was known.[7] It lacked the weight of convincing research, however, to cause great anxiety. More disturbing, although at the same time exhilarating to many, were the developments in the study of archaeology stimulated by the geological researches of Lyell and others. Archaeology became the popular science of mid-Victorian England – awesome in its challenge to the Mosaic cosmology but, in its revelations of the gradual evolution of technology from the use of flint, bronze and iron to the astounding achievements of their own time, a demonstration to Victorians that their belief in progress was being triumphantly confirmed. Sir Austen Layard, the excavator of Nineveh, found himself famous overnight after the publication of his findings in 1848. Two years later, an abridgement for railway bookstalls was commissioned by John Murray for his series entitled 'Reading for the Rail, or Cheap Books in a large readable type published occasionally'.[8]

Scientific advance creates its own momentum. Geology stimulated studies in archaeology; and as the century progressed, archaeology in turn stimulated researches into anthropology, ethnology, and philology, each contributing its knife-thrust into those still clinging to fundamentalist, Old Testament accounts of the Creation. The leading philologist of his day, Max Müller, with his insights into the degree in which language is the clue to history, arising from the 'identity of language and thought',[9] was deemed in 1860 to constitute a threat to orthodoxy in Oxford, still trying to come to grips with Darwin, and he consequently failed to gain the Chair of Sanskrit. Eight years later the climate had changed sufficiently to secure for him the Oxford Professorship of Comparative Philology.

Darwin's great work was very nearly forestalled by the publication of similar conclusions by the eccentric Alfred Russell Wallace, who had espoused a theory of natural selection as well as a host of other more questionable and fashionable enthusiasms including phrenology, mesmerism and spiritualism. He was also a disciple of Tom Paine and Robert Owen. Lyell warned Darwin that he might not succeed in getting in first. 'All my originality ... will be smashed,' Darwin wrote in despair in 1858, after reading a paper of Wallace's written three years earlier.[10] Hooker offered to act as mediator, and Wallace was mollified by an invitation to give a joint paper with Darwin to the Linnean Society. Darwin duly published a year later, expressing some disappointment at the initially modest sales of the book. But Huxley was to be his champion. His first reaction on reading the *Origin of Species* was: 'How extremely stupid not to have thought of that!'[11] His proselytism, together with highly controversial reviews of the book, ensured an immediate boost to its sales. By the end of the century, nearly 50,000 copies had been sold.

It would appear from the careful, almost devout, tone of the book, and from Darwin's own (surely naïve) statement towards its conclusion that he saw 'no good reason why the views given in this volume should shock the religious feelings of any one',[12] that he was unprepared for the onslaughts that awaited him. Huxley was more realistic. 'I am sharpening up my claws and beak in readiness,' he assured his friend.[13] How effective those claws and beak were, in his allegedly blistering riposte to Samuel Wilberforce, Bishop of Oxford, at the meeting of the British Association at Oxford in 1860, has been for many years a matter of debate. Wilberforce, in a moment of misjudgement, had concluded a not very convincing defence of orthodoxy against the implications of Darwin's theories with what he thought would score a smart debating point, posing the question (to whom directed, no one could accurately recall) whether 'it was through his grandfather or his grandmother that he claimed ... descent from a monkey?' Various versions of what Huxley actually said in reply have been offered; and J.R. Green, who was present, claimed an exact recollection which, when subsequently transcribed, suggests a far more finished piece of prose than could actually have been either uttered or committed to memory at the time:

> A man has no reason to be ashamed of having an ape for his grandfather. If there were to be an ancestor whom I should feel shame in recalling, it would rather be a man – a man of restless and versatile intellect, who, not content with an equivocal success in his own sphere of activity, plunges into scientific questions with which he has no real acquaintance, only to obscure them by an aimless rhetoric, and distract the attention of his hearers from the real point at issue by eloquent digressions and skilled appeals to religious prejudice.[14]

More recent investigations, based largely on press reports, have cast doubts on whether Huxley ever said anything of the sort. According to the report in *The Athenaeum*, the truly effective reply to Wilberforce's speech came not from Huxley at all, but from Joseph Hooker.[15]

What is not a matter of doubt is that Darwin had seemed to deliver body blows to Christian orthodoxy in three main respects. In the first place, his careful analysis of the transmutation of species made it impossible to adhere to the traditional view of 'special creation' – the notion that at some historic moment God determined that birds should be birds, beasts should be particular beasts, and that man should be man. Secondly, the process by which organisms developed and modified, through adaptation, was not according to some benevolent design, but in response to the exigencies of chance. What determined the survival and evolution of one species and the death of another was natural selection. 'Nature', as Basil Willey has explained, '... takes advantage of the favourable variations, and suppresses the unfavourable; creatures that happen to put forth variations advantageous to them in the struggle, survive and perpetuate themselves; the rest perish.'[16]

The third disquieting element was Darwin's picture of the amorality of nature: the survival of the fittest, suggesting that it was certainly not the meek who inherited the earth. Darwin was not intending to say that there was no possible role for God in this, admittedly unbiblical, scenario. As Walter Cannon has pointed out, Darwin rejected Design, but he did not repudiate the concept of some underlying purpose in the way in which *Homo sapiens* evolved.[17] Inevitably, however, the rejection of the account of the Creation in Genesis fostered an escalating scepticism. If there was no Adam and Eve, there was no Garden of Eden. If no Eden, there was no Temptation, and no Fall of Man. If no Fall of Man, what became of original sin and the requirement of redemption? So, a thirteen-year-old schoolboy named George Macaulay Trevelyan reasoned, from hearing that Darwin had proved the Bible to be untrue, 'the fabric of Christian doctrine instantaneously fell away in ruin.'[18]

How far this sort of thinking percolated to the 'man in the pew' is difficult to gauge. *The Origin of Species* is a very substantial volume, and although elegantly written, it is by no means simple reading. But the substance of Darwin's teaching and of Huxley's own contribution – *Evidence as to Man's Place in Nature* – was widely known. There can be little doubt that the theory of evolution was popularized among the earnest self-improving members of the Mechanics' Institutes, whose reaction was likely to be similar to the young Trevelyan's. But not all churchmen were discountenanced. The Catholic Newman, for example, distanced himself from an attempt by one of his co-religionists in 1868 to undermine Darwin's conclusions.

> I do not fear the theory so much as he seems to do [he wrote] ... It does not seem to me to follow that creation is denied because the Creator, millions of years ago, gave laws to matter. He first created matter and then he created laws for it – laws which should *construct* it into its present wonderful beauty, and accurate adjustment and harmony of parts *gradually* ... Mr Darwin's theory *need* not then be atheistical, be it true or not; it may simply be suggesting a larger idea of Divine Prescience and Skill.[19]

It is interesting to note that Kingsley, Newman's great adversary, came to precisely the same conclusion.[20] Earlier than either of them, only months after Darwin's book had appeared, the young F.J.A. Hort, who was to play a not insignificant role years later in correcting some of the errors of the Tübingen school, wrote to his friend Brooke Foss Westcott: 'Have you read Darwin? How I should like a talk with you about it! In spite of difficulties, I am inclined to think it unanswerable. In any case it is a treat to read such a book.'[21] What each of these three men were saying, at least by implication, was 'your God is too small'. The extraordinary picture presented by Darwin, far from diminishing the stature of God, enlarged it. Certainly the barber whom the young A.J. Balfour visited in the 1860s – full of the chatter of his kind – thought that it was all very exciting: 'the doctrine of evolution, Darwin and Huxley and the lot of them – hashed up somehow with the good time coming and the universal brotherhood, and I don't know what else.'[22]

For the majority of the clergy, it is probable that the advent of Darwinism immeasurably intensified their anxieties. They were being presented with questions they were unable satisfactorily to answer. Many will have swallowed their own doubts and misgivings and put a brave face on things. Tennyson's father, long before Darwin, did his duty as a parish priest, while having lost his faith.[23] Leslie Stephen, on the other hand, could not live a lie. He ceased to officiate as a priest when he found that he no longer believed; but he was quite certain that many of his Cambridge contemporaries 'shared my scepticism, but continued to be clergymen'. They were 'rational enough to see that the old orthodox position was untenable ... but also thought that religious belief of some kind was necessary or valuable'.[24] Perhaps not without a little struggle of conscience, they took heart from the advice which the cynical and scep-tical Roger Wendover gave to the over-scrupulous Robert Elsmere in Mrs Humphry Ward's novel: 'Good God, what nonsense! As if any one inquired what an English parson believed nowadays, so long as he per-forms all the usual antics decently!'[25]

The loss to the Church of many men of stature who – in different cir-cumstances – might have been expected to become its staunchest defenders, cannot, of course, be measured. While Leslie Stephen aban-doned his Orders without a struggle, J.A. Froude felt it necessary to make a loud noise about his loss of faith. Mark Pattison continued to officiate half-heartedly, but he became soured and peevish; and the Rugby of Arnold, Tait and Temple – the nursery of talented, ardent young Christians – produced more than its fair share of disenchanted souls, A.H. Clough, Matthew Arnold himself, Henry Sidgwick and T.H. Green the most celebrated among others. Green found a new cause in preaching a religion of humanity; Sidgwick felt an intense sense of responsibility lest his own scepticism should influence others, and was totally honest about his personal sense of loss. 'I still hunger and thirst after orthodoxy,' he wrote in 1862, while yet in his early twenties; 'but I am, I trust, firm not to barter my intellectual birthright for a mess of mystical pottage.'[26]

When Clough and Matthew Arnold lost their faith, they seemed to lose too all sense of joy, never really to be recovered.[27] They both became wanderers, as Arnold expressed it in *Stanzas from the Grande Chartreuse*:

> Wandering between two worlds, one dead
> The other powerless to be born,
> With nowhere yet to rest my head.

But then, one never quite knows with Arnold. Did he, as George Landow suggests, have a secret wish – in spite of his predilection for 'metaphors of isolation and helplessness' – to find himself wandering back home?[28] R.H. Hutton suspected that Arnold was 'never quite at his best except when ... delineating a mood of regret'. This was not quite joylessness, but rather a sort of melancholy joy in the midst of pain.[29]

None of these men was an atheist. They had no wish to try to prove that God did not exist, even if that were possible. Some agnostics believed, with Huxley, that the release from Christianity enabled one to aspire to a superior moral code. In an article on 'Science and the Bishops' in 1887, Huxley wrote:

> Theological apologists who insist that morality will vanish if their dogmas are exploded, would do well to consider the fact that, in the matter of intellectual veracity, science is already a long way ahead of the Churches; and that, in this particular, it is exerting an educational influence on mankind of which the Churches have shown themselves utterly incapable.[30]

Was there a future for human kind in the beyond? Some of the agnostics hankered after some convincing evidence of life after death. Huxley was not one of them. He unburdened himself at length to Charles Kingsley in 1860, pointing out that he neither denied nor affirmed the immortality of man; and as for ultimate judgement of man's actions, why should it be necessary – he asked – to believe in anything so improbable when, in this life on earth, 'the gravitation of sin to sorrow is as certain as that of the earth to the sun'? He had frankly been revolted, at the recent funeral of his little son, by the words of the officiating minister: 'If the dead rise not again, let us eat and drink, for tomorrow we die.'

> I cannot tell you how inexpressibly they shocked me ... What! because I am face to face with irreparable loss ... I am to renounce my manhood, and, howling, grovel in bestiality? Why, the very apes know better, and if you shoot their young, the poor brutes grieve their grief out and do not immediately seek distraction in a gorge.[31]

On the other hand – many agnostics seemed to argue – granted the unparalleled advance of knowledge of natural phenomena in their own lifetime, civilization could well be on the threshold of equally amazing discoveries about the supernatural, the extra-sensory and the paranormal. The 'science' of phrenology, associated with the name of George Combe, was not exactly paranormal, nor was it in any sense avowedly anti-Christian. Its scientific status has been defined as 'half-way between anatomy and a primitive form of psychology'.[32] Combe's conviction that each human being's character and natural disposition could be discerned by an examination of cranial bumps (corresponding to the respective organs of the brain, each determining particular mental faculties) seemed to him to revolutionize the whole concept of metaphysics, ethics, education, bodily health and social behaviour. Its application could prove to be the panacea of the world's ills.

Combe's triumphant exposition of his discovery in *The Constitution of Man*, published in 1828, created such an impact, both in Britain and America, that – Boyd Hilton maintains – 'it was possibly the most widely-read book after the Bible, *Pilgrim's Progress*, and *Robinson Crusoe* during the second quarter of the nineteenth century.'[33] Richard Cobden was an early convert and founded one of the first phrenological societies in Manchester in 1838. He was apt, in making new acquaintances, to look first at the shape of their skulls, so that he could determine the type of person he was addressing. The loathsome Mahomet Ali, whom Cobden met on a visit to Cairo in 1836, was minutely observed and the diagnosis duly recorded:

> I glanced at the form of his head ... confirmatory of the science of phrenology – its huge size according with the extraordinary force of character displayed by this successful soldier, whilst a broad and massive forehead harmonizes with the powerful intellect he has displayed in his schemes of personal aggrandizement.[34]

Perhaps it is not surprising that those questing for new insights into human behaviour, for new truths to replace outmoded ones, should want to explore everything that offered explanations of the workings of the human mind. George Eliot pressed her friend Charles Bray (a disciple of Combe) to examine and diagnose her bumps, deemed to be so extraordinary that she arranged for Combe himself to make a second examination.[35] Harriet Martineau eagerly embraced both phrenology and mesmerism, enthusiasms which brought about her estrangement from her Unitarian brother, James.[36] Mesmerism, or Animal Magnetism, as it was sometimes called, tended to appeal to exactly the same clientele. It was something new. It promised limitless therapeutic possibilities. More than that, it unfolded further revelations about the nature of the human mind and possible extra-sensory forces. Lord Amberley, yet another agnostic, was fascinated by it. He tried his hand at it himself, and – to his great satisfaction – succeeded in mesmerizing one of their housemaids who complained of a pain in her face, and actually cured it.[37]

It seems strange in retrospect, even ironical, that free thinkers who rejected the irrational element in Christian belief should have become so possessed of a credulous compulsion to investigate the paranormal. From phrenology and mesmerism it was but a step to earnest explorations into the 'beyond' through the experience of spiritualism. There was nothing new, of course, in the fascination with anything suggestive of the supernatural. The 'Ghost Society' in Cambridge, for instance, was founded in 1851 by the most orthodox of young Anglicans, including E.W. Benson, Lightfoot and Westcott, partly for thrills, but also partly from an earnest desire to exchange information about the seemingly inexplicable.[38] It was in the next decade that attempts to make contact with the spirit world by seances became almost a vogue. Jowett confessed to Huxley that he was seriously worried by the extent to which it was absorbing the interests of Oxford undergraduates in the early 1870s.[39] Huxley himself attended a seance in 1874, coming to the conclusion that he had been the victim of 'mere trickery'.[40] Matthew Arnold was equally dismissive of 'our modern sorcerers'.[41] Kate Stanley was singularly unimpressed by a charlatan called 'Mr Squires' in 1860, and in 1873, in the company of Amberley, left a seance conducted by a Mrs Acworth, a good deal 'perplexed but not convinced'.[42] Harriet Beecher Stowe and George Eliot corresponded with each other in 1872 about a variety of extraordinary alleged manifestations on both sides of the Atlantic, including the materialization of live eels and lobsters by a Mrs Samuel Guppy. But when Mrs Beecher Stowe claimed to have had a planchette conversation with Charlotte Brontë, lasting two hours, George Eliot was so persuaded of its 'enormous' improbability that she made so bold as to tell her friend that 'it seems to me that to rest any fundamental part of religion on such a basis is a melancholy misguidance of men's minds from the true sources of high and pure emotion.'[43]

Henry Sidgwick could not leave the paranormal alone, satisfied that there was sufficient prima facie evidence to warrant dispassionate scientific enquiry. He found a soul-mate in F.W.H. Myers in 1869, and in Nora Balfour whom he first met at a seance and subsequently married. In February 1882 they all became founder members of the Society for Psychical Research. If Christianity had seemed no more than a mess of mystical pottage to this scrupulously honest and truth-loving man, then he had to convince himself that other claims, either for the reality of the spirit world or for the transmigration of souls, were equally invalid. So, in 1884, in Oscar Browning's rooms in King's College, Cambridge, he met the co-founder of the cult of Theosophy, Madame H.P. Blavatsky, for earnest discussion. 'If she is a humbug,' he wrote, 'she is a consummate one.' So impressed were he and his wife that they despatched a member of the SPR to Madras, which had become the headquarters of what its adherents hoped would prove a world-wide movement. The report came back: 'a fraud from beginning to end'.[44]

During the 1870s and 1880s, unbelief was reaching its peak. W.H. Mallock's 'Mr Leslie' in *The New Republic* (1877) observed to the assembled company: 'I certainly think that our age in some ways could not possibly be worse. Nobody knows what to believe, and most people believe nothing.'[45] The protracted conflict over the election to Parliament in 1880 of the avowed atheist Charles Bradlaugh, who refused to take the required oath 'on the faith of a Christian', degenerated almost into farce, to the embarrassment of Gladstone's ill-starred second administration. It lasted until 1886, by which time the whole country was talking about it and taking sides, the working classes on the whole firmly supporting Bradlaugh.[46] In the same year, Sidgwick recorded in his diary: 'I do not think the spirit of the age, in its most religious phase, is really Christian; I think it is Theistic.'[47]

This may have been wishful thinking on the part of a somewhat disillusioned agnostic. In fact, through these same decades and well into the next century, all the Christian churches were showing signs of a new vitality. From some quarters there was a decided counter-attack. Unquestionably, too, Christian defences were being reappraised and reorganized. Much of what had seemed shocking to Christians at first had had time to be absorbed and appreciated for its positive rather than its potentially destructive significance. Darwinism, for instance, by the close of the century had become so much part of the accepted thinking within the Establishment that Darwin's remains were interred in Westminster Abbey. In 1894 Huxley had cause to marvel at the extent to which the old conflicts had subsided. The British Association had met again in Oxford, and Huxley reported on events to his lifelong friend, Joseph Hooker:

> It was very queer to sit there and hear the doctrines you and I were damned for advocating thirty-five years ago at Oxford, enunciated as matters of course – disputed by no reasonable man! – in the Sheldonian Theatre by the Chancellor.[48]

This had required from the churches some shifting of ground; and for the most part they had responded, the notable exceptions being the Evangelicals and the Weslyan Methodists.[49] One traditional argument in particular – the notion that the abandonment of Christian belief would inevitably lead to moral collapse – was less confidently asserted. At least for the educated classes, this would no longer serve. J.E.C. Welldon, later to become Bishop of Calcutta, was ill-advised enough in 1885, in the hearing of Henry Bradshaw, the University Librarian, to state publicly that the spread of unbelief in Cambridge had been invariably accompanied by 'loss of morality'. Bradshaw knew the undergraduates well. They were as honest, decent and caring as they had ever been. He also knew Sidgwick well, whose influence in Cambridge was little less than that of T.H. Green in Oxford. Sidgwick might have encouraged agnosticism, but never a lowering of morals. So Bradshaw gave Welldon a little lesson in morality in return. 'Well, Welldon,' he said. 'You lied; and what is worse, you knew you lied!'[50]

III

'This world's no blot for us
Nor blank; it means intensely, and means good:
To find its meaning is my meat and drink.'

Robert Browning, *Fra Lippo Lippi*

R.H. Hutton, commenting in the 1870s on the fear of certain of his contemporaries that 'the dark shadow of Atheism' threatened 'to envelop the earth', called to mind 'a very obvious but strangely-forgotten truth, that human trust does not create God, and that human distrust would not annihilate him'.[1] John Keble, twenty years earlier, expressed the same sentiment even more strongly, quoting the words of St Basil, 'that God be true, but every man a liar'.[2] In whatever form God had revealed divine truth, the truth could not be rendered less divine by the hands of men. Among the churches at the time, there were three different stances on the understanding of the nature of revelation, two firmly traditional and one very much the product of nineteenth-century thinking. The influence of Coleridge and Thomas Arnold lay behind the perception of Anglican Broad Church thinkers, that man's discoveries through his God-given intellect were actually vehicles of a progressive revelation, truth being apprehended about the nature of God's creation and his purposes for man, which God intended that the mind of man should bring to light at some appointed time. This might be described as a dynamic concept of revelation.

By contrast, the traditionalist Protestant stance was that the revelation had been delivered once and for all in the Word of God in the Scriptures and was therefore complete in itself. As John Knox once testily explained to the unconvinced Catholic Mary, Queen of Scots:

> Ye shall believe God that plainly speaketh in his word ... The word of God is plain in the self, and if there appear any obscurity in one place, the Holy Ghost, which is never contrarious to himself, explains the same more clearly in other places; so that there can remain no doubt.[3]

The Roman Catholic stance was equally authoritarian. The Church was the interpreter of Scripture, and – guided by the Holy Spirit – might in its own good time clarify its divine teaching by rendering explicit what had always been implicit, if never previously defined, according to the needs of the faithful. In that sense the Romanists (as opposed to Anglo-Catholics, who rested authority on the doctrines of the primitive Church) admitted the possibility of the development of doctrine, always resting on a divinely authoritative basis.

There is no doubt that both the Evangelical wing of the Anglican Church (with also the Evangelical Dissenting Churches) and the Catholic Church possessed a power to withstand the impact of unbelief which they could immediately invoke to ease the mind of waverers, and this was their particular strength. An Evangelical who had had the experience of personal conversion, and who revered the Scriptures as the instrument of his salvation, was not likely to be seriously bothered by Darwin's excursions into the pre-history of man. That was Darwin's problem, not his. Similarly, if F.C. Baur chose to have doubts about the authenticity of the Gospels, then that was his misfortune, the penalty of supposing that intellect had anything remotely to do with the claims of faith. A devout Catholic, too, could confidently leave it to his Church, when it thought the moment right, to declare how Catholics were to react to notions that were causing turmoil in other people's minds. To this extent, both the Evangelicals and the Catholics had in their favour the disposition of the mass of men, in times of crisis and doubt, to yearn for an authoritative voice.

Archbishop Manning saw this clearly. It was the trump card that he played in the debates in Rome in 1870, during the first Vatican Council, when the dogma of Papal Infallibility came to be defined.

> The religious Protestant in England [he said] desired an escape from the confusion and chaos of the innumerable sects, and the lack of any tribunal able to teach with authority; so far as England is concerned, the definition will more than anything else promote conversions and the return of the country to the Faith.[4]

This was a little sanguine, but also possessed a grain of truth. In fact, Newman's mollifying genius was needed to ease the minds of the more intellectual spirits among English Catholics. It would therefore be true to say that while the Evangelicals' assurance that the Word of God was sacrosanct and the Catholic Church's defiant dogmatism proved an effective antidote to the doubts of the many, neither stance was likely to cut much ice with intellectuals like Henry Sidgwick or Matthew Arnold.

History suggests that the evangelical spirit can never be quiescent for long; and that it thrives on moments of crisis. During the 1860s, possibly as a reaction against Darwinism, spontaneous outbreaks of revivalism took place in Cornwall, the Midlands, even – in the form of prayer meetings – at Oxford and Cambridge, much of them the result of lay initiatives. Whether these were influenced by a more dramatic 'Evangelical Awakening' in the USA, following a financial crash of appalling dimensions in the autumn of 1858, as maintained by Edwin Orr,[5] is questionable. What is certain is that the impact of the revivalist preaching of C.H. Spurgeon, for whom the Metropolitan Tabernacle had to be built to house his vast congregations, testified to the large number, chiefly within the lower-middle and working classes, who recognized in themselves 'the hungry sheep who look up and are not fed'. The ground was being well prepared for the sensational success of the mission of two American revivalists – D.L. Moody and I.D. Sankey – who came to London in 1875 to conduct mass meetings in the Agricultural Hall. These were all un-denominational gatherings, from which the Nonconformist Churches benefited most of all, gaining during the 'Awakening' some 370,000 accessions.[6]

The Anglican hierarchy viewed all this evangelistic activity with mixed feelings. Archbishop Tait rather guardedly gave it his blessing.

What worried him was the effect of crowd psychology in inducing people to come forward to declare their conversion without realizing the full implications of what they were doing. Furthermore, Tait had misgivings about the unprofessional nature of the 'after-care' such converts were likely to receive.[7] The Moody and Sankey approach, at least, eschewed the Hell-fire tactics of the earlier generation. Nevertheless, the theology of the revivalist movement remained confidently fundamentalist; and on the vexed question of eternal punishment there was no indication that the Evangelicals found it in the least vexing. The Calvinist emphasis, however, seems to have been silently dropped, in particular the doctrine of predestination to salvation or damnation. The influence of the Wesleyan Methodists in repudiating that 'hateful, horrible decree' (Charles Wesley's own words) gradually prevailed. A popular Evangelical hymn of the period left no doubt that redemption was available to all who repented.

> Come, sinners, to the gospel feast:
> Let every soul be Jesu's guest:
> Ye need not one be left behind,
> For God hath bidden all mankind.[8]

There were significant lessons to be learnt from the imaginativeness and wide-ranging appeal of this revivalist campaign. It was obviously sensible to tailor the missionary approach to young people – the particular undertaking of the American evangelist Paysan Hammond. It was perceptive to exploit the presence of holiday crowds on the beaches at seaside resorts by holding informal services on the sands. But it was positively inspired of William Booth to create a force of militant evangelists, with a special uniform and a band to accompany the hymn-singing, processing into the poorest areas of London, bringing colour into drab lives as well as compelling attention and provoking a response (even a hostile one). The military discipline of the Salvation Army was itself an attraction, appealing in a subtle way to the yearning for authority; and William Booth was a convinced authoritarian. 'Despotism is essential to most enterprises,' he wrote in his *In Darkest England and the Way Out.*[9] His methods were crude, as was his evangelism. He had come to rescue sinners from Hell; and to Hell they would surely go if tempted by the demon drink. The Salvationists had one object only: to save souls by whatever rough and ready means lay to hand.

When we go fishing [Booth informed a rally of his 'troops'], we bait our hooks with the most enticing bait we can find. If one bait does not take, then we try another, and another, and another, and if they won't take any, then, as one of our Officers said the other day, *we go down and hook them on.*[10]

This was good fighting talk; but Booth came to see in time that trying to capture the souls of the destitute before something had been done to improve their social conditions was to engage in a battle that he could not win; and there was little to gain by making threats of Hell-fire to those who were living in a sort of hell already.

Archbishop Manning, who was elevated to the cardinalate in 1875, had come to the same conclusion, while at the same time amazing his fellow Catholics by unashamedly adopting evangelical tactics and the methods of the Salvation Army in his own missionary work and his crusade against the evils of intemperance, the chief cause – as he believed – of poverty, misery and vice. In the earliest days of his Anglican ministry Manning had been an Evangelical, and although he became one of the leading High Churchmen of his day before his conversion to Rome, something of that evangelical fervour and pietism was never lost. He had himself founded an order of mission priests, working among the poor in Bayswater, before he succeeded Cardinal Wiseman as Archbishop in 1865.

He castigated his fellow Catholics for their failure to involve themselves in the great social causes of their times. 'All the great works of charity in England have had their beginning out of the Church,' he observed.[11] Why could they not learn from the example of the 'Evangelicals, Methodists and Salvationists? ... Why then do we not draw men as Spurgeon and "General" Booth and Hugh Price Hughes?'[12] He set a personal example by founding the League of the Cross to proselytize for total abstinence, which – like the Salvation Army – held open-air meetings, complete with processions and banners. He happily shared a platform with Bramwell Booth. Convinced that the Church should be seen to be the protector of the people, who could so easily fall prey to the communists if the Church failed to take the initiative, he served on the Cross Committee on elementary education and became a member of the Royal Commission on the Housing of the Working Classes. It is significant that he was granted precedence on that Commission next below the Prince of Wales and above Lord Salisbury, a remarkable indication of his success in gaining public acknowledgement of Roman Catholicism which, only thirty years earlier, had been the butt of 'No Popery' riots. His final service to the working classes was his successful last-minute intervention in the crippling London dock strike of 1889, using his personal influence with the strike leaders to secure a satisfactory settlement.

Both Evangelicals and Anglo-Catholics, in their different ways, were responding to the desperate need for missionary work in the poorest areas of London. The Evangelical approach tended to fasten on specific groups in the metropolis, establishing missions to, for instance, the seamen of the Port of London or the street traders of the East End. As early as 1835 the London City Mission had been set up, consisting of Anglican Evangelicals and Nonconformists, resolved to ignore denominational distinctions both in their composition and in the souls whom they were reaching out to save. Under the chairmanship of Baptist Noel the Mission recruited a little army of lay evangelists, committed to regular nightly stands in railway stations, all-night coffee-stalls, public houses and gin-palaces. They even sought out 'the pathetic creatures who scavenged on the refuse tips'.[13]

The Anglo-Catholic approach differed in two significant respects. Whereas the Evangelicals distributed bibles on every possible occasion, the Anglo-Catholic clergy sought, in the worship they offered, to bring colour into drab and dingy lives – light, warmth, ceremonial, vestments – not only to offer an escape from the squalor of the areas in which they ministered, but also to inculcate a sense of Catholic devotion and some understanding of Catholic doctrine, which – to an illiterate congregation – could best be conveyed by visual acts, symbols and ceremonial. A.H. Mackonochie, of St Alban's, Holborn, rejected the label 'ritualist' which was levelled derisively at him and at other like-minded mission priests.

> People have taken to call us 'Ritualists' [Mackonochie wrote] ... I confess to thinking the name a somewhat unsuitable one ... We feel that a gorgeously conducted service ought to mean something. It does mean something – it means that the Holy Eucharist is the Sacrament of Christ's Body and Blood – 'the Body and Blood of Christ' under the Form of Bread and Wine.[14]

Their concept of mission, too, was different from that of the revivalists. They meant by 'mission' a permanent settlement in order to live and to

work among the souls whom they were striving to convert. Charles
Lowder, when he founded the Society of the Holy Cross, defined his
order as 'the establishment of a permanent mission in the first practically heathen district they could get admission to'; and just such a propitious, or daunting, district was found for them in the parish of St
George's-in-the-East in the heart of London dockland. It was an area
of 6,000 houses in which as many as 48,000 had to find shelter.[15]

In time the concept of missionary settlements caught on, demonstrating an early example of the way in which different religious traditions came to be fused in order to meet a common objective. After all,
it had been the Broad Church party of F.D. Maurice, Kingsley, J.M.
Ludlow and Tom Hughes who had been the pioneers of Christian
Socialism in the 1840s and 50s. Two decades later, when the consciences
of the more privileged classes were stirred by the plight of the outcasts
living in what has since come to be known as the 'inner city', public
school and college missions came to be a new fashion, with the building
of recreational centres adjoining the mission churches. These offered
the sort of robust, physical outlets to engage the energies of poor
boys that Kingsley and Hughes, in their proselytism of 'muscular
Christianity', believed to be the ideal therapy for both body and soul. It
was not long before the Evangelical YMCA fastened upon the same
idea. Norman Vance discovered a superb example of latter-day
Evangelical muscularity in a publication by a devotee of the YMCA –
Frederick Atkins – in 1890, entitled *Moral Muscle and how to use it. A brotherly chat with young men.*[16]

But this was not enough, said humanitarian crusaders like T.H.
Green and John Ruskin. What was needed above all was the commit-
ment to 'become a Jacob in Esau's need': the educated should be prepared to live in the midst of the uneducated. Unless places like Stepney
and Whitechapel had a 'resident gentry', prepared to perform 'a social
function complementary to the religious work of missions', the inhabitants would continue to live in squalor.[17] It was to this call that Arnold
Toynbee responded; and, after his early death, Samuel Barnett, the
founder of Toynbee Hall in memory of his friend. The revelations of
the horrors of the East End in *The Bitter Cry of Outcast London*, the work
of a Congregationalist minister, Andrew Mearns, published in 1883,
came at a timely moment; and Barnett admitted the first residents of
Toynbee Hall in the following year.

To their credit, the Evangelicals could point to the success of the Sunday school as a prime agency in the conversion of the working classes. Although its origins went back to the 1780s, it was during the nineteenth century that the phenomenal increase in the number of children attending Sunday schools took place, crossing all denominational borders. In 1888 it was calculated that in many areas of England and Wales about three children out of four regularly attended; and since many of the upper classes felt that their ambience, both socially and educationally, was inappropriate for their offspring, this suggests that the majority of working class families patronized them. John Bright saluted the achievement in rapturous terms: 'I don't believe that all the statesmen in existence – I don't believe all the efforts they have ever made – have tended so much to the greatness and true happiness, the security and glory of this country, as have the efforts of Sunday school teachers.'[18]

Closer investigation has revealed a degree of regional variation in attendance. The north (the north-east in particular) comes out easily top of the list; the statistics for Birmingham are less impressive; and London – not surprisingly – has the lowest figures.[19] Furthermore, a very sobering fact has to be taken into account, casting Bright's enthusiasm in a rather less sanguine light. At a time when the number of children attending Sunday school was increasing, the attendance figure for both church and chapel-goers declined and continued to fall until – and beyond – the end of the century. The idealism behind the movement has never been better expressed than by a United Methodist in 1858: 'The primary design of the Sabbath-school is the communication of religious knowledge, the implantation of right principles, the culture of the heart and, as the climax of all, conversion of the soul.'[20] Sadly, however, the evidence suggests a very limited long-term effect.

A number of explanations for the failure of the Sunday schools to rear adult worshippers can be offered. Children obliged by their non-church-going parents to 'get out from under their feet' on a Sunday morning were not likely to adopt a different stance from their parents when freed from compulsion. More to the point, perhaps, was the changing nature of weekend life for the lower classes during the second half of the century. When there had been no alternative on offer for social concourse or relaxation on a Sunday, church or chapel attendance constituted a not altogether unwelcome break from the domestic environment. Probably the Sunday openings of museums and art galleries were not exactly magnetic counter-attractions to working-class families, although anti-Sabbatarian artisans were prepared to demonstrate for their right to enjoy such cultural pleasures, more – one fancies – for reasons of principle than from any genuine desire for intellectual uplift.[21] But the late-Victorian Saturday had pleasures to offer which were unknown earlier in the century and had repercussions on how the following day of rest might be spent. More money in the pocket at a time of a rising standard of living meant more money to be spent in a public house on Saturday nights. In a survey of Bristol (population: 206,513) over the years 1881 and 1882, it was reckoned that the number of drinkers in public-houses on a Saturday night practically equalled the total number attending worship – morning or evening or both – on a Sunday.[22] They were not likely to be the same people, of course. Most sizeable cities had music-halls, with ticket prices within the reach of most wage-earners. But the greatest threat of all was the diversion offered to all classes, and the lower classes most of all, by the advent of professional football. This is what the working-man regarded as the highlight of his weekend. To many representatives of the different churches, it seemed as if the passion engendered by football was rapidly becoming the working-man's religion. In any event, the pattern of his Saturday recreation meant that he took to his bed so late that he was too often tempted to keep to it on a Sunday morning.[23] In such a changed situation, the churches were likely to be the losers.

This did not mean that the child who had dutifully attended Sunday school became either anti-Christian or hostile to church or chapel when, as an adult, he put away childish things. If asked, he would probably claim to be a Christian, even if he no longer attended worship at all. And some dim residuum of what he had been taught would still linger in his mind, sufficiently, at least, to influence his personal moral code. This is the conclusion that Elizabeth Roberts arrived at during her researches into the lives of Lancashire women at the close of the century. Whether they went to a place of worship or not, 'religion had not lost its hold on the urban working class in the north-west of England, and it is questionable whether it had in other areas.'[24]

As for the various denominations, there was no relaxation of their efforts to meet the challenge of changing circumstances. If Manning had been prepared to inject into Roman Catholicism something of the revivalism of the Salvation Army, so the Anglo-Catholic clergy working in slum parishes were equally prepared to borrow from the Evangelicals some of their aspects of worship, in order to combine every possible element that might serve to attract a working-class congregation. No pew-rents, of course; and the services themselves would be likely to contain an extraordinary mixture of the formal and the informal: lively hymn-singing, reverently-conducted ritual, splendid vestments, but also extempore intercessions offered at will by members of the congregation. It cannot be said that the Evangelicals responded in like manner. They were the main instigators of the series of prosecutions against the ritualists, rendered the more vexatious by the Public Worship Amendment Act of 1874.

In 1880 William Magee, Bishop of Peterborough, chaired the Church Congress at Leicester and declared that 'the religious condition of the masses [was] the one great Church question of our time, before which all others fade into insignificance.'[25] If one were to devise a collage depicting typical scenes in which the various churches were responding to the challenges of social reform and religious indifference, the medley of cameos would tell its tale of how the religious life of late Victorian England had changed almost out of recognition since the 1850s. Within that collage might be seen: Salvationists on parade with a brass band and a woman in uniform presuming to call upon a throng of down-and-outs to repent of their sins; pipe-smoking young Oxonians in loose-fitting blazers and flannel bags, slightly concertina-ed at the ankles, endeavouring to adjust to speaking a language intelligible to their less-favoured neighbours in Whitechapel; a priest in cotta and biretta listening with amused solemnity to improbable supplications from a ragged member of his congregation; Etonians at Hackney Wick trying to instruct street-wise lads how to use their fists according to the Queensberry rules; and – most improbable of all – an octogenarian Cardinal of the Roman Church trundling through the streets of London in a little dark horse-drawn carriage, alighting in Kensington High Street (as the young G.K. Chesterton once saw Manning), looking like a 'ghost clad in flames' as the assembled crowd dropped to their knees in reverence.[26]

If religious indifference had evoked a positive response, the phenomenon of unbelief among the more educated classes was still a thorn in the flesh of all the churches. The role of the Unitarians was of some significance here. As Geoffrey Rowell observed: 'For most of the nineteenth century Unitarianism served as a kind of half-way house for those who found themselves no longer able to accept orthodox Christian belief and who did not as yet wish to pass entirely into agnosticism.'[27] For a while George Eliot had been on the fringes of the Unitarian circle through a close friendship with Harriet Martineau, a relationship which later turned sour.[28] J.A. Froude, after publishing *The Nemesis of Faith*, virtually took refuge with the Unitarians in Manchester, befriended by Samuel Darbishire and making the acquaintance of the Martineaus, Charles Hallé and Elizabeth Gaskell. His subsequent marriage to Charlotte Grenfell, who appears to have detested Manchester, caused him to withdraw from that influence altogether. He confessed to disliking the 'gracelessness of their manner'.[29]

This was a curious accusation: the last epithet one would have thought applicable to James Martineau, who – more than anyone else – wrought a complete change in the status of the Unitarians during the course of his long life. When Thomas Arnold wrote his *Principles of Church Reform* he rejected the Unitarians, along with Quakers and Roman Catholics, as fit members of his ideally-based 'national Christian church'.[30] By the middle years of the century, however, Unitarianism had shed the dry, rationalistic, 'cerebral grey' tone of its earlier teaching;[31] and it was a measure of the new respect accorded to Unitarianism that, when the decision was made by Convocation in 1870 to proceed with a new translation of the Bible, a Unitarian – Dr George Vance Smith – was included (not without some opposition) among the revisers. Furthermore, Dean Stanley invited him to join all the others to receive Holy Communion in Westminster Abbey.

F.D. Maurice had been born and bred a Unitarian, forsaking that denomination when he was baptized and ordained into the Anglican Church in 1831. Although he abandoned the Unitarian belief in universal restitution (or 'universalism', the belief that all in the end would be saved), there seems little doubt that his later views on the nature of eternal punishment were influenced by his Unitarian upbringing. The bold publication of his views had, at the time, seemed almost a life-saver for those who revolted against the traditional interpretation. But where did this leave the question of divine judgement, and how might the perplexity about what lay beyond the grave be resolved? Traditional

Protestant teaching was quite categorical. You went either to Heaven or to Hell, although there was some difference of opinion on whether you were despatched immediately after death or whether you had to wait in a deep sleep until all the dead should rise on the Day of Judgement. A second possibility was annihilation, either at death or after some suitable penalty, for all except those privileged to enter the ranks of the blessed. The third, Roman Catholic, solution was the doctrine of the intermediate state, which at least offered a satisfactory solution to the problem of death-bed repentance. The sinner who left it so late would have to serve some indefinite spell in Purgatory. The Unitarian belief was that all would find salvation in the end; or – as Martineau put it – 'redemption ... shall restore to all at length the image and the immortality of God.'[32]

Maurice found this difficult, but his heart wanted to accept it; and the young F.J.A. Hort pressed him for an answer. In a very long letter, Maurice wrestled with the impossibility of providing a satisfactory one.

> I am bound to believe that the eternal life into which the righteous go is that knowledge of God which *is* eternal life; I am bound to suppose that the eternal punishment into which those on the left hand go, is the loss of that eternal life – what is elsewhere called eternal death ... A man ... feels that God is altogether Love, Light with no darkness at all. But then that which is without God, that which loves darkness, that which resists Love, must not it be miserable? ... Has it not a power of defying that which seeks to subdue it? ... I know that we may struggle with the Light, that we may choose death. But I know also that Love does overcome this rebellion. I know that I am bound to believe that its power is greater than every other ... How can I reconcile these contradictory discoveries? I cannot reconcile them. I know no theory which can. But ... I dare not fix any limits to the power of His love.[33]

It is, of course, the only answer that a man can give; and Maurice expressed it superbly. Hort was a disciple of Maurice to the end of his life. He was also the chief link between Maurice's teaching and the strikingly similar theology of the celebrated 'Cambridge trio' of biblical scholars – Hort himself, Brooke Foss Westcott and J.B. Lightfoot – who did more than any others to supply a scholarly riposte to the destructive criticism of the Tübingen school.[34]

In a review of Mrs Humphry Ward's *Robert Elsmere*, R.W. Church assessed the strengths and weaknesses of the Tübingen school as follows:

> German learning is decidedly imposing. But ... with all that there has been of great in German work there has been also a large proportion of what is bad – conceited, arrogant, shallow, childish. ... Those who have been so eager to destroy have not been so successful in construction. Clever theories come to nothing; streams which began with much noise at last lose themselves in the sand ... Criticism has pulled about the Bible without restraint or scruple ... Have its leaders yet given us an account which it is reasonable to receive, clear, intelligible, self-consistent and consistent with all the facts, of what this mysterious book is?[35]

This is what many English theologians felt in their bones; but only meticulous research could answer the Germans in their own kind. Of the three Cambridge scholars, J.B. Lightfoot was the chief force in countering the claims of F.C. Baur and his disciples. His researches into the early dating of the first epistle of Clement and the much-disputed letters of Ignatius, published under the title *Apostolic Fathers* in 1885, at least for a time called into question Baur's contention of the non-apostolic authorship of the Gospels.

In 1870 a young Fellow of Merton by the name of Mandell Creighton, later to become Bishop of London, decided to seek ordination. Henry Scott Holland, looking back years later, thought that he had made a very brave decision 'at that extreme hour of intellectual tension ... It is difficult for us now to gauge the dismay of that bad hour. At the close of the sixties it seemed to us at Oxford almost incredible that a young don of any intellectual reputation for modernity should be on the Christian side.'[36] The Church had been made to look either feeble or foolish over the prosecution of two of the contributors to *Essays and Reviews*, the judgment overruled by the Judical Committee of the Privy Council. This had been followed by the fiasco of the excommunication of the Bishop of Natal, J.W. Colenso, for raising doubts about the Mosaic authorship of the Pentateuch, the prelude to years of schism within the Church in South Afica. It was actually from Oxford, nearly thirty years after the publication of *Essays and Reviews*, that a second attempt was made to reappraise Christian doctrine and the interpretation of the Scriptures, and Scott Holland himself was one of the group of young Anglican scholars who took part in the exercise. This was the symposium volume edited by Charles Gore and published in 1889, enti-tled *Lux Mundi* and significantly sub-titled 'A Series of Studies in the doc-trine of the Incarnation'.

This was not a quarter from which such a reappraisal might have been expected to come. None of the contributors was a Broad Church-man. They all belonged to the Catholic wing of the Establishment, and two of them – Gore as Principal of Pusey House, and E.S. Talbot, Vicar of Leeds and formerly first Warden of Keble College – were regarded as latter-day Tractarians, the protégés of Liddon and Pusey. But they had other mentors too; and notably T.H. Green, from whom they had derived their strong social conscience and also a touch of Green's moderate Hegelianism. *Lux Mundi* was to prove a seminal work; and it caused a considerable stir at the time. There were even mutterings of prosecution. Newman was so dismayed on reading it that he declared: 'It is the end of Tractarianism. They are giving up everything.'[37] Clearly some of the views expressed needed time for the Church to absorb them. The most significant departures from traditional teaching, and the most influential in the long run, were four.

The first was the unequivocal acceptance of the doctrine of evolu-tion, as Darwin had given it to the world. This was expressed in an essay by Aubrey Moore.

> The one absolutely impossible concept of God, in the present day, is that which represents Him as an occasional Visitor. Science had pushed the deist's God farther and farther away, and at the moment when it seemed as if He would be thrust out altogether, Darwinism appeared, and, under the guise of a foe, did the work of a friend ... Either God is everywhere present in nature, or He is nowhere ... It remains then for Christianity to claim the new truth – the old almost forgotten truth of the immanence of the Word, the belief in God as 'creation's secret force', illuminated and confirmed as that is by the advance of science, till it comes to us with all the power of a new discovery.[38]

Secondly, Gore – in his essay on 'The Holy Spirit and Inspiration' – boldly faced the fact that difficulties over the understanding of the Old Testament arose from the error in supposing it to be a strictly historical narrative. Furthermore, in acknowledging the mythical character of the opening chapters of Genesis, it was important to understand what myth really meant. 'A myth is not a falsehood; it is a product of mental activity, as instructive and rich as any later product.'[39] This had been well understood by theologians of earlier times; and Gore cited Origen, Clement of Alexandria and St Anselm in support of the allegorical interpretation of Genesis. Five years earlier, in his Bampton Lectures of 1884, Frederick Temple, then Bishop of Exeter, had made precisely the same claim on the basis of Christian antiquity.[40]

Thirdly, Gore fastened upon the significance of the doctrine of *kenosis* (the self-emptying of God's omnipotence and omniscience in the person of the Son) to explain the occasions when Jesus commits actual error in his references to the Scriptures – the assumption, for instance, of the Davidic authorship of Psalm CX.[41] In speaking to those with whom he was living, he could not anticipate something that would not be known until centuries later. The fourth major thesis of *Lux Mundi* – the unifying element in all the essays – was the emphatic conviction of the centrality of the doctrine of the Incarnation, which, when properly understood, was the most elevating and exhilarating revelation of God's purposes for man. God, by becoming man in the person of His Son, had ennobled his own creation, had – as it were – consecrated the works of man.[42]

Oxford and Cambridge spoke with one voice here. The elevating nature of the Incarnation, the sanguine message which it delivered to mankind, was exactly the conclusion that Westcott had arrived at, and from similar sources, notably Origen and the Gospel of St John.[43] Although there is very little evidence of cross-fertilization between the contributors to *Lux Mundi* and their Cambridge contemporaries, they had one other enthusiasm in common: a veneration for the poetry of Robert Browning. He was – to them – 'the poet of the Incarnation'.

Both Westcott and Scott Holland delivered papers to the Browning Society. Time and again Westcott laced his writings with Browning quotations, the most favoured coming from *Fra Lippo Lippi*:

> This world's no blot for us
> Nor blank; it means intensely, and means good:
> To find its meaning is my meat and drink.

And again:

> We're made so that we love,
> First when we see them painted, things we have passed
> Perhaps a hundred times nor cared to see; ...

> ... Art was given for that:
> God uses us to help each other so,
> Lending our minds out.

The doctrine of Incarnation, so interpreted, came very soon to be the dominant tone of Anglican theology, lasting for some three decades, into the twentieth century. It was, for instance, the enduring inspiration of William Temple. Like Westcott and all the incarnationalists, he revered the Gospel of St John. As for poets, F.A. Iremonger has written: 'Browning soars above them all ... There was a completeness in Browning which he [Temple] found nowhere else ... To Browning the climax of history, the crown of philosophy, and the consummation of poetry, is unquestionably the Incarnation.'[44]

This was a phase of Anglicanism. It could not last for ever. Too many disasters on an almost cosmic scale occurred during the first half of the twentieth century to allow Christians sincerely to suppose that 'this world's no blot for us'; too many reminders of the sinfulness of man to obscure the figure of Christ the Redeemer on the Cross. It was, however, a very significant phase. The Church had suffered many wounding blows during the nineteenth century; but in one respect the wheel appeared to have gone full circle. There had been a genuine joyousness in the vitality of the Evangelicals of the Clapham Sect. There was an inspiring and infectious buoyancy among the Anglican incarnationalists at the century's end. Scott Holland's rhapsodic description of the mood, in his tribute to Francis Paget, one of the *Lux Mundi* essayists and later Bishop of Oxford, has a very dated ring to it. He recalled how they were

> ... always laughing. Life was all unbuttoned ... There were no invading cares ... We were complete in ourselves ... We were a band of friends who were sufficient for each other; and we wanted nothing more ... The hills waited upon us; the rivers ran for us; the great sea laughed as we plunged into its green Cornish waters. Nature was on our side: and we were one with it.[45]

Pessimism and disillusionment could be found in plentiful supply in other quarters of the country, but the world was no blot for these happy souls. They may not have succeeded in bringing a committed unbeliever back into the fold; but there is no doubt that they rendered the Anglican Church an inestimable service in stemming the tide of unbelief among the educated classes, and in raising the morale of the clergy as a whole.

And there is one service that they rendered which was enduring. It was no small achievement to have convinced so many of their contemporaries that Science and Christianity were not locked in war; and to have demonstrated so effectively that Darwin, consciously or not, had actually been their friend and certainly not their foe.

CHAPTER 5

Looking Ahead

I

'Mammon-worship is a melancholy creed.'
Thomas Carlyle, *Past and Present*

JOHN BRIGHT, during the last ten years of a long life that ended in
1889, came to the unhappy conclusion that the world was passing him
by. Within the Liberal party, he had always been his own man – 'the last
great lone wolf', as John Vincent has described him.[1] But as he looked
ahead in 1879, on the eve of Gladstone's Midlothian campaign, the
great Victorian reformer whose watchwords had been liberation, paci-
fication and non-intervention saw nothing to bring him comfort. New
men were entering the political scene bringing with them 'not only a
startling uprising of new issues' – in the words of the editor of Bright's
diaries – '... but a subtle change in the temper of politics and a new
alignment of minds which altered the very texture of parties.' Between
1879 and 1882 a sort of 'chemical transformation' was taking place, with
the Radical–Imperialism of Joseph Chamberlain and Charles Dilke.
The changing role of the state in matters of social reform, and the seemingly inevitable advance towards centralization and collectivism, were
unmistakeable signals that the days of Victorian voluntaryism and
laissez-faire were gone for ever.[2]

Gladstone's own position was a curious one. At odd moments
during the 1860s he had felt himself a relic of a past age, something of a
'political dinosaur';[3] and in his social philosophy he never lost his deep-
seated respect for individualism. Nevertheless his first administration of

1868–1874 saw more additions to the statute book in terms of state intervention, paving the way for the collectivism of the future, than any previous government had achieved in the nineteenth century. There had been W.E. Forster's Education Act of 1870, creating – not before time – a national system of education; Cardwell's reforms of the Army; the imposition of competitive entry to the Civil Service; the abolition of religious tests for entry to Oxford and for proceeding to a degree at Cambridge; the introduction of the secret ballot. In addition, the first of his pledges to do something for Ireland had been secured, in the Disestablishment of the Irish Church and the first major Land Act.

Disraeli's six years of power saw an even more substantial packet of social legislation carried through Parliament, partly to redeem electoral promises, partly to woo the working classes by two highly significant measures: the Employer and Workmen Act (1875), which made breaches of contract by workers no longer liable to criminal prosecution, and the Conspiracy and Protection of Property Act of the same year, which released trades unions from prosecution for conspiracy, permitting them to resort to peaceful picketing in the course of a strike. But these reforms did not constitute a decided shift in policy. Indeed, it has been suggested that Disraeli embarked upon his administration without any defined policy at all:

> The great conservative champion of social reform and the reconciliation of classes came into office in 1874 without a single concrete proposal in his head ... Disraeli's role was to dream the dreams, not to implement them.[4]

'Collectivism' was neither a part of his dream, nor a word in his, or anybody else's, vocabulary.

During these years out of office Gladstone was on the war-path again, his passions aroused by the Turkish massacres of Bulgarian Christians; and this was the Gladstone of old, using much the same invective as he had employed against the atrocities of King 'Bomba' in the Two Sicilies in 1851. The passage of nearly thirty years, however, had wrought one significant difference. His concern for the plight of Ireland had developed into an obsession; and his determination to secure Home Rule – as has been seen earlier – so divided his party that he unwittingly created for the Liberals a situation that threatened eventual political suicide. The last years of the Grand Old Man have been described as a 'heroic squandering of heroic endowments on a problem which ... the intellectual equipment of the age was not capable of solving.' Like John Bright, he found himself 'in a world which was passing beyond his comprehension, the world of Empire, of Science, of wealth without tradition, of armed power acknowledging no restraint'.[5]

The new men on the political scene, whose advent was altering the texture of parties, were Joseph Chamberlain and Lord Randolph Churchill. Their backgrounds could hardly have been more different. Chamberlain was the son of a Dissenting shopkeeper, and made his fortune as a manufacturer of screws in Birmingham. Churchill was born to the purple, the Eton-educated third son of the 6th Duke of Marlborough. Their careers, however, and the impact each made on the destinies of their respective parties, had a remarkable similarity. Chamberlain, the successful Mayor of Birmingham, represented in his person the civic pride and assured municipal status of a city which, by the mid-Victorian period, had come to occupy the place which had hitherto unchallengeably belonged to Manchester. It would almost seem that when John Bright, having been rejected by Manchester, became MP for Birmingham in 1857 – a seat which he was to hold until 1885 – he carried with him from 'Cottonopolis' the mantle of Elijah to cast over that rapidly thriving Midlands city. Somewhat ironically, by so doing he helped to create the situation which Chamberlain, whose Radical policies were beyond Bright's understanding, was able to exploit to his own political advantage.

Chamberlain's rise to power is always, and quite rightly, associated with the so-called Birmingham 'caucus'. He was not, however, its creator, but rather its product. The caucus was an association of Nonconformist bourgeoisie in alliance with artisans, shopkeepers and the working class, with a sophisticated machinery of a controlling representative commit-tee, with branches in every ward of the city, to ensure that carefully chosen Liberal candidates would be elected to promote an agreed pro-gramme of reform. Its background and origins have been explored in detail by Dr T.R. Tholfsen, who has shown that it was 'not an abrupt innovation, but the end-product of a long and gradual process', going back to the insights and influence of men like Thomas Attwood, Joseph Sturge and John Bright himself, acquiring an institutional status in 1867.[6] Chamberlain's role was to revolutionize an established organization with his 'resurgent Radicalism',[7] and – more significantly – in 1877 to extend its influence by the founding of the National Liberal Federation, with a network of constituency associations which rapidly became a powerful pressure-group within the Liberal party. So powerful did it become, with the acknowledged political expertise of Chamberlain as a consummate parliamentarian, that the more radical, municipal, Nonconformist voice threatened to wrest control of the party from the old traditional 'Whig' aristocracy.

David Cannadine has observed that, although the great Whig families comprised the largest group in the cabinet of Gladstone's second ministry in 1880, by the 1890s they had 'virtually disappeared'.

> Two centuries of Whig tradition was dissolved in little more than a decade … It was a veritable cataclysm in the history of the landed elite … The difficulty to the Whigs was that although they were the defenders of liberty, they were not the champions of equality. They feared democracy as much as they hated despotism. They would 'go with the people', but 'not to extremes'. And so, as politics in late nineteenth-century Britain became increasingly democratic in its tone and reformist in its preoccupations, they gradually ceased to be the leaders of progress, and became instead its opponents.[8]

The future of Liberalism, therefore, was not to lie with them. Indeed, if the issue of Home Rule had not split the party asunder, its future would surely have lain with Chamberlain, the obvious successor to Gladstone as the party's leader. But in 1886, Chamberlain's opposition to Home Rule compelled him to resign from the cabinet. He was later to change his political colour by taking office under Lord Salisbury in 1895 as Colonial Secretary.

To create a populist base for the Conservative party, emulating Chamberlain's methods, was also Lord Randolph Churchill's objective. He was thirteen years younger than Chamberlain, but quite his match as a parliamentarian, rising within his party to become Chancellor of the Exchequer and leader of the Commons under Salisbury at the age of 37. An avowed Tory democrat, he brought to the party something of the spirit of Young England, a little older and somewhat wiser, and certainly not to the taste of the party's old guard. If the Liberals could create a caucus machinery, involving the active participation of the working classes, so could the Conservatives. Churchill was able to achieve a change in the social structure of the National Union of Conservative Associations, so that the two rival parties could woo an electorate enlarged by a further two million after the Franchise Bill of 1884 on reasonably equal terms. He also founded the Primrose League (Disraeli's favourite flower) as an organ of party propaganda. Although many of his colleagues, including Salisbury himself, questioned the wisdom of allowing women to become members, Churchill shrewdly perceived that, though without the vote, they could often exercise a decisive influence on their husbands. Here again was a Prime Minister in the making, a possible successor to Salisbury. He committed, however, one act of extraordinary political folly in resigning from the chancellorship over a budget dispute with W.H. Smith, in the overconfident expectation that either Salisbury or the nation at large, or both together, would insist on his return. But no call came. He slipped into political oblivion until his early death from paralysis in 1894.

Both political parties had, then, in the closing decades of the century, devised an organization and propaganda techniques which, at least implicitly, acknowledged that Britain was fast becoming a democracy. Indeed, from the moment that the franchise had been tampered with in 1832, warnings of what this might lead to had been voiced. Peel justified his opposition to the Reform Bill by saying that 'I was unwilling to open a door which I saw no prospect of being able to close.'[9] For years thereafter the political equilibrium effectively remained the same as it had ever been. As recent research has shown, the much-contested Reform Bill 'far from granting power to the middle classes, in fact served to preserve the predominance of the landed interest and of the aristocracy in English politics and society.'[10] It was in 1867, with the granting of the franchise to urban artisans, that the writing on the wall became plain to see.

Education Acts had therefore to become a priority, to ensure that the future masters of the nation's destiny should be at least able to read and write; and notwithstanding the headaches over denominational religious teaching, some million and a half new school places were provided within six years of the Forster Act.[11] One person of consequence, however, refused to concede that a change in the political landscape was inevitable. Democracy was not to the liking of Queen Victoria.

A *Democratic* Monarchy [she wrote to Earl Granville in 1880] ... she will not *consent to belong to. Others* must be found, *if* that is to be, and she *thinks* we are on a dangerous and doubtful slope which may become too rapid for us to stop, when it is too late.[12]

As early as 1859, Gladstone had declared rather grandly that 'every man who is not presumably incapacitated by some constitutional consideration of personal unfitness or of political danger, is morally entitled to come within the pale of the constitution.'[13] This left open, however, the definition of personal unfitness and political danger; and many Victorians – and notably Lord Salisbury himself – found it difficult to envisage a prosperous and stable future for the state if votes were counted rather than weighed. Would not universal suffrage lead inevitably to socialism? By the 1880s, this word had come to mean different things to different people. To T.H. Green and his Oxford disciples, who were later to found the Christian Social Union, socialism was an altruistic ideal, the realization of a moral and social order in conformity with Christian teaching. As Charles Gore expressed it in 1891:

> There exists what can rightly be called a Christian socialism, by the very fact that the law of brotherhood is the law of Christ. It is quite beyond all question that ... the Christian Church should at all times represent a body living not only by a certain rule of faith, but also by a certain moral law, which puts the sternest restriction on the spirit of competition, on the acquisition of wealth, on selfish aggrandizement: which bids every man, in the simplest sense, love his neighbour as himself.[14]

This was pulpit language, and certainly far removed from the tone of Karl Marx's writings, which were beginning to have their effect upon left-wing intellectuals in the 1880s. During this decade socialism, understood as the political and economic antithesis of capitalism, assumed a more belligerent form. This was the inevitable consequence of, on the one hand, the organization of labour, with the new nation-wide unions and a common mouthpiece in the Trades Union Congress – and, on the other, seemingly ranged against them, the Leviathan-like aspect of capitalism, becoming increasingly monopolistic and thereby widening the gulf between management and employees. On both sides of some invisible barrier, forces of unprecedented strength could now be marshalled in the event of industrial confrontation. H.M. Hyndman, the founder of the Social Democratic Federation, was a convert to Marxism, and his influence lay behind the Trafalgar Square riots of 1887. William Morris, too, became more and more convinced that capitalism could only be overthrown by violent means.

This was not the way of the Fabian Society, however – the brain-child of Sidney and Beatrice Webb, tireless researchers into the social problems of their day whose objective was to gain the classless society by a process of gradualism. Their influence was directed towards the existing political structure, which effectively meant gaining a dominant voice within the Liberal party. This was a more cerebral approach, and they attracted powerful left-wing propagandists in George Bernard Shaw and H.G. Wells, and – at a more popular level – in Robert Blatchford, whose weekly paper, the *Clarion*, dating from 1891, was aimed at gaining converts from the reasonably literate sections of the working class. How far the policy of gradualism might have succeeded through such Trades Union spokesmen as were able to gain seats on the Liberal benches in the Commons – men such as Joseph Arch, John Burns and Henry Broadhurst – is a question to which history has no answer. Although it could not have been foreseen at the time, the socialist programme was to pass into other hands. The significant moment was the appearance in the Commons in 1892 of an ex-miner by the name of James Keir Hardie, MP for South-West Ham, who one year after his election formed the Independent Labour Party. Unlike his forerunners who found themselves in Westminster from humble origins, he refused to purchase for himself the appropriate silk hat. He came into the Commons, cloth cap and all, a portent of stirring events to come. That story, however, belongs to the twentieth century.

A socialist state is almost by definition also collectivist; but collectivism does not necessarily mean socialism. By 1889, socialism was a phenomenon much talked about; but its reality was little more than a potential threat from the activists and a collection of essays produced during that year by the Fabian Society. Collectivism, on the other hand, had already won the battle against *laissez-faire*. How it had done so is a more complex problem. Whereas the progress towards democracy can be charted by various legislative landmarks – three Reform Acts, the introduction of the secret ballot, the redistribution of constituencies – there were no such milestones to mark what was perhaps the most significant transformation in the sphere of politics and administration during the course of Victoria's reign. It is almost true to say that, like the accumulation of England's overseas possessions into an empire, it came about in a fit of absence of mind. As Oliver MacDonagh has expressed it, the transformation was 'scarcely glimpsed till it was well secured'.[15]

For at least half the span of Gladstone's political career, government had been implicitly regarded as having two paramount duties: to legislate as little as possible, and to reduce public expenditure. But not even the most ideally inactive government could ignore certain problems brought about by a rapidly changing society; and there were at least two forces at work which were difficult, if not impossible, to withstand. The first was simple humanitarianism. When appalling instances of deprivation, exploitation or negligence came to light, so that public opinion demanded remedial action, an administration would be forced to take notice. Secondly, the pressure of Utilitarianism, not always humanitarian and sometimes coldly rational only to be kind, was never quiescent during the whole of the Victorian period; and certain 'useful' ends could only be achieved by governmental action. In most cases, however, it seems – as W.L. Burn observed – that 'the State was disinclined to formulate long-term plans and policies. Usually it waited to be jogged into action, and that along paths which private initiative had marked out for it.'[16]

It took a long time for governments to realize that a law is no more than words in a statute book if no provision is made for it to be enforced. The Benthamites knew better; and the timidity of governments in framing permissive legislation, which allowed local authorities to take action to alleviate a problem rather than compelling them to do so, was a cross that a dedicated Benthamite like Edwin Chadwick found difficult to bear. A law can only be effectively enforced if there is an executive organization armed with privileges of immunity and with delegated powers. It requires immunity from a civil action of trespass for an inspector checking on a factory-owner's compliance with the law; and it needs at least a limited amount of delegated power to cope with loopholes which the original law-makers had not foreseen. The Northcote–Trevelyan major shake-up of the Civil Service was to prove in the long run the most effective measure to strengthen the power and efficiency of the executive, but the main purpose of these reforms had been to weaken the control of the aristocracy, to eliminate corruption and to effect economies. Dr MacDonagh has concluded that 'there was a total absence of either bureaucratic or collectivist intention'.[17] In so far as the executive was becoming steadily, if slowly, stronger, the evidence is best seen in 'the silent metamorphosis taking place within such long-established arms of government as the Colonial or Home Offices, or the

Board of Trade, as new areas of administration were placed under or ... grew into their jurisdiction.'[18]

The one moment when actual governmental initiative – of set purpose to create some centralized executive control – can be confidently acknowledged came in 1888, when many of the traditional powers of local JPs were removed by C.T. Ritchie's Local Government Bill during Salisbury's second administration. By that time, collectivism had won the day. A contemporary observer, looking around him, recorded the transformation as follows:

> A minute and far-reaching system of bureaucratic control is exercised from Whitehall, within a radius equal in extent to the length and breadth of the United Kingdom. Modern legislation has created new departments of State. We have entire armies of official inspectors of all kinds. We accumulate annual libraries of local reports.[19]

Not everyone saluted these changes with enthusiasm. Even those whom the law and the executive had been devised to protect might resent interference in their working conditions.

In November 1897 there appeared in *The Nineteenth Century* an article by Edith Hogg on the plight of 'The Fur-Pullers of South London', describing the appalling conditions in which elderly women worked long hours for a pittance, removing the fur from the skins of rabbits to provide the material for making felt hats. Any visitor was regarded with suspicion:

> They imagine that you are an emissary of the London County Council – in their eyes, the embodiment of unlimited and tyrannical power. The County Council and the law are their standing dread; for, if these take it upon them to interfere and deprive the fur-puller of her employment, there is nothing left but starvation.[20]

On a different level altogether, the new county councils and the emasculation of the powers and status of the local justices brought a protest, in one of his most famous essays, from the revered medievalist F.W. Maitland.

> As a governor he is doomed [he wrote]; but there has been no accusation. He is cheap, he is pure, he is capable, but he is doomed; he is to be sacrificed to a theory, on the altar of the spirit of the age.[21]

Yet another medieval historian, John Neville Figgis, was much more forthright. A Christian Socialist like Gore, whose Community of the

Resurrection at Mirfield he joined in 1907, Figgis became more and more attracted to guild-socialism and the right of lesser communities within the state to enjoy their own autonomous existence without governmental interference. Looking ahead, he saw a very bleak picture of ever-increasing centralization. The state was setting itself up as 'The Great Leviathan'.

> Now the State did not create the family, nor did it create the Churches; nor even in any real sense can it be said to have created the club or the trades union ... They have all arisen out of the natural associative instincts of mankind, and should all be treated by the supreme authority as having a life original and guaranteed.[22]

Gladstone was not entirely happy either. He was too old to accept changes, especially changes of convention, introduced supposedly for the purpose of increased efficiency. He told Henry Sidgwick in 1885 that he was greatly irritated at discovering that Salisbury conducted cabinet meetings on a different pattern. 'They now sit round a table, whereas they used to sit on chairs in a circle.' It was a great mistake.[23]

Inevitably, as the power of the state increased, so all lesser authorities within the nation saw their influence diminishing; it was equally true that as democracy advanced, and the nature of the two parties was to become more conscious of the need of a populist base, so the influence of the aristocracy declined.

The Great Depression had left its mark on the landed aristocracy, quite apart from this shifting power-base. As has been noted earlier, the great landed families could retain their wealth, even perhaps increase it, by selling unprofitable land and reinvesting the proceeds, by exploiting their urban acres or mineral rights, and by obtaining directorships of companies. Nevertheless, their social and political influence dwindled with the erosion of their estates. Peers and country gentlemen not so handsomely advantaged 'became too poor to maintain the standard of living which was now expected of Society people', Professor Hanham has written, 'and gave way as arbiters of taste to the *nouveaux riches*.'[24] The result was that the change in composition of the aristocracy, through the elevation to peerages of new men whose wealth had been acquired through business, manufacturing and finance, was threatening to turn the higher echelons of late Victorian society into a plutocracy.

As early as 1871, Gladstone had expressed his fears on this disturbing trend to Monckton Milnes (Lord Houghton, as he had become).

I think [he wrote] that in a political view the spirit of plutocracy requires to be vigilantly watched and checked. It is a bastard aristocracy and aristocracy shows too much disposition, in Parliament, to join hands with this bastard. In a religious point of view I believe the case to be yet worse, and I groan over the silence and impotence of the pulpit. I almost wish for a Savonarola or part of one. Manning has said some good things about it.[25]

This was all very well. He had already, two years earlier, urged upon the Queen the need 'in a few carefully selected cases' to 'connect the House of Lords . . . with the great representatives of the commerce of the country'.[26] He had the Rothschilds in mind, and found the Queen unwilling to support him. The situation was soon to change, however. No one could complain over the elevation of men of outstanding distinction – Tennyson, for instance, ennobled by Gladstone, or William Thompson, the first scientist to become a peer (Lord Kelvin), at the instigation of Lord Salisbury. But what were the grounds for ennobling successful brewers (Sir Arthur Guinness was the first), newspaper proprietors and financiers, if not to bring funds and powerful support to a political party – suggestive of some underhand bargaining for the sale of honours, which became so notorious under Lloyd George? Gladstone himself, in 1891, faced with the grave financial straits of his party, agreed to sell two peerages 'in return for substantial contributions to the Liberal party funds'.[27] The phenomenon of the financier was not new, although the word itself, to describe someone who 'profitably manipulates risk capital', was not coined until 1867 (in the *Pall Mall Gazette*).[28] Trollope then popularized this new breed in his unflattering portrait of Melmotte in *The Way We Live Now* (1873). Whatever personal distaste Gladstone felt for the plutocrat, he elevated two to the peerage: 'Ned' Baring became Lord Revelstoke, before bringing ruin to Baring's; the other was his first, unsuccessful candidate, Nathan Meyer Rothschild, ennobled in 1885.

F.M.L. Thompson and David Cannadine have supplied further details of the *nouveaux riches* who received peerages in the 'Indian Summer' of the late Victorian and early Edwardian aristocracy. On the Conservative side, three newspaper barons, three brewers and eight (possibly nine) bankers were ennobled; for the Liberals, three bankers, two brewers, one newspaper baron and seven industrialists.[29] Some of the 'new men' became great landowners. William Armstrong acquired the huge estate of Cragside in Northumberland, and then Bambrough Castle; Samuel Cunliffe-Lister (Lord Masham), whose fortune had been made from wool-combing, secured 34,000 acres of land from the estate of the Marquess of Aylesbury. It was calculated in 1896 that, taking the aristocracy as a whole, 167 peers had become directors of companies, railways topping the list, constituting a quarter of the House of Lords.[30] No wonder W.S. Gilbert raised a smile in *The Gondoliers*, when the Duke of Plaza-Toro described the happy change in his fortunes:

> I sit, by selection,
> Upon the direction
> Of several companies' bubble –
> As soon as they're floated
> I'm freely banknoted –
> I'm pretty well paid for my trouble.[31]

The Victorian horror of 'Mammonism' can be traced back to the earliest years of the Queen's reign. Robert Southey described 'Mammon' as the 'god of the nineteenth century'.[32] Carlyle, in *Past and Present*, inveighed against England's special 'Hell', which 'belongs naturally to the Gospel of Mammon ... Verily Mammon-worship is a melancholy creed.'[33] J.A. Froude was appalled by 'the rage to become rich' which had 'infected all classes'.[34] 'Oh! what a frightful business is this modern society', he wrote in *The Nemesis of Faith*; 'the race for wealth – *wealth*. I am ashamed to write the word.'[35] Henry George prophesied ominous consequences:

> Where population is densest, wealth greatest ... we find the deepest poverty, the sharpest struggle for existence, and the most of enforced idleness.

What modern society was contriving, in its blindness, was simply the widening of 'the gulf between Dives and Lazarus'.[36]

In 1871 Gladstone had lamented that the pulpit was too silent and too impotent on the issue, but Charles Gore did not hold his tongue. In 1894, he preached the University Sermon at Oxford on the text 'Look carefully how you walk, not as unwise but as wise; buying up the opportunity because the days are evil'. What had Mammonism brought upon contemporary society? he asked – moral slackness, lawlessness, selfishness and luxury. In a scarcely veiled reference to the circle of the Prince of Wales, he declared that the time had come to speak 'stern words in the King's sanctuary and the royal house'.[37] J.E.C. Bodley, in a lecture delivered in 1911, looked back on some of the things that the late Victorians might have observed when they looked ahead. His thesis was that the growth of materialism leads to the decay of idealism. His particular concern was the Western European dimension of this phenomenon, arising from his study of what was happening to French society in the closing decades of the nineteenth century, reflected also in England by the currency of the French term *fin de siècle* as descriptive of the last ten years of Victoria's reign. Something of the *malaise* implicit in that phrase was evident in all the major countries of Western Europe. Visit any of the great cities of Europe, and what did one find? They had become 'gaudy pleasure-resorts'.[38] This, at least, was what one saw on the surface. More hidden was the insidious influence of international financiers, and more submerged and unspoken-of was the groaning poverty of those to whom the opulence and luxury were no more than an occasional alluring spectacle.

How could one account for it? Was it just the spirit of the age, or could its source be located? John Ruskin, as early as 1870, when he wrote *Sesame and Lilies*, was convinced that decadence (although he did not use that term) was beginning to spread into England from France. It was Napoleon III's last unwanted gift from the Second Empire now fallen into ruin at the hands of the Prussian army. He quoted a letter to *The Times* written by a French lady who felt it her duty to warn English society to learn the lessons from the fate of her own country, before it was too late.

> It is the shame, the sad and large shame, that French society and its recent habits of luxury, of expenses, of dress, of indulgence in every kind of extravagant dissipation, has to lay to its own door in its actual crisis of ruin, misery, and humiliation. If our *ménagères* can be cited as an example to English housewives, so, alas! can other classes of our society be set up as an example – *not* to be followed.[39]

Ruskin reiterated this warning with increasing stridency to the end of his life, which closed in the first year of the new century. If his words were largely ignored during his lifetime, they were not likely to be heeded a year later when, as it would have seemed to him, Mammon personified was crowned King.

II

'Everything was going to be different.'

Virginia Woolf, 1904

The *Annual Register* for the year 1900 gives no suggestion that the new century was ushered in with a flourish of trumpets and a beating of drums. Quite the reverse. Its review of so significant a milestone is unremittingly muted, the prevailing note being one of sober reflection:

> The political position of Great Britain in the first and last year of the nineteenth century [the review begins] had many points of resemblance. On both dates she was engaged in a war of which the difficulties and the duration had been misjudged by her rulers, and at the close as at the opening of the century she was without a continental ally ... At home there were also to be found many points of analogy in the state of affairs at the beginning and at the end of the century.[1]

There was no attempt to dwell on the extraordinary transformation that had taken place in the course of the last hundred years; no comment on the acceleration of the changes, social, cultural and technological, over the preceding ten years. Even the frenzied rejoicing at the relief of Mafeking on 17 May after 217 days of siege was played down. The theme of the review was summed up in the statement that 'the interest aroused by the war, with all its side issues, was sufficient to occupy public attention to the exclusion of all other subjects.'[2]

To a man who was in his twenties during that last decade – E.F. Benson, the third son of the Archbishop of Canterbury (until 1896) – the 1890s seemed in retrospect, however, to be the moment when 'the long-retarded spring burst into fullest summer ... I confess that I was then tipsy with the joy of life and the horns of Elfland were continually blowing.'[3] And he blew them the more lustily when the new century dawned. But when he reflected that, during the 1890s, 'Victorianism was already dead and buried, and nobody was concerned to meddle with what was decaying so nicely',[4] he nevertheless shared with the mass of his contemporaries a proud consciousness that his salad days had been spent during the reign of the Queen. The 1890s may well appear as a curiously un-Victorian epilogue, as so much that was anticipatory of Edwardianism was manifested in the temper of the times, but while the Queen lived – and she did not die until 22 January 1901 – her subjects were still Victorians; and in a certain respect, they were never more consciously Victorian than during these last years of her life.

After all, these were the Jubilee years. There had been times during the Queen's protracted mourning after the death of the Prince Consort in 1861 when she had effectively withdrawn from public life, and had been in danger of forfeiting the affection and sympathy of her subjects. People had been saying 'what do we pay her for if she will not do her work?' and 'she had better abdicate if she is incompetent to do her duty'.[5] If Disraeli had done nothing else of consequence in the course of his political career, he had at least drawn his sovereign, somewhat fitfully and guardedly at first, out of retirement at Balmoral or Osborne; and, felicitously coincidental with a mood of emancipation from the conventions of the past evident in so many respects throughout the country, the Queen herself seemed to be emancipated from at least some of the burdens that had thrown her into her self-imposed isolation. She was seen to smile again, on occasions. Although she dreaded the ordeal of the first of her Jubilees in 1887, she was so moved by the demonstrations of affection and respect from Londoners in their thousands that she discovered a new delight in public functions. Her subjects – in turn – came to regard the sheer longevity of her reign, breaking all records as the Golden Jubilee advanced to the Diamond, as a source of national pride. With the full realization that so many of the crowned heads of Europe – Germany, Greece, Russia, Spain, Rumania, Norway – came to pay deference to her, not only as Queen of England and Empress of India, but also as grandmother or mother-in-law, that sense of national pride soared to new heights.

It was very clear, too, that the Queen's enthusiasms were those of her subjects. She was tenaciously proud of her Empire; the Duke of Wellington had been her hero, and she loved her Army and her Navy, especially the Seaforth Highlanders with their pipers and her Indian troops, conspicuously present among the 50,000-strong armed escort in the procession to St Paul's at the Diamond Jubilee. The mood of the nation in the 1890s – once described as 'a period of amazing swaggering', the crowds singing 'Soldiers of the Queen' and 'Ta-ra-ra-boom-de-ay'[6] – undoubtedly had an ugly and unhealthy side to it; and the Queen was inclined, metaphorically at least, to indulge in some swaggering herself. The reverses of the Boer War nearly broke her heart, but the evidence suggests that her judgement on military matters was shrewd, and that if she had been War Minister, she might well have brought the campaign to a successful conclusion rather earlier.[7]

Victoria could be imperious, demanding, selfish and self-willed. The royal household held her in awe. But they loved her, too. Arthur Benson (the elder brother of E.F.), while a housemaster at Eton, saw a great deal of the Court at Windsor because he became a sort of unofficial poet-laureate to both Victoria and Edward VII, having the exceptional facility of producing appropriate verses almost on the spur of the moment. He never approved of the pleasure-loving Edward VII (he described the King's coronation as 'the Apotheosis of Buttons, not the consecration of life to service'),[8] and noticed at once the changes that came over the royal household under Victoria's son.

> It is much more genial, considerate, *equal* [he wrote] – it lacks the grim and ugly stateliness of the old time; but it also lacks the dignity. When it was said that the Queen is coming – that she wd receive, courtiers ran about like frightened hens – and were horribly afraid of her, knowing that she would notice everything. Now, no one could be exactly *afraid* of the King.[9]

When the old Queen died, and the immediate shock had passed (after all, practically no one, except the very old, could recall what life was like without her), there came – according to E.E. Kellett, 'amid all the other feelings a sense of relief'[10] – the prospect of a new century, a new sovereign. As Virginia Woolf put it, emancipated from the Stephen family home in Kensington as she moved to Bloomsbury in 1904: 'Everything was going to be new; everything was going to be different; everything was on trial. We are going to do without napkins ... to have coffee after dinner, instead of tea at nine o'clock.'[11] As for the King himself, he was in his sixtieth year when at last he gained his inheritance. As the years had passed and that long-expected day seemed never to come, with his mother persistently refusing to allow him to undertake any public responsibilities much more onerous than laying foundation-stones, it is not surprising that he gathered round him his own entourage at Marlborough House, who shared his taste for luxurious habits. They also shared his enthusiasms for gambling, philandering and the Turf: a way of life in embarrassing contrast to the standards of Court behaviour so rigorously upheld by his mother.

It cannot be said that Victoria's family were always a credit to her. The

years from 1889 to 1891 were the worst for scandals, the full circumstances of which the Queen probably never knew. The period began
with the coming to light of the lascivious activities of certain well-known
society figures who had been frequenting a brothel in Cleveland Street
where London telegraph boys offered their sexual services at a price. On
12 November 1889 a warrant was issued – after a suspiciously long delay
– for the arrest of Lord Arthur Somerset, the third son of the 8th Duke
of Beaufort and also Superintendant of the Stables and Extra-Equerry
to the Prince of Wales. Worse was to follow, during 1890, as rumours
began to circulate that the Prince's eldest son, Prince Albert Edward
('Eddy'), later Duke of Clarence, had also patronized the Cleveland
Street establishment.[12] No charges were brought against Prince Eddy,
and Lord Arthur Somerset evaded arrest by fleeing the country, remaining in permanent exile for thirty-six years. Accusations of a cover-up and
of a 'criminal conspiracy to defeat the ends of justice' by unwarrantable
pressure put upon the law officers and the police by those in high places
(in order to avoid the possibility of truly horrific publicity) were made in
the House of Commons by Henry Labouchère in February 1890. The
Attorney-General, Sir Richard Webster, was hard pressed to refute the
charges.[13]

In 1891 the further scandal of the Tranby Croft affair hit the head-
lines, publicizing to the world the Prince of Wales's passion for gambling.
He was summoned as a witness for the defence in a defamatory libel
action brought by Sir William Gordon-Cumming against those who had
accused him of cheating at baccarat while the guest (with the Prince of
Wales and others) of a wealthy shipowner, Arthur Wilson, at his home,
Tranby Croft in Yorkshire. The Prince of Wales was pilloried in
the witness box by Gordon-Cumming's counsel, Sir Edward Clarke.
Although his evidence was largely instrumental in the prosecution
failing, he had done his public reputation considerable harm. He was
subjected to such a degree of obloquy from the press, and from pulpits
throughout the land, that the Queen confessed that the Monarchy itself
was 'almost in danger'.[14]

Even then the Prince's troubles were not over. He became embroiled
in an unseemly personal quarrel with Lord Charles Beresford concerning Beresford's relations with Lady ['Daisy'] Brooke, Countess of
Warwick, which threatened to lead to divorce proceedings. It did not
help the Prince that Daisy Brooke had quite obviously taken the place

of Lillie Langtry in the heir to the throne's extra-marital dalliances.[15] One can well understand the sentiment that he expressed to his sister, the Empress Frederick, on 30 December: 'I cannot regret that the year '91 is about to close, as during it, I have experienced many worries and annoyances which ought to last me for a long time.'[16] His only consolation was to have secured the engagement of the curiously listless (even perhaps a little feeble-minded) Eddy to Princess Victoria Mary of Teck. It may have been a mercy for the future wife of George V, and for the nation at large, that Prince Eddy died in the following year, reportedly from influenza turning to pneumonia. It took five years for the opprobrium which the Prince of Wales had brought upon himself to subside; but such is the fickleness of public opinion, and the enthusiasm that his future subjects shared with him for the Turf, that when he won the Derby with Persimmon in 1896, he was restored to favour on the instant.

The example set by the Prince's circle at Marlborough House may have contributed to the undoubted loosening of the moral rigidities of the Victorian age, but can hardly be accused of causing it. The cult of respectability was under fire from other quarters, notably from the cultural movement known as aestheticism, with its ideology of 'decadence'. Although this is often represented as the most typical of the emancipatory forces of the *fin de siècle*, its origins go back to the later stages of Pre-Raphaelitism, from which it grew through the combined influences of Whistler, Swinburne and Walter Pater, in their different fields, to become a recognized (and to many, unwelcome) cult by the late 1870s. Indisputably the slogans of the decadents were imported from France. It was Théophile Gautier who coined the phrase 'art for art's sake'. It was Charles Baudelaire who, by his poems in *Les Fleurs du Mal* (1857) extolling the glories of vice and the pursuit of 'sensation for sensation's sake', provided the decadents with their bible:[17] a shocking, but also thrilling, exhibition of the sheer perversity and nerve of this tortured soul, whose objective seemed to be to shatter and ridicule every convention, social and sexual, that had been advanced as conducive to respectability and decency. It certainly captivated the American artist James McNeill Whistler, who had through his experience of a Bohemian life in Paris from 1855 become convinced that this was the ideal existence for the true artist, the perfect atmosphere for the creation of genuine art.

Swinburne first read Baudelaire in 1861, and his own *Poems and Ballads* appeared one year later, causing a sensation with its hints of satanism and its rejection of the inhibiting bourgeois sexual mores of the age; all profoundly distasteful to conservative critics, but eagerly received by the younger generation. Cambridge undergraduates selected the most offensive passages of 'Dolores' to chant in the streets in the hope of bringing a blush to the cheek of elder persons.[18] Matthew Arnold was not in the least impressed when he met this young rebel at All Souls in 1863. He dismissed him as a sort of 'pseudo-Shelley'. Swinburne's riposte, when he came to hear of this, was to describe Arnold as a sort of 'pseudo-Wordsworth'.[19]

It was Walter Pater who supplied aestheticism with its philosophy. It was not the function of the artist to teach or to prophesy or to indulge in nostalgic sentimentalism. His true duty was 'to live in the experience of the moment'.

> Our one chance [he wrote in *The Renaissance* in 1873] lies in ... getting as many pulsations as possible into the given time. Great passions give us this quickened sense of life ... The love of art for art's sake has most, for art comes to you proposing frankly to give nothing but the highest quality to your moments as they pass, and simply for those moments' sake.[20]

From this philosophy can be discerned two features of this cultural movement which were to leave their mark on the *fin de siècle*, even though the influence of aestheticism was actually on the wane. The first was the deliberate distancing of the artist or the poet from his public. The object of creative work was to satisfy its creator. If others within the artistic élite appreciated and understood the product, well and good. True art was not created for the masses. It has been suggested that the response of the aesthetes and decadents to the expansion of the popular press and 'to the onslaught of popular culture was a fastidious distaste, and if anything a stiffening of the barriers between – indeed, perhaps the invention of the distinction between – high and low culture'.[21] Graham Hough has argued similarly on the particular emphasis in Pater's writings on 'withdrawal'.

> There were more than enough influences at work in late Victorian life to drag the arts into the commonplace of day-to-day existence. In an age that was boiling up for the Boer War and the windy degradation of the daily press it was necessary that a small group of hierophants should keep the sacred flame burning in some still retreat.[22]

Secondly, there was in almost all the productions of the aesthetes a flavour of homo-eroticism: so much so that the word 'decadent' came to acquire a meaning synonymous with 'unnatural' and therefore homosexual, before that last word obtained general currency. Krafft-Ebing's *Psychopathia Sexualis* was not published until 1886 and was hardly a book to appeal to a wide public.[23] The homosexual bond that linked the members of John Addington Symonds' circle in the 1860s, involving figures like Arthur Sidgwick at Oxford and Roden Noel and H.G. Dakyns at Cambridge, has been established beyond doubt by Phyllis Grosskurth.[24] Nor, from the constant tone of homo-eroticism in his writings, can there be any doubt about Walter Pater's sexual orientation.[25]

The rise and fall of Oscar Wilde complete the picture. His notorious trial and subsequent imprisonment in 1895, with the unlovely public explosion of outrage and derision, compounded of genuine affront and not a little of guilt on the part of those who murmured to themselves 'there, but for the grace of God, go I', was to prove of crucial significance to the fortunes of the aesthetic movement. It led, for instance, to the decision by the editors of *The Yellow Book* to dispense with the services of Aubrey Beardsley, actually the only one of its contributors who could remotely be described as 'decadent'.[26] By the end of the century 'aestheticism' had become virtually an historical phenomenon. The concept of 'decadence', however, had a longer life and acquired a new twist to its meaning, passing from individual application to the idea of civilization in decay.[27] Walter Pater's 'sacred flame' was not entirely extinguished, but it was certainly burning less brightly in the new century. He was read as a stylist, but he had ceased to be a figure of influence. T.S. Eliot went so far as to say that he did 'not believe that Pater ... has influenced a single first-rate mind of a later generation.'[28]

The homo-eroticism of the aesthetic movement was not, it seems, unconnected with another significant movement towards emancipation from traditional Victorian restraints. While the decadents claimed complete freedom for themselves to defy every requirement of decorum, they regarded with repugnance the emergence, in the closing decades of the century, of the 'New Woman'; even worse, 'the wild woman', with her assertion of robust independence, often manifested in an unnatural masculinity. It was almost as if they were 'unnerved and unbalanced', and certainly threatened, by behaviour that they could not understand.[29]

Indeed, the male reaction of barely rationalized distaste was not confined to the aesthetes. Militant feminism coincided with the relatively new institution of 'Clubland'. The leading anti-feminists, being products of all-male public schools,

> lived in privileged enclaves of men's colleges, men's holidays, men's professional brotherhoods, all symbolized and perpetuated in men's clubs, and they found it painful to contemplate their boyish world being invaded by the females whom their favourite institutions had deliberately, so far successfully, excluded.[30]

The conventional role of women in Victorian society was given classical expression in the words of Sir John Vesey to his daughter, Georgina, in Bulwer Lytton's play *Money*:

> I never grudged anything to make a show. Never stuffed your head with history and homilies; but you draw, you sing, you dance, you walk well into a room; and that's the way young ladies are educated nowadays, in order to become a pride to their parents and a blessing to their husbands – that is, when they have caught him.[31]

From the early years of the century dissentient voices were to be heard, even among men. Sydney Smith was one, for instance. 'Why are we necessarily to doom a girl, whatever her taste or her capacity, to one unvaried line of petty and frivolous occupation?' he asked.[32] J.S. Mill described the continual subjection of women as 'the single relic of the past discordant with the future'. It therefore 'must necessarily disappear'.[33] The problem, as the century advanced, resolved itself into four related aims.

The first was to secure the removal of the offensive anomalies of the law which denied to a married woman any economic independence. On marriage, all her property and any earnings belonged thereafter to her husband. And greatly did Charlotte Brontë resent the transference of her copyright and all her royalties to her father's curate whom she married in 1854.[34] Perhaps this was one of the reasons why George Eliot, always watchful of her literary earnings, decided to live with G.H. Lewes, rather than marry him. Women had to wait until as late as 1882 for this injustice to be redressed, in the Married Women's Property Act of that year. The divorce laws were equally inequitable. At least in 1857 jurisdiction was removed from church courts to the civil courts, but – even so – while a man could obtain divorce on the ground of adultery, a wife was obliged to prove 'aggravated enormity' on the part of her husband.

The second target was to obtain equal educational opportunities for women. Until this was secured, the third objective of gaining the vote was an impossibility; and this was well perceived by such pioneers as Emily Davies and Josephine Butler. 'Education was what the slave-owners most dreaded for their slaves,' Josephine Butler wrote, 'for they knew it to be the sure way to emancipation.'[35] F.D. Maurice, typically, was sympathetic. So was Mill. Tennyson debated the opposing attitudes in *The Princess*, while in his heart adhering to the traditional view that moral influence was the natural role of women, intellectual influence belonging exclusively to men. Frederic Harrison insisted that 'the moral superiority of women was a fundamental tenet of the Positivist credo', and that her place was therefore properly in the home, where she could escape from the taint of a man's professional world.[36] This was precisely the attitude that the pioneers of women's eduction were striving to resist. They felt like Bella Rokesmith in *Our Mutual Friend*, who told her husband that 'I want to be something so much worthier than the doll in the doll's house.'[37]

Florence Nightingale could admittedly exercise an inspiring influence as a nurse, but why should women be denied the right to train as doctors? When Queen Victoria was told of such a suggestion, she recoiled in horror:

> To tear away all the barriers wh surround a woman, & to propose that they shld study with *men* – things wh cld not be named before them – certainly not in a *mixed* audience – wd be to introduce a total disregard of what must be considered as belonging to the rules and principles of morality.[38]

Nothing of significance was achieved in this battle until 1869, when the Endowed Schools Act stipulated that endowments should not be restricted to boys, also recommending that every town should endeavour to set up a day-school for girls, charging only moderate fees. These provisions owed much to the determined stance of Frances Buss and Dorothea Beale (the founders respectively of North London Collegiate School for girls and the only proprietary girls' boarding school in the country, at Cheltenham). Both had given evidence before the Commissioners in 1865. Higher education for women was confined to Queen's College, London, founded in 1848 by F.D. Maurice, until – in the 1870s

– the persistent pressure of Emily Davies, with the strong support of Henry Sidgwick, bore fruit in the founding of two women's colleges in Cambridge (Girton and Newnham). Oxford soon followed suit, with the founding of Lady Margaret Hall and Somerville College in 1878 and 1879. Neither university, however, was prepared to admit women to degrees; but at least a foothold had been gained in what was still overwhelmingly a man's world.

Progress towards the third objective – the enfranchisement of women – was seriously impeded by the inability to gain a united front, even among the most respected and influential members of their own sex. George Eliot, a strong supporter of equal educational opportunities, could not bring herself to join ranks with Josephine Butler, Harriet Martineau and Emily Davies.[39] Almost all the leading women writers of the day dissociated themselves from the suffragists – Charlotte Brontë, Elizabeth Gaskell, Charlotte Yonge, Elizabeth Browning and Mrs Humphry Ward. Florence Nightingale took the same stand, as did Beatrice Webb and Octavia Hill. Even at the height of the Suffragette Movement in 1910, Octavia Hill expressed her opinion very frankly in *The Times*. 'I believe men and women help one another because they are different, have different gifts and different spheres; one is the complement of the other.'[40] The one political party that might have embraced the women's cause was the Liberals, but their fiercest opponent, whose vehemence amounted almost to hysteria, was – perhaps surprisingly – John Bright. As Bright's sister recalled: 'he could praise women, but not Woman ... he could *never* bear women to assert themselves.'[41] There was just one moment when the activists thought they might succeed, by the inclusion of a women's amendment to the Reform Bill of 1884, having received a sufficient number of pledges of support to raise their hopes. But Gladstone would have none of it, and his influence prevailed.

The cry 'Votes for Women' seems to have been muted by this rebuff. The 1890s proved to be – in the words of Lady Frances Balfour – 'the doldrum years' for the suffragists.[42] On the other hand, this same decade witnessed the most articulate campaign for the fourth objective of those who sought emancipation for their sex. The 'new woman' of the 1890s was determined to secure release from the tyranny of 'bourgeois domesticity';[43] escape from the stifling obligations of the home, whether from parents or from husbands. As Alys Pearsall-Smith wrote in March 1894, in an article in *The Nineteenth Century*, speaking on behalf of the repressed daughters of her generation, today's daughter 'wants to belong to herself ... Her capacities were not given to her parents, but to herself; her life is not their possession, but her own.'[44] What a boon to the 'new woman' was the invention of the bicycle. She could escape from the attentions of a chaperone and explore the world as she pleased.[45] What a boon, too, to the married woman was the (unofficial) acquiescence in the use of contraceptives, so freeing her from what could seem an endless cycle of childbirth.

The fact that as late as 1877 Charles Bradlaugh and Annie Besant were prosecuted for obscene libel (and acquitted only on a technicality) for proselytizing birth-control, is a reminder that late Victorian society was still watchful, even irrationally so, over matters of sexual morality. A combination of circumstances in the 1880s and 1890s precipitated something of a backlash against libertinism, in the formation of the National Vigilance Association for the Repression of Criminal Vice and Immorality: Henry Mayhew's revelations (actually exaggerated) of the disturbing number of prostitutes in London; W.T. Stead's exposé in *The Pall Mall Gazette* of the extent of child prostitution; the Cleveland Street scandals and the publicity accorded to the trial of Oscar Wilde; the dire warnings by doctors of the spread of syphilis, interpreted by many as divine retribution on a society that was wilfully defying the God-given moral code. Who were the chief culprits? In so far as the 1890s were notoriously 'naughty', the least respectable section of society could well be represented as those who, from their position, ought to have been the most.

'Hardly a week passes without some new scandal,' Lady Ambrose observed cheerfully in Mallock's *New Republic*. 'However – that sort of thing, I believe, is confined to us. The middle classes are all right – at least, one always hears so.'[46] W.T. Stead, horrified at the extent of corruption in London, came to the conclusion that the best hope for the capital was to enlist the purifying help of the provinces and to turn its gaze northwards. There would be found 'the soundest part of the realm – the sober, hard-working, intelligent men who in North and central England constitute the saving strength of our land.'[47]

Lady Ambrose was, of course, a caricature. But there was no hint of tongue-in-cheek in what Stead was saying. Indeed, Elizabeth Roberts, in her researches into working-class attitudes and habits in north-west England during the 1890s, has supplied striking confirmation of Stead's conviction that the mood of emancipation had made not the slightest impression on the urban poor in these areas. There were no 'new women' – and certainly no 'wild women' – to be found in Barrow, Preston or Lancaster; no interest, either, in feminist causes. In a typical working-class family, why should there be? The mother was very often the dominant figure in the home, controlling the family budget and making the most important decisions affecting the family as a whole. Children were brought up to know 'at a very young age the difference between right and wrong', and to learn the habit of obedience. One Preston woman recalled: 'I was fifty-six before I answered my mother back.'[48] There was no indication, either, of the weakening hold of religion, which seemed still to provide for working-class families 'fundamental underpinning and comfort in what were often hard and troubled times'.[49] As for sexual morals:

> Not only were lengthy courtships an indication of the priority given to sustaining the family budget by working children; they were also an indication of the strict sexual self-control exercised by the great majority of young couples. In all families ... there was unanimous condemnation of sex outside marriage, although the vehemence of the condemnation varied considerably.[50]

Ignorance about contraception was widespread, partly because doctors seemed reluctant to give advice. The most usual control appears to have been abstinence or *coitus interruptus*. Dr Roberts quotes the advice of a bus conductor to a young recently-married man, Harold: 'Don't forget, always get off the bus at South Shore, don't go all the way to Blackpool.'[51]

The period of the *fin de siècle*, then, should be seen in perspective. The rejection of Victorian standards tended to be confined to the upper classes and the intellectuals. The thought of a new age dawning could be very exhilarating to some, as they looked ahead. What future wonders lay in store? many would ask, as they observed the extraordinary transformation in material benefits within a single decade. In 1895, for instance, Henry James 'acquired electric lighting; in 1896 he rode a bicycle; in 1897 he wrote on a typewriter; in 1898 he saw a cinematograph'.[52] But accompanying this awareness of a new century about to be born, there was also a sense that the old century would very shortly die; and perhaps a whole way of life would die with it. When one contemplates the new style of fashionable living which reached its peak in the 1890s, the glitter and careless rapture of the weekend country-house parties, the flashy social circles that radiated round the great hostesses – Ettie Grenfell (Lady Desborough), Lady Elcho, Lady Ribblesdale – there comes to mind de Gaulle's telling description of France during the same decade, recovering from the hysteria of the Panama scandal: 'like the Infanta, weeping in the Palace gardens, overcome with melancholy, while enjoying the good things of life'.[53]

One thing had not changed during the course of the nineteenth century. England was still two nations, and perhaps never more so than at its close, when opulence, frivolity, smart talk, slightly *risqué* affairs and flirtations set the tone of high society, concealing from its members, whether consciously or not, a sense of *hubris*, or – if not that – a fear of sheer boredom. It is significant that in 1894 and 1895, H.G. Wells published his *The Time Machine* in serial form; and it has been said of its message that: 'Wells projects the notion of "two nations" ... into a ghastly nemesis.' He pictures, on the one hand, the working class of London descending into violent anarchy, while the ruling class, on the other, is sliding 'into the cloistered world of fantasy, decadence, neurosis'.[54]

Doubtless no reference in this to themselves would have been seen by the members of the exclusive group known as 'The Souls' – the circle of the young and 'most self-regarding and self-assured of *fin de siècle* social groups',[55] so christened by Lord Charles Beresford in 1888. It included Arthur Balfour, George Curzon, George Wyndham, Evan Charteris, Margot Tennant (the future wife of H.H. Asquith), Harry Cust (editor of *The Pall Mall Gazette*). They prided themselves on their wit and sociability, which made them the most favoured guests at house parties, and saw themselves destined to make the Edwardian age virtually their own. There were those outside this circle of mutual self-esteem who believed that they were riding for a fall. One such was Field Marshal Lord Wolseley, who confessed to his wife that he saw no prospect of salvation for the nation in the hands of people such as these.

> I feel that a country whose upper classes live as a certain set of men and women do, can only be saved from annihilation by some such upheaval as a great war, which will cost all the best families their sons.[56]

'The Souls' were not entirely right in their expectation that they would rise to eminence; but the Field Marshal was uncomfortably near the truth in his prophecy of the tragedies that would befall them. The Great War took a terrible toll of the 'golden boys' from these very families. These were the 'doomed genteel youth' as David Cannadine has described them, who went out with such confidence as subalterns to face the might of Germany.[57]

Rudyard Kipling, who lost his only son – a subaltern in the Irish Guards – in the carnage that was to come, had in certain memorable lines of his poem *Recessional*, written for the Queen's Diamond Jubilee, thought it expedient to hint at a possible nemesis, if Jingoism were carried too far.

> Judge of the nations, spare us yet,
> Lest we forget, lest we forget.

When congratulated by J.W. Mackail on his prudent warning, he too expressed his conviction that 'a great smash', sooner or later, was bound to come. As to its eventual outcome, he had no doubt. 'We shall pull through not without credit.' And then he added, in words reminiscent of W.T. Stead's faith in the soundness of heart of the less-privileged members of England's other nation: 'It will be the common people – the third-class carriages – that'll save us.'[58]

CONCLUSION

Looking Retrospectively

'And yet the wiser mind
Mourns less for what age takes away
Than what it leaves behind.'
Wordsworth: *The Fountain*

It has been maintained that Edward FitzGerald's translation of *The Rubáiyát of Omar Khayyám* became in the 1890s the most popular poem of the nineteenth century. On what basis such a judgement has been arrived at is not clear. But even if it can be challenged, there is sufficient truth in the statement to allow one to take this 'very breviary of epicurean hedonism'[1] as representative of the tastes, opinions and mood of Queen Victoria's twilight years. Comparable poetic works, as representative of the middle and early periods, offer an interesting contrast. For the 1850s and 1860s, Tennyson's *In Memoriam* or Matthew Arnold's 'Dover Beach' would serve very well; and could one improve upon Wordsworth's *The Prelude* and John Keble's *The Christian Year* for the opening decade of the Queen's reign? These titles alone chart the extent to which the felt needs of contemporaries changed during the course of a little over sixty years. They suggest, too, very different world pictures.

Leslie Stephen, whose life spanned these years, chose another, equally significant, measuring rod. The whole vocabulary of politics had acquired new meanings. In 1899 he reflected in a letter to an American friend, C.F. Adams, on 'the singular change which has come over British opinion ... The people who still call themselves liberal have disavowed all the doctrines which used to be called liberal in my youth. Cobden and Bright and J.S. Mill and all the old idols have been deposed.'[2]

Perhaps less noticed at the time, but more evident in a retrospective survey, were changes in the whole approach to the disciplines of scholarship which were serving to make it increasingly difficult to speak about a world picture ever again.

During the nineteeth century knowledge was sufficiently unfragmented to allow scholars and thinkers to presume to have an overall view of their times. The polymath, sage or seer could not only pronounce oracularly about the state of the world and of civilization, but also – in some instances, but by no means all – could communicate his message to others in a language intelligible to most literate people. Coleridge was unquestionably a polymath, with a universal knowledge unequalled by any thinker of his day. It has to be admitted, however, that his efforts to explain the unity of knowledge, through his favourite device of trichotamous logic, led him into such convolutions of verbiage that he seemed to lose the power to communicate at the very moment when he discovered a truth eminently worth communicating. Carlyle tried to understand everything and convinced most of his readers that he really did; but he, too, served up less palatable offerings in his last years, as his colourful prose turned into authoritarian ranting. John Stuart Mill was the most lucid of the polymaths, but he too had his blind spots, never really being able to comprehend the element of the spiritual in people's lives. Matthew Arnold would have liked to have been acknowledged as a polymath, but never quite succeeded in elevating himself above the rank of critic.

Newman, but for his ignorance of German, had a better claim than most; and at least in his *Idea of a University* made perhaps the last great serious attempt to represent knowledge as a circular phenomenon, with all the separate branches of study neatly interlocking and inter-relating in such a way that some ultimate 'science of sciences' could be discovered and apprehended.[3] Thereby he hoped to reveal what Coleridge had tried to prove in his *Encyclopaedia Metropolitana*, that all Truth is essentially one. John Ruskin had a wide-ranging mind, and at a time when specialist scholars were beginning to resent the intrusion of amateurs on to their territories, irritated the professional practitioners of the 'dismal science' by his anachronistic assumption that he could lay down the law on economic issues as well as on art and culture. Ruskin was the quintessential 'seer', but – as has been said of him – 'it was Ruskin's peculiar fate to be the seer for an age which no longer wanted to see so much.'[4]

By the late nineteenth century people were not inclined to see as much as Ruskin might wish, for the simple reason that so much could no longer be seen by one master mind. Specialization, the fragmentation of the various sciences into a multitude of different branches, each developing its own technical language, killed the polymath. In his demise, universal world views perished too. It should be remembered that the professional scholar, probing deeply into his own chosen specialism, was a rarity in the nineteenth century until the closing decades. Charles Darwin, for instance, as his son recorded, 'was a Naturalist in the old sense of the word, that is, a man who works at many branches of science, not merely a specialist in one'.[5] The same was true of T.H. Huxley. The professional historian was practically unknown until Oxford produced a William Stubbs, Maitland maintained. Macaulay was an essayist and a statesman who wrote history as a hobby. 'The active labourers' in the historical field, Maitland wrote, were 'Grote and Carlyle, Buckle and Palgrave, men in whom neither Oxford nor Cambridge could claim anything, and Edinburgh could not claim much'.[6]

Specialism was bound to come; bound also to increase to the extent that it has reached in the twentieth century, when even a scientist in one particular field may be unable to comprehend, or even to communicate with, a scientist working in another. Such a change was, in itself, sufficient to render the modern world so far removed from the Victorian age that no prophet of those times could have envisaged the completeness of the fragmentation of individual disciplines from its first manifestations. Perhaps all the Victorians' predictions turned out either to become advances beyond their comprehension or to be vain hopes never fulfilled. That there would be technological progress, the late Victorian had no doubt whatever. But what else?

Dr Kitson Clark has written:

> If it were possible to add up the numbers of hours spent by human beings hoping, planning and working for selected objectives in the reign of Queen Victoria, it seems possible that the re-conversion of England and the achievement of democracy and the abolition of privilege would come highest on the list.[7]

Efforts to stem the tide of secularization have never ceased throughout the twentieth century. But the number of men and women 'in the pew' has continued to decline, with – as was probably always so – fewer men at regular worship than women. As for democracy, its complete fulfilment was realized rather more swiftly than many anticipated, especially with the gaining of the enfranchisement of women, a process which in time was sure to lead to further claims for equality between the sexes. No Victorian could have supposed that a day would dawn when women were ordained to the priesthood. Such a notion would have elicited from the vast majority the sentiment of that mild, good-hearted man, Septimus Harding, who – in *Barchester Towers* – remarked to his daughter, Eleanor, when she mooted the hypothetical case of a 'sacred lady' at work within a parish: 'No priestly pride has ever exceeded that of sacerdotal females.'[8]

Universal education and democracy might have been supposed to lead to a raising of moral standards. Fitzjames Stephen was dismissive of such a notion. No amount of freedom of discussion would ever enable the mass of mankind to rise above the acceptance of vaguely-understood half-truths.

> Estimate the proportion of men and women [he wrote] who are selfish, sensual, frivolous, idle, absolutely commonplace and wrapped up in the smallest of petty routines, and consider how far the freest of free discussion is likely to improve them. The only way by which it is practically possible to act upon them at all is by compulsion or restraint ... I confine myself to saying that the utmost conceivable liberty which could be bestowed upon them would not in the least degree tend to improve them.[9]

This may sound very cynical. But one has to ask whether, in fact, universal education and the enormous expansion of the media, with their powerful influence on public opinion, have ministered to a general raising of moral standards. Gertrude Himmelfarb could never be accused of nostalgic sentimentalism in her many significant contributions to the history of the Victorian age; but in her most recent study on *The Demoralisation of Society: From Victorian Virtues to Modern Values*, she has expressed her views very emphatically. In the present century, values have taken the place of virtues; and values reject absolutes such as right and wrong, virtue and vice. The notion of values, she writes, 'brought with it the assumption that all moral ideas are subjective and relative, that they are mere customs and conventions ... peculiar to specific individuals and societies'. To impose a moral code upon the young is only to inhibit them, therefore they are encouraged 'to discuss their own values by exploring their likes and dislikes, preferences and feelings'.[10]

She is not, of course, writing of Britain alone; the shift of emphasis from virtues to values can be seen – to a greater or lesser extent – in the USA and in most countries of Western Europe. It reflects a fundamental change in the nature of modern society, to some degree presaged by the reaction against the precepts and restraints of the early and mid Victorian periods during the 1880s and 1890s. As the reaction gathered strength and momentum, especially in the second half of the twentieth century, so many of the cherished assumptions of the Victorians have turned into quaint historical phenomena. Time was, for instance, when society prided itself on having few laws and an abundance of moral imperatives; modern society has a profusion of laws and an emasculated moral code. The Victorian age believed devoutly in the centrality and sanctity of family life. The revolt against 'bourgeois domesticity' has seen society becoming less and less home-centred, especially among the middle classes, where once the family ethic had been so strong. Whether in small ways – like the tendency to patronize restaurants in place of meals at home – or in much more significant ones – such as the pressure upon married women to seek the earliest opportunity to return to employment after childbirth – the effect of the diminution of the habit of 'doing things as a family' has inevitably led to an increase in broken homes and also the greater permissiveness extended to the young. The transference of paternalism from a personal preceptor or benefactor to the impersonal state has tended to weaken the sense of duty, so constantly urged by all Victorian moralists, and to encourage a stronger sense of individual rights.

It may be recalled that Thomas Arnold, when teaching history, was wont to raise the question 'What does this remind you of?', believing that analogies could be useful pointers, provided they were not taken completely out of context. If the same question were put today to a student of the *fin de siècle*, he could offer some interesting reflections. What might he notice? The long reign of a queen, the majority of whose subjects had no memory of life before her accession; the heir to the throne, left waiting in the wings until advanced middle age; the unhappy fact that certain members of the royal family, by their behaviour, were damaging the reputation of the monarchy; a general loosening of moral standards, especially among the upper classes and the better educated; a consequent fear of venereal diseases, interpreted by many as a divine judgement on deviant sexual behaviour; a frightening widening of the gulf between the luxury-loving affluent and the underprivileged denizens of the inner city; the increasing power of the popular press in the manipulation of public opinion; the damage inflicted upon the reputation of the City by the rash speculation and consequent fall of the house of Baring. These were all observations of their times, looking inwards, by those who lived in the last years of Queen Victoria. Looking outwards, they could hardly fail to notice the collapse of all efforts to cope with the intractable problem of Ireland. Perhaps only the 'Jingoism' and the ominous massing of armed forces on the Continent were observations which have no parallel in the 1990s. Not so certain, because only time will tell, was the evidence of an incipient moral backlash that followed upon the fall from grace (if grace there ever was) of the decadents.

But this is a dangerous game for an historian to play. History can never actually repeat itself. The furthest that one can go is to notice that sometimes similar circumstances lead to similar results. Equally suspect is the inclination to romanticize the past, without appreciating its uglier features. A recent symposium, *In Search of Victorian Values*, has poured scorn on the temptation to eulogize Victorian values as the necessary therapy for curing some of the ills of the present day, dismissing such an attitude as naïve sentimentalism.[11] There is some truth in this. On the other hand, it would be wrong to fail to acknowledge some of the insights of the Victorians which the twentieth century – for better or for worse – has ignored or forgotten. The Victorians were properly anxious lest technological advance should carry in its wake a corresponding increase in materialism. They were doubtless indulging in nostalgic fantasy in looking back with a certain longing to the Middle Ages, yearning for the recovery of the personal bond of loyalty and obligation that seemed to them implicit in feudalism. But Carlyle's anxieties about the relationship between employer and employee becoming one of a 'cash-nexus' were real and pertinent. Nothing is more destructive of loyalty than the attitude which puts profit-making before every other consideration and sacrifices personal obligations, without hesitation, to commercial interests. The erosion of the sentiment of loyalty weakens society at every level, because it creates a vacuum immediately filled by cynical self-interest.

This is not to say that the Victorians were guiltless of a sometimes ruthless quest for prosperity, both for themselves and for the nation. Were it otherwise, Carlyle would not have felt the need to inveigh so vehemently against it. Their sense of duty was unbending, and they showed little sympathy for weakness, and none at all for idleness. It has been observed that the major contrast between the noonday of Victorianism and the twentieth century was not the optimism of the one and the pessimism of the other, but the extraordinary faith that the Victorians possessed in 'the power of the human will'. In the closing years of the century this was diminishing, and with it much of the idealism that lay behind it. One does not hear so much about Self-Help in the 1880s and 1890s. They seemed to be losing, too, one of the most attractive features of their idealism – the quest for heroes. W.E.H. Lecky put this down to a weakening of backbone. The nation seemed to be losing 'the power of breasting the current of desires and doing for long periods what is distasteful and painful', and this could only be to the detriment of the interests of both individuals and the country as a whole.[12]

Learning from the insights of a past age, and also from its defects, does not, then, invite a romanticizing of it in the way that so many of the Victorians romanticized the Middle Ages. Was this what Wordsworth was trying to say in the beautiful verse of his poem 'The Fountain'?

> Thus fares it still in our decay;
> And yet the wiser mind
> Mourns less for what age takes away
> Than what it leaves behind.

R.H. Hutton comments on this verse:

> And thus meditating, he [Wordsworth] wrings from the temporary sadness fresh conviction that the ebbing away, both in spirit and in appearance, of the brightest part, sad as it must ever be, is not so sad a thing as the weak yearning which, in departing, it often leaves stranded on the soul, to cling to the appearance when the spirit is irretrievably lost.[13]

Were a time-traveller from the twentieth century, in his admiration for all things Victorian, to have his wish granted and to be transported back, say, to the 1860s, and landed in the midst of London, what would strike him first of all? G.M. Young has suggested that his ears would register the first impression: 'the noise – the noise of the traffic, of wheels on granite setts'. Then his nose would begin to twitch as he caught 'a sudden puff of tainted air'.[14] Hippolyte Taine's own experience, on first visiting London, was not the sound or the smell, but the sight: the grime – 'porticos foul with soot ... columns ... full of greasy filth, as if sticky mud had been set flowing down them ... In this livid smoke, objects are no more than phantoms and nature looks like a bad drawing in charcoal on which someone has rubbed his sleeve.'[15] Fascinated as he might be, the time-traveller would not wish to linger; certainly not to remain.

If the time-travel were inverted – if a Victorian were transported to England in the late twentieth century – the shock would, of course, be greater still: a different sort of traffic noise, and a form of traffic beyond his imaginings. But when the first bewilderment had subsided, and he had ceased to marvel at the changed appearance of the buildings, he would very probably stop and stare at the extraordinary sight of men walking the streets without hats.

Would the people themselves, however, be identifiably the same, notwithstanding the weirdness of their dress? Macaulay, in his essay on Sir James Mackintosh, was aware of the necessity to try to understand figures of the past by a conscious effort to see them in the context of their times:

> In order to form a correct estimate of their merits [he wrote], we ought to place ourselves in their situation, to put out of our minds, for a time, all that knowledge which they, however eager in their pursuit of truth, could not have, and which we, however negligent we may have been, could not help having.[16]

C.S. Lewis, in his *Preface to Paradise Lost*, added the warning to historians to guard against the erroneous doctrine of the 'Unchanging Human Heart'. A man's anatomy may not change over the centuries, but his heart, his emotions and his sensibilities are moulded by the culture and mores of his times.

The Victorians tended to wear their hearts upon their sleeves. They cried more openly and more frequently than modern men and women; and both their weeping and their laughter could be provoked by cir-

cumstances which would not elicit the same response from later generations. A twentieth-century reader can still be moved by Dickens' account
of the death of Paul Dombey in *Dombey and Son*, although many may find
it too obviously sentimental for their taste. But the seventy-five-year-old
Lord Jeffrey wrote to Dickens, after reading the book, to tell him that he
had sobbed and cried all night over the death of little Paul.[18] There are
passages in Dickens which are enduringly funny, but there are also some
at which his public would have laughed that appear to a reader of today
as humour of such blackness that the stomach turns over. Two instances
in *Pickwick*, both from Sam Weller's inexhaustible stock of absurd stories,
come to mind: the 'clever pieman' who kept a diminishing number of
cats –

> 'noble animals,' says he, a-pointin' to a wery nice little tabby kitten, 'and I
> season 'em for beefsteak, weal, or kidney, 'cordin to the demand.'[19]

In the same genre, there is the horrible tale of the inventor of a 'patent-
never-leavin-off sassage ingine' who mysteriously disappeared one day
because he had fallen into his own machine. His fate came to light a little
later when his customers discovered buttons in their sausages.[20]

This is all of a piece with a society that lived much closer to the stark
realities of life than later generations who have developed both a protective technology and a sensibility to insulate themselves against the
horrors, elemental vicissitudes and barbarisms that were all part of the
Victorians' *mise-en-scène*. It was a very different world. Just occasionally
in the course of one's delving into the nineteeth-century past, however,
a little vignette presents itself which, although it might speak of anonymous figures of flesh and blood about which history can have nothing
more to say, yet conjures up such a vivid picture of a moment of authentic life that one experiences a sense of identity and yearns to know what
happens next. What happened, for instance, to the 'villainous-looking'
little rogue in a reformatory at Redhill, which Monckton Milnes once
visited, who sidled up to Milnes and 'stole a dirty paw' into his hand,
saying not a word, because he could not think of any other way of
thanking the man who had actually rescued him off the streets?[21] Did
he ever make good, one wonders? No name is recorded; his ultimate fate
will never be known.

Sometimes, too, one encounters a vignette that conveys the sheer joy
of being alive – some spontaneous expression of happiness, transmitting

to a reader the mood of the moment with an almost infectious vividness: the charming picture, for instance, of little Annie Darwin, out walking with her famous father, who liked to set a cracking pace on his daily constitutional; but his daughter would always run ahead, 'pirouetting in the most elegant way', smiling brightly all the while.[22] Alas, what happened next is only too tragically known. She died at the age of ten – another reminder of the realities of Victorian life. Even more vivid was a walk taken by Hippolyte Taine with the two teenage daughters of the hostess with whom he once stayed, at a house some thirty miles from London. The girls were 'real little goats, for ever leaping and cavorting, even while we were climbing stiff, stony slopes … The youngest had a lovely colour in her cheeks, like an apple.' They told Taine that their nurse had been teaching them some German, but as yet they knew no French. Taine looked rather solemn at this, and reminded them that their governess was actually a French lady.

'Yes [they replied], but then we're so stupid!' which was followed by a burst of laughter.[23]

Who were the girls? What happened to them next? Again, history does not record.

The consciousness of a shared experience, the characters delineated so clearly across the barrier of time, provides the material for empathy. The Victorians' observations of their times, however, offer something of real value in helping the present and future generations to tackle their own challenges and predicaments; and this for two good reasons. In many ways the Victorians were wiser than their posterity; and, secondly, their priorities make those of today look shallow and short-sighted. But the clock can never be put back; nor is it desirable to attempt to do so. Shortly before he died, Julius Hare, Archdeacon of Lewes – one of the most enlightened and influential Broad Churchmen of the middle years of the century – delivered what was to be his final Charge to the clergy of his archdeaconry. The date was September 1854. He felt it expedient to warn them that learning from the past, which all right-minded people should do, is a very different thing from trying to take refuge in the past, for the simple reason that the past is past. Old remedies are not always necessarily the best for new situations.

As time advances [he said], circumstances change: new wants spring up, and multiply; that which may have been perfectly suited for one form of society, for one mode of human thought and feeling, becomes, in certain respects, inappropriate for others.

He then reminded them of an old adage: 'The clothes of the boy will not fit the man: and the attempt to force them on him will only disclose their unfitness more and more.'[24]

References

(Place of publication is London, unless otherwise stated)

INTRODUCTION: 'Observation of one's times'

1. G.M. Young, *Portrait of an Age: Victorian England*, annotated edition, ed. G. Kitson Clark (1977), p. 96.
2. Raymond Williams, *Culture and Society, 1780–1950* (1966 edn), p. 123.
3. E. Bulwer [Lytton], *England and the English* (1833), vol. II, p. 165.
4. W.E. Houghton, *The Victorian Frame of Mind, 1830–1870* (Yale, New Haven, Connecticut, 1957), p. 1.
5. T.H.S. Escott, *England. Its People, Polity, and Pursuits* (1891), p. 6.
6. C. Gore (ed.), *Lux Mundi: A Series of Studies in the Religion of the Incarnation* (1891 edn), p. viii.
7. R.W. Harris, *Romanticism and the Social Order, 1780–1830* (1969), p. 22.
8. J.S. Mill, *Collected Works*, ed. A.P. and J.M. Robson (Toronto, 1986), vol. xxii, p. 228.
9. John Clive, *Thomas Babington Macaulay: The Shaping of the Historian* (1973), p. 123.
10. Benjamin Disraeli, *Coningsby* (1983 edn), Bk III, ch. 1.
11. R.H. Hutton, *Essays on some of the Modern Guides to English Thought* (1888), p. 107.
12. G. Kitson Clark, *The Making of Victorian England* (1962), p. 66.
13. J.M. Golby (ed.), *Culture and Society in Britain, 1850–1890* (Oxford, 1987), p. 1.
14. Walter Bagehot, *Literary Studies*, ed. R.H. Hutton (1879), vol. II, pp. 56–7.
15. A.P. Stanley, *The Life and Correspondence of Thomas Arnold* (1858 edn), vol. I, p. 164.
16. Charles Dickens, *Hard Times*, Bk II, ch. v.
17. W.M. Thackeray, *Vanity Fair*, ch. 2.
18. A.O.J. Cockshutt, *Truth to Life: The Art of Biography in the Nineteenth Century* (1974), p. 88.
19. J.S. Mill, *Dissertations and*

Discussions, Political, Philosophical, and Historical (1875 edn), vol. I. p. 437.

20. C. Stephen (ed.), *Sir James Stephen. Letters with biographical notes* (privately printed, 1906), p. 87.

21. Joseph E. Baker, *The Reinterpretation of Victorian Literature* (Princeton, 1950), p. 212.

22. J.C. Thirlwall, *Connop Thirlwall, Historian and Theologian* (1936), p. 27.

23. T. Wemyss Reid, *The Life, Letters and Friendships of Richard Monckton Milnes, 1st Lord Houghton* (1890), vol. I, p. 171.

24. F.W. Maitland, *The Life and Letters of Leslie Stephen* (1906), p. 341.

25. Young, *op.cit.*, p. 184.

26. E.E. Kellett, *As I Remember* (1936), pp. 105–6.

27. Quoted in Asa Briggs, *Victorian Cities* (1986 edn), p. 14.

28. Goldwin Smith, *Reminiscences* (New York, 1910), p. 4.

29. *Ibid.*, p. 11.

30. Anthony Trollope, *An Autobiography* (1950 edn), p. 222.

31. R.H. Tawney, *Religion and the Rise of Capitalism* (1926), p. 61.

32. W.L. Burn, *The Age of Equipoise: A Study of the Mid-Victorian Generation* (1964), p. 41.

33. Michael Mason, *The Making of Victorian Sexual Attitudes* (Oxford, 1994), p. 58.

34. Keith Robbins, *Nineteenth-Century Britain. Integration and Diversity* (Oxford, 1995), pp. 9–10.

35. Humphrey House, *The Dickens World* (1942), pp. 32–3.

36. P.J. Keating, *The Working Classes in Victorian Fiction* (1971), p. 2.

37. C.S. Peel in *Early Victorian England 1830–1865*, ed. G.M. Young, (1934), vol. I, p. 126.

38. Mark Pattison, *Sermons* (1885), p. 128.

39. E.F. Benson, *As We Were. A Victorian Peep-Show* (1930), p. 333.

CHAPTER 1: Looking Inwards

SECTION 1: 'It has all been so sudden'

1. G. Tracey (ed.), *Letters and Diaries of John Henry Newman* (Oxford, 1984), vol. vi, p. 10.

2. *Annual Register of the year 1837* (1838), pp. 8–9.

3. *Ibid.*, pp. 45–6.

4. *Ibid.*, p. 56.

5. Stanley, *op.cit.*, vol. II, p. 198.

6. *Ibid.*, vol. II, pp. 161–2.

7. Duncan Forbes, *The Liberal Anglican Idea of History* (Cambridge, 1952), p. 96.

8. *Ibid.*, p. 168, n. 101.

9. Statistics from Burn, *op.cit.*, pp. 112–3, and *Early Victorian England* vol. I, p. 13.

10. M.J. Daunton, *Progress and Poverty: An Economic and Social History of Britain 1700–1850*

11. *Ibid.*, p. 401; the statistics are taken from R.I. Woods and P.R.A. Hinde, 'Nuptuality and Age of Marriage in Nineteenth-Century England', in *Journal of Family History*, vol. 10 (1985), p. 125.

12. Quoted in E. Halévy, *A History of the English People in 1815* (1924), vol. I, p. 498.

13. Boyd Hilton, *The Age of Atonement. The Influence of Evangelicalism on Social and Economic Thought, 1785–1863* (Oxford, 1988), p. 81.

14. Mason, *op.cit.*, p. 175.

15. Gertrude Himmelfarb, *The Demoralisation of Society. From Victorian Virtues to Modern Values* (1995), p. 130.

16. Quoted in Williams, *op.cit.*, p. 222.

17. Thomas Carlyle, *Sartor Resartus* (1908 edn), p. 170.

18. Quoted in Harris, *op.cit.*, p. 74.

19. Humphrey House in *Ideas and Beliefs of the Victorians: an historic revaluation of the Victorian Age* (1949), p. 74.

20. Williams, *op.cit.*, p. 13.

21. *Ibid.*, pp. 90–1.

22. Quoted in E.P. Thompson, *The Making of the English Working Class* (1991 edn), p. 208.

23. Alan Everitt, 'County, Country and Town: Patterns of Regional Evolution in England', in *Transactions of the Royal Historical Society*, 5th series, vol. 29 (1979), p. 104.

24. Quoted in Williams, *op.cit.*, p. 73.

25. R.H. Mottram in *Early Victorian England*, vol. I, p. 169.

26. Charles Dickens, *Barnaby Rudge*, Bk I, ch. iii.

27. Francis Sheppard, 'London and the Nation in the Nineteenth Century', in *Transactions of the Royal Historical Society*, 5th series, vol. 35 (1985), p. 55.

28. Charles Dickens, *Dombey and Son*, vol. II, ch. xxxiii.

29. Hippolyte Taine, *Notes on England*, trans. E. Hyams (1957 edn), p. 13.

30. Briggs, *Victorian Cities*, p. 96.

31. Alexis de Tocqueville, *Journeys in England and Ireland*, trans. G. Lawrence and K.P. Mayer, (1958), pp. 107–8.

32. Taine, *op.cit.*, p. 219.

33. Daunton, *op.cit.*, p. 141.

34. de Tocqueville, *op.cit.*, p. 94.

35. Peter Ackroyd, *Dickens* (1990), p. 692.

36. Dickens, *Hard Times*, Bk II, ch. ii.

37. Statistics in S.E. Finer, *The Life and Times of Sir Edwin Chadwick* (1952), p. 213.

38. H. Perkin, *The Origins of Modern English Society, 1780–1880* (1969), pp. 124–5.

39. J.H. Clapham in *Early Victorian England*, vol. I, p. 62.

40. The opinion of E.P. Thompson, *op.cit.*, p. 237 is challenged by J.D. Chambers, 'Enclosure and the Labour Supply in the Industrial Revolution', in *Economic History*

Review, 2nd series, vol. 5 (1952–3), pp. 332–3; see Daunton, *op. cit*, p. 110.

41. Taine, *op.cit.*, p. 134.

42. Bulwer, *op.cit*, vol. I, pp. 174–5.

43. Elizabeth Gaskell, *Mary Barton*, ch. iii.

44. J.R.T. Hughes, 'Patterns of Industrial Change', in *1859: Entering an Age of Crisis*, ed. P. Appleman, W.A. Madden and M. Wolf (Bloomington, Indiana, 1959), p. 135.

45. Geoffrey Best, *Mid-Victorian Britain, 1851–1875* (1979), pp. 122–3.

46. Perkin, *op.cit.*, p. 143.

47. Paul Johnson, 'Conspicuous Consumption and Working-Class Culture in late Victorian and Edwardian Britain', in *Transactions of the Royal Historical Society*, 5th series, vol. 38 (1988), p. 28.

48. N. McKendrick (ed.), *Historical Perspectives. Studies in English Thought and Society, in honour of J.H. Plumb* (1974), p. 175.

49. Daunton, *op.cit.*, pp. 440–1 .

50. Elizabeth Gaskell, *North and South*, ch. xxxiii.

51. F.M.L. Thompson, *English Landed Society in the Nineteenth Century* (1963), p. 239.

52. Elizabeth Gaskell, *Mary Barton*, ch. viii.

53. Asa Briggs, *Victorian People. A Reassessment of Persons and Themes, 1851–67* (1965 edn), p. 31.

SECTION II: 'It's this steam, you see'

1. Mona Wilson in *Early Victorian England*, vol. II, p. 289.

2. Wemyss Reid, *op.cit.*, vol. I, p. 110.

3. John Morley, *The Life of Richard Cobden* (1881), vol. I, p. 15.

4. Philip Bright (ed.), *The Diaries of John Bright* (1930), p. 13.

5. R. Sopwith, *Thomas Sopwith, Surveyor. An Exercise in Self-Help* (Durham, 1994), p. 73.

6. Peter Levi, *Tennyson* (1993), p. 123.

7. *Charles Kingsley: His Letters and Memories of his Life*, edited by his Wife (1877), vol. II, p. 21.

8. Charles Dickens, *Master Humphrey's Clock*, ch. iii.

9. Charles Dickens, *Pickwick Papers*, vol. I, ch. xx.

10. Charles Dickens, *Master Humphrey's Clock*, ch. iii.

11. E.J. Hobsbawm, *Industry and Empire: From 1750 to the Present Day* (1990), p. 113 n.

12. William Johnston, *England as it is, Political, Social and Industrial in the Middle of the Nineteenth Century* (Irish UP, 1971 edn), vol. I, p. 263.

13. Escott, *op.cit.*, p. 257.

14. Statistics from Johnston, *op.cit.*, vol. I, p. 260, and Escott, *op.cit.*, p. 258.

15. Robbins, *op.cit.*, p. 27.

16. Young, *Portrait of an Age*, p. 67.

17. Escott, *op.cit.*, p. 259.

18. Quoted in Briggs, *Victorian People*, p. 8.

19. Wolfgang Kemp, *The Desire of my Eyes. The Life and Work of John Ruskin* (1991), p. 256.

20. Quoted in J.H. Buckley, *The Triumph of Time: A Study of the Victorian Concept of Time, History, Progress and Decadence* (Cambridge, Mass., 1967), p. 65.

21. Houghton, *op.cit.*, p. 7.

22. Mona Wilson in *Early Victorian England*, vol. II, p. 291.

23. *The Household Narrative of Current Events for the Year 1852*, p. 111; ... *for the Year 1853*, p. 44.

24. A.C. Benson and Viscount Esher (eds), *The Letters of Queen Victoria, 1837–1861* (1908), vol. I, p. 369.

25. Elizabeth Gaskell, *Cranford*, ch. 2.

26. Ackroyd, *op.cit.*, pp. 959–61; see also Charles Dickens, *Our Mutual Friend*, epilogue.

27. Charles Dickens, *Dombey and Son*, vol. II, ch. lv.

28. Charles Dickens, *Hard Times*, ch. xi.

29. House, *The Dickens World*, pp. 145–6.

30. Johnston, *op.cit.*, vol. I, p. 260.

31. Hobsbawm, *op.cit.*, p. 114.

32. C.S. Peel in *Early Victorian England*, vol. I, p. 81.

33. C.R. Fay, *Great Britain from Adam Smith to the Present Day* (1948), p. 146.

34. P.J.G. Ransom, *The Victorian Railway, and How it Evolved* (1990), pp. 141–2.

35. Fay, *op.cit.*, p. 213.

36. Lucy Brown, 'The Treatment of the News in Mid-Victorian Newspapers', in *Transactions of the Royal Historical Society*, 5th series, vol. 27 (1977), p. 26.

37. Mona Wilson in *Early Victorian England*, vol. II, p. 285.

38. R.H. Mottram in *ibid.*, vol. I, p. 172.

39. Briggs, *Victorian Cities*, p. 15.

40. Roy Jenkins, *Gladstone* (1995), p. 507.

41. R.S. Surtees, *Mr Facey Romford's Hounds* (1864), p. 66.

42. Quoted in Houghton, *op.cit.*, p. 41.

43. Anthony Trollope, *Phineas Finn*, ch. 35.

44. Matthew Arnold, *Culture and Anarchy: An Essay in Political and Social Criticism* (1961 edn), p. 12.

45. John Ruskin, *The Crown of Wild Olive. Four Lectures on Industry and War* (1895 edn), p. 158.

46. S. Gilley, 'Edward Irving: Prophet of the Millennium', in *Revival and Religion since 1700: Essays for John Walsh*, eds J. Garnett and C. Matthew (1993), p. 107.

47. David Newsome, *The Parting of Friends. The Wilberforces and Henry Manning* (1966), p. 7.

48. Elizabeth Gaskell, *North and South*, ch. xlvi.

SECTION III: 'The poor in a loomp is bad'

1. Elizabeth Gaskell, *Mary Barton*, ch. 1.

2. G. Rudé, 'The Gordon Riots: A Study of the Rioters and their

Victims', in *Transactions of the Royal Historical Society*, 5th series, vol. 6 (1956), p. 102.

3. Magdalen Goffin (ed.), *The Diaries of Absolom Watkin. A Manchester Man, 1787–1861* (1993), p. 41.

4. *Ibid.*, p. 69.

5. House, *Dickens World*, p. 49.

6. Charles Dickens, *The Old Curiosity Shop*, vol. II, ch. xlv.

7. de Tocqueville, *op.cit.*, p. 95.

8. J.T. Ward, *The Factory Movement, 1830–1855* (1962), p. 32.

9. Clive, *op.cit.*, p. 127.

10. *Ibid.*, p. 150.

11. Levi, *op.cit.*, p. 79.

12. *Kingsley: Letters*, vol. I, pp. 307–8.

13. D.J. Rowe, 'Francis Place and the Historians', in *The Historical Journal*, vol. xiii, no.1 (1973), p. 60.

14. Perkin, *op.cit.*, pp. 367–8.

15. de Tocqueville, *op.cit.*, pp. 79–80.

16. C.S. Peel in *Early Victorian England*, vol. I, p. 83.

17. *Kingsley: Letters*, vol. I, p. 302.

18. F.M.L. Thompson, *op.cit.*, p. 271.

19. Johnston, *op.cit.*, vol. I, pp. 90–1.

20. E.P. Thompson, *op.cit.*, p. 687.

21. Alice Chandler, *A Dream of Order: The Medieval Ideal in Nineteenth-Century English Literature* (1971), p. 137.

22. *Letters of Queen Victoria*, vol. I, p. 425.

23. Williams, *op.cit.*, p. 122.

24. Goffin, *op.cit.*, p. 272.

25. Gordon S. Haight, *Selections from George Eliot's Letters* (Yale, 1985), p. 47.

26. E. Abbott and L. Campbell, *The Life and Letters of Benjamin Jowett* (1897), vol. I, p. 134.

27. Brian Harrison, 'Teetotal Chartism', in *History*, vol. 58, no.193 (June 1973), pp. 206–7.

28. Perkin, *op.cit.*, p. 317.

29. Best, *op.cit.*, p. 293.

30. D.J. Rowe, 'The Failure of London Chartism', in *The Historical Journal*, vol. xi, no.3 (1968), p. 483.

31. Shepperd, *art.cit.* in *TRHS*, p. 58.

32. *Letters of Queen Victoria*, vol. II, p. 164.

33. G. Kitson Clark, *An Expanding Society. Britain 1830–1900* (Cambridge, 1967), p. 20.

34. Walter Bagehot, *The English Constitution* (Oxford, 1949 edn), p. 235.

35. Bertrand Russell in *Ideas and Beliefs of the Victorians*, p. 20.

36. Golby, *op.cit.*, p. 3.

37. V.A.C. Gatrell, 'The Decline of Theft and Violence in Victorian and Edwardian England', in *Crime and the Law: The Social History of Crime in Western Europe since 1500*, eds. V.A.C. Gatrell, B. Lennam, S.G. Parker (1980).

38. D.J.V. Jones, 'The New Police, Crime and People in England and Wales, 1829–1888', in *Transactions of the Royal Historical Society*, 5th series, vol. 33 (1983), p. 162.

39. Briggs, *Victorian People*, p. 204.

40. Quoted in Sheldon Rothblatt, *The Revolution of the Dons: Cambridge and Society in Victorian*

England (New York, 1968), p. 124.

41. William Morris, *News from Nowhere* (1928 edn), pp. 130–53.

42. Lord Lee of Fareham, *A Good Innings. Autobiography* (1974), p. 47.

43. Quoted in Briggs, *Victorian Cities*, p. 353.

SECTION IV: 'The spirit of Utility'

1. Mark Pattison, *Memoirs* (1885), p. 244.

2. Young, *Portrait*, p. 87.

3. *Letters of Queen Victoria*, vol. II, pp. 317–8.

4. R.E. Prothero, *The Life and Correspondence of Arthur Penrhyn Stanley* (1893), vol. I, p. 425.

5. Waldo Hilary Dunn, *James Anthony Froude: A Biography* (Oxford, 1961), vol. I, p. 202.

6. *Early Victorian England*, vol. I, p. 265.

7. Goffin, *op.cit.*, p. 325.

8. Quoted in Houghton, *op.cit.*, p. 39.

9. Quoted in Buckley, *op.cit.*, p. 35.

10. Mill, *Dissertations and Discussions*, vol. I, p. 331.

11. Clive, *op.cit.*, p. 130.

12. J.W. Burrow, *Evolution and Society: A Study in Victorian Social Theory* (Cambridge, 1968), pp. 71–2.

13. J.S. Mill, *Utilitarianism, Liberty and Representative Government*, ed. A.D. Lindsay (1968 edn), 6, n.

14. *Ibid.*, p. 6.

15. Henry Sidgwick, *Miscellaneous Essays and Addresses* (1904), p. 151.

16. J.R. Dinwiddy, 'Early Nineteenth-Century Reactions to Benthamism', in *Transactions of the Royal Historical Society*, 5th series, vol. 34 (1984), p. 50.

17. *Ibid.*, p. 49.

18. Clive, *op.cit.*, p. 126.

19. *Ibid.*, pp. 62–3.

20. Fay, *op.cit.*, p. 367.

21. Halévy, *op.cit.*, vol. I, p. 505.

22. Bulwer, *op.cit.*, vol. I, p. 62.

23. Fay, *op.cit.*, p. 367.

24. Clive, *op.cit.*, pp. 310–11.

25. *Ibid.*, p. 347.

26. B. Hilton, *Corn, Cash, Commerce: The Economic Policies of the Tory Government, 1815–1830* (Oxford, 1977), p. 304, quoted in E.T. Stokes, 'Bureaucracy and Ideology: Britain and India in the Nineteenth Century', in *Transactions of the Royal Historical Society*, 5th series, vol. 30 (1980), p. 135.

27. *Ibid.*, p. 135.

28. *Ibid.*, p. 155.

29. Mill, *On Liberty*, ch. 1.

30. Mill, *Dissertations and Discussions*, vol. I, p. 381.

31. S.T. Coleridge, *Table-Talk*, 20 August 1831 (in Harris, *op.cit.*, p. 221).

32. Thomas Carlyle, *On Heroes, Hero-Worship and the Heroic in History* (1840), lecture V.

33. Carlyle, *Sartor Resartus*, pp. 50, 126, 166, 177.

34. John Ruskin, *Unto This Last, and other writings* (1985 edn), pp. 167, 222.

35. Basil Willey, *Nineteenth-Century*

Studies. Coleridge to Matthew Arnold (1964), p. 152.

36. Gertrude Himmelfarb, *Marriage and Morals among the Victorians: Essays* (1986), p. 191.
37. Dinwiddy, *art.cit.* in *TRHS*, p. 69.
38. Willey, *op.cit.*, p. 154.
39. In *1859* ... p. 159.
40. Hilton, *op.cit.*, p. 39.
41. *Ibid.*, p. 17.
42. Houghton, *op.cit.*, pp. 249–50.
43. Clive, *op.cit.*, p. 345.
44. Quoted in Hilton, *op.cit.*, p. viii.
45. Oliver MacDonagh in R. Robson (ed.), *Ideas and Institutions of Victorian Britain: Essays in Honour of George Kitson Clark* (1967), p. 76.
46. Noel Annan, *Leslie Stephen: The Godless Victorian* (1984), p. 175.
47. Willey, *op.cit.*, pp. 152–3.
48. Gertrude Himmelfarb, *Victorian Minds: Essays on Nineteenth-Century Intellectuals* (1968), p. 132.
49. B. Russell and P. Russell (eds), *The Amberley Papers. Bertrand Russell's Family Background* (1937), vol. II, p. 375.
50. Mill, *Collected Works*, vol. xxii, p. 244.
51. S.T. Coleridge, *On the Constitution of the Church and State, according to the Idea of Each* (1839 edn), p. 49.
52. Maurice Cowling, *Mill and Liberalism* (Cambridge, 1983), p. 19.
53. *Ibid.*, pp. 34–5.
54. Disraeli, *Coningsby*, Bk iii, ch. 3.
55. Robbins, *op.cit.*, p. 100.

SECTION V: 'What is it to be a gentleman?'

1. Bagehot, *Literary Studies*, vol. II, p. 142.
2. Bulwer, *op.cit.*, vol. I, pp. 24–30.
3. Young, *Portrait*, p. 25, n.
4. Brian Harrison, *Peaceable Kingdom. Stability and Change in Modern Britain* (Oxford, 1982), pp. 159–60.
5. Elizabeth Roberts, *A Woman's Place: An Oral History of Working-Class Women, 1890–1940* (Oxford, 1984), p. 6.
6. Kitson Clark, *Making of Victorian England*, p. 5.
7. Norman Gash, *Politics in the Age of Peel: A Study in the Technique of Parliamentary Representation, 1830–1850* (1953), p. 15.
8. Perkin, *op.cit.*, p. 230.
9. Burn, *op.cit.*, p. 315.
10. Matthew Arnold, *Essays in Criticism*, 1st series (1900), p. ix.
11. Kellett, *op.cit.*, p. 182.
12. George Eliot, *The Mill on the Floss*, ch. xii.
13. George Eliot, *Middlemarch*, ch. 17.
14. Quoted in D.G. James, *Matthew Arnold and the Decline of English Romanticism* (Oxford, 1961), p. 11.
15. R.M. Ogilvie, *Latin and Greek. A History of the Influence of the Classics on English Life from 1600 to 1918* (1964), p. 103.
16. Wemyss Reid, *op.cit.*, vol. I, p. 80.
17. Charles Dickens, *Pickwick Papers*, vol. I, ch. xvi.
18. W.M. Thackeray, *Vanity Fair*, ch. v.

19. Norman Vance, *The Sinews of the Spirit: The Ideal of Christian Manliness in Victorian Literature and Religious Thought* (Cambridge, 1985), p. 25.

20. Stanley, *op.cit.*, vol. I, p. 71.

21. Quoted in Burn, *op.cit.*, p. 260.

22. Anthony Trollope, *The Duke's Children*, ch. viii.

23. Anthony Trollope, *An Autobiography*, p. 39.

24. Anthony Trollope, *The Last Chronicle of Barset*, ch. 83.

25. Arthur Pollard, *Anthony Trollope* (1978), p. 137.

26. T.H. Green, *Works*, ed. R.L. Nettleship (1888), vol. III, pp. 459–60.

27. Quoted in Martin J. Wiener, *English Culture and The Decline of the Industrial Spirit 1850–1980* (Cambridge, 1992 edn), p. 18.

28. *Ibid.*, p. 18.

29. G.M. Young, *Daylight and Champaign. Essays* (1937), pp. 87–8.

30. Escott, *op.cit.*, pp. 334–5.

31. Anthony Trollope, *Doctor Thorne*, ch. iii.

32. Taine, *op.cit.*, p. 195.

33. Wemyss Reid, *op.cit.*, vol. I, p. 246.

34. David Newsome, *On the Edge of Paradise: A.C. Benson the Diarist* (1980), pp. 110–1.

35. Arthur Westcott, *The Life and Letters of Brooke Foss Westcott* (1903), vol. I, p. 50.

36. D. Newsome, *Edge of Paradise*, pp. 52, 56.

37. Leonard Huxley, *The Life and Letters of Thomas Henry Huxley* (1900), vol. I, p. 68.

38. David Kynaston, *The City of London: A World of its Own, 1815–1890* (1994), p. 92.

39. Clive Dewey, *The Passing of Barchester* (1991), p. 4.

40. Noel Annan in J.H. Plumb (ed.), *Studies in Social History: A Tribute to G.M. Trevelyan* (1955), pp. 243–87.

41. Kellett, *op.cit.*, p. 211.

42. T. Carlyle, *Past and Present* (1912 edn), p. 189.

43. Stanley, *Life of Arnold*, vol. I, p. 33.

44. Burn, *op.cit.*, p. 106.

45. John Ruskin, *Sesame and Lilies* (1893 edn), p. xv.

46. George Eliot, *Middlemarch*, ch. 14.

47. Charles Dickens, *Little Dorrit*, ch. xiii.

48. Geoffrey Faber, *Jowett. A Portrait with Background* (1957), p. 359.

49. Quoted in Briggs, *Victorian People*, pp. 124, 133.

50. Barry Supple in N. McKendrick (ed.), *Historical Perspectives: Studies in English Thought and Society in honour of J.H. Plumb* (1974), p. 216.

51. Harrison, *op.cit.*, p. 136.

52. Bulwer, *op.cit.*, vol. I, p. 33.

53. Golby, *op.cit.*, p. 12.

54. Kitson Clark, *An Expanding Society*, p. 42.

55. Edward Royle, 'Mechanics' Institutes and the Working Classes, 1840–1860', in *The Historical Journal*, vol. xiv, no. 2 (1971), p. 305.

56. Harrison, *op.cit.*, p. 163.
57. Roberts, *op.cit.*, p. 131; other examples of the way in which poverty might be disguised from one's neighbour are cited in Paul Johnson, *art.cit.* in *TRHS*, pp. 32–4.
58. Quoted in Houghton, *op.cit.*, p. 397.
59. *Diaries of John Bright*, p. 391.
60. Goffin, *op.cit.*, p. 235.

SECTION VI: 'God preserve me from being poor'

1. George Eliot, *Middlemarch*, ch. 12.
2. Bagehot, *Literary Studies*, vol. II, p. 2.
3. Kynaston, *op.cit.*, p. 63.
4. Mark Pattison, *Essays*, ed. H. Nettleship (Oxford, 1889), vol. II, p. 217.
5. *Portrait*, p. 67.
6. C. and F. Brookfield, *Mrs Brookfield and her Circle* (1905), vol. I, pp. 202, 212.
7. Wemyss Reid, *op.cit.*, vol. II, p. 12.
8. *Ibid.*, vol. I, p. 525.
9. H.A. Shannon, 'The Coming of General Limited Liability', in E.M. Carus-Wilson, *Essays in Economic History* (1954), p. 376.
10. *Ibid.*, p. 391.
11. Kynaston, *op.cit.*, p. 240.
12. Levi, *op.cit.*, pp. 156–7.
13. Goffin, *op.cit.*, p. 64.
14. Hilton, *op.cit.*, p. 145.
15. *Household Narrative for 1852*, pp. 24, 48, 72, 96, 120, 144.

16. V. Markham Lester, *Victorian Insolvency: Bankruptcy, Imprisonment for Debt and Company Winding-up in Nineteenth-Century England* (Oxford, 1995), p. 314.
17. Dickens, *Dombey and Son*, ch. iv.
18. Thackeray, *Vanity Fair*, ch. xxxvii.
19. Michael Goodwin, *Nineteenth Century Opinion* (1951), pp. 38–43.
20. Dickens, *Our Mutual Friend*, ch. xvi.
21. Roberts, *op.cit.*, p. 170.
22. F. Darwin, *The Life and Letters of Charles Darwin*, 1888, vol. I, p. 37.
23. E.M. Forster, *Marianne Thornton, 1797–1887: A Domestic Biography* (1956), p. 134.
24. F. Darwin, *op.cit.*, vol. I, p. 385.
25. Haight, *op.cit.*, p. 122.
26. Burn, *op.cit.*, p. 32.
27. W. Benham (ed.), *Catharine and Crauford Tait. A Memoir* (1879), pp. 282–393.
28. James Drummond and C.B. Upton, *The Life and Letters of James Martineau* (1902), vol. I, p. 184.
29. Levi, *op.cit.*, pp. 172–3.
30. Young, *Portrait*, p. 226.
31. E.P. Thompson, *op.cit.*, pp. 359–61.
32. Roberts, *op.cit.*, p. 94.
33. Stanley, *Life of Arnold*, vol. I, p. 163.
34. George Prevost (ed.), *The Autobiography of Isaac Williams* (1892 edn), prefatory note.
35. *Amberley Papers*, vol. II, p. 405.
36. Finer, *op.cit.*, p. 333.

37. *Ibid.*, p. 460.
38. *Kingsley Letters*, vol. I, pp. 414–15.
39. Osbert Wyndham Hewett (ed.), *Chichester Fortescue, Lord Carlingford, and Mr Fortescue* (1958), p. 134.
40. *Kingsley Letters*, vol. II, p. 330, n.
41. *Ibid.*, vol. II, p. 109.
42. Taine, *op.cit.*, p. 150.
43. Briggs, *Victorian Cities*, p. 375.
44. Finer, *op.cit.*, pp. 341–2.
45. Nicholas Edsall, 'Varieties of Radicalism: Attwood, Cobden and the Local Politics of Municipal Incorporation', in

The Historical Journal, vol. xvi, no.1 (1973), pp. 93–4.
46. Stokes, *art.cit.* in *TRHS*, p. 142.
47. Finer, *op.cit.*, pp. 507–9.
48. Kathleen Tillotson, *Novels of the Eighteen-Forties* (Oxford, 1954), pp. 55–7.
49. G.M. Young, *Today and Yesterday. Collected Essays and Addresses* (1948), p. 245.
50. L. Huxley, *op.cit.*, vol. II, p. 65.
51. Annan, *Leslie Stephen*, p. 141.
52. Kemp, *op.cit.*, p. 408

CHAPTER 2: Looking Outwards

SECTION I: 'Rule, Britannia!'

1. Allen McLaurin in Eric M. Sigsworth (ed.), *In Search of Victorian Values: Aspects of Nineteenth-Century Thought and Society* (Manchester, 1988), pp. 35–7.
2. In *Ideas and Beliefs of the Victorians*, p. 55.
3. Alfred, Lord Tennyson, *The Princess*, conclusion.
4. Richard Jenkyns, *The Victorians and Ancient Greece* (Oxford, 1981), p. 165; the quotation from Matthew Arnold may be found in *Essays in Criticism*, p. 21.
5. Stanley, *Life of Arnold*, vol. II, p. 344.
6. Quoted in Houghton, *op.cit.*, pp. 44–5.
7. Dickens, *Great Expectations*, ch. xx.

8. S. Strewbridge in Sigsworth, *op.cit.*, pp. 108–9.
9. Burrow, *Evolution and Society*, pp. 50–1.
10. *Henry Sidgwick: A Memoir*, by 'A.S. and E.M.S.' (1906), p. 140.
11. In *1859: ...* pp. 128–9.
12. William Gaunt, *The Aesthetic Adventure* (1945), p. 32.
13. Haight, *op.cit.*, p. 476.
14. Derek Hudson, *Lewis Carroll* (1995), pp. 163–5; J.O. Johnston, *Life and Letters of Henry Parry Liddon* (1904), pp. 100–1.
15. *Early Victorian England*, vol. II, p. 298.
16. Golby, *op.cit.*, p. 5.
17. Jane Austen, *Pride and Prejudice*, ch. viii.
18. Pattison, *Essays*, vol. II, p. 400.
19. Quoted in Kemp, *op.cit.*, p. 152.
20. *Letters and Diaries of J.H. Newman*, vol. XV, p. 416.

21. A.C. Benson, *The Life of Edward White Benson, sometime Archbishop of Canterbury* (1899), vol. I, p. 123.
22. Vance, *op.cit.*, p. 12.
23. Briggs, *Victorian People*, p. 121.
24. Sidgwick, *Memoir*, p. 126.
25. Finer, *op.cit.*, p. 177.
26. Burn, *op.cit.*, p. 171.
27. Quoted in *Ideas and Beliefs of the Victorians*, p. 389.
28. Dickens, *Our Mutual Friend*, ch. xi.
29. P.M. Kennedy, 'Idealists and Realists: British Views of Germany, 1804–1939', in *Transactions of the Royal Historical Society*, 5th series, vol. 25 (1975), p. 139.
30. Thirlwall, *op.cit.*, p. 35.
31. Wemyss Reid, *op.cit.*, vol. I, p. 99.
32. *Life and Letters of James Martineau*, vol. I, p. 191.
33. Haight, *op.cit.*, pp. 144–5.
34. J.A. Froude, *Short Studies on Great Subjects* (1891 edn), vol. II, p. 367.
35. Matthew Arnold, *Discourses in America* (1912 edn), p. 145.
36. Hutton, *Essays Theological and Literary*, vol. II, p. 416.
37. Ackroyd, *op.cit.*, p. 369.
38. Dickens, *Martin Chuzzlewit*, ch. xxxiv.
39. *Diaries of John Bright*, p. 254.
40. John Morley, *The Life of Richard Cobden* (1881), vol. I, p. 33.
41. Kenneth Allott (ed.), *Five Uncollected Essays of Matthew Arnold* (Liverpool, 1953), p. 6.
42. Arnold, *Discourses in America*, pp. 69–70.
43. Matthew Arnold, *The Study of Celtic Literature* (1891 edn), p. 82.
44. *Letters of Matthew Arnold*, vol. I, p. 309–10.
45. Melvin Richter, *The Politics of Conscience: T.H. Green and his Age* (1964), pp. 24–5.
46. *Life and Letters of Benjamin Jowett*, vol. I, p. 191.
47. Eliot, *Middlemarch*, ch. 21.
48. *Letters of Matthew Arnold*, vol. I, p. 4.
49. Stefan Collini, 'Arnold', in K. Thomas (ed.), *Victorian Thinkers* (Oxford, 1993), p. 273.

SECTION II: 'Entering upon most dangerous times'

1. Thackeray, *Vanity Fair*, ch. xxxii.
2. H.A.L. Fisher, *Bonapartism. Six Lectures* (1928), p. 139.
3. *Ibid.*, p. 151.
4. *Life of Richard Cobden*, vol. I, p. 101.
5. *Ibid.*, vol. I, p. 103.
6. N. McCord, 'Cobden and Bright in Politics, 1846–1857', in *Ideas and Institutions*, p. 104.
7. *The Greville Memoirs*, ed. C. Lloyd (1948), p. 234.
8. Norman Gash, 'After Waterloo: British Society and the Legacy of the Napoleonic Wars', in *Transactions of the Royal Historical Society*, 5th series, vol. 28 (1978), p. 148.
9. Briggs, *Victorian People*, p. 70.
10. *Diaries of John Bright*, p. 184.
11. N. McCord, *art.cit.* in *Ideas and Institutions*, p. 114.

12. In *Early Victorian England*, vol. I, p. 364.

13. David Cannadine, *The Decline and Fall of the British Aristocracy* (1990), p. 265.

14. See the reference to Correlli Barnett, *The Swordbearers* (1963), p. 186, in Wiener, *op.cit.*, p. 10.

15. Froude, *Short Studies*, vol. I, p. 27.

16. Andrew Ward, *Our Bones are Scattered: The Cawnpore Massacres and the Indian Mutiny of 1857* (1996), pp. 48–9.

17. *Ibid.*, p. 65.

18. Quoted in *Early Victorian England*, vol. I, pp. 404–5.

19. *Ibid.*, vol. II, pp. 405–6.

20. *Ibid.*, vol. I, p. 367.

21. Clive Dewey, *Anglo-Indian Attitudes. The Mind of the Indian Civil Service* (1993), pp. 15–16.

22. Elizabeth Longford, *Victoria R.I.* (1964), p. 253.

23. *Ibid.*, p. 255.

24. *Letters of Queen Victoria*, vol. III, pp. 309–10.

25. Derek Beales, 'An International Crisis: the Italian Question', in *1859 ...* , p. 189.

26. *Letters of Queen Victoria*, vol. III, p. 399.

27. Noel Blakiston, *The Roman Question. Extracts from the Despatches of Odo Russell from Rome, 1858–1870* (1962), p. 39.

28. Quoted in Beales, *art.cit.* in *1859 ...* , pp. 192–3.

29. Jenkins, *op.cit.*, p. 213.

30. E.L. Woodward, *The Age of Reform (1815–1870)* (Oxford, 1949), p. 296.

31. *Diaries of John Bright*, p. 261.

32. James Bryce, *Studies in Contemporary Biography* (1903), p. 90, n.

33. Wemyss Reid, *op.cit.*, vol. II, p. 76.

34. John Morley, *The Life of William Ewart Gladstone* (1903), vol. II, p. 79.

35. Briggs, *Victorian People*, p. 233.

36. Robbins, *op.cit.*, p. 97.

37. *Diaries of John Bright*, p. 61.

38. Robert Blake, *Disraeli* (1966), pp. 450–1.

39. Lucy Brown, *art.cit.* in *TRHS*, pp. 38–9.

40. L. Huxley, *op.cit.*, vol. I, p. 334.

41. Christopher Hibbert, *Queen Victoria in her Letters and Journals* (1984), p. 220.

42. Kennedy, *art.cit.* in *TRHS*, p. 140.

SECTION III: 'Our approaching decrepitude'

1. Froude, *Short Studies*, vol. II, p. 479.

2. N. McCord, *art.cit.* in *Ideas and Institutions*, p. 91; *Life of Cobden*, vol. I, pp. 107–8, for a similar sentiment.

3. George Haines, 'Technology and Liberal Education', in *1859 ...* , p. 97.

4. David Newsome, *A History of Wellington College, 1859–1959* (1959), p. 75.

5. Haines, *art.cit.* in *1859 ...* , p. 97.

6. *Ibid.*, p. 104.

7. Quoted in Burn, *op.cit.*, p. 299.

8. H.L. Beales, 'The Great Depression in Industry and Trade', in Carus-Wilson, *op.cit.*, p. 411.

9. Hobsbawm, *op.cit.*, p. 127.

10. Quoted in Beales, in Carus-Wilson, *op.cit.*, p. 409.

11. Statistics in Young, *Portrait*, p. 147.

12. Cannadine, *op.cit.*, p. 448.

13. Robbins, *op.cit.*, p. 167.

14. Quoted in Fay, *op.cit.*, p. 244.

15. F.M.L. Thompson, *op.cit.*, p. 256.

16. *Ibid.*, p. 290.

17. Hobsbawm, *op.cit.*, p. 199.

18. Cannadine, *op.cit.*, p. 16.

19. *Ibid.*, p. 27; cf. p. 391.

20. L.E. Jones, *A Victorian Boyhood* (1955), pp. 69–70.

21. Sidgwick, *op.cit.*, pp. 422–3.

22. Hobsbawm, *op.cit.*, p. 200.

23. Haines in *1859* ... , pp. 102–3.

24. R.C.K. Ensor, *England 1870–1914* (Oxford, 1952), p. 106.

25. Philip Ziegler, *The Sixth Great Power: Baring's, 1762–1929* (1988), p. 85.

26. Kynaston, *op.cit.*, pp. 424–37.

27. Ziegler, *op.cit.*, p. 254.

28. Escott, *op.cit.*, p. 116.

29. *Amberley Papers*, vol. I, p. 462.

30. Wiener, *op.cit.*, p. 19.

31. Jenkyns, *op.cit.*, p. 267.

32. Wiener, *op.cit.*, p. 33.

33. John Gross, *The Rise and Fall of the Man of Letters. Aspects of English Literary Life since 1800* (1969), pp. 56–7.

34. Arnold, *Essays in Criticism*, p. xi.

35. Wiener, *op.cit.*, p. 52.

36. Henry Pelling, *Modern Britain, 1885–1955* (Edinburgh, 1960), p. 15.

37. Beales in Carus-Wilson, *op.cit.*, pp. 414–15.

SECTION IV: 'The British Empire divinely ordained'

1. R.T. Shannon, 'John Robert Seeley and the Idea of a National Church', in Robson, *op.cit.*, p. 257.

2. Gaskell, *Mary Barton*, ch. xv; *North and South*, ch. xvii.

3. H.E. Manning, *Miscellanies* (1877–88), vol. I, p. 233.

4. Alan O'Day, *Parnell and the First Home Rule Episode, 1884–87* (Dublin, 1986), pp. 44–6.

5. Jenkins, *op.cit.*, p. 570.

6. Quoted in Roger Hudson (ed.), *The Jubilee Years, 1887–1897* (1996), p. 33.

7. Douglas Woodruff, 'Expansion and Emigration', in *Early Victorian England*, vol. II, p. 353.

8. Pelling. *op.cit.*, p. 5.

9. D. Woodruff in *Early Victorian England*, vol. II, p. 357.

10. J.W. Davidson, 'The Idea of Empire', in *Ideas and Beliefs*, p. 322.

11. M.I. Finley, 'Colonies – An Attempt at a Typology', in *Transactions of the Royal Historical Society*, 5th series, vol. 26 (1976), pp. 170–1 .

12. Froude, *Short Studies*, vol. II, pp. 208–10.

13. Davidson in *Ideas and Beliefs*, p. 323.

14. MS letter, dated 4 November 1823, in author's private possession.

15. A.R. Ashwell and R.G. Wilberforce, *The Life of Samuel Wilberforce* (1881), vol. II, pp. 197–8.

16. Jack Simmons, 'The Proconsuls', in *Ideas and Beliefs*, pp. 415–16.

17. *Kingsley. Letters*, vol. I, p. 445 .

18. Davidson in *Ideas and Beliefs*, p. 324.

19. Blake, *op.cit.*, p. 523.

20 Escott, *op.cit.*, p. 159.

21. *Ibid.*, p. 6.

22. Quoted in Davidson, in *Ideas and Beliefs*, p. 327.

23. R.C. Mowat, 'From Liberalism to Imperialism: the Case of Egypt, 1875–1887' in *Historical Journal*, vol xvi, no.1, (1973), pp. 110–12.

24. Young, *Portrait*, p. 176.

25. John Saville, 'Imperialism and the Victorians', in Sigsworth, *op.cit.*, pp. 167–8.

26. Elaine Showalter, *Sexual Anarchy. Gender and Culture in the Fin de Siècle*, (1991), p. 79.

27. Quoted in Vance, *op.cit.*, p. 197.

28. Shannon in Robson, *op. cit.*, p. 240.

29. Maisie Ward, *Unfinished Business* (1964), p. 18.

30. Noel Annan, 'Kipling's Place in the History of Ideas', in *Victorian Studies*, vol. iii, no. 4 (June 1960), pp. 323–48.

31. Dewey, *op.cit.*, p. 13.

32. Quoted in R. Hudson, *op.cit.*, p. 186.

33. Shannon in Robson, *op. cit.*, p. 257.

34. Alfred Cobban, 'The Idea of Empire', in *Ideas and Beliefs*, pp. 329–30.

CHAPTER 3: Looking Before and After

SECTION 1: 'The favourite reading'

1. John Kenyon, *The History Men: The Historical Profession in England since the Renaissance* (1993), pp. 149–53.

2. Kellett in *Early Victorian England*, vol. II, p. 60.

3. Morley, *Life of Gladstone*, vol. I, p. 169.

4. Robbins, *op.cit.*, p. 67.

5. Both instances described in Horton Davies, *Worship and Theology in England. From Newman to Martineau* (1962), p. 286.

6. *Diaries of John Bright*, p. 430.

7. *Amberley Papers*, vol. I, p. 155.

8. Francis Doyle, *Reminiscences and Opinions, 1813–1885* (1886), p. 101.

9. Kellett, *As I Remember*, p. 196.

10. Amy Cruse, *The Victorians and their Books* (1935), p. 118.

11. Wemyss Reid, *op.cit.*, vol. I, p. 192.

12. *Amberley Papers*, vol. II, p. 11.

13. Pattison, *Essays*, vol. II, p. 413.

14. Tillotson, *op.cit.*, p. 125.

15. Gross, *op.cit.*, p. 76.
16. *Ibid.*, pp. 76–7.
17. In *Early Victorian England*, vol. II, pp. 36–7.
18. Harrison, *Peaceable Kingdom*, p. 138.
19. Owen Chadwick, *The Secularization of the European Mind in the Nineteenth Century* (Cambridge, 1975), pp. 38, 40.
20. *Letters of Queen Victoria*, vol. III, p. 347.
21. *Ibid.*, vol. III, p. 462.
22. *Ibid.*, vol. III, p. 5.
23. Quoted in Briggs, *Victorian Cities*, p. 356.
24. In *Early Victorian England*, vol. II, p. 3.
25. R.K. Webb, 'Working-Class Readers in Early Victorian England', in *English Historical Review*, vol. lxv (1950), p. 349.
26. In *Early Victorian England*, vol. II, p. 65.
27. Harrison, *Peaceable Kingdom*, p. 163.
28. Young, *Portrait*, p. 161.
29. Himmelfarb, *Marriage and Morals*, p. 164.
30. Harrison, *Peaceable Kingdom*, pp. 162, 177.
31. Edward Alexander, *Matthew Arnold and John Stuart Mill* (1965), p. 18.
32. Kellett, *As I Remember*, p. 35.
33. *Diaries of John Bright*, p. 115.
34. In *Early Victorian England*, vol. II, p. 48, n.
35. Prothero, *op.cit.*, vol. I, p. 113.
36. *Amberley Papers*, vol. I, pp. 77–80; 386.
37. F. Darwin, *op.cit.*, vol. I, p. 101.
38. Thirlwall, *op.cit.*, p. 90.
39. G.W.E. Russell, *Collections and Recollections* (1903), p. 327.
40. Michael Wheeler, 'Gladstone and Ruskin', Annual Hawarden Lecture, 1991, p. 18.
41. Jenkins, *op.cit.*, xiv.
42. Morley, *Life of Gladstone*, vol. I, p. 207, n.; vol. III, p. 423.
43. Clive, *op.cit.*, p. 70.
44. Michael Wheeler, *Death and the Future Life in Victorian Literature and Theology* (Cambridge, 1990), p. 231.
45. Mary Church, *Life and Letters of Dean Church* (1895), p. 133.
46. Graham Hough, *The Last Romantics* (1961), p. 68.
47. Wheeler, *op.cit.*, pp. 223, 231.
48. Stopford A. Brooke (ed.). *Life and Letters of F.W. Robertson* (1906), p. 48.
49. Morley, *Life of Gladstone*, vol. III, p. 424.
50. R.H. Hutton, *Essays Theological and Literary* (1880), vol. II, p. 175.
51. Rothblatt, *op.cit.*, p. 117.
52. Cruse, *op.cit.*, 260.
53. Bagehot, *Literary Studies*, vol. II, p. 185.
54. Cruse, *op.cit.*, p. 154.
55. *Ibid.*, p. 158.
56. *Ibid.*, pp. 168–9.
57. Ian Bradley, *The Call to Seriousness. The Evangelical Impact on the Victorians* (1976), p. 98.
58. Cruse, *op.cit.*, pp. 315–22, 327–9.
59. R.D. Altick, 'The Literature of

an imminent Democracy', in *1859* ... , p. 217.

60. Taine, *op.cit.*, p. 235.
61. Young, *Daylight and Champaign*, p. 171.

SECTION II: 'Great men are profitable company'

1. J.W. Burgon, *Lives of Twelve Good Men* (1888), vol. I, p. 379.
2. *Letters of Queen Victoria*, vol. II, p. 394.
3. Young, *Daylight and Champaign*, p. 168.
4. Mary Church, *op.cit.*, p. 19; H.P. Liddon, *The Life of Edward Bouverie Pusey* (1895), vol. I, p. 67.
5. William Tuckwell, *Reminiscences of Oxford* (1900), pp. 84–5.
6. Baker, *op.cit.*, pp. 219–20.
7. R.W. Church, *The Oxford Movement. Twelve Years, 1833–1845* (1891), p. 141.
8. Quoted in Buckley, *op.cit.*, pp. 97–8.
9. Charles Wordsworth, *Annals of my Early Life, 1806–1846* (1891), p. vii.
10. Burn, *op.cit.*, p. 62.
11. R. Davidson and W. Benham, *Life of Archibald Campbell Tait* (1891), vol. I, pp. 112–13.
12. *Mrs Brookfield and her Circle*, vol. II, p. 505.
13. Disraeli, *Coningsby*, Bk iii, ch. 1.
14. Carlyle, *On Heroes*, lecture 1.
15. *Ibid.*, lecture 1.
16. *Ibid.*, lectures 2–6.
17. Ruskin, *Crown of Wild Olive*, lecture iv.
18. Houghton, *op.cit.*, p. 209.
19. Kenyon, *op.cit.*, 111.
20. A.L. Le Quesne, 'Carlyle' in *Victorian Thinkers*, ed. K. Thomas (Oxford, 1993), p. 89.
21. Houghton, *op.cit.*, p. 330.
22. *Ibid.*, p. 298.
23. Kitson Clark, *An Expanding Society*, p. 19.
24. Vance, *op.cit.*, p. 78.
25. Houghton, *op.cit.*, p. 122.
26. Charles Kingsley, *Hereward the Wake*, ch. 1.
27. Vance, *op.cit.*, p. 109.
28. Tillotson, *op.cit.*, p. 141.
29. George Eliot, *Felix Holt*, ch. v.
30. Roy Strong, *And when did you last see your Father? The Victorian Painter and British History* (1978), p. 141.
31. *Ibid.*, p. 126.
32. *Ibid.*, p. 129.
33. J.R. Green, *A Short History of the English People* (1874), Preface.
34. Dunn, *op.cit.*, vol. I, pp. 202–3.
35. Andrew Browning, 'Lord Macaulay, 1800–1859', in *The Historical Journal*, vol. II, no. 2 (1959), pp. 156–7.
36. Clive, *op.cit.*, p. 34.
37. J.W. Burrow, *A Liberal Descent. Victorian Historians and the English Past* (Cambridge, 1981), pp. 61–2.
38. *Ibid.*, p. 55.
39. Samuel Smiles, *Self-Help*, ch. 1.
40. Young, *Today and Yesterday*, p. 44.
41. Original in author's possession.
42. Burrow, *Liberal Descent*, pp. 199, 207.
43. John Kent, *The Age of Disunity* (1966), p. 110.
44. Kenyon, *op.cit.*, p. 142.

45. V.H.H. Green, *Oxford Common Room. A Study of Lincoln College and Mark Pattison* (1957), p. 190.

SECTION III: 'For was, and is, and will be'

1. Carroll, *Alice in Wonderland*, ch. vii (I must confess that I had not perceived the significance of this famous exchange until my attention was drawn to it in Buckley, *op.cit.*, p. 2).
2. Carlyle, *Sartor Resartus*, Bk III, ch. i.
3. Le Quesne, in *Victorian Thinkers*, pp. 44–5.
4. Chandler, *op.cit.*, p. 131.
5. Himmelfarb, *The Demoralisation of Society*, p. 13.
6. Maitland, *Leslie Stephen*, p. 13.
7. *Life of Jowett*, vol. II, p. 303.
8. *Letters of Matthew Arnold*, vol. II, p. 144.
9. R.H. Hutton, *Modern Guides*, p. 3.
10. *Life of James Martineau*, vol. I, p. 340.
11. Froude, *Short Studies* , vol. I, pp. 21, 37.
12. Bulwer, *op.cit.*, vol. II, p. 53.
13. Forbes, *op.cit.*, p. 13.
14. Stanley, *op.cit.*, vol. II, pp. 49–50.
15. Coleridge, *Table-Talk*, 4 August 1833.
16. R. Preyer, in K. Coburn, *Coleridge: A Collection of Critical Essays* (New Jersey, 1967), p. 155.
17. Owen Barfield, *What Coleridge Thought* (1971), p. 161.
18. Coleridge, *The Statesman's Manual* (2nd edn, 1839), p. 212.

19. Coleridge, *On the Constitution of the Church and State according to the Idea of Each* (1839), p. 34.
20. Forbes, *op.cit.*, p. 13.
21. Prothero, *op.cit.*, vol. I, p. 362.
22. Ogilvie, *op.cit.*, ch. 2 and ch. 4.
23. David Newsome, *Two Classes of Men: Platonism and English Romantic Thought* (1974), pp. 73–7.
24. Quoted in Richard Jenkyns, *op.cit.*, p. 62.
25. Thomas Arnold, *Miscellaneous Works* (ed. A.P. Stanley) (1858), p. 399.
26. Forbes, *op.cit.*, p. 93.
27. Stanley, *Life of Arnold*, vol. I, p. 26.
28. *Ibid.*, vol. II, p. 160.
29. T. Arnold, *Introductory Lectures on Modern History* (1874), pp. 30–1.
30. Forbes, *op.cit.*, p. 38.
31. *Ibid.*, p. 4.
32. Andrew Browning, *art.cit.* in *HJ*, p. 159.
33. T.B. Macaulay, *Miscellaneous Essays* (1910 edn), pp. 16–17.
34. Clive, *op.cit.*, p. 481.
35. *Ibid.*, pp. 483–5.
36. Himmelfarb, *Marriage and Morals*, p. 164.
37. Quoted in *Ideas and Beliefs*, p. 49.
38. Burrow, *A Liberal Descent*, p. 77.
39. Mill, *Works*, vol. XXII, pp. 228–9; 234.
40. Trollope, *The Way We Live Now*, ch. iv.
41. Owen Chadwick, *The Victorian Church* (1970), vol. II, pp. 114–15.
42. Buckley, *op.cit.*, p. 67.
43. Chadwick, *Secularization of the European Mind*, pp. 132–3.

44. Shannon in Robson, *op. cit.*, p. 250.

45. F.W. Maitland, *Collected Papers* (Cambridge, 1911), vol. III, pp. 505–7.

46. Annan, *Leslie Stephen*, p. 172.

47. Haight, *op.cit.*, pp. 46, 49.

48. Faber, *op.cit.*, p. 180.

49. Richter, *op.cit.*, p. 203.

50. T.H. Green, *Works*, ed. R.L. Nettleship (1888), vol. III, p. 141.

51. Robert Young, in A. Symondson (ed.), *The Victorian Crisis of Faith* (1970), p. 29.

52. L. Huxley, *op.cit.*, vol. II, p. 229.

53. Sidgwick, *op.cit.*, p. 421.

54. W.H. Mallock, *The New Republic, or Culture, Faith and Philosophy in an English Country House* (1878 edn), pp. 214–15.

55. Quoted in Buckley, *op.cit.*, pp. 9–10.

56. Pattison, *Essays*, vol. II, p. 405.

57. Pattison, *Sermons*, esp. 124–5.

58. Pattison, *Essays*, vol. II, p. 406.

SECTION IV: 'Doat upon the Middle Ages'

1. Stanley, *Life of Arnold*, vol. II, p. 242.

2. J.A. Froude, *History of England*, vol. 1, p. 62

3. John Livingson Lowes, *The Road to Xanadu. A Study in the Ways of the Imagination* (1964 edn), p. 223.

4. Wordsworth, *The Prelude*, Bk I, ll. 351–5.

5. Keats, *Endymion*, Bk I, ll. 795–7.

6. E.D. Hirsch, *Wordsworth and Schelling: A Typological Study of Romanticism* (New Haven, 1969), p. 4.

7. J.H. Newman, *Essays Critical and Historical* (1872), vol. I, p. 272.

8. Chandler, *op.cit.*, p. 12.

9. Hough, *op.cit.*, p. 84.

10. Carlyle, *Past and Present*, Bk II, ch. xvii.

11. *Ibid.*, Bk II, ch xv.

12. Quoted in Chandler, *op.cit.*, p. 167.

13. *Ibid.*, p. 160.

14. Disraeli, *Coningsby*, Bk vii, ch. 2.

15. *Ibid.*, Bk iii, ch. 3.

16. Quoted in Chandler, *op.cit.*, p. 177.

17. *Letters of Queen Victoria*, vol. II, p. 16.

18. Dickens, *Dombey and Son*, vol. I, ch. xxvii.

19. Dickens, *Nicholas Nickleby*, vol. I, ch. xxviii.

20. Dickens, *Great Expectations*, ch. xxv.

21. Forbes, *op.cit.*, p. 107.

22. Newman, *Essays Critical and Historical*, vol. I, p. 268.

23. J.H. Newman, *Apologia pro Vita sua* (W. Ward's edn, 1913), p. 120.

24. Giles Worsley, 'The Origin of the Gothic Revival: A Reappraisal', in *Transactions of the Royal Historical Society*, 6th series, vol. III, (1993), p. 106.

25. Kitson Clark, *Making of Victorian England*, p. 169.

26. James F. White, *The Cambridge Movement. The Ecclesiologist and the Gothic Revival* (Cambridge, 1962), p. 8.

27. Quoted in Kemp, *op.cit.*, p. 211.

28. *Ibid.*, p. 214.
29. Ruskin, *The Crown of Wild Olive*, p. 181.
30. Ruskin, *Unto this Last*, Essay I.
31. Ruskin, 'The Nature of Gothic' in *Unto this Last*, p. 86.
32. Quoted in Golby, *op.cit.*, p. 161.
33. Peter Stansky, 'William Morris', in *Victorian Thinkers*, p. 348.
34. Morris, *News from Nowhere*, ch. xviii.
35. Burrow, *A Liberal Descent*, pp. 121–3.
36. Christopher Hill, 'The Norman Yoke', in *Puritanism and Revolution. Studies in Interpretation of the English Revolution of the 17th Century* (1958), pp. 55, 65, 77.
37. E.P. Thompson, *op.cit.*, pp. 726, 756, 779.
38. *Kingsley Letters* vol. I, p. 157.

39. Dickens, *Little Dorrit*, vol. II, ch. xxii.
40. Dickens, *Our Mutual Friend*, vol. I, ch. viii.
41. Quoted in Burrow, *Liberal Descent*,p. 102.
42. *Ibid.*, p. 171.
43. *Ibid.*, pp. 139–40.
44. C.H.S. Fifoot (ed.), *The Letters of Frederic William Maitland* (Cambridge, 1965), p. 36.
45. F.W. Maitland, *Domesday Book and Beyond: Three Essays in the Early History of England* (Cambridge, 1921 edn), p. 9.
46. *Ibid.*, p. 340.
47. Fifoot, *op.cit.*, p. 498.
48. Thirlwall, *op.cit.*, p. 108.
49. Chadwick, *Secularization of the European Mind*, p. 251.
50. Strong, *op.cit.*, p. 118.

CHAPTER 4: Looking Beyond

SECTION I: 'An after-life?'

1. Himmelfarb, *Victorian Minds*, p. 280.
2. Bradley, *op.cit.*, p. 40.
3. J.H. Newman, *Parochial and Plain Sermons* (1868 edn), vol. I, p. 7.
4. Wheeler, *op.cit*, pp. 135, 143.
5. Perkin, *op.cit.*, p. 287.
6. Young, *Today and Yesterday*, p. 238.
7. Mason, *op.cit.*, p. 2.
8. Annan, *Leslie Stephen*, p. 2.
9. *Ibid.*, p. 265.
10. *Amberley Papers*, vol. II, pp. 482–3.
11. *Ibid.*, vol. II, p. 427.
12. Matthew Arnold, 'Literature

and Dogma' in P.H. Soper (ed.), *Dissent and Dogma* (Ann Arbor, 1968), pp. 407, 409.
13. Statistics in Kitson Clark, *Making of Victorian England*, pp. 148–9; analysis and revised statistics in Best, *op.cit.*, pp. 197–202.
14. K.S. Inglis, *Churches and the Working Classes in Victorian England* (1963), p. 1.
15. Chadwick, *Secularization*, p. 184.
16. Pattison, *Memoir*, pp. 236–7.
17. Prothero, *op.cit.*, vol. II, p. 14.
18. *Kingsley Letters*, vol. II, p. 129.
19. Taine, *op.cit.*, pp. 192–3.
20. de Tocqueville, *op.cit.*, p. 54.

21. *Life of Cobden*, vol. II, pp. 78, 82.
22. Kitson Clark, *Making of Victorian England*, p. 20.
23. J.A. Froude, *The Nemesis of Faith* (1849), pp. 12–13.
24. *Ibid.*, pp. 14–15.
25. T. Mozley, *Reminiscences, chiefly of Oriel College and the Oxford Movement* (1882), vol. II, pp. 221–2.
26. J.J. Stewart Perowne (ed.), *Letters, Literary and Theological, of Connop Thirlwall* (1881), vol. I, p. 327.
27. Henry Crabb Robinson, *Diary, Reminiscences, and Correspondence*, ed. T. Sadler, (1869), vol. II, p. 371.
28. H.G. Wood, *Belief and Unbelief since 1850*, (Cambridge, 1955), p. 11.
29. Geoffrey Rowell, *Hell and the Victorians. A Study of the nineteenth-century theological controversies concerning eternal punishment and the future life* (Oxford, 1974), p. 3.
30. *Ibid.*, p. 81.
31. *Ibid.*, p. 75; Wheeler, *op.cit.*, p. 187.
32. Wheeler, *op.cit.*, p. 188.
33. J.B. Mozley, *Essays Historical and Theological* (1878), vol. II, p. 299.
34. *Ibid.*, II. 297.
35. Chadwick, *Secularization*, p. 105.
36. Quoted in E.P. Thompson, *op.cit.*, p. 413.
37. Bradley, *op.cit.*, p. 187.
38. Quoted in Rowell, *op.cit.*, p. 172.
39. Quoted from C. Gore, 'Belief in God', in Hilton, *op.cit.*, p. 278.

40. Stanley, *op.cit.*, vol. I, p. 38.
41. *Letters of Matthew Arnold*, vol. II, p. 20.
42. B.A. Smith, *Dean Church. The Anglican Response to Newman* (1958), p. 140, n.
43. *Letters and Diaries of John Henry Newman*, vol. XIX, p. 488.
44. Annan, *op.cit.*, p. 156.
45. Pattison, *Essays*, vol. II, pp. 227–8.
46. Mrs Humphry Ward, *Robert Elsmere*, ch. 5.

SECTION 11: 'Mr Darwin's theory not atheistical'

1. *Life of T.H. Huxley*, vol. I, p. 168.
2. *Ibid.*, vol. I, p. 320; *Life of Darwin*, vol. I, p. 333.
3. *Life of Darwin*, vol. I, p. 313.
4. *Ibid.*, vol. I, p. 304.
5. *Life of Huxley*, vol. II, p. 65.
6. *Ibid.*, vol. I, pp. 67–8.
7. R.M. Young, 'The impact of Darwin on Conventional Thought', in *The Victorian Crisis of Faith*, ed. A. Symondson (1970), p. 16.
8. Glyn Daniel, 'Archaeology links Geology to History', in *Ideas and Beliefs*, p. 198.
9. J.W. Burrow, 'The Uses of Philology in Victorian England', in *Ideas and Institutions*, p. 199.
10. *Life of Darwin*, vol. II, p. 116.
11. *Ibid.*, vol. II, p. 197.
12. C. Darwin, *On the Origins of Species by Means of Natural Selection* (1866 edn), p. 567.

13. *Life of Darwin*, vol. II, pp. 230–1.

14. *Life of Huxley*, vol. I, pp. 183–5.

15. Steven Jay Gould, *Bully for Brontosaurus* (1991), p. 391.

16. Basil Willey, 'Darwin and Clerical Orthodoxy', in *1859: ...* , pp. 53–4.

17. Walter F. Cannon, 'The Basis of Darwin's Achievement: A Reassessment', in *Victorian Studies*, V, no. 2 (Dec.1961), p. 121.

18. Chadwick, *The Victorian Church*, vol. II, p. 1.

19. *Newman Letters*, vol. XXIV, p. 77.

20. *Kingsley Letters*, vol. II, p. 347.

21. A.F. Hort, *Life and Letters of Fenton John Anthony Hort* (1896), vol. I, p. 414.

22. Quoted in Houghton, *op.cit.*, p. 38.

23. Levi, *op.cit.*, p. 18.

24. Maitland, *Leslie Stephen*, pp. 150–1.

25. *Robert Elsmere*, Bk i., ch. xxvi.

26. Sidgwick, *Memoir*, p. 90.

27. Leon Gottfried, *Matthew Arnold and the Romantics* (1963), p. 22.

28. George P. Landow, *Images of Crisis. Literary Iconography, 1750 to the Present* (1982), p. 26.

29. Hutton, *Modern Guides*, pp. 139–40.

30. Quoted in Goodwin, *op.cit.*, p. 146.

31. *Life of Huxley*, vol. I, pp. 217–20.

32. Hilton, *op.cit.*, p. 191.

33. *Ibid.*, p. 198.

34. *Life of Cobden*, vol. I, p. 62.

35. Haight, *op.cit.*, pp. 20, 82.

36. *Life of James Martineau*, vol. I, pp. 118–20; 220.

37. *Amberley Papers*, vol. II, p. 379.

38. *Life of E.W. Benson*, vol. I, p. 98.

39. *Life of B. Jowett*, vol. II, p. 76.

40. *Life of Huxley*, vol. I, pp. 420–3.

41. Matthew Arnold, *Last Essays on Church and Religion* (1877), p. 7.

42. *Amberley Papers*, vol. I, p. 83; vol. II, p. 537.

43. Haight, *op.cit.*, pp. 400, 403.

44. Sidgwick, *Memoir*, pp. 384–5, 405, 410.

45. Mallock, *The New Republic*, p. 50.

46. Chadwick, *Victorian Church*, vol. II, p. 113.

47. Sidgwick, *Memoir*, p. 437.

48. *Life of Huxley*, vol. II, p. 379.

49. John Kent, 'From Darwin to Blatchford: The Role of Darwinism in Christian Apologetic', in Annual Lecture to The Friends of Dr William's Library (1966), p. 7, summarizing the conclusions of A. Ellegard, *Darwin and the General Reader, 1859–1872* (Göteborg, 1958).

50. Annan, *Leslie Stephen*, p. 234.

SECTION III: 'The world's no blot for us'

1. Hutton, *Essays Theological and Literary*, vol. I, p. 3.

2. Newsome, *Parting of Friends*, pp. 394–5.

3. J.W. Allen, *A History of Political Thought in the Sixteenth Century* (1951), p. 115.

4. Cuthbert Butler, *The Vatican Council* (1930), vol. II, p. 50.
5. J. Edwin Orr, *The Second Evangelical Awakening* (1955), p. 12.
6. *Ibid.*, p. 81.
7. *Life of A.C. Tait*, vol. II, pp. 507–10.
8. Wood, *op.cit.*, p. 10.
9. Quoted in K.S. Inglis, *Churches and the Working Classes in Victorian England* (1963), p. 183.
10. *Ibid.*, p. 186.
11. E.S. Purcell, *The Life of Cardinal Manning, Archbishop of Westminster* (1896), vol. II., p. 81.
12. *Ibid.*, vol. II, p. 777.
13. Bradley, *op.cit.*, pp. 45–6.
14. Michael Reynolds, *Martyr of Ritualism. Father Mackonochie of St Albans, Holborn* (1965), p. 109.
15. *Ibid.*, pp. 39–41.
16. Vance, *op.cit.*, p. 168.
17. Inglis, *op.cit.*, p. 144.
18. Chadwick, *Victorian Church*, vol. II, p. 257.
19. *Ibid.*, vol. II, p. 258.
20. Trygve R. Tholfsen, 'Moral Education in the Victorian Sunday School', in *History of Education Quarterly*, Spring 1980, p. 79.
21. Harrison, *Peaceable Kingdom*, p. 141.
22. *Ibid.*, pp. 123–4.
23. John Kent, 'The Role of Religion in the Cultural Structure of the Late Victorian City', in *Transactions of the Royal Historical Society*, 5th series, vol. 23 (1973), pp. 162–7.
24. Roberts, *op.cit.*, p. 4.
25. Inglis, *op.cit.*, p. 23.
26. Sheridan Gilley, 'Manning and Chesterton' in *The Chesterton Review*, vol. xviii, no. 4. (Saskatoon,1992), p. 487.
27. Rowell, *op.cit.*, p. 32.
28. Haight, *op.cit.*, pp. 483–4.
29. Dunn, *op.cit.*, vol. I, pp. 152–3; 162; 167–8.
30. Thomas Arnold, 'The Principles of Church Reform', in *Miscellaneous Works*, p. 281.
31. Davies, *op.cit.*, p. 266.
32. *Life of James Martineau*, vol. I, p. 99.
33. F. Maurice, *The Life of Frederick Denison Maurice* (1884), vol. II, pp. 18–19.
34. A.R. Vidler, *F.D. Maurice and Company: Nineteenth-Century Studies* (1966), pp. 274–5.
35. R.W. Church. *Occasional Papers* (1897) vol. II, pp. 185–7.
36. Louise Creighton, *The Life and Letters of Mandell Creighton* (1905), vol. I, p. 75.
37. Newman, *Letters*, vol. xxxi, p. 294, n.
38. Gore, *Lux Mundi*, pp. 73, 75–6.
39. *Ibid.*, p. 262.
40. *Ibid.*, p. 263; Kent, 'From Darwin to Blatchford', p. 9.
41. *Ibid.*, p. 264 .
42. *Ibid.*, pp. 143–4.
43. B.F. Westcott, *Essays in the History of Religious Thought in the West* (1891), p. 238.
44. F.A. Iremonger, *William Temple. His Life and Letters* (1948), p. 47.
45. H. Scott Holland, *A Bundle of Memories* (1915), pp. 63–4.

CHAPTER 5: Looking Ahead

SECTION I: 'Mammon worship a
                melancholy creed'

1. John Vincent, *The Formation of
   the Liberal Party, 1857–1868* (1966),
   p. 199.
2. *Dairies of John Bright*, p. 415.
3. Hilton, *op.cit.*, p. 359.
4. Paul Smith, *Disraelian
   Conservatism and Social Reform*
   (1967), pp. 199–200.
5. Young, *Today and Yesterday*,
   p. 39.
6. Trygve R. Tholfsen, 'The
   Origins of the Birmingham
   Caucus', in *Historical Journal*, vol.
   II, no.2 (1959), p. 184.
7. *Ibid.*, p. 184.
8. Cannadine, *op.cit.*, p. 506.
9. Gash, *op.cit.*, p. 7–8.
10. Clive, *op.cit.*, p. 142.
11. E. Salter Davies, 'The
    Development of Education', in
    Ideas and Beliefs, p. 308.
12. Note by Kitson Clark in Young,
    Portrait, p. 365.
13. K.B. Smellie, 'Victorian
    Democracy: Good Luck or
    Good Management', in *Ideas and
    Beliefs*, p. 292.
14. Charles Gore, *The Incarnation and
    the Son of God* (1896), p. 211.
15. Oliver MacDonagh, 'The
    Nineteenth-Century Revolution
    in Government: A Re-appraisal'
    in *Historical Journal*, vol. I, no. I,
    (1958), p. 57.
16. Burn, *op.cit.*, p. 219.
17. MacDonagh, *art.cit.* in *HJ*, 64–5;

see also Stokes, *art.cit.* in *TRHS*,
pp. 141–2.
18. MacDonagh, *art.cit.* in *HJ*, p. 55.
19. Escott, *op.cit.*, p. 3.
20. Goodwin, *op.cit.*, p. 22.
21. Maitland, *Collected Papers*, vol. I,
    p. 472.
22. J.N. Figgis, *Churches in the Modern
    State* (1913), p. 47.
23. Sidgwick, *Memoir*, p. 425.
24. H.J. Hanham, 'The Sale of
    Honours in Late Victorian
    England', in *Victorian Studies*, vol.
    III, no.3 (March 1960), p. 279.
25. Quoted in Hilton, *op.cit.*, pp.
    359–60.
26. Cannadine, *op.cit.*, p. 196 .
27. Hanham, *art.cit.*, in *Victorian
    Studies*, p. 277.
28. John Sutherland, editorial note
    in Trollope, *The Way we Live Now*
    (World Classics, 1982), p. xviii.
29. F.M.L. Thompson, *op.cit.*, p. 296;
    a fuller list is given in
    Cannadine, *op.cit.*, pp. 406–20.
30. F.M.L. Thompson, *op.cit.*, pp.
    306–7.
31. Quoted in Cannadine, *op.cit.*, p.
    412.
32. Houghton, *op.cit.*, p. 183.
33. Carlyle, *Past and Present*, Bk III,
    ch. ii.
34. Froude, *Short Studies*, vol. II, p.
    195.
35. Froude, *Nemesis of Faith*, Letter
    vii.
36. Quoted in Buckley, *op.cit.*, p. 55.
37. Charles Gore, *Buying up the
    Opportunity* (1895), pp. 13,15.

38. J.E.C. Bodley, 'The Decay of Idealism in France', in *Cardinal Manning and other Essays* (1912), p. 108.

39. Ruskin, *Sesame and Lilies*, Preface, p. xxix.

SECTION II: 'Everything was going to be different'

1. *Annual Register of the year 1900* (1901), pp. 1–2.
2. *Ibid.*, p. 17.
3. E.F. Benson, *As We Were*, pp. 330–1.
4. *Ibid.*, p. 317.
5. *Amberley Papers*, vol. I, p. 515.
6. David Thomson, *England in the Nineteenth Century* (1950), p. 212.
7. E.F. Benson, *op.cit.*, pp. 333–4.
8. Newsome, *Edge of Paradise*, p. 109.
9. *Ibid.*, p. 109.
10. Kellett, *op.cit.*, pp. 90–91.
11. Quoted in Himmelfarb, *Marriage and Morals*, p. 28.
12. The fullest account of the background, details and court proceedings may be found in Theo Aronson, *Prince Eddy and the Homosexual Underground* (1994), *passim*; see also J. Lees-Milne, *The Enigmatic Edwardian: The Life of Reginald, 2nd Viscount Esher* (1986), pp. 78–83.
13. Aronson, *op.cit.*, pp. 173–4.
14. Philip Magnus, *King Edward the Seventh* (1964), p. 228.
15. *Ibid.*, p. 232.
16. *Ibid.*, p. 222.
17. Gaunt, *op.cit.*, p. 16.

18. Wheeler, *op.cit.*, p. 207.
19. *Letters of Matthew Arnold*, vol. I, p. 196.
20. Quoted in Showalter, *op.cit.*, pp. 169–70.
21. Susan Pederson and Peter Mander (eds), *After the Victorians. Private Conscience and Public Duty in Modern Britain. Essays in memory of John Clive* (1994), pp. 18–19.
22. Hough, *op.cit.*, p. 173.
23. Daniel Pick, *Faces of Degeneration. A European Disorder, c. 1848–1918* (Cambridge, 1989), p. 167.
24. Phyllis Grosskurth, *The Woeful Victorian* (New York, 1965), p. 28.
25. Hough, *op.cit.*, p. 170.
26. E.F. Benson, *op.cit.*, p. 313.
27. Buckley, *op.cit.*, pp. 88–9.
28. T.S. Eliot, *Selected Essays* (1951), p. 442.
29. Showalter, *op.cit.*, p. 170.
30. Quoted in *ibid.*, p. 12.
31. Quoted in Cruse, *op.cit.*, p. 233.
32. Harris, *op.cit.*, p. 55.
33. R. Glynn Grylls, 'The Emancipation of Women', in *Ideas and Beliefs*, p. 254.
34. McKendrick, *op.cit.*, p. 153.
35. Quoted in Rosamund Billington, 'The Dominant Values of Victorian Feminism', in Sigsworth, *op.cit.*, p. 119.
36. Himmelfarb, *Demoralisation of Society*, p. 62.
37. Dickens, *Our Mutual Friend*, vol. iv, ch. 5.
38. Quoted in Jenkins, *op.cit.*, pp. 341–2.

39. Haight, *op.cit.*, pp. 350–1.
40. Himmelfarb, *Demoralisation of Society*, pp. 102–3.
41. Vincent, *op.cit.*, p. 210.
42. Showalter, *op.cit.*, p. 7.
43. Pederson and Mander, *op.cit.*, p. 14.
44. Goodwin, *op.cit.*, 90.
45. Himmelfarb, *Demoralisation of Society*, p. 190.
46. Mallock, *op.cit.*, p. 126.
47. Harrison, *op.cit.*, p. 189.
48. Roberts, *op.cit.*, pp. 10–11.
49. *Ibid.*, p. 4.

50. *Ibid.*, p. 73.
51. *Ibid.*, p. 95.
52. Norman Stone, *Europe Transformed* (1983), p. 15.
53. J.P.T. Bury, *France, 1814–1940* (1949), p. 188.
54. Pick, *op.cit.*, pp. 158–9.
55. Cannadine, *op.cit.*, pp. 350.
56. Quoted from Lord and Lady Wolseley, *Letters* (1923), in Roger Hudson, *op.cit.*, p. 67.
57. Cannadine, *op.cit.*, p. 82.
58. Quoted in Roger Hudson, *op.cit.*, p. 228.

CONCLUSION: Looking Retrospectively

1. Buckley, *op.cit.*, p. 127.
2. Maitland, *Leslie Stephen*, p. 451.
3. John Coulson, *Newman and the Common Tradition. A Study in the Language of Church and Society* (Oxford, 1970), pp. 88–9.
4. Kemp, *op.cit.*, p. 470.
5. *Life of Darwin*, vol. I, pp. 155–6.
6. Maitland, *Collected Papers*, vol. III, p. 497.
7. Kitson Clark, *Making of Victorian England*, p. 284.
8. Trollope, *Barchester Towers*, ch. xxi.
9. James Fitzjames Stephen, *Liberty, Equality, Fraternity*, ed. R.J. White, (Cambridge, 1967), pp. 71–3.
10. Himmelfarb, *Demoralisation of Society*, pp. 10–12.

11. Sigsworth, *op.cit.*, pp. 2–5.
12. Quoted in Burn, *op.cit.*, p. 21.
13. Hutton, *Essays*, vol. II, p. 88.
14. Young, *Last Essays*, p. 214.
15. Taine, *op.cit.*, p. 9.
16. Quoted in Clive, *op.cit.*, p. 480.
17. C.S. Lewis, *A Preface to Paradise Lost* (Oxford, 1942), pp. 61–2.
18. Tillotson, *op.cit.*, pp. 48–9.
19. Dickens, *Pickwick Papers*, vol. I, ch. xix.
20. *Ibid.*, vol. II, ch. xxxi.
21. *Life of Monckton Milnes*, vol. II, p. 7.
22. *Life of Darwin*, vol. I, p. 133.
23. Taine, *op.cit.*, p. 71.
24. Julius Hare, *A Charge to the Clergy of the Archdeaconry of Lewes, 1854* (1855), pp. 11–12.

Index